FAITH & PHILOSOPHY OF ISLAM

INDIAN RELIGIONS SERIES: 2

FAITH & PHILOSOPHY OF ISLAM

Shamim Akhter

KALPAZ

Faith & Philosophy of Islam

ISBN: 978-81-7835-855-0

Published in 2010 in India by
Kalpaz Publications
C-30, Satyawati Nagar,
Delhi-110052
E-mail: kalpaz@hotmail.com
Phone: 9212729499

Printed at : Salasar Imaging System, Delhi

Contents

Preface

Islam is a monotheistic religion arising from the teachings of the prophet Muhammad. The word Islam means submission, or the total surrender of oneself to God. Islam is a complete system in itself. For knowing Islam, it is all-important to study its doctrine, theory, principles, and tradition. It is not possible for every one to refer to the original sources, which were written in Arabic. Hence, a need was felt for a comprehensive work on Islam. This is the aim of this volume.

Islam is a scientific religion, based on logic and reasoning, with a rational attitude towards life and the world. Islam is far more democratic and scientific religion than many other religions of the world. Islam believes in equality of humanity without any discrimination on the basis of caste, creed, race, or gender. It was the first religion to grant equal rights to women. Islam teaches its followers to respect other religions. There is no concept of idol worship in Islam and it believes in one God and his superiority.

This volume covers all these topics in a systematic manner. This volume on Islam covers all important aspects of Islam in a nutshell. Knowledge is provided in such a way that it make this volume reader friendly. This volume is indispensable for all scholars, researchers, students, and lay man.

A comprehensive bibliography, along with references at the end of each chapter is provided to prove the authenticity of the work and in order to guide the scholars and readers for further studies. Hopefully, this volume would be able to satisfy the urge of students, scholars, researchers, and all those who desire to know about Islam. This volume will prove of uttermost value to the scholars and laymen alike who wish to have a comprehensive knowledge of Islam.

1

Islam: An Introduction

The name of Allah is the greatest of the Names of God for Muslims. It is an Arabic word of varied meaning, indicating the one who is worshiped, who creates all that lives, which had precedence over all creation, which is towering and hidden, who confounds all human understanding. Islam teaches that all faiths have, in spirit, one common message, the existence of a Supreme Being, the one and only God, whose dominion is to be acknowledged in worship and in the pledge to obey His teaching and commandments, conveyed through His envoys and prophets who were sent at various times and in lots of places throughout history.

Islam in Arabic means affluent. Commitment to Islam demands striving for harmony through a struggle for justice, equality of opportunity, mutual caring and thoughtfulness for the rights of others, and continuous research and attainment of knowledge for the better protection and use of the resources of Creation. Islam teaches that the aim of the Commandment of God is that peace should be established in the human societies of this world, in preparation for an additional dimension of human continuation in the world to come, i.e. the Afterlife. Islam's verdict of peace is therefore truly global.

Islam does not say that it is different or apart from that of other world religions. It is the reaffirmation of the ancient yet living truth of all religions, which can be expressed in the viewpoints such as, the uniqueness of the one and only God who is supreme ruler of the universe. The exposure of the teaching and commandments of God through Angels in heaven to Prophets on earth, and written in holy writings which all have the same transcendent source; these contain the will of God which results the way of peace for the whole universe and all of humanity.

Islam affirms these simple beliefs as the basis for the decent, educated society, which is its aim. Its vision of society is; in essence, not unlike from that upheld by all monotheistic religions. This is particularly true of Judaism and Christianity, which share with Islam the direct spiritual lineage of the Prophet Abraham. Islam asserts the divinely ordained assignments of the Prophet Moses, through whom God revealed the sacred scripture called the Torah, and of the Prophet Jesus, through whom God revealed the scripture known as the Gospel. The message of Islam is in essence the same as that which God revealed to all His prophets and messengers.

The accomplishment of civilizations and cultures is directly connected to the extent of their practice of the righteous way of life revealed in the philosophy and commandments of God, and set forth in the monotheistic religions which are affirmed by Islam. God's revelation enshrines the most renowned values of humanity, and the celestial commandments are essentially no different from the values which human beings have cherished and endeavoured to maintain throughout history, disregard less of cultural, racial, linguistic and socioeconomic differences. Success in this life is directly related to the practice of these treasures. The irreducible minimum of religious belief is to have faith in God as the exclusive sovereign Lord of this world and the next, and to believe in the reality of the Afterlife for which human beings are to prepare by living righteously in this world. God is the only Judge of human morality, and it is God who rewards and punishes in this life and in the life afterlife.

The Scripture "Quran", which was disclosed to the Prophet Muhammad in the 7th century, and which, after 1400 years, remains unquestionable in its original Arabic text, in the language which is still used and understood by millions of people all around the world today; it contains God's counselling in teachings and commandments which are effectual for all times and all places, and which covers all areas of human life.

The Prophet Muhammad, who according to the Quran is the last of the Prophets, and of whose life and aim there is complete and genuine evidence in the Sira and the Hadith. He exemplified the teachings and commandments of God in practice, and taught the principles laid down in the Quran in order to provide a sure guidance for their interpretation and application for later times.

The Sacred Law (Shariah) dictates the way of worship prescribed in the Quran; it goes beyond the common understanding of worship as the performance of religious rituals, and encompasses the whole of human life, individual as well as social. Thus all so-called secular activities become acts of worship, provided they are performed with pure and righteous intention, seeking God's pleasure. Muslims are told to organize their lives on the basis of of ritual acts of worship which are explained in the Quran as ways which discipline human beings to remember God constantly, accepting his Sovereignty and pledging to obey his commandments. These are:

Shahada (Proclamation of belief): This is the primary act of faith. It testifies to one's allegiance to following the straight path of God's guidance.

Salat (Prayer): It is offered five times a day and has the effect of reminding the faithful that remembring God is the greatest virtue, and helps them to hold fast the path of morality and to hold back from evil.

Sawm (Fasting): It is observed throughout the Islamic month of Ramazan. It call for abstinence from eating, drinking, smoking and marital intercourse; this reminds the believers of their dependency upon God, as well as their relationship with human beings who lack food.

Zakat (Purification of wealth): It requires the giving of excess personal assets to the poor; it serves to remind Muslims that all benevolence comes from the God; sharing becomes an act of purification both of the wealth itself, and of the giver whose soul is disciplined against rapacity by the practice of selflessness.

Haj (Pilgrimage): All Muslims should perform Haj at least once in a lifetime. They perform decreed acts of worship at the Kaaba in Mecca which, according to the Quran, was originally built by the prophet Abraham and his son Ishmael; and at Mount Arafat, where they remember the pure and original way of life of Adam, the ancestor of human race.

Concept of Worship

The theory of worship in Islam is different from other religions. In general, worship is understood to mean the observance of certain rituals such as praying, fasting, charity, etc. In Islam, worship is much more, it is one's entire life. Worship is an all-embracing term for those sayings and activities of a person that are delighting to Allah. In other words, worship is that which is done in respect to Allah's will, which includes rituals but goes far beyond to the borders of ones beliefs, social activities, and personal contributions to society and fellow human beings. Islam looks at the person as a whole. Islam says that its followers behave every facet of their lives according to its instructions. The Prophet instructed his followers that Islam is far more than a religion. Islam gives no value to rituals that are performed and have no authority on one's inner life.

Faith, according to the Prophet, is the base of worship and is made up of sixty and about branches: the upmost of which is the notion in the Oneness of Allah, i.e., there is no God but Allah and the lowest in the scale of worship is removing impediment. In Islam, the executing one's duties is also considered an act of worship. The Prophet told us that whatsoever one spends for his family will be counted as an human action of worship for which he will be rewarded, provided that he has assumed it through Islamically acceptable means. Kindness to family members, irrespective how small, is also deemed acts of worship. Even activities that we love very much, are believed acts of worship as long as they are executed in accordance with the applicable Quranic and prophetic rules. Islam has various ritualistic activities that all Muslims are expected to execute. The most crucial one is the prayer (salah), which mustbe performed according to a particular style. Its importance comesfrom the fact that it serves as the typical trait of a Muslim andbecause it prevents a Muslim from employing sinful activities byplacing him into direct liaison with Allah five times a day. Thus, theritual prayer is an opportunity for him to renew his compact with Allah and to seek His direction.

Zakat

The second most significant pillar of Islam is zakat, a term that means giving to the less fortunate a sure part of one's net income and holdings. Giving the poor-due and doing the prayer are usually mentioned together in the Quran, for they are both visible expressions of one's Islamic trust and notion that Allah is the sole owner of everything in the cosmos, which he allows man to enjoy as His trustee for a particular period of time: In addition, this act provides a way to distribute a society's riches in a way that reduces differences between classes and groups.

It makes an important share to social stability, for by flushing the soul of the rich person from selfishness and the soul of the poor from begrudge and resentment against society, it blocks the channels leading to class hate and makes it possible for the outflow of brotherhood and commonness to spout forth. Such stability is not merely based on the personal impressions of the rich: it stands on a firmly based right that, if denied by the rich, would be demanded by force, if necessary.

The fast of Ramazan (siyam) is the third pillar of Islam. Its main purpose is to make the Muslim pure from inside, just as the legal code (the Shariah) makes his external activities pure. This action of purification makes it possible for him to respond to what is true and good and to banish what is false and evil.

Fasting, awakens an individual's moral sense and gives it scope for exercise in a communal feel that is engaged in by the full Muslim world at the same time. Such a ritual strengthens the individual's resolve to improve himself and to realize the purpose of the whole undertaking. Fasting offers a mandatory rest to the over-worked human body for the length of one full month, and also reminds Muslims of those who are deprived of life's necessities throughout the year or throughout one's life. It makes him recognise the suffering of his less fortunate Muslim brothers, a feeling that encourages in him a sense of understanding and kindness towards Muslims and other people generally.

Haj

Finally, comes the the annual pilgrimage to the House of Allah (the Kaaba) in Mecca. This rite, known as the Haj, is singular to Islam. Muslims from all niches of the world and all dressed up in the same clothing answer in one voice and one language with the following phrase upon entering the sacred precincts: "labbayk Allahuma Labbayk" (I am at your service O Lord). This is a time of rigorous self-control where not only sacred things are venerated, but even the life of plants and birds is made secure: And he that venerates the sacred things of God, it shall be better for him with his Lord as well as he that venerates the way marks of God, it surely is from veneration of the heart.

Pilgrimage gives a chance for all Muslims, regardless of their associations with certain groups, classes, organizations, and governments, to meet annually in a great meeting. The time and locus of this gathering has been set by God. All Muslims are asked to attend, for no person or government can refuse any Muslim the right to do so. Every Muslim who attends is assured full safety and freedom as long as he does not breach its holiness.

Thus, worship in Islam, whether rites or non-ritual, trains the person in such a way that he loves his Creator even more, which causes him to acquire a determined will and spins to clean out all evil and repression from his society and to make the word of God victorious.

Belief in one God

The central theme of Islam, is that there is one God. The Muslim name for God is Allah, which is in Arabic.

Muslims think that God is the omnipotent Creator of a consummate, ordered universe. He is inspirational and not a part of his conception, and is most often denoted to in terms and with names that stress his majesty and high quality. Although the God of Islam has revealed his will through the prophets, his literal nature remains ultimately transcendent. God's will is all we have, and we have it in flawlessness in the Quran. But Islam does not compare the Quran with the nature or heart and soul of God. It is the Word of God, the Teaching of God, the Will of God. But God does not disclose Himself to anyone.

Despite God's superiority and utmost unknowability, however, the Quran does not instruct that God does not know us, nor that he remains aloof in some distant heaven.

The one matter that is made profusely clear, however, is that Allah is One. He is unparalleled and indivisible. The Quran repeatedly stresses severe monotheism, explicitly declining both polytheism and the Christian conception of the Trinity. Along with Judaism and Christianity, Islam belongs to the religious family of "honourable monotheism." Allah is a God of justness, who expects righteous demeanour and submission to the divine will and penalizes unrighteousness. Yet divine mercy is not missing from the Quran. It teaches that God will react to anyone who cries out to him in suffering and that he mercifully provides direction to humanity so they can follow "the direct path." The chief way God has done this is through his prophets or couriers, the last and most significant is the Prophet Muhammad.

The Prophets

Muhammad, the founder of Islam, is revered as the last and most sterling of the messengers of God. He is not divine in any way, for the rigorous monotheism that qualifies Islam does not allow for such a rendition. Other prophets are significant in Islam as well, all of which are common with the Jews and the Christians.

Traditionally, five prophets are accepted by Islam as having been sent by God are:

Noah (Nuh)

Abraham (Ibrahim)

Moses (Musa)

Jesus (Isa)

Muhammad

Muslims trace their inheritance to the Hebrew people and prophets. The term "Semite" comes from Shem, the son of Noah, and both Jews and Arabs believe themselves Semitic people. Particularly, they trace their bloodline to Ishmael, the firstborn son of Abraham.

According to the Hebrew Scriptures, Abraham and Sarah, had trouble bearing a child. This problem was made even more grievous by the fact that God had promised Abraham that he would become the forefather of many nations. So, Abraham took Hagar as a second wife. Hagar gave birth to a son, named Ishmael. Before long thereafter, Sarah also bore Abraham a son, Isaac. Having fulfilled her matrimonial duty and God's promise, Sarah asked that Abraham reject Hagar and Ishmael. Abraham did so, and from this point, the Quran deviates from the biblical story to comply the story of Ishmael. According to the Quran, Ishmael went to the place that would later be known as Mecca. His heirs would be the Muslims, while Isaac's heirs became the Jews.

Allah

Allah is the standard Arabic word for God. It is used by Arabic-speakers of all Abrahamic religious beliefs in reference to God. In pre-Islamic Arabia, Allah was not the exclusive divinity, having companions, sons and daughters. In Islam, Allah is the sovereign and all-comprehensive celestial name. All other godly names are believed to refer to Allah. Allah is unparalleled, the only God, supreme creator of the universe and all-powerful. Arab today, having no other word for 'God' than Allah',use terms such as Allah al-ab to mean God the father. There are both similarities and deviations between the concept of God as depicted in the Quran and the Hebrew Bible.

The term Allah is most likely deduced from a contraction of the Arabic article al and ilah; to al-lah meaning "the only deity. Another hypothesis traces the account of the word to the Aramaic Alaha. Cognates of the name "Allah" exist in other Semitic languages, including Hebrew and Aramaic.The matching Aramaic form is Elaha in Biblical Aramaic and Alaha or Aloho in Syriac. The term Allah is invariably used in the singular form; the plural form of the term is not there in Arabic language.

In pre-Islamic Arabia, Allah was used by Meccans as a denotation to the the supreme deity.Allah was not the exclusive divinity and the impression of the term may have been undefined in the Meccan religion. Allah had associates and companions, whom pre-Islamic Arabs considered as underling deities. Meccans held that a kind of relationship existed between Allah and the jinn. Allah had sons and the local deities of al-Uzza, Manat and al-Lat were his daughters. The Meccans possibly connected angels with Allah. Allah was appealed to in times of suffering.

In Islam, Allah is the name of the nameless God,the pivot of the Muslim faith. "He is the only God, transcendent creator of the universe, and the judge of humankind." "He is unique (wahid) and inherently one (ahad), all-merciful and omnipotent." The Quran insists upon "the reality of Allah, His inaccessible mystery, His various names, and His actions on behalf of His creatures."

According to the tradition of Islam there are 99 Names of God (al-asma al-husna lit. meaning: "The best names") each of which evoke a distinct characteristic of Allah.All these names refer to Allah, the supreme and all-comprehensive divine name. Among the 99 names of God, the most famous and most frequent of these names are "the Merciful" (al-rahman) and "the Compassionate" (al-rahim). Most Muslims use the untranslated Arabic phrase "insha Allah" (meaning "God willing") after references to future events.

Prophets of Islam

Prophets of Islam are humans who are considered by Muslims to be prophets selected by God. All prophets preached the same teachings; to think that there is only one God, not to commit idolatry, and to follow the word of God, not to perpetrate sin, etc, and that they all came to advocate Islam and to tell of the coming of the last prophet and messenger of God; Muhammad. They were, however, just dissimilar in Sharia (or the practice of religion) that they taught to their nations. Islamic custom dictates that messengers were sent by God to all nations. In Islam, only Muhammad was sent to communicate God's message to all world, whereas other messengers (rasuls) were sent to bring their messages to a particular group of people or nation. Unlike Judaism and Christianity, Islam discerns between a direct courier of God and a prophet. Both are divinely inspired receivers of God's disclosure.

Muslims consider that the first prophet was Adam, while the final prophet was Muhammad. In Islam, Jesus is looked upon as nabi and a rasul because he received wahi (divine revelation) from God, through which God disclosed the Injil (Gospel) to him. Opposite to Christianity, though, in Islam, it is unorthodoxy to claim that God had a son. Muslims believe that God has sent out over 124,000 messengers all over the world as mentioned in the Sahih Hadith. Five (Ulul Azmi) are allotted the highest veneration for their perseverance and unusually strong commitment to God in the face of great suffering. These five are Nuh (Noah), Ibrahim (Abraham), Musa (Moses), Isa (Jesus), and Muhammad.

The Quran, as in the New Testament, grades apostles (rasul) higher than prophets. For instance, in the Quran whenever both titles come along together, messenger comes foremost. The Quranic commentators state that a messenger is a prophet who is additionally given a message, which must be delivered. A messenger installs a novel religious law (sharia) whereas a prophet continues an old one. Moreover, a prophet experiences divine revelation only in dreams whereas a messenger obtains it from an angel. These would mean that prophets were more numerous than messengers and filled a lower rank. Both prophets and messengers are sent out by God as preachers to their people. In the case of messengers however, there seems to be a deep relation between them and their people.God sends only one messenger for each one people. This messenger will be the attestator that God will take from that society on the Day of Judgment. According to the Quran, Muhammad is sent to a people to whom no messenger has been sent. Lastly, a differentiation should be made between heavenly and human messengers. In the Quran, God has made the angels couriers but not prophets. The human messengers nevertheless are also prophets while not every prophet is a messenger.

Principal Duties

Kalimah: Islam is divided up into iman, i.e belief of a Muslim, and din, the exercise of his religion. Muhammad is said to have defined these pillars according to the subsequent tradition:

To prove that none has the right to be worshipped but Allah and Muhammad is Allah's messenger.

To offer prayers dutifully and absolutely.

To pay Zakat (charity).

To perform Haj.

To maintain fast during the month of Ramazan.

The complete religion of Islam is concisely summed up in these sentences, "La ilaha ill-Allah", i.e. there is no god but Allah, and Muhammad-un Rasulullah, i.e. Muhammad is the Messenger of Allah. It is simply by attesting to the truth of these two uncomplicated proposals that a man enters the congregation of Islam.

As soon as a child is born into a Muslim family these words are spoken into his ears and all efforts is made to get a dying Muslim to say this testimony. Muhammad is said to have claimed that whosoever actually professed this testimonial would never be affected by the Fire of Hell, though he was evidently unwilling to bring out this lest his followers relied on it alone for their redemption.

Another custom states that on the Judgment Day, despite the fact that ninety-nine scrolls naming Muslim's sins should be produced, each scroll extending as far as the eye can see, yet even a shard the size of an ant assuming the Kalimah, recited during his lifetime, would outbalance the scrolls and assure his admission to justification by faith of a very different kind to that which Christians profess. Nevertheless all these customs and practices show how spectacular the Kalimah is in the exercise of the Muslim's faith.

Salaah: Five times a day a Muslim is obligated to execute the Salaah, the defined ritual of the Islamic prayer-worship. He should decently go to the nearest mosque to offer his prayers collectively the whole fold. Each of the five periods is preceded by the adhaan (azaan). After the call to the god during the Fajr prayer, the crier calls up out twice: "Prayer is better than sleep". Then comes the real performance of prayer itself in which anything between two or four rites (rakah) are performed. The worshipper starts with the qiyam, the standing position. He raises his hands to his ears and then closes them, right over left, on his breast. Coming after this is the ruku in which he prostrates and places his hands on his knees, thereafter returning to the standing posture. Then comes the sajdah, the prostration on the ground. This is performed twice with a brief sitting in between. He then takes the sitting position, the qadah and passes the greeting as-salaamu alaykum wa rahmatullah. It is known as the taslim and it is said that the believer is greeting his fellow Muslims.

In between these positions various expressions and transitions of the Quran are recited. These include the takbir (Allah is Most Great), the tahmid (Praise be to Allah), the tahlil (There is no god but Allah) and the tasbih (May Allah be Glorified). There are versions of these, for example subhaana rabbiyyal Adhiim (Glorified be the Lord, the Most High). This fixed ceremony of prayer is so strict in Islam that there may be no deviation from it and the pious Muslim will slavishly follow it day after day. Muslims say that the whole procedure is a necessary discipline to bring the remembrance of God perpetually before the minds of those who otherwise would soon forget him. The truth is that the august idea of holding manduction with God or recognising the Divine within man, which is so necessary to the moral elevation of man, could not have been kept alive unless there was an outward form to which all people should try to adapt. In the first place, no thought can live unless there is a foundation to keep it alive. Secondly, the flocks in any society, even though it may be civilized, can be awakened to the acknowledgment of a truth only through some outward form, which reminds them of the fundamental idea.

The great emphasis is placed on the outward configuration in Islam however, not only tends to lull dull worshippers into a sense of complacency and reliance on the rituals themselves, but also implies that the true knowledge of God and witness of the Holy Spirit is absent in Islam for, when these are present, there is no need for a strict outward form, a regulation to compel the devotion of men who otherwise would probably go astray.

In addition to the five daily prayers there are the taHajud prayers, a late-night ritual practiced by Muhāmmad but not commanded by him, as well as tarawih prayers after the last prayer, salaut-al-isha, during the month of Ramazan. Furthermore on Fridays the great congregational prayer dust after midday, the Juma prayer, replaces the midday prayer. In all of these the ritualistic performance of rakaat continues but, apart from these prescribed prayers, Muslims also have a more extemporaneous form of prayer, the dua. This takes the form either of set Arabic phrases or of personal devotions which may also be in Arabic or in the worshipper's language.

The growth of Islam as a religion of established rituals and practices did not stop at the death of Muhammad. On the contrary much growth was still needed before the rough edges could be smoothed out into determined system that we find now.

The Salaah is possibly the pivot around which all else revolves in ritualistic Islam. The times are fajr, the morning prayer just before sunrise; zuhr, the prayer just after noon; asr, the afternoon prayer; maghrib, the prayer just after sundown; and isha, the evening prayer. All Muslim hold that the observance of these prayers is compulsory. Nevertheless, while the forms of ritual are defined in the Quran, neither the five times of prayer nor the process of each rakah is dictated in the book. The Quran does observe both the salaatal-fajr and salaatal-ishaa in Surah by name but in this case it is unlikely that these were actual titles of prescribed prayer. It is far more likely that the manifestations simply mean the "morning prayer" and the "evening prayer" in that order. This interpretation is backed by the form of the only other prayer mentioned in the Quran, namely salaatal-wusta in Surah, which means the middle prayer. Even though the Quran only mentions three times of prayer, Muslim scholars attempt to make the Quran prescribe the five fixed periods of prayer. The Quran urge worshippers to set up steady prayers at stated times, but it is rather loose in its discourse of the daily prayers.

God is said to have declared that those who observed the five prayers would have the value of fifty mattered to them. In Hadith it is said that Gabriel particularly came to Muhammad one day and executed the fajr, zuhr, asr, maghrib and isha prayers with Muhammad and said to him he that he was ordered to show them to him so that he would know when and how to perform the decreed prayers.

Zakaah and Saum: The Quran invariably enjoins on believers the duty of giving Zakaah, a prescribed almsgiving. The book often connects the duty of charity with the observance of Salaah and denotes to it as an act of piousness to purify the believer and as an act of gratitude to God. The fixed offering in Islam has been installed as two-and-a-half per cent but, whereas the Old Testament charge of ten per cent was calculated simply in terms of a man's financial gain, zakaah is fixed chiefly as a surcharge or a man's wealth and possessions. The other form of charity in Islam, of a less irremissible nature, is known as sadaqah, a voluntary offering showing the sincerity of a man's disposition towards unselfishness. Apart from the even prescribed alms, there is also a extra charity known as zakatal-fitr, being a contribution made at the end of the fast month of Ramazan on the function of the festival Eid-ul-Fitr. This charge is also known as sadaqatal-fitr as it is not necessarily an irremissible charity.

Zakaah can be used for dispersion to the poor, aid towards those who have lately embraced Islam and the freeing of slaves. Fasting is also dictated as an obligatory duty of Islam and the Muslim is duty-bound to fast from sunrise to sunset during the thirty days of the month of Ramazan. The statement about fast is found in the Quran:

The worshipper must declare his niyyah before dawn each day and must refrain from all foods, liquids and other pleasures throughout the day. He should share a proper breakfast, a sehri, before the morning prayer. At sunset he should also break off his fast as soon as he can. The fast-month ends with the sighting of the new moon announcing the month of Shawwal and the Eid festival. All over the Muslim world this fast, although commanded only once in the Quran, is strictly observed, even by those who are otherwise loose in religious observations. In some Muslim lands it is a crime to fail to keep it. Finally it may be said that

Salaah and the Ramazan fast have a bigger effect on the Muslim's religious awareness than all the other dictated duties of Islam.

The Prayer

Worship is common to all faiths. What differs is only the fashion and manner of worship. That which is singular in Islamic mode of worship is that it incorporates features from the mode of prayers found in other religions. Some people pray to God in a standing position and some in a sitting position. In some religions individuals remember God by kneeling to Him, while others prostrate to Him. Some stand before Him with closed arms, and others with arms dangling at their sides. In brief there is no single way of worship common to all religions as a whole. It is interesting to note that Islam teaches its followers regarding the manner of prayer so comprehensively, that all the positions of worship found in other religions are symbolically represented in the manner of Muslim prayer.

The establishment of Islamic prayer is a most highly-developed system, covering every human necessity. It should be remembered at the beginning that the aim of worship is not just bowing to a superior being and paying homage to God, as if God created man only for fulfilling His desire of being praised. All the intentions mentioned in relation to the doctrine of worship and the way in which a Muslim is commanded to conduct his prayer, makes it plainly clear that the benefit of prayer is drawn by the believer himself and in no way can it be accepted as a favour to God. The Holy Quran announces that God does not need mens' praises. He is so great in His nobility and so elevated in His character that the praises of His creatures do not add anything to His largess and magnificence. The Holy Prophet of Islam once said that if the total mankind turnes away from God and perpetrated the worst possible sins, they would not diminish His collective magnificence.

So, worship in the Holy Quran is only decreed for the sake of the believer himself. It is a huge subject, and we can only illustrate a few points in relation to this as cited in the Holy Quran and the traditions of the Holy Prophet of Islam.

Worshiping of God and musing over His attributes during the prayer helps man in elaborating his spirit, bringing it more into harmoniousness with the nature of God. This is fundamental to the Islamic prayer. Man was made in the image of his Almighty, and he must ever endeavour to gain closeness to Him. This is a example in nobility which is ultimate. Those who develop themselves to think and to act like Him within the restrictions of the human sphere, constantly amend in their relation to all other human beings and even other classes of life.

In human conditions it can be better understood by taking example of mother's position towards her babies. For the one who truly gains closeness to a mother, all that is beloved to the mother will naturally become dear to him as well. Developing the attitude of the creator is like gaining the attitude of an artist to his arts. It is unimaginable for one to be near God and distance himself from His institution. Again, the term used for worship in the Quran is descended from a word which is so substantial and different from terms used in other religions. Ain, Be, Dael are the three original letters which have the introductory meaning of slavery. Like a slave who loses all things to his master and follows him in all regards, the worshipper in Islam must do the same in his relation to God. The verb used for worship has the intension of following in the footsteps of someone. That is the ultimate in the imitation of God's dimensions.

This verse has both positive and negative meanings, both extremely essential for educating perfect human manner. Thus in its negative implication, it helps the worshipper by releasing him from sins of all types. In its positive connotation it educates man, fines his character and cultivates his qualities to such grandeur as he becomes suitable of communion with God.

Another field which is highly noteworthy in this regard is the role worship plays in formulating one's soul. According to Islam, each human soul in relation to the sensual human body can be likened to a child in the uterus of the mother. To deliver a healthy child requires so many influences that are always channelized from the mother to the embryo and the child at a posterior stage. If the mother's influence on the embryo is unhealthy, the child is born as innately ill; if they are healthy then the child is born in a perfect health. Of all the acts that work towards the building and change of the human soul, prayer is the most significant individual factor.

The tradition of Islamic prayer is loaded in so many fundamental lessons which are not found even minorly in other religions. Islam discourages both congregational and personal prayer. The congregational prayers are held in a manner which is astonishingly well coordinated and meaningful.

There is single leader who guides the congregation in all such prayers. Anybody whom the people believe worthy of this job is chosen as the 'Imam'. The assembly is warned to be set out behind the Imam in perfectly straight lines, each worshipper standing close to the other, without any space between the two worshippers. They follow the Imam absolutely in everything that he does. Even if the Imam commits a fault and does not excuse it even after a reminder, all followers must duplicate the same. To question the Imam during the prayer is not tolerated. All face the same direction without exclusion, facing the Mecca. No-one is permitted to reserve any particular place behind the Imam. In this regard the rich and poor are treated with absolute equivalence, and also the old and the young. Whoever reaches the mosque before others has the prior choice to sit wherever he pleases. None has the right to bump off others from the place that they occupy, except on grounds of security etc., in which case it becomes an administration matter. Thus the Islamic structure of prayer is well-off not only in spiritual command, but also in common and organisational order.

All mosques are visited five times a day, a chore which appears to be over-much necessitating to a cursory observer. This aspect should be further expanded to build a broader picture of the role of congregational prayers in the Muslim's life. In an ideal Muslim order, where mosques are within reach of almost every citizen, the five time prayer becomes a mundane way of all Muslim's life. The midday prayer is executed in Muslim societies during the noon break from work. Thus it is not only a lunch break, but is slightly extended to adapt the performance of prayer as well. The next prayer after the midday prayer is the afternoon prayer, which is executed almost immediately after return from an average day's work. Then no prayer is permitted until after sunset. The time among the two is passed in outdoor activities like sports, shopping, walks, calls to friends and relatives etc. It is a period of rest in which prayers are practically prohibited, except for the quiet remembrance of God which becomes a ceaseless feature with some believers. At sunset, the night of the worshipper begins with the sunset prayer, after which there is again a time for rest, dining, and so on. The night is crested before retirement with the final prayer which is called Isha. It is discouraged to stay awake after Isha in tasks of gossip and futile talk etc.

The Muslims are promoted to develop a habit of early to bed and early to rise. The day, next morning, begins routinely in the time of day before dawn. The prayer which is performed at the end of the night is called TaHajud. It is not obligatory, but is a very highly emphatic voluntary prayer. The dawn ushers in the time for Morning Prayer, which is called Al-Fajar. Nonmandatory prayers are not recommended between Fajar and sunrise. Then till Zuhar, the midday prayer, only two nonobligatory prayers are mentioned; otherwise the pre-Zuhar period is expected to be spent in normal day to day natural processes.

Looking at the establishment of prayer in Islam from some other angle, it is fascinating to note how well organised, conditioned and comprehensive it is. There are some prayers of congregation in which recital of the Quran is done in a loud, clear voice, in a semi-singing tone, which does not exactly meet the concept of singing, but which has a rhythmical tone that is profoundly penetrating.

The Holy Prophet also advised that there should be a shade of sadness in the tone in which the Quran is narrated; this makes it more affecting, with the meaning of the verses burying deeper into the recesses of the heart. In prayers, specially the two afternoon prayers, there is no loud chanting; this goes well with the universal mood of the time. There is a general air of silence covering the uproar of normal work. The Morning Prayer, the prayer after sunset and the prayer after the fall of night all admit periods where chanting of verses is the everyday practice.

The prayers can be again divided into two categories. As against congregational prayers, individual prayers are also highly stressed. In congregational prayers, society pays respect to God conjointly and openly. In individual prayers, emphasis is laid on seclusion, and there should be no effort to exhibit such prayers to anyone. Similarly the late night prayer is performed in complete privacy. Members of the same house try to find their own corners, and even husband and wife try to say their prayers individually so that communion with God becomes a highly personal matter.

It has been observed that the institution of the five time congregational prayer has figured out very well, for over fourteen hundred years or so, for the shelter and conservation of this holy institution. The mosques have been the backbone in keeping this stately institution alive. They also serve as education centres and during history they have played the most spectacular role in religious teachings and education.

The places of worship in Islam are kept painstakingly clean. Everyone has to take his shoes off before entering such places. Though in every prayer the worshipper has to touch the floor with his forehead, it is surprising that no skin disorder have been transmitted in the Muslim society. Some may assign this to the high criterion of cleanliness and some to the benedictions of God, but this is a well detected fact.

As far as the messages of the prayer, they are of two types:

1. A conventional reading of verses of the Quran and other prayers which are done basically in the language of the Quran, Arabic. All believers are required to know the meaning of what they are reciting; otherwise they will deprive themselves of the vast benefit which they may draw from the significant recitation.
2. In the second family belong the personal prayers in one's own language, in which one is free to pray as he pleases. This second category is arguable in the sense that many a school of philosophy disallow such practices and insist on the reading of only the prescribed form, regardless of whether the worshipper realizes that or not. However, they do take account the need for private and personal prayers, so they propose praying in one's own it language after the formal prayer has ended and not throughout its course.

Mosque

The Masjid (Mosque) is the base and the foundation for Muslim society. It is the place where believers assemble to get to know each other and share their joys and their troubles. It is the hub from where the sound of the Oneness of Allah is raised and commitment to His Oneness is exercised. It is the place where the remembrance of Allah takes place ceaselessly. It is the centre from where the light of cognition and wiseness exhales and illuminate the surroundings.

A Mosque is a place devoted to the worship of God. Muslims are ordered to observe Salat in fold. If one is unable to reach a Mosque handily, or the journey to the mosque is unsafe, the Salat may be observed wherever suitable. The Holy prophet, has said that the all earth has been blessed and made a Mosque for Muslims.

The Mosque plays an exceedingly crucial role in a Muslim's life. Islam stresses that congregational prayers should be said in the Mosque. In the former state of Islam, when the Muslims were still unable to construct a Mosque of their own, the Holy Prophet selected Arqam's house who was a fellow of the Holy Prophet as the gathering place for the worshippers to say their prayers. This house was also used by the Holy Prophet as the focus for the preaching and spreading of Islam.

When the Holy Prophet migrated to Medina, the first activity he took was to construct a Mosque there, which is now acknowledged as the Prophet's Mosque. This Mosque became the focus of all Muslim actions. Deputations coming from other countries were invited there and were generally put up in this Mosque. This Mosque also served well as the centre for educational activity, knowledge, and training.

Muslim Mosques are therefore, not only for the intention of worship alone but, also serve as the focus for all social, cultural, political and versatile activities. There is no particular design or construction for a Mosque. Any building set up or used for congregational prayers is a Mosque.

Mosques are not only centres for worship but are also the manifestation of the features of Muslim society and its culture. Due to this fact, the Muslims have been called for to follow some rules which can be regarded to be the earliest state for the growth of Muslim character and to form true Muslim social system. The Mosques are centres of Islamic social growth, therefore, there are quite a few directions for a Muslim to follow when he comes to the Mosque.

When a Muslim attends the Mosque, he should wear clean, humble, and dignified cloths. There is no special dress decreed for the Muslims when the prayer is being offered.

- A Muslim should not consume any odorous foods such as onions, garlic or raw radish ahead of coming to the Mosque.
- Worshippers should not come in the Mosque with their shoes on.
- Making noise is also prohibited in the Mosque.
- Penalties are not allowed to be executed in the Mosque.
- Mosques are required to be kept absolutely clean.
- As prayer demands immersion and full attention, it is therefore prohibited to pass in front of the worshippers.

Mosques are centres for the worship of Allah, therefore, no body should be prevented admission to the Mosque. Allah states in the Quran; "All Mosques belong to Allah, so call not on anyone besides Allah." This verse line of the Holy Quran distinctly orders that Mosques are the place of Allah and Allah Alone. Thus, no one is allowed to keep anybody from entering the Mosques for the intention of worship.

Khutbah

Khutbah serves as the elementary formal occasion for public discourse in the Islamic custom. Such preachings occur on a regular basis, as dictated by the teachings of all legal schools, at the dhuhr (i.e.

noon) congregation prayer on Friday. In addition, alike sermons are called for on the two festival days, or in reaction to an eclipse or undue drought.

Religious oratory, including sermons, may be enunciated in a variety of settings and at diverse times. The khutbah, however, refers to khutbat al-juma, normally meaning the address delivered in the mosque at weekly and annual rituals. Other religious speech and affairs of preaching are depicted as dars (lesson) or waz (admonition), and their arrangments differ accordingly.

The khutbah developed from the practice of the prophet Muhammad, who used to deliver words of stimulation, direction, or command at assemblies for worship in the mosque, which comprised of the court of his house in Medina. Though khutba is not cited by name in the Quran, one passage clearly adverts to the Friday noon prayer, and calls believers to dhikr Allah (the remembrance of God). This is interpreted to be a saying that some commentators have regarded as referring the sermon.

After the takeover of Mecca, Muhammad introduced himself as a khatib to the city in AD. 630. The first four caliphs, and the Ummayads caliphs and governors all presented Sermons. There were not necessarily stimulating, but addressed pragmatic questions of government and sometimes even included direct decrees. Beneath the Abbasids, the caliph himself no longer preached, but allotted the task to the spiritual judges. The Abbasids asserted they were clearing Islam of the secularism of the Umayads, and this likely helped in strengthening the spiritual aspect of the Sermon.

At the commencing of the religious service the adhan is given, during which the khatib remains sitting. The iqama is given when the khatib comes down. The Sermon is presented in two parts. Both parts are delivered while khatib is standing and punctuated by a pause in between them when the khatib sits down. During the sermon itself, it is irremissible to enunciate the following:

The hamdala, saying to praise Allah and demonstrate feeling towards Him; enunciating al-hamdu li'llah "Praise belongs to Allah" at the origin of the Sermon is usually enough.

The salat on the Prophet.

Reading of a part of the Quran in the first part of the Sermon.

Warnings to devoutness in both parts of the Sermon,

Dua (prayer) on behalf of the faithful.

The khatib must be in a state of ritual purity; his dress must be in accordance with the situation. It is laudable for the khatib to be on a podium or an elevated place; to salute the fold when directing himself towards them; to sit down until the adhan is pronounced by the muadhdhin and to direct himself directly to his audience. In the end the khatib should make the Preaching short.

In medieval Islam, Preachings were generally in Arabic. This lingual necessity required substantial training on the part of the khatib, and a noteworthy degree of education on the part of listeners, particularly non-Arab Muslims. This prospect added to the growth of a writing style consisting of model sermons, such as those by the famous Ibn Nubata. Afterward, however, preaching in conversational languages, while often holding certain Arabic expressions, has become increasingly general.

One of the considerations for the validness of the Friday service is that it must be introduced by two sermons. The Sermon is when number of attenders expected for a valid Jumua are there. Traditionally, as taught in classic Islamic legal writings, Friday congregational prayers in which preachings were delivered were limited to urban centres and commonly to one major mosque in each city. Such a mosque is referred to as a jama masjid, i.e. a "Friday Mosque". These mosques were marked by their central position, large proportions, monumental architecture, and emblematic furnishings indicative of its grand stature, and, the most promonant of all, the minbar (ritual pulpit).

In present-day times, Friday Congregationalist prayers are common in mosques of all sizes and considerations, and not just limited to a few central positions. Sermons are also meted out through newspapers and broadcasted on radio and television.

Sermons on particular social occasions generally contain characteristics that are applicable to the celebrations at whose reaching they are presented. For example, on Eid-ul-Fitr, the preacher has a responsibility to instruct the congregation regarding the zakat, or alms-giving. On Eid-ul-Adha the preacher admits remarks defining the rules for the sacrifice.

There is a little difference in the Sermon delivered on Eid. The sermon's first part must start with nine takbirs, the second part with seven takbirs. The Sermon may also be said while sitting. Concerning the Sermons delivered during eclipse or drought, authoritative texts suggest that such sermons must warn the audience and ask God's forgiveness.

REFERENCES

Abdullah, S.: *Adabiyyat-i Farsi men Hinduwon ka hòissa,* Delhi, 1942.

Abid Husain: *The Destiny of Indian Muslims,* London, 1965.

Babur: *Tuzuk,* Leyden and Erskine, London, 1921.

Bada'uni, 'Abd-al-Qadir: *Muntakhab at-tawarikh,* Calcutta, 1868-1869.

Farid Bhakkari: *Dhakhira al-khawanin,* Karachi, 1961.

Farquhar, J. N.: *Modern Religious Movements in India*, London, 1924.

Fat'hò-ad-din: *Shajra-i Naqshbandiyya,* Rawalpindi, 1904.

Fergusson, James: *History of Indian and Eastern Architecture*, London., 1910.

Lentz, W.: "Sammlungen zur afghanischen Literatur — und Zeitgeschichte", *ZDMG* (1937), 711-32.

Leyden, J.: "On the Roshenian Sect and its Founder Bayazid Ansari", *Asiatic Researches.*

Lokhandwalla, Sh. T.: "The Bohras, a Muslim Community of Gujarat", SI, 1955.

Madani, Hòusayn. Ahmad: *Naqsh-i hòayat,* Delhi, 1953.

Simnani, Ashraf Jahangir: *Latòa'if-i Ashrqfi,* Delhi, 1882.

Smith, V. A.: *Akbar, the Great Mughal*, Oxford, 1919.

Temple, R. C.: *The Legends of the Punjab*, Bombay, 1884.

The Founder of the Ahòmadivya Movement, Lahore, n.d.

The Imperial Gayetteer of India, London, 1907-1909.

Titus, Murray T.: *Islam in India and Pakistan*, Calcutta, 1959.

Wa'izòshifi: *Rashhòat*, Cawnpore, 1912.

Wahid Mirza: *The Life and Works of Amir Khusrau*, Calcutta, 1935.

Wajia 'Ali Shah: *Sòawt-i mubarak*, Lucknow, 1853.

Wakil Ahòmad: *Nusrat al-mujtahdin,* Lucknow, 1896.

Wali-Allah, Shah *Hòusn al-'aqida* (Urdu tr. *Mera aqida*), in *Ar-Rahim* 1964.

Walter, H. A.: *The Ahmadiyya Movement*, Calcutta/ London, 1918.

Wellesz, Emmy: *Akbar's Religious Thought reflected in Mughal Painting*, London, 1952.

Wilkinson, J. V. S. and Gray, B.: *Persian Miniature Painting*, London, 1933.

Yusuf Husain: *L'Inde Mystique au Moyen Age*, Paris, 1929.

Zaehner, R. C.: *Hindu and Muslim Mysticism*, London, 1960.

Zahid 'Ali: *Hamara Isma'ili madhhab awr uski hòaqiqat,* Hyderabad, 1954.

Zubayd M. G. Ahmad: *The Contribution of India to Arabic Literature*, PH.D. dissertation, University of London.

2

History

The Arabia, place of birth of Islam is one of the hottest and driest areas in the world, comprising mainly of deserts. Since ancient times tribes of the wandering races had inhabited the region.

Considered the descendents of Noah's son Shem they are addressed as Semites. Over the years, theses Semitic people have migrated into the Geographic area and were absorbed to into existing civilizations.

In the sixth century AD., due north of the Arabian Peninsula two major powers were locked in a power conflict. The Christian Byzantine kingdom, heirs of the Roman Empire was to the northwest and in the northeast was the Zoroastrian Persian kingdom.

Both the Byzantine and Persian kingdoms had Arab tribes confederate to their cause of trade and subjugation.The Arabian Peninsula became a ground of sanctuary for those looking for escape from both of these empires. Christian sects like the Nestorians, and Jewish tribes getting away from the tyrannical Byzantines found sanctuary in the defensive deserts and cities of the Peninsula. Arabian Peninsula was separated into tribes and cities.

Each city had own deities. At one time in year the tribes and cities of Arabia would converge in the city of Mecca during an event acknowledged as the Haj. In Mecca, the Kaaba, a large cube shaped edifice housed 360 idols from all the clans of Arabia.

The Kaaba was the focus of Arabian spiritual life. Here all the war-ridden tribes would put away their conflicts. From the Kaaba they would continue to the other shrines outside Mecca during this five day spiritual event. The Haj was a custom that Arabs of the peninsula recalled going back hundreds of years.

ORIGIN

Muhammad

It was in this part of the world Muhammad Ibn Abdallah was born in 570 AD. in Mecca. His father died before his birth and his mother Amina expired when he was 6 years of age. His grandfather raised him but he also died two years later. Abu Talib his uncle took Muhammad into his family and nurtured him as his own son. At the age of 12, youthful Muhammad was taken on a wagon train-trading business to Syria and he saw the external world of Arabia for the first time. Christian monk named Buhaira, announced Talib's young nephew as the last prophet and warns him about the Jews. For the following 13 years little is known of his life except that he was involved in caravan trade.

At the age of 25, Muhammad weds a 40 year old affluent, widow named Khadijah who possesses trading caravans. During the next 15 years of his life he moves with Arabs known as the Hanefites. Hanefites were Arabs who disapproved idol worship and were looking for the true religion. They looked to the faith of the Jews and Christians as being close to the goal. The Hanefites deserted their idols and retreated to the caves of Mecca in contemplation and supplication.

At age 40 Muhammad had, for the first time, vision in the year 610 AD. He was in a cave on Mt. Hera and believed he was demon possessed. He went to Khadijah and told her more or less about the event. She checked with with her uncle Waraca, a Hanefite who had converted to Christianity, who reassured them that Muhammad vision was from God. Waraca announced Muhammad was a prophet to the Arab peoples.

Muhammad announced Allah as the one rightful god and spurned the idol worship of Mecca. Hardly any listened to Muhammad's message and bad blood developed against him as he confronted the idol believers and advocated his religion to Mecca. Abu Talib his uncle and his clan the Hasims saved him during this early Meccan period. In 619 Khadijah and Abu Talib died. Abu Talib headed the Hasim clan, of which Muhammad was a fellow member. The new leader of the Hasim tribe his uncle Abu Lahab declined to protect Muhammad. During the next three years Muhammad was constantly in danger. He sought asylum and protection in nearby cities from those looking for his life.

Then in 621 AD. during the Haj, Arab tribes from the city of Medina, came for the yearly pilgrimage. They encountered Muhammad and thought him to be a prophesier and invited him to their city to bring peacefulness and decide disputes between the war-ridden tribes. The Arabs of Medina had been assured by Jewish tribesmen about the approaching Messiah who would one day suppress the world including the Arabs. The Arab tribes hoped to find this person before the Jews. After meeting Muhammad they believed he was the one.

The Hejira (Flight): The following year the position became unbearable for the Muslims and in June 622 AD. they did what is now known as the Hejira (flight). In little groups the 150 Muslims of Mecca got out of the city of Medina 280 miles to the north. When word reached those of Mecca about the get away to Medina they tried to kill Muhammad. Muhammad and Abu Bakr were able to slip away of the city and get away to Medina by another road in September 622 AD.

In Medina the war-ridden Arab tribes presented to Muhammad leadership and prophet-hood. The Jewish tribes scorned his claims of prophet and laughed at his divine revelation. With most of the new arrivers from Mecca without employment they needed to earn a living. Ghazu or caravan marauding was a way tribes would keep one tribe from becoming too mighty. The Muslims in Medina began to hold up the caravans leading toward Mecca. This is from where the Muslim philosophy of Jihad was created.

With their caravan occupation being jeopardized, Mecca answers with one thousand soldiers at the battle of Bedr in March 624, the Muslims fielded 300 soldiers. The battle was won by the Muslims. Muhammad announced his victory was a sign from Allah and his status in Medina was amplified. The lack of ebullience by one of the Jewish tribes induced them to be expelled by the winning Muslim army. The focus of prayer was also altered from Jerusalem to Mecca as the Jews declined Muhammad's prophet-hood.

Precisely one year latter Mecca gathered 3000 soldiers at the battle of Uhud and the Muslims answered by 1000 soldiers. The fight did not go as plotted. The Muslims beaten by Mecca drew back to Medina. Demoralized, Muslims blamed the second Jewish tribe as plotters against their cause. Their homes and belongings were impounded, and they were expelled from the city in 626 AD.

The Meccans in the hope of ending the caravan forays by the Muslims gathered 10,000 soldiers to assault the city of Medina in the year 627. After a two weeks military blockade, they were unable to get through the fortress of city. They came back to Mecca. After this failed attack,

Muslims attacked the last left over Jewish tribe. The tribe gave up to the mercy of Muhammad. The men were disposed off and the women and children were traded into bondage. The Muslims then begin to strengthen their power with the neighbour Arab tribes and cities.

Mecca started to feel the economical impact of its business losses and Muhammad's might grew in the north. They unenthusiastically signed the 10 year Hudaybiah peace agreement with Muhammad in March 628 AD. Muslims were allowed to return to Mecca and worship at the Kaaba one time in a year. The citizenry of Mecca would leave their city so the Muslim could come in and worship.

Two years later, in January 630 AD., Muhammad heads 10,000 soldiers to Mecca and invalidates the treaty of Hudaybiah because Muslims were killed. The city bows to Muhammad and his warriors and admits him as prophet. Muhammad goes to the Kaaba and demolishes the 360 idols. From Mecca, the Muslims waged Jihad on the bordering cities coercing them to accept Islam as their religion and Muhammad as their prophet. Muhammad made his final Haj in 632 AD. and died three months later in June. His father in law Abu Bakr followed him as leader of the Muslims.

EARLY HISTORY

From the cities of Mecca and Medina, the message of Islam went into the world with moving speed. Within half a century of the Prophet's death, Islam had outspread to three continents. Islam is not a faith of the sword nor did it spread out chiefly by means of war. It was only within Arabia, where a crude form of idolatry was rearing, that Islam was spread by warring against those tribes which did not consent the message of God, whereas Christians and Jews were not pressured to convert. Outside from Arabia also the immense grounds, conquered by the Arab armies in a little time, became Muslim not by force but by the charm of the new faith. It was trust in One God and stress upon His Mercy that brought huge numbers of people into the congregation of Islam. The new religion did not force people to convert. Many remained Jews and Christians and even now significant communities of these faiths are found in Muslim lands.

Furthermore, the spread of Islam was not confined to its providential early expansion outside of Arabia. During later centuries the Turks adopted Islam peacefully as did a large number of the individuals of the Indian sub-continent. In Africa also, Islam has spread out throughout the past two centuries even under the powerful power of European rulers. Nowadays Islam goes on to grow not only in Africa but also in Europe and America where Muslims now constitute a noteworthy minority.

Islam was intended to become a world religion and to produce a civilization which extended from one end of the globe to the other. Already throughout the early Muslim caliphates, first Arabs, then Persians and later the Turks set out to make classical Islamic civilization. Later, in the 13th century, both Africa and India became great focuses of Islamic civilization and soon thenceforth Muslim kingdoms were founded in the Malay-Indonesian world while Chinese Muslims prospered throughout China.

Islam is a faith for all people from whatsoever race or background they might be. That is why Islamic civilization is founded on a unity which stands entirely against any racial or ethnic favouritism. Such major racial and ethnic groups as the Arabs, Africans, Indians, and Malays in addition to several smaller social units adopted Islam and contributed to the building of Islamic civilization. Moreover, Islam was not opposed to teaching from the earlier civilizations and integrating their learning, and culture into its own world, as long as they did not contradict the principles of Islam. Each cultural and racial group which adopted Islam made its contribution to the one Islamic civilization to which everyone belonged to. The feel of brotherhood and sisterhood was so much accentuated that it overcame all local adherences to a particular tribe, race, or language, all of which became submissive to the world of Islam.

The world-wide civilization hence produced by Islam permitted people of various cultural backgrounds to work together in refining assorted arts and sciences. Though the civilization was deeply Islamic, even non-Muslim people took part in the rational activity whose fruits belonged to everybody. The scientific mood was evocative of the present situation in world where scientists are active in the progress of knowledge which belongs to everyone.

This civilization of Islam also succeeded in setting off the mind and reflection of the people who entered its congregation. As a result of Islam, the wandering Arabs turned pallbearers of learning. The Persians who had produced a great culture before the rise of Islam however produced much more learning in the Islamic period than before. The same can be said of the Turks and other peoples who adopted Islam. The faith of Islam was itself responsible for not only for the introduction of a world civilization in which individuals of many different cultural backdrops participated, but it played a fundamental role in developing rational and cultural life on a size not seen before. For some eight hundred years Arabic continued the major scientific language of the world. During the centuries coming after the rise of Islam, Muslim dynasties ruling in several parts of the Islamic universe proved the rise of Islamic culture. As a matter of fact this tradition of rational activity was overshadowed only at the beginning of modern times as a result of the breaking of faith among Muslims combined with outside domination.

MEDIEVAL HISTORY

Caliphs

On the death of the Prophet, Abu Bakr, the supporter of the Prophet and the first man to embrace Islam, became caliph. Abu Bakr reigned for two years to be followed by Umar who was caliph for a decade and throughout whose rule Islam propagated extensively. It was Umar who advanced foot at the end of his army into Jerusalem and ordained the protection of Christian sites. Umar also founded the first public treasury and an advanced financial organization. He founded many of the introductory practices of Islamic administration.

Umar was followed by Uthman who ruled for twelve years during which time the Islamic expansion went forward. He is also recognized as the caliph who had the text of the Quran replicated and sent to all corners of the Islamic world. He was in turn followed by Ali who is acknowledged to this day for his fluent sermons, and also for his courage. With his demise the reign of the rightly guided caliphs, who hold an exceptional place of deference in the hearts of Muslims, came to an conclusion.

The Caliphate

Umayyad: The Umayyad era founded in 661 AD. was to last for more or less a century. During this time Damascus became the capital of an Islamic world which extended from the western borders of China to southern France. Not only did the Islamic conquerings continue during this period of time through North Africa to Spain, France in the West and to Sind, Central Asia and Transoxiana in the East, but the fundamental social institutions of the freshly established Islamic world were founded.

Abbasids: The Abbasids, who followed the Umayyads, changed the capital to Baghdad which soon grew into an incomparable centre of learning and culture as well as the administrative and policy-making centre of a huge world.

They reigned for over 500 years but bit by bit their power declined and they remained only symbolical rulers bestowing authenticity upon various sultans and princes who maintained actual military power. The Abbasid caliphate was finally eliminated when Hulagu, the Mongol ruler, conquered Baghdad in 1258, demolishing much of the city including its libraries.

While the Abbasids ruled in Baghdad, a number of mighty families such as the Fatimids, Ayyubids and Mamluks held magnate in Egypt, Syria and Palestine. The most crucial event in this area as far as the relation between Islam and the Western world was related was the series of Campaigns declared by the Pope and adopted by various European kings. The aim, although political, was outwardly to retake the Holy Land and particularly Jerusalem for Christianity. While there was at the outset some success and local European rule was established in parts of Syria and Palestine, Muslims finally dominated and in 1187 AD. Saladin recaptured Jerusalem and overcame the Crusaders.

North Africa And Spain

When the Abbasids conquered Damascus, one of the Umayyad princes got away and made the long travel from there to Spain to found Umayyad rule there, thus commencing the golden age of Islam in Spain. Cordoba was founded as the capital and soon became Europe's most outstanding city not only in population but from the viewpoint of its cultural and intellect life. The Umayyads reigned over two centuries until they weakened and were substituted by local rulers.

In the meantime, in North Africa, various neighbouring dynasties commanded until two mighty Berber dynasties succeeded in combining much of North Africa and Spain in the 12th and 13th centuries. After them this area was governed once again by local dynasties such as the Sharifids of Morocco who still reign in that country. As for Spain, Muslim might continued to decline until the last Muslim dynasty was overcame in Granada in 1492 AD. thus bringing eight hundred years of Muslim rule in Spain to a finish.

After Mangol Invasion

The Mongols laid waste the eastern lands of Islam and ruled from the Sinai Desert to India for a period of time of 100 years. But they soon embraced Islam and got known as the Il-Khanids. They were in turn followed by Timur and his lineage who made Samarqand their capital and reigned from 1369 to 1500 AD. The unexpected rise of Timur checked the formation and enlargement of the Ottoman Empire but before long the Ottomans became the prevailing power in the Islamic world.

Ottoman Empire

From modest blood line the Turks rose to prevail over the whole of Anatolia and even parts of Europe. In 1453 AD. Mehmet conquered Constantinople and finished the Byzantine Empire. The Ottomans seized much of Eastern Europe and nearly the whole of the Arab world, only Morocco and Mauritania in the West and Yemen. They reached their peak of power with Suleyman the Magnificent whose forces reached Hungary and Austria. From the 17th century onwards with the rise of Western European forces and later Russia, the might of the Ottomans began to decline. But they however remained a force to be considered with until the First World War when they were overcame by the Western nations. Soon thereafter Kamal Ataturk gained magnate in Turkey and got rid of the Ottomans in 1924.

Persia

While the Ottomans were interested mostly with the western face of their empire, to the east in Persia a young dynasty called the Safavids came to might in 1502 AD. The Safavids founded a powerful state of their own which prospered for over two centuries. Their capital, Isfahan, became one of the most glorious cities with its blue tiled mosques and beautiful houses.

The Afghan intrusion of 1736 put an end to Safavid rule and prepared the independency of Afghanistan which happened officially in the 19th century. Persia itself fell into turmoil until Nader Shah, reunified the state and even conquered India. But the rule of the dynasty founded by him was short-lived. The Zand dynasty soon took over to be brought down by the Qajars in 1779 who made Tehran their capital and reigned until 1921 when they were successively replaced by the Pahlavis.

India

While for India, Islam came to it from east of the Indus River peacefully. Step by step Muslims acquired political power in the early 13th century. But this period which marked the growth of both Islam and Islamic culture came to an end with the conquering of much of India in 1526 AD. by Babur. He established the powerful Mughal Empire which gave rise to such famous rulers as Akbar, Jahangir, and Shah Jahan and which survived, in spite of the gradual rise of British power in India, until 1857 when it was formally abolished.

Malaysia and Indonesia

Islam began to propagate in the 12th century in northern Sumatra and before long Muslim kingdoms were founded in Java, Sumatra and Malaysia. In spite of the colonization of the Malay world, Islam multiplied in that area covering Indonesia, Malaysia, the southern Philippines and southern Thailand, and is even extending in islands farther east.

Africa

Islam came into East Africa at the very commencement of the Islamic period but stayed confined to the coast for some time, only the Sudan and Somaliland becoming bit by bit both Islamized. West Africa experienced the presence of Islam through North African dealers who travelled with their caravans south of the Sahara. By the 14th century there were already Muslim states in areas as Mali, and Timbuktu in West Africa and Harar in East Africa.

Step by step Islam infiltrated both interior and southward. There also came along major magnetic figures who enlivened intense opposition against European supremacy. The process of the Islamization of Africa did not end during the colonial time period and goes on even today with the consequence that most Africans are now Muslims preserving a tradition which has had much as long a history in certain regions of sub-Saharan Africa as Islam itself.

MODERN HISTORY

After Colonial Period

At the peak of European colonial growth in the 19th century, most of the Islamic world was under colonial dominion with the exclusion of a few regions such as the Ottoman empire, Persia, Afghanistan, Yemen and certain parts of Arabian Peninsula. But even these areas were under alien influence or, in the case of the Ottomans, under ceaseless menace. After the First World War with the break down of the Ottoman empire, a number of Arab states such as Iraq became autonomous, others like Jordan were made as a new entity and so far others like Palestine, Syria and Lebanon were either assigned or became French colonies. As for Arabian Peninsula, it was at this time that Saudi Arabia became finally amalgamated. As for other regions of the Islamic world, Egypt became more independent as a consequence of the fall of the Ottomans, Turkey was turned into a secular democracy by Kemal Ataturk, and the Pahlavi dynasty began a new phase in Persia where its name returned to its eastern conventional form of Iran. But rest of the Islamic world stayed under colonial dominion.

Arab

It was only after the Second World War and the break down of the British, French, Dutch and Spanish empires that the rest of the Islamic world acquired its independency. In the Arab world, Syria and Lebanon became autonomous at the end of the war as did Libya and the sheikhdoms around the Gulf and the Arabian Sea by the 1960's. The North African nations of Tunisia, Morocco and Algeria had to fight a hard end, in the case of Algeria, lengthy war to gain their freedom which did not arrived until a decade later for Tunisia and Morocco and two decades later for Algeria. Only Palestine did not become sovereign but was zoned in 1948 with the constitution of the state of Israel.

India

In India Muslims took part in the freedom crusade against British rule along with Hindus and when independency finally came in 1947, they were able to make their own homeland, Pakistan, which came to life for the sake of Islam and became the most inhabited Muslim state though many Muslims stayed in India. In 1971, however, the two parts of the Pakistan broke up and East Pakistan becoming Bangladesh.

Far East

Further east still, the Indonesians at last gained their independency from the Dutch and the Malays from Britain. At first Singapore was part of Malaysia but it broke in 1963 to become an autonomous state. Small colonies still continued in the area and persisted in seeking their independence, the land of Brunei becoming autonomous only just in 1984.

Africa

In Africa countries with large Muslim populations such as Nigeria, began to gain their independence in the 1950's and 1960's with the result that by the end of the 60's most parts of the Islamic world were formed into autonomous nations. The Muslim states in the Soviet Union failed to earn their liberty or independence. The same holds true for Sinkiang while in southern Philippines Muslim independence campaigns still continue.

National States

While the cosmos of Islam has entered into the contemporary world in the form of national states, uninterrupted attempts are made to produce closer cooperation within the Islamic world completely and to bring about bigger integrity. This is seen not only in the get together of the Muslim chiefs of state and the constitution of the OIC (Organization of Islamic Countries) with its own secretariate, but also in the founding of institutions dealing with the whole of the Islamic world. Among the most significant of these is the Muslim World League with its main office in Mecca. Saudi Arabia has in fact acted a key role in the foundation and maintenance of such establishments.

Islam in the United States

It is almost unfeasible to generalize about American Muslims. They are converts, migrants, factory workers, doctors; all are building their own share to America's future. This composite society is unified by a general faith, supported by a nationwide web of a thousand mosques.

Muslims were early arrivers in North America. By the eighteenth century there were thousands of them, working as slaves on plantations. These early societies cut off from their inheritance and families, without doubt lost their Islamic uniqueness as time went by. In the present day many American Muslims play a significant role in the Islamic society.

The nineteenth century, saw the early expansion of incursion of Arab Muslims, most of whom established in the main industrial centres where they worshipped in borrowed rooms. Near the beginning of twentieth century, we witnessed the influx of hundred thousands of Muslims from Eastern Europe: the first Albanian mosque was opened in 1915; others soon followed, and Polish Muslims opened a mosque in Brooklyn in 1928. During the time of President Truman, in 1947 the Washington Islamic Centre was established, and various nationwide establishments were founded in the fifties. More lately, numerous fellow members of these assemblies have figured in the congregation of Muslim orientation. Today there are approximately five million Muslims in America.

Revival of Islam

Muslims did not like to acquire only their political independency. They also wished to maintain their own religious and ethnical personal identity. From the 18th century onwards Muslim reformists appeared in the picture who attempted to confirm the teachings of Islam and to straighten out society on the basis of Islamic commandments. One of the first within this group was Muhammad ibn Abd al-Wahhab. This reformist was backed by Muhammad ibn al-Saud, the founding father of the first Saudi state. With this backing Muhammad ibn Abd al-Wahhab was able to extend his precepts not only in Arabian Peninsula but even outside its borders where his restructuring persist to exert authority to this day.

In the 19th century Islamic affirmation took various forms such as the Mahdi movement of the Sudan, informative movements such as that of Aligarh movement in India aspiring to re-educate Muslims. Egypt continues to this day centre of Islamic learning. A number of reformists came along, each dealing with some view of Islamic thought. Some were interested in law, others economics, and yet others the challenges laid by Western civilization with its potent technology. These included Jamal al-Din al-Afghani who was the great hero of Pan-Islamism, which was the social movement to unite the Islamic world politically and religiously. Muhammad Abduh, who was the rector of al-Azhar was also very authoritative in Islamic theological system. Also of significant authority was his student, Rashid Rida, who held a place closer to that of Abd al-Wahhab and represented the rigid application of the Shariah. Among the most celebrated of these creative thinkers is Muhammad Iqbal, the prominent poet and philosopher who is looked at as the father of Pakistan.

Reform Organizations

As Western authority began to infiltrate more profoundly into the character of Islamic society, establishments gradually grew up whose destination was to regenerate society in practice on Islamic lines and forestall its secularization. These included the Muslim Brotherhood established in Egypt and with branches in numerous Muslim countries, and the Jamaat-i Islami of Pakistan established by the Mawlana Mawdudi. These organizations have been normally peaceful and have sought to reinstate an Islamic order through teaching. Throughout the last two decades, as a result of the foiling of many Muslims in the face of forces coming from a secularized external world, some have sought to refuse the damaging aspects of Western thought process and culture and to return to an Islamic order based totally on the application of the Shariah.

Today in all Muslim countries there are substantial movements to maintain and spread Islamic teachings. In countries such as Saudi Arabia Islamic Law is already being employed and in fact is the reason for the successfulness, growth and stability of the country.

In erstwhile countries where Islamic Law is not enforced, however, most of the attempt of Islamic movements is used up in making possible the full use of the Shariah so that the country can enjoy successfulness along with the fulfilment of the trust of its people. Anyhow the far-flung desire for Muslims to have the spiritual law of Islam applied and to confirm their religious values and their own individuality must not be equated with particular violent outbreaks which do exist but which are usually treated sensationally and taken out of proportionality by the mass media in the West.

In seeking to live fruitfully in the modern world, in sovereignty and concording to Islamic principles, Muslim countries have been stressing a great deal the implication of the role of educational activity and the importance of mastering Western education. Already in the 19th century, many Muslim countries such as Egypt, Turkey and Persia founded institutions of higher teachings where the advanced sciences and particularly medicine were taught. During this century establishments at all levels have multiplied across the Islamic world. Nearly every science ranging from mathematics to biology as well as various fields of modern technology are taught in these establishments and some famous scientists come out in the Islamic world, who have often united teaching in these establishments with training of the West.

In several parts of the Islamic world there is a sense that educational institutions must be spread out and also their standards should be bettered to the degree of the best establishments in the world in respective fields of learning particularly science and technology. Simultaneously there is an consciousness that the educational system must be based totally on Islamic precepts and the influence of foreign cultural and values and norms, to the degree that they are negative, be lessened. To cure this difficulty a number of international Islamic informative conferences have been held, the first one in Mecca in 1977, and the world-class minds of the Islamic world have been drew together to study and contemplate over the question of the relation between Islam and modern science. This is an on-going procedure which is at the centre of attention in many parts of the Islamic world and which points to the implication of educational questions in the Islamic world today.

The oldest educational institution in the world which is still running is the eleven hundred year old Islamic university of Fez, Morocco (Qarawiyyin). This old custom of Islamic learning shaped the West greatly through the way of Spain. In this realm where Muslims, Christians and Jews lived for the most part peacefully for many years, interlingual rendition began to be created in the 11th century for the most part in Toledo of Islamic works into Latin through the mediator of Jewish scholarly persons most of whom had the knowledge of Arabic and frequently wrote in

Arabic. As a result of these versions, Islamic thought process and through it much of Greek view became known to the West. Even the Islamic educational system was imitated in Europe and to this day the term chair in an educational institution comes from the Arabic kursi (seat) upon which a teacher would sit to instruct his students in the madrasa (school). As European culture grew and arrived at the high Middle Ages, there was few field of learning, whether it was literature or science, where there was not some authority of Islam present.

Islamic teaching became in this way part of Western civilization even if with the coming of the Renaissance, the West not only turned against its own medieval past times but also attempted to forget the long relation it had had with the Islamic cosmos, one which was based on rational respect notwithstanding religious resistance.

The Islamic cosmos remains nowadays a vast land stretching out from the Atlantic to the Pacific, with an existence in western world, inspired by the teachings of Islam and seeking to maintain its own identity. In spite of the bearing of patriotism and various secular orientations in their middle, Muslims wish to live in the modern world but without simply copying blindly the manners adopted by the West. The Islamic world wishes to live at peace but simultaneously not to be overshadowed by them. It wishes to dedicate its resources and energies to constructing a better life for its people on the foundation of the commandments of Islam and not to waste its resources in conflicts. It looks to create better understanding with the West and to be better realized by the West. The fates of the Islamic world and the West cannot be totally differentiated and thus it is only in understanding each other better that they can supply their own people more fruitfully and also lead to a better liveliness for the entire humanity.

REFERENCES

Abu-l-Layth Siddiqi: *Lakhna'u ka dabistan-i sha'iri,* Lahore, 1955.

Ahmad Ali Batalawi: *Nusrat al-mujtahidin,* Lucknow, 1895.

Bahra'ichi, Na'im-Allah: *Ma'lumat-i Mazhariyya,* Cawnpore, 1858.

Bailey, T. Grahame: *A History of Urdu Literature*, Calcutta, 1932.

Firishta, Abu-l-Qasim: *Gulshan-i Ibrahimi* (*Ta'rikh-i Firishta),* Bombay, 1832; Lucknow, 1905; Eng. tr. J. Briggs (*History of the Rise of Muhammadan Power in India*), London, 1829.

Firuz Tughluq: *Futhòhòat-i Firuz Shahi*, ed. S. Abdur-Rashid, Aligarh, 1954.

Fisher, Humphrey J.: *Ahòmadiyyah: A Study in Contemporary Islam on the West Afirican Coast*, London, 1963.

Fyzee, A. A. A. (ed.): *A Shïte Creed*, Bombay, 1942.

Mançri, Sharaf-ad-din Ahòmad ibn-Yahòya: *Maktubat,* Lucknow, 1868; Cawnpore, 1911.

Massignon, L.: *Essai sur les origines du Lexique Technique de la Mystique musulmane,* Paris, 1922.

Mawdudi, A. A.: *Towards Understanding Islam*, Lahore, 1960.

Mawdudi, Abu-l-A'la: *Ta'limat,* Lahore, 1955.

Roychoudhuri, M.: *The Din-i Ilahi,* Calcutta, 1941.

Sabir, M.: "Cultural and Linguistic Affinities Between Turkey, Iran and Pakistan", in *Papers read at the R.C.D. Seminar on Common Cultural Heritage*, Tehran, 1965.

Sadiq, Muhammad: *A History of Urdu Literature*, London, 1964.

Saksena, R. B.: *A History of Urdu Literature*, Allahabad, 1940.

Saqi Musta'id Khan: *Ma'athir-i 'Aamgiri,* Calcutta, 1947.

Sarwar Muhòammad: *Panjabidab,* Karachi, n.d.

Sayyid, Ahòmad Khan: *Tafsir al-Qur'an,* Lahore, 1880-1895.

Sell, E.: *The Religious Orders of Islam*, Madras, 1908.

Sen, D. C.: *History of Bengali Language and Literature*, Calcutta, 1911.

Shatòtòari, Baha'ad-din: *Risala-i Shatòtòariyya,* 10 Pers. MS 2257.

Shçr Khan Lodi: *Mir'at al-khayal,* Calcutta, 1831.

Shçrani, M.: *Panjab mçn Urdu*, Lahore, 1928.

Shibli Nu'mani: *Rasa'il,* Delhi, 1898.

Shustari, Nur-Allah: *Majalis al-mu'minin,* Tehran, 1852.

Sijzi, Amir Hòasan: *Fawa'id al-fu'ad,* Delhi, 1865.

Sikander ibn-Muhòammad 'Manjhu': *Mir'at-i Sikandari,* Baroda, 1961.

Simnani, 'Ali'-ad-dawla: *Chihil Majalis,* BM Or. MS 9725.

Simnani, Ashraf Jahangir: *Latòa'if-i Ashrqfi,* Delhi, 1882.

Smith, V. A.: *Akbar, the Great Mughal*, Oxford, 1919.

Smith, Wilfrid Cantwell: *Pakistan as an Islamic State*, Lahore, 1951.

Sòabah-ad-din 'Abd-at-Rahòman: *Bazm-i Sòhòfiyya,* A'zamgarh, 1949.

Sorley, H. T.: *Shah Abdul Latif of Bhit*, London, 1940.

Stchoukine, Ivan: *La Peinture Indienne,* Paris, 1929.

Storey, C. A.: *Persian Literature, A Bio-Bibliographical Survey*, London, 1927-58.

Suhrawardi, Diya'-ad-din Abu-Najib ' Abd-al-Qahir: *Adab al-muridin,* Urdu tr. Delhi, 1901.

Tara Chand: *The Influence of Islam on Hindu Culture*, Allahabad, 1936.

3

Philosophy

The correct purpose of embracing a religion follows that we ought to derive such certainty pertaining to God, who is the source of redemption, as though one can discover him with one's eyes. The unholy spirit of sinfulness seeks to destruct a person cannot escape the fateful poison of sin till he trusts with full certainty in the complete God and till he knows for sure that God exists, Who penalizes the offender and confers upon a righteous one every long-lasting pleasure. It is a general experience that when one believes in the fateful consequences of anything one does not have refuge to it. Then why does somebody commit sin intentionally? The reason is that he has not that confidence in this thing as he has in other subjects of the kind that we have cited. The first obligation of a person, therefore, is to develop certainty with regard to the beingness of God, and to assume a religion through which this certainty can be gained so that he should fear God and banish sin. How can such belief be developed? It cannot be gained through mere narratives. It cannot be acquired through mere argumentations. The only way of acquiring assurance is to live God repeatedly through discourse with Him or through seeing his amazing signs, or by keeping company with person who has that knowledge.

The aim of religion is that man should obtain liberation from his fervour and should develop special love for God through certain confidence in His existence and His perfect dimensions. Such affection for God is the heaven which will appear in various shapes in the afterlife. To be incognizant of the true God and to keep at bay from Him and not to have any affection for Him is the hell which will appear in various shapes in the afterlife. Therefore the exact reason is to have full faith in Him.

The purpose of accepting a religion is that God, Who is self- adequate and is in no requirement of His creation or its adoration, may be delighted with us, and that we should go through such grace and clemency as should erase our inner blots and rusts so that our heart may be filled with conviction and reason. This is not possible for a man to accomplish through his own methods. Hence, God, keeping concealed primarily His own Being and the marvels of His macrocosm, for instance, mortals and bodies, saints, paradise, hell, resurgence and envoy ship etc. and yet revealing them partly through rationality, appointed his retainers to believe all these enigmas.

BASIC PHILOSOPHY

To recognize a genuine faith it is necessary to look at three issues. In the first place, we must look what the precept of a faith concerning to God is. That is to say, what does a religion state with regard to the unity, might, knowledge, perfection, greatness, punishment, clemency and other attributes of the God. Second, it is essential that a seeker after truth should investigate what does a religion teach with respect to his individual self and with respect to human behavior. Is there anything in its commandment which would disrupt human kinships, or would draw a soul into courses which are inconsistent with modesty and honour, or would be opposite to the law of nature, or would be impossible to conform to or carry out, or make it dangerous to do so. It would also be essential to look whether some important teaching required to control disorderliness has been left out. It would also be necessary to learn whether a faith presents God as a Great Benefactor with Whom a kinship of personal love should be built and whether it sets down precepts which lead from darkness into light and from inadvertence to remembrance.

Third, it is essential for a seeker after truth to satisfy himself that the God presented by a religion should not be one Who is considered in on the basis of tales and stories and resembles a dead being. To trust in a God who resembles a dead being, belief in whom is not by virtue of His having manifested Himself but is due to one's own good faith, would be to put Him under an responsibility. It is useless to believe in a God whose abilities are not felt and who does not Himself make manifest the signs of His own existence and spirit.

The religion that claims to be from God must show Preindication of being from Divinity and should bear the seal of God which should attest the fact that it is from God. Islam is such a faith. That God Who is hidden is known through this religion and demonstrates Himself to the genuine followers of this religion. A true religion is supported by the hand of God, and through such religion God manifests Himself that He exists. The religions that depend completely upon narratives are only a kind of idol worship. Such religions do not possess the spirit of truth. If God is alive as He was, and speaks and hears as He did, there is no reason why He should continue silent as if He does not exist. If He does not speak in this age, then evenly and certainly He does not hear either. In other words, He is now naught. That religion alone is true which demonstrates that God hears and speaks in this age also. In a true religion, God certifies His existence through His speaking. Search for God is a hard subject. It is not an affair of worldly philosophers and informed men. Observation of the spheres and world only leads to the decision that although orderliness indicates that the universe should have a Creator yet it is not impervious that such Creator in fact exists. There is a deal of difference between ought to be and is. The Sacred Quran is the only book which places forth His existence as a fact and not only advocates the seeking of God but gives Him apparent. There is no other book which makes transparent the Hidden Being.

Faith does not mean conflicts, abuse and loose words which are spoilt, in the name of religious belief. In this linguistic context, no one pays attention to the inhibition of inner frailties or the establishment of true kinship with the Beloved. One party attacks another party and every kind of ill conduct is exhibited in support of religion. Such people do not see why they arrived into this world and what is the important function of their lives. They continue blind and ill-natured and give their intolerant opinions the name of religion. They exhibit their bad manners and use their loose tongues in support of a fictitious god of whose existence they have no proof. Of what use is a religion which does not teach the worship of a Living God? The God that they present is no better than a cadaver. He walks with the backup of others. When that support is removed, he falls to the earth. The only thing they benefit from such a faith is bigotry. They lack completely true fear of God and true sympathy with humanity which is the greatest of features.

The second feature of Islam, which is not shared by any other religion and which demonstrates its truth, is that it manifests its living benedictions and miracles of which different religions are wholly stripped. The marks that Islam exhibits not only establish its transcendency over other religions but enable it to attract the hearts of the people by demonstrating its perfect light. The first feature of Islam which we have stated above, that is to say, the flawlessness of its teaching, is not quite definitive in establishing that Islam is a true religion disclosed by God. A bigoted opponent who is not clear-sighted may assert that it is possible that a teaching might be perfect and yet it may not proceed from God Almighty. This first characteristic relieves a wise seeker after truth of many doubts and brings him close to certainty, but does not establish the matter conclusively and beyond doubt till it is combined with the second feature. By their combination the light of the true faith reaches its perfection. A true faith represents thousands of proofs and sparkles but these two characteristics are enough to carry strong belief to the spirit of a searcher after truth and elaborate the matter to the gratification of all deniers of trueness. Nothing more is needed in accession.

God Almighty is not held back in exposition of the claim of the Holy Prophet. He came like a sunlight and demonstrated his light from every degree of position. He who turns away from this true sun, will come to no good. We cannot credit such a one with esteemed faith. Can anyone who is afflicted with disease and whose arms are defective, lay claim that he is healthy and is not in need of treatment? Should he say so, can we accredit him with complete trust? Should such a person insist that he cannot arrive at the truth of Islam, despite good faith and despite every attempt such as he puts onward in his worldly affairs, his subject rests with God. We have not come across any such person and we consider it impossible that anyone equipped with understanding and a sense of justice should prefer some other religion to Islam. Foolish and ignorant people adopt the position under the dictates of their lower egos that notion in the Unity of God is enough, and that it is not necessary to the Holy Prophet, but it is to be taken in mind that a Prophet shows the existence of God.

Who knows the exposition of the trueness better than God Himself. He filled heaven and earth with signs to prove the truth of the Holy Prophet. What then is lacking in the full exposition of the truth. He who has sense plenty to oppose why can he not think out the path of acceptance? He who professes that he can see at nighttime, why can he not see in the complete light of daytime? Indeed the way of acceptance is much easier than the way of rejection. The case of a person whose reason is defective and whose faculties are not normal should be committed to God, and we have nothing to do pertaining to him. He is like children who die at an early age. But a bad denier cannot exempt himself on the ground that he is acting in good faith. It should be considered whether his mental faculties are such that he can value questions of Unity and Prophet Hood. If he is capable of appreciating them and denies out of ill-will, he cannot be apologized. Can we apologize a person who observes the light of the sun and yet persists in insisting that it is not daytime but night. In the identical way, we cannot exempt those who deliberately indulge in wrong rational and are unable to rebuff the arguments that are put onward on behalf of Islam. Islam is a practical faith.

DIVINE LAWS

The God of Islam is the same God who is visible in the natural law of nature and is discernible in the book of nature. Islam has not presented a new God but has presented the same God who is introduced by the light of man's heart, by the moral sense of man, and by promised land and earth.

Our soul and every particle of our beingness are flat before the Mighty, True and Perfect God from whose hand each soul and every speck of creation together with all its mental faculties came into being, and through whose support every being is sustained. Nothing is outside His knowledge, or outside His control, or outside His creation. We call thousands of blessings and peace and mercy on the Holy Prophet Muhammad, the chosen one, through whom we have seen the living God who gives us proof of His existence through His Word. He presents to us through extraordinary signs His shining countenance which possesses eternal and perfect power. We found the Messenger who demonstrated God to us and we found the God who created everything through His perfect power. How majestic is His might that nothing came into beingness without it and nothing can remain to exist without its backup. That genuine God of ours features infinite benedictions, numberless powers, numberless beauties, and beneficences.

The Beingness of God is invisible upon invisible and beyond and is most private and cannot be found by the ability of human rational alone, and no debate can prove it once and for all; inasmuch as ground can travel only so far that contemplating the universe it feels the demand of a Creator. But the feeling of a need is one thing and it is quite another to arrive at the certainty that the God whose need has been felt does in fact exist. As the operation of reason is abnormal, incomplete, and doubtful, a philosopher cannot recognize God purely through reason. Most individuals who try to determine the existence of God Almighty purely through the exercise of reason, in the end become atheists. Reflecting over the creation of the heavens and the earth does not avail them much and they begin to deride and laugh at the men of God. One of their arguments is that there are thousands of things in the universe which have no use and the making of which does not indicate the beingness of a fashioner.

They exist merely as vain and useless things. These people do not seem to figure that lack of knowledge of something does not needfully negative its beingness. There are millions of people in the world who regard themselves as very informed philosophers and who absolutely deny the existence of God. It is obvious that if they had discovered a strong reason for the existence of God, they would not have refused it. If they had discovered a conclusive argument in support of the existence God, they would not have rejected it shamelessly and in derision. It is obvious, therefore, that no one boarding the ark the philosophers can find saving from the storm of doubts, but is bound to be drowned, and such a one would ever have admittance to the toasting of complete Wholeness.

It is a wrong and stinking notion that belief in the Unity of God can be achieved otherwise than through with the Holy Prophet, nor can man achieve redemption without it. How can there be a faith in the Unity of God unless there is complete certainty with regard to His beingness? Be sure, therefore, that belief in the Unity of God can be achieved only through a Prophet, as our Holy Prophet, peace be on him, convinced the atheists and infidels of Arabia of the existence of God Almighty by showing them thousands of heavenly signs. Up till today the true and perfect followers of the Holy Prophet, show those signs to the atheists. The truth is that till a person observes the living powers of the living God, Satan does not part from his heart, nor does true Unity enter into it, nor can he believe with certainty in the existence of God. This holy and ideal Unity is appreciated only through the Holy Prophet.

It is not within the ability of man to perceive all the actions of the Divine. They are above reason and understanding and resource. A man should not be proud of his cognition that he has to some degree comprehended the system of case and effect, inasmuch as that knowledge of his is very specific, as if it were a millionth part of one drop out of the sea. The truth is that as God Almighty is unbounded and His activities are unbounded also. It is beyond and above human ability to reach the reality of every action of God.

Contemplating His eternal attributes we can, however, affirm that as Divine properties have never fallen into disuse, therefore, in God's creation some species have always come into existence; but any personal co-existence is wrong. It is to be remembered that, like His attribute of creation, His attribute of devastation has always been in operation all the time and that also has never fallen into disuse. The philosophers have put forth every effort to bring the creation of heavenly and earthly bodies within the horizon of their physical laws and to demonstrate the source of all creation, but they have utterly failed to do so. Whatsoever they have gathered together as the result of their material research is rather incomplete and flawed.

This is why they have not been effective to adhere to their theories throughout and have always modified them around. As their enquiry is confined entirely to their understanding and speculation and they receive no assistance from God, they cannot emerge out of their dark. No one can truly recognize God till he understands that there are countless activities of the Divine which are far beyond and above human power and reason and speculation. Before reaching this stage of understanding a person is either an atheistic and has no faith in God, or if he does believe in God, that God is the result of his own reasoning and is not the God Who manifests His own Being and the mysteries of Whose powers are so numerous that human reason cannot encompass them. Since God has conferred the knowledge that His powers are wonderful, that they have deepness upon depth and are beyond of beyond, and are outside understanding. He who has not observed this wonder of Divine power has found nothing. We do not believe in a God whose powers are specific by our reason and speculation and there is nothing beyond. We conceive in the God whose powers, like His Being, are unlimited, available, and permanent.

The Holy Quran comprises teachings which work towards endearing God. They exhibit His holiness and prompt us of His beneficence, inasmuch as love is made either by the observation of beauty or by the commemoration of beneficence. The Quran teaches that by virtue of His excellences God is One, without associate. He suffers from no fault. He comprehends all good qualities and manifests all holy powers. He is the Conceiver of all creation and is the fountain-head of all goodwill. He is the Master of all recompense and everything returns to Him. He is near and yet far, and He is far and yet close. He is above all, but it cannot be said that there is somebody below Him.

He is more hidden than everything else but it cannot be said that there is something more manifest than Him. He is Self Existing in His Being and everything is live through Him. He is Self Existing and everything exists through with Him. He is All Sustaining and there is nothing that supports Him. There is nothing that has come into being on its own, or can live without Him on its own. He comprehends everything, but it cannot be said what is the nature of that comprehension. He is the brain of everything in heaven and world and every light has reflected forth from His hand and is a expression of His Being.

There is no mortal that is not maintained by Him and exists by itself. No soul has any power which it has not received from Him and which exists by itself. His mercy is of two forms. One, which has been eternally demonstrated without being the result of any action on the part of anyone. For example, heaven and earth, the sun and moon and planets, water and fire and air and all the molecules of the universe which were created for our comfort, and all those things that were needed by us, were provided before our coming into being. All this was done when we were not even present. No action had proceeded from us. Who can say that the sun was produced on account of some activity of his, or that the earth was created in consequence of some good action of his? This is the mercy which came into operation before the existence of man and is not the effect of anyone's activities. The second kind of Spiritual clemency comes into process in consequence of human action. This requires no example.

The Holy Quran places forth that God is free from all defects and is not subject to several loss; and He wants that man should purge himself from shortcomings by working upon His teachings. He has said: He who is irrational in this world will be irrational in the hereafter. This means that he who has no insight in this world and is not able to see the peerless Being, will be blind after death and will be wrapped in darkness, inasmuch as man is bestowed insight in this life with which to see God and he who will not take that insight with him from this world will not be able to see God in the future. God Almighty has made it clear in this verse what progress He desires man to achieve and how far can man proceed by following His teaching. God sets forth in the Holy Quran the teaching by following which a person can see God in this very life. Let him who hopes to meet his Lord work righteously and let him relate no one in the adoration of his Lord.

This means that he who wants to see God in this same life-time, should work righteously, that is to say, his conduct should exhibit no default and his activities should not be for demonstrate, nor should he take pridefulness in them that he is such and such, nor should his actions be wrong and incomplete, nor should they feel of anything which is inconsistent with his own love of God. All his actions should breathe seriousness and faithfulness. He should abstain from associating anything with God and should worship neither sun nor moon, nor stars, nor air, nor fire, nor water, nor any other thing whatsoever.

He should not exalt worldly means so as to depend upon them as if they were God's associates, nor should he depend upon his own endeavor and effort, for this is also a species of association. Having done everything he should consider that he has done nothing. He should have no pride in his knowledge, nor have dependence upon his actions. He should consider himself truly ignorant and slothful and his soul should be prostrate all the time at the threshold of God Almighty. He should draw the grace of God to himself through his supplications. He should grow like a soul who is thirsty and is helpless and finds food in front of him, the water which is clear and sweet, and he crawls up to the spring and applies his lips to it and does not let go till he is fully satisfied.

In the Holy Quran God describes His dimensions as thus: Proclaim: He is Allah, the Single; Allah, the Self Active and Besought of all. He begets not, nor is He begotten; and there is none one like Him. This implies that our God is one in His Beingness and in His Dimensions. No other being is eternal and everlasting and self- existing like His Being, nor are the attributes of any being like His attributes. A person's knowledge needs a teacher and yet is limited. God's knowledge needs no teacher and is unlimited. A person's hearing is dependent upon air and is limited, but God's hearing is inherent and is unlimited.

A person's seeing is dependent upon the light of the sun or some other light and is limited, but God's seeing is by His inherent light and is unlimited. The power of man to create is dependent upon some matter and needs time and is limited. God's power to create is neither dependent on any matter nor does it need time and is unlimited. All His attributes are without equal and as He has no equal in His Being, no one is His equal in His attributes. If one of His attributes were to be defective, all His attributes would be defective and therefore his Unity cannot be established unless He were without any equal in His attributes as He is without any equal in His Being. He is not anyone's son, nor is anyone His son. He is Self-Sufficient and needs neither father nor son. This is the Unity which the Holy Quran instructs and which is the basis of our faith.

PRIMARY BELIEFS

Islam is established on five towers or five fundamental clauses of faith. These five articles or pillars of Islamic religion have been derived from saying (Hadith) of Prophet Muhammad which has been recorded by Bukhari and Muslim on the authority of Ibn Omar. The Prophet is accounted to have said: "Islam is built on five things; to bear witness that there is no god only Allah and that Muhammad is His messenger and servant, to maintain up supplication, to pay Zakat, to make Pilgrimage and to keep fast in Ramazan".

So following are the five pillars upon which the edifice of Islam is founded according to the above custom of the Prophet:

1. Iman (profession of belief).
2. Salat (to show prayer).
3. Zakat (to give poor-due or compulsory charity).
4. Saum (to keep fast during the month of Ramazan).
5. Haj (to execute pilgrimage to Mecca).

Iman

Belief is the first and the foremost article of Islamic faith. The Holy Quran says: "But chaste is he who believe in Allah and the End Day and the Angels, and the Sacred Scripture and the Prophets. " At different site the Holy Book says "who so disbelieve in Allah and His Angels and His Scriptures and His couriers and the Last Day, he verily hath wandered far wide. (al-Quran 4:136). Thus the Quran has established for the followers of Islam to trust in Allah, His Courier, His Angels, His Scriptures and the Afterlife. To these five elements of belief, Prophet Muhammad has added another element and that is belief in fortune.

Iman or feeling, is to shown by exalting the following Kalima (formula) with the tongue and affirm its truth with the heart:

"There is no god but Allah; Muhammad is the Apostle of Allah."

Moreover one has to testify the truth of the above referred Kalima with the following words:

"I attest that there is no god but Allah who is One and has no collaborator. And I also testify that Muhammad is His retainer and His messenger".

As said above, there are six components or ingredients of belief which have been prescribed by the Quran and the Sunnah. These are: Notion in Allah, belief in messengers, belief in Sacred Scriptures or books, belief in Angels, belief in the Hereafter or the Last Day, and belief in Preordination or Taqdir. All these constituents of belief are briefly discussed here:

Belief in Allah

Allah is the Potent and only one God of the entire world. He is the Creator of everything in the cosmos. He is Endless and Ever-Living. He has no collaborator, no children, no parents, no partners. He is Potent, One in Substance and Attributes, All-Perfect, Sovereign Lord, Existing, Omniscient, All-Knowing, the Gracious and the Forgiving. The heavens and world are full of His signs and blessings. He gives life and death and resurrects the dead. He sent Prophets and revealed Sacred Scriptures for the direction of man. He is the Superior of the Day of Judgment. He is only to be preferred. Followers of Islam have been enjoined by the Quran and by the Prophet Muhammad to believe in Allah and serve Him only.

Belief in Messengers

For counseling of humanity Allah sent messengers called Prophets or Apostles of Allah who brought to humanity Spiritual message and also acted upon the message themselves setting model for their followers. The Prophets were human beings and they did not claim to any contribution in Godhead. The Muslims have to trust in all the Prophets without making any differentiation between them and without declining anyone of them. Belief is to be showed in all the Prophets, whether mentioned in the Quran or not, from Adam to Muhammad. Life and teachings of some of these Prophets along with stories of their tribes or states have been accounted in detail by the Quran such as that of Abraham, Nuh, Hud, Salih, Lut, Shoaib, Moses and Jesus.

Belief in Scriptures

Allah revealed books or scriptures and gave them to the Prophets for guidance and education of humankind. These are:Sahifahs (Scrols) passed to Abraham; the Torah given to Moses; the Psalms given to David; the Gospel given to Jesus Christ, and the Quran given to Muhammad. Followers of Islam are required to trust all these Holy Scriptures.

Belief in Angels

Allah made Angels from light. They are invisible to human eye, have no gender and are equipped to carry out Allah's commands and glorify Him. They are not daughters of Allah as the heathen Arabs held. Most famous of them are: Gabriel charged with the duty of bringing divine revelations and messages of Allah to the Prophets; Israfil who will blast the Trumpet on the Day of Resurrection; Mickael charged for arranging rainfall, Izrael charged to take souls. Some other angels mentioned in the Quran and Hadith are: Harut and Marut; sent by God to test the belief of some nation, Kiraman Katibin; the esteemed recorders who record the acts of human beings); Munkir and Nakeer who would question the dead in graves; angel who brought good tidings of birth of a son to Mary;

angels who brought great news about birth of Isaac to Abraham; angels who destroyed the people of Lut; angels in direction of Hell and Angels who would receive the chaste in Paradise. Muslims are expected to trust in all angels of God.

Belief in the Hereafter

This universe would end on the Last Day (Doomsday) when every last living soul would perish. The Hereafter would start after the demise. On the Doomsday (Day of Judgment/ Day of Resurrection), every dead person would be revived by Allah. Allah would judge between humankind on that day and would reward the devotional with Paradise and penalize the wicked with Hell. The life in the Hereafter would be genuine and eternal life. Muslims are asked to believe in the Last Day and in the Hereafter, in life after end and in Paradise and Hell.

Belief in Fate

This belief is virtually whole part of belief in Allah and so it is not regarded as an individual component. This notion implies that all good and sinful is from Allah and is in the knowledge of Allah.

ETHICS

Islam instructs that the only God is Allah, and that it is a sin (shirk) to make other individuals equal to Allah by looking up to them, worshipping them, or putting improper effort and want into acquiring them. Other activities that are strictly prohibited include slaying, theft, fornication, lending money, the magic, cowardliness in fulfilling Allah's wishings, bad mouthing other people, and using drugs or alcohol. The spiritual volume, the Koran, encourages faith in God, encouraging justness for everyone, forgiving to others, and being compassionate, gracious, generous, modest, and liberal. Muslims are also expected to take responsibility for the well-being of all life, and to be courageous in following God's laws and in standing up to injustice and tyranny.

The family is the central place where Islamic practices are passed on. Bringing up children in the faith is extremely important, and extended families are close. The concept of pity and care for others is a important Islamic belief, and all humans are seen to be equal.

The word Islam has the same meaning as "peace" in Arabic. Islam is a religion that came to offer humanity a life filled with the serenity and well-being in which God's eternal clemency and pity is attested in the world. God invites all people to accept the moral commandments of the

Quran as model whereby clemency, compassion, tolerance, and peace may be received in the world.

METAPHYSICS

Advanced science sees things as mere things, and that it has cut the study of the special world to an end in itself. For Certain this has contributed physical benefits, however it is companied by an uncontrolled and unquenchable propensity to destruct nature itself. To study and use nature without higher spiritual end has brought mankind to the state of thought that men are divinities.

Islamic metaphysics is a integrated system that discovers the ultimate nature of Realism in positive terms, mixing reason and experience with other broad orders in the worldwide and transempirical degrees of human cognizance. He sees this from the perspective of philosophical Sufism. Essentialist and the Existentialist Philosophers of the Islamic tradition address the nature of reality. The first is presented by philosophers and theologists, and the latter by Sufis. The Essentialists hang to the precept of quiddity(mahiyyah), whereas the Existentialists are fixed in the fundamental reality of existence(wujud) which is direct spontaneous experience, not merely supported on moral analytic thinking or logical reasoning. This has undoubtedly led philosophic and scientific hypotheses to be concerned with things and their substances at the expense of existence itself, thereby making the study of nature an end in itself. In the extra-mental reality, it is wujud that is the real essences of things and that what is conceptually posited as mahiyyah are in reality accidents of world.

The process of creation or working into beingness and disintegration or returning to non-existence, and recreation of akin is a ever-changing observational movement. There is a principle of integrity and a principle of diversity in creation. The numerosity of existents that effects is not in the one reality of existence, but in the manifold prospects of the recipients of beingness in the several levels, each according to its durability or helplessness, perfection or imperfectness, and precedency or posteriority.

Thus the multiplicity of existents does not mar the integrity of creation, for each effective is a mode of existence and does not have a distinguish ontological position. Kernel of God is absolutely greatest and is unknown and unknowable, except to Himself, whereas the substance or realism of a thing consists of a mode of creation providing the lasting prospect of the thing, and its essence, endowing it with its varying characters.

REFERENCES

Ahòmad Shaykh Sirhindi: *Mabda wa ma'ad, Cawnpore,* 1891.

Akhund Darwiza: *Tadhkirat al-abrar wa-l-ashrar,* BM Or. MS 222.

Bains, A.: *Ethnography of the Castes and Tribes of India*, Strassburg, 1912.

Bakhtawar Khan: *Mir'at al-'alam,* BM Add. MS 7657.

Gait, E. A.: *Census Report: Bengal*, Calcutta, 1902.

Ghani, A. R. and Nur K. Ilahi: *Bibliography of Iqbal*, Lahore, 1955.

Ghani, A.: *A History of Persian Language and Literature in the Mughal Court*, Allahabad, 1929-1930.

Ghosh, J. C.: *Bengali Literature*, London, 1948.

Mazòhar, Mirza Jan-i Janan: *Kalimat-i Tòayyibat,* Delhi, 1891.

Menant, D.: "Les Bohras du Guzarate", *RMM*, 1910.

Mihr, Ghulam-Rasul: *Sayyid, Ahòmad Shahid*, Lahore, 1952.

Ministry of Education, Government of Pakistan: *Report of the Commission on National Education*, Karachi, 1959.

Misra, S. C.: *Muslim Communities in Gujarat*, Bombay, 1964.

Nizami, K. A.: "Some Aspects of Khanqah Life in Medieval India", *SI*, 1957.

Nizami, K. A.: *The Life and Times of Shaykh Farid-u'd Din Ganj-i Shakar,* Aligarh, 1955.

Nurul M. Karim: "Part played by Haji Shari'atullah and his son in the socio-political history of East Bengal", *Proceedings of the Pakistan History Conference*, Karachi, 1955.

O'Malley, L. S. S.: *Census Report: Bengal, Bihar, Orissa, Sikkim*, Calcutta, 1913.

Oman, J. C.: *The Mystics, Ascetics and Saints of India*, London, 1905.

Pakistan ki 'ilaqa'i zabanon par farsi ka athar, Karachi, n.d.

Philips, C. H.: *Historians of India, Pakistan and Ceylon*, London, 1961.

Punjab Notes and Queries, Allahabad, 1883-7.

Qadiri, Shams-ad-din: *Urda-yi qadim,* Lucknow, 1930.

Qani', Ali Shir: *Tuhòfat al-karam,* Delhi, 1886.

Qidwa'i, J. A.: *Pashto Adab*, Karachi, 1951.

Qurayshi, 'Abd-ar-Razzaq: *Mirza Maz'har Jan-i Janan awr unka Urdu kalam*, Bombay, 1961.

Qureshi, I. H.: *The Muslim Community of the Indo-Pakistan Sub-Continent*, 'S-Gravenhage, 1962.

Rahòman 'Ali: *Tadhkira-i 'ulama-i Hind,* Lucknow, 1914; Urdu tr. by M. Ayyub Qadiri, Karachi, 1961.

Ram Lajwanti Krishna: *Panjabi Sufi Poets*, Calcutta, 1938.

Rashidi, Hòusam-ad-Din: *Sindhi Adab,* Karachi, n.d.

Raverty, H. G.: *Selections From the Poetry of the Afghans*, London, 1864.

Razvi, S. N. Haidar: "Music in Muslim India", *IC*, 1941.

Rieu, C.: *Catalogue of the Persian Manuscripts in the British Museum*, London, 1879-95.

Rizvi, S. A. A.: *Muslim Revivalist Movements in Northern India in the Sixteenth and Seventeenth Centuries*, Agra, 1965.

Rose, H. A.: *A Glossary of Tribes and Castes of the Punjab and North-West Frontier Province*, Lahore, 1911-19.

Rosenthal, E. I. J.: *Islam in the Modern National State*, Cambridge, 1965.

Stchoukine, Ivan: *La Peinture Indienne,* Paris, 1929.

Storey, C. A.: *Persian Literature, A Bio-Bibliographical Survey*, London, 1927-58.

4

Concept of God

In Islam, Supreme Being is considered to be the sole true God, omnipotent and omniscient Almighty, maintainer, Ordainer, and evaluator of the cosmos Islamism places an accented stress upon the formulation of God as rigorously unique (tawhid). He is singular (wahid) and inherently one and only (ahad), all-merciful and all-powerful. Concording to the custom of Islam there are ninety-nine Names of Supreme Being (al-asma al-husna) all of which arouse a clear-cut feature of God. All these adverts pertain to Allah, the sovereign and all-comprehensive Almighty name. Amongst the ninety-nine names of God, the most notable and most predominant of these names are "the compassionate" (al-rahman) and "the caring" (al-rahim). Universe and ordination of the cosmos are visualized as a work of superior clemency for which every creature sing his glorifications and attest to his integrity and lordship. Consorting to the Muslim commandments, God is ever-present all over without having embodied in anything. According to the Book, "nary visual sense could comprehend Him, simply His grasp is across altogether imagination. He's above all comprehension, all the same is familiar with whole affairs."

God in Islam isn't exclusively superior and supreme, but as well a individualized God: agreeing to the Quran, he's closer to human beings than man's jugular. He answers to those in want or suffering if they call him. Most importantly, he leads humankind to the justly path, "the direct course." Islam instructs that its God is the one and the same god revered by the members of another Abrahamic religions such as Christian religion and Judaism. This is not universally acknowledged by non-Muslims.

DEFINING GOD

Oneness of Supreme Being or Tawhid is the act of trusting and asserting that God (Allah) is matchless and unparalleled (wahid). The Quran insists the being of an individual and inviolable Sojourner Truth that surpasses the cosmos; a singular and indiscrete being who's independent of the total creation.

The Quran as well allows a monist figure of God by drawing the truth as a integrated unit, with Supreme Being being an exclusive conception that would describe or assign every living things:"he's the first of all and the ultimate, the external and the inwards; he's the apprehender of everything. A few Muslims have nonetheless vigorously criticized readings that would extend to a monist aspect of God since what they encounter as smudging the differentiation between the Almighty and the creature, and its inconsistency with the immoderate monotheism of Islam.

The indivisibility of Supreme Being means the indivisibility of God's reign which successively leads to the concept of cosmos as a fair and lucid ethical world instead of an empirical and moralistic bedlam (as in polytheism). Likewise the Quran rejects the binary modes of thinking such as the idea of duality of God by arguing that both good and evil generate from God's creative act and that the evil forces have no power to create anything. Supreme Being in Islam is a cosmopolitan god instead of a localized, tribal or provincial one; an inviolable who incorporates altogether optimistic values and bears no wickedness.

Tawhid comprises the frontmost articles of the Muslim community. To ascribe divinity to a made entity is the solely inexcusable sin referred in the Quran. Muslims consider that the totality of the Islamic teaching builds on the rationale of Tawhid.

DIMENSIONS OF GOD

The Quran mentions the dimensions of God as God's handsomest names. They're traditionally numbered as ninety-nine to which is bestowed as the highest name, the sovereign name of God, Allah. The names of God include:

- The Most Gracious
- The Most Merciful
- The Ever Forgiving
- The Ever Providing
- The Lord and Cherisher of the Worlds
- The Self Subsisting (upon whom all creatures depend for sustenance)
- The Eternal Lord (who never dies)
- The Supremely Wise

Muslim theological system makes a differentiation between the dimensions of God and the heavenly substance.

The Quran identifies God equally being fully knowledgeable of everything that takes place in the world, including secret thinkings and notions, and insists that nothing can be concealed from Allah:

In whatsoever thyself mayest be, and whatsoever part thyself mayest be narrating from the Quran,- and whatsoever effort ye (humanity) possibly doing,- we're attestators thence whilst ye are profoundly absorbed in this. Nor is concealed from thy Lord (such as) the burden of a corpuscle on the earth or in paradise. And not the smallest and not the biggest of these matters but are registered in a clean-cut register.

A few western scholarly persons have painted a picture that Muhammad applied the full term Allah in addressing both heathen Arabs and Jews or Christians so to instal a familiar background for the understanding of the name for Supreme Being.

In direct contrast with Pre-Islamic Arab polytheism, God in Islam doesn't accept affiliates and associates nor is there whatsoever relationship between God and jinn. Pre-Islamic heathen Arabs trusted in an unreasoning, potent, adamant and senseless destiny over which humankind had none control. This was substituted with the Islamic belief of a almighty but farsighted and kind God.

The Quran asserts, Muslims think, and historians assert that Muhammad and his following worship the same God as the Jews. The Quran's Allah is the same Almighty God who covenanted with Abraham. Quran depicts Allah as both more cogent and more distant than Jehovah, and as a cosmopolitan divinity, unlike Jehovah who intimately follows Israelites.

God loves those who do goodness, and two passages in the Quran convey a common love between God and humanity, but the Judeo-Christian principle to "love God with wholly thy bosom" is nowhere contrived in Islam. The stress is instead on God's cryptical sovereignty, to which one must forsake oneself. Basically, the "capitulation to Allah" (Islam) is the faith itself.

Islam vehemently declines the Christian notion that God is three individuals in one content. In Islamic conception of God, no mediators between God and the cosmos subsists and God's bearing is considered to be all over, and all the same he's not embodied in anything.

A lot of passages in the Old testament pertain to God's love. A fundamental composition in the New Testament is God's love in sending out of Jesus. In Islam, God's love is demonstrated through his signs and the creation of the earth where human beings can live in moderate comfortableness. The standard Muslim invocation of God is 'the caring, the kind'. Two of the "aesthetic names" of God are 'the very loving' and 'the ceaseless donor'. Christianity has however much more emphasis on God's active role as a shepherd who gets out to look for the lost sheep and delivering it. On the other hand, Islam holds a few hope for those who have gone astray. In Islam, God has furnished the chance for each community to attain the great success (i.e. the life in Heaven) by sending messengers or prophets to them. Islam has also acquired a philosophy of intervention of Muhammad on the Day of Judgement that would be invited favourably, although the sinners could be penalized for their sinfulnesses either therein life or for a bounded time in hell.

DEITIES

In Islam, Muhammad, approximately 1400 years ago, received the sanctified words of the deity. The Quran, given to Muhammad by the deity by the Archangel Jibraeel, establishes direction for an accomplished path that's the will of the deity and is to finally involve altogether multitude on earth. "Compliance to Allah" is a fundamental vision. Honoring of witness, supplication, alms-giving, fast and pilgrim's journey are central points for Islam and the individual Muslim. Friday is the day for assembling at the mosque for gathering, prayers and sermons. Primary Holy Day observances are Eid-ul-Fitr and Eid-ul-Adha. Muslims believe in the beingness of the angels and that they are respected creatures. The angels idolize God exclusively, obey Him, and work entirely by His bidding. Amongst the angels is Gabriel, who brought down the Quran to Muhammad.

PHILOSOPHY OF GOD

Philosophical system is related with the central motions about nature and fact. Al-Kindi (first Arab philosopher) called philosophy the most idealistic scientific discipline, because it addressed subjects which are comprehensive. Al-Kindi is accepted as the first Arab or Muslim philosopher.

Ibn Rushd goesfurther and expresses that the Quran establishes the study of philosophical system compulsory on all worshippers. Ibn Rushd is regarded a great Aristotelean Muslim and Spanish philosopher. He says that philosophy is nothing more than the study of organisms and manifestation upon them. The Quran promotes mankind to "Reflect, you have imagination." At another place it states, "have they not studied the kingdom of the heavens and the earth and whatever things God has created?" Here God is advocating the readers to study the world and how and why objects and beings survive. Ibn Rushd concludes that God requires man to try to obtain illustrative knowledge of His existence. But before having demonstrative knowledge, Man must be able to have dialectic, theoritical and coherent knowledge. That is for man to learn he must recognize the base of abstract thought. Hence, philosophy is not only essential but also required by the God Almighty.

Al-Ghazzali detects grievous troubles with the philosophers of his epoch. He pens, "they've deserted all the spiritual obligations of Islam enforces on its followers." He believes that the sort of reasoning out applied by philosophers would never result in the proof of the beingness of God. Al-Ghazzali was an exceedingly authoritative orthodox Islamic thinker who fought off many of the claims of the 'philosphers' who claimed they could give proof of God by understanding entirely.

Ibn Rushd accepts that philosophy could have its impairments as a branch of knowledge, but these damages are no bigger than those ensuing from the study of medical specialty or practice of law. Since, the study of philosophical system is compelled by God Himself, it's compulsory, although it is possible to misuse the science for other purposes. As Al-Kindi and most Islamic philosophers agree philosophy can't accomplish as far as revealation can. Hence, the foundation of our actions should be founded on Islam, whereas doctrine ought to be considered as an autonomous branch of knowledge. It should also be noted that the thrust of Ghazzali's argument isn't against philosophy, but instead its function. His main concern is that the philosophers are getting conclusions from their argumentations that are not legitimate.

Muhammad Iqbal ascertains no contradiction in terms between religion and rationality. Iqbal, believed to be the poet-philosopher of Islam, his pieces of work have been exceedingly authoritative in the resurgence of Muslim thought. He was born in (what is at present) Pakistan but studied in Britian and Germany, thus allowing for perceptiveness into both philosophical customs. He thinks that both thought and intuition arise from the identical source and do not contradict one another, but rather are complimentary. Reason aspires at understanding the material world and beingness, whereas religious experience aspires at surpassing these cosmos and accomplishing the cognition of the highest. Iqbal then thinks that it's essential for Muslims to absorb themselves in the field of study and scientific discipline of philosophical system in order to redefine Muslim civilization, which is now faced with a more innovative Western culture. If Islamic thinkers fail in that challenge, then Islamic thought may be engulfed by Western doctrine, as the two civilizations get down to incorporate further.

This argumentation isn't unambiguously Islamic, alike argumentations have persisted in Christian thought also. Whilst spiritual latent hostility in Europe were blockading analytic thought, it was booming in Islamic lands. As the Christian church influence diminished a more active social movement came forth in Europe bringing with it an altogether fresh worldview moving toward reason and away from tenet. Nowadays a lot of Christian theologists also use philosophy to excuse their attitudes, as is like amidst certain Islamic groups. The annoying problem, all the same, is to carry on the decision of these theists on strictly philosophic bases, in the face of a challenge from extremist skepticism.

Muslim doctrine bloomed as a afterward development of Islamic thought. It was predated by the kalam (debate) science, the field of study of affirming the Islamic religious doctrine and maintaining it against revolutionary sects. It developed in the theological disputations of the 8th century over God's wholeness and dimensions. Like the Jewish Holy Scripture, the Koran too stresses the wholeness of God, the resurrection of the dead, and the answerability of man. But it is the first article-the integrity of God-that has come to occupy a fundamental place in Islamic ideological and theological rational.

The earlier debatable doubt addressed the kinship between God and his dimensions, that is, whether God is one without sectionalization or calibre, or one in effect but manifold in dimensions. Contending this matter added in a few of the centuries-old ontological and epistemic questions, such as: What is the nature of God's existence? Does Supreme Being, for example, subsist as a concept in one's judgement, or does he also live in an extra-mental (or transcendental) world? And anyhow, what is the kinship between God and humanity, and between God and the cosmos, and how could a human know him and interpret his biddings?

The argument could have carried on peacefully had not the Mutazilites, who adopted an utmost positivist attitude, resorted to force. Changing the Abbasid caliph al-Mamun to their cause, they acquired a grasp on the most eminent berths in the caliphate and used that power to enforce their views. The Islamic world as a whole was appalled by the way they addressed their adversaries, especially Ahmad ibn Hanbal (780-855), a distinguished scholarly person and founding father of one of the four schools of shariah law, who was subjugated to caning and captivity because of his resistance to the Mutazilites' views on the nature of God's words.

Distancing themselves from the abhorrent Mutazilite politics and uttermost interpretings, most legal experts took a central attitude, making a true attempt to keep close to the Koranic and Sunnah texts bila kaifa, i.e., without calling for a "how" question. Their objective was to shift the argumentation from theological system to jurisprudence and law. Besides centering on God's dimensions and substance, attention should be addressed, they debated, to man's demeanour and actions in abidance (or lack therefrom) with God's law. But when al-Ashari dramatically broke off from the Mutazilites, came back to the mcderationist position of the citizenry of the Sunna, and, thence, administered the coup de grace to Mutazilism, followers of the conservative law school bestowed him their backup. The Asharite school became the theological representative of the mainstream Sunnite Muslims.

With the advance of Asharism a few theological issues lost their charm, although fresh ones have came forth, for example, pertaining the question of sensing as an autonomous generator of knowledge in direct contrast to revelation. Like the Mutazilites before them, most of the Asharite scholars debated that percept is a reservoir of cognition. None of them, however, maintained that sensing is the exclusive source of knowledge. According to Asharism, cognition that is deduced from the senses is established, but it must be subdued to the revealed fact, if certainty is to be achieved.

In this view, revealing has an epistemic as well as a cultural social function. Likewise enlightening the wider picture of oneself, the creation, human macrocosm, and supreme human ends, it also attends to free the individual from illogical reverence of natural forces, and instils in him a tendency to attempt a orderly understanding of these forces and their affect on human life. The revealed imagination, furthermore, sets free the individual from hyponymy to the ego and ethnocentrism and the dehumanisation of the other that blockades intellectual argumentation and agreement.

But this equilibrium between the unveiled vision and the speculative brain has not always been asserted. In contrast to the Sunnis, who battle to preserve a differentiation between God and human beings, the Shia argue that the distance that distinguishes God from human persons is the seed of all evil. Absorbed in matter, and cut off from their beginnings, human souls have no hope of being relieved except through cognition (irfan). But the redemptive cognition, wherein God reveals himself and his Almighty aims, is attainable only through the guardians whom God assigns to company the prophets. Prophets bring the outer (zahir) ecclesiastic bidding, whereas the guardians initiate citizenry into the batin, or internal dictations.

Adopting this component of batin, the Sufis, then again, developed a slightly dissimilar hypothesis of knowledge. For them, realizing the heavenly sources of Islam rests neither in holy protectors nor in terminology, but on the people of reality. They retained that the Koran admits certain heavenly mysteries and niceties that only the people of reality-Sufis-are capable of agreement.

It was chiefly due to such tendencies of batini (cryptical) interpretings that a barrier of suspicion developed amid Shia, Sufi, and Sunni jurists in Muslim chronicle. Besides contending the nature of God's dimensions, the new questions for argumentation asked what it means for a term to have a particular meaning, and how one can know that a statement is true. These interrogatives resulted finally to the development of the doctrine of language, religious mysticism, system of logic, and legal philosophy as new Islamic studies. Contradicting these Shia and Sufi tendencies of rendition, most Sunni jurists fell back to the custom of the Prophet and standard Arabic usage of language, applying the first as an explicit code of behavior and the second as an objective code of meaning. Both were entailed to restrain intense propensities of rendition.

Closely accompanying these argumentations was the issue of the source of ethical cognition and responsibility. Believing God as the finally wise and just Being, the Mutazilites declined to build a relation between God and evil. Empowered with a free will, they contended, humans are the authors of their own actions and should to be honoured or penalized consequently. Ethical judgment and cognition, in their view, stems from individual reason, which can severally recognize between good and bad.

For Sunni scholarly persons, it was all very well to emphasise a person's capability to argue. What they found unacceptable, however, was the affirmation that human reason is the exclusive standard of accuracy and behaviour, or that by following the dictates of rationality alone one can be upright and attain felicity. This freethinking was thought to be unreconcilable with Islam's sources of counselling, reason, and revelation.

It's peculiar, however, that the Mutazilites' philosophic technique, as well as some of the unsolved problems they left alone, have become, in spite of their political defeat, a crucial source of educated agitation in Muslim thought. Some of the issues they brought up persisted and were followed, with more moderateness, by other distinguished linguists, observers, and philosophers. And most of those-Ibn Tufayl, Ibn Rushd and Ibn Khaldun, among others-came along in the Muslim West and not in the East, as could be acknowledged.

Ninety-Nine Names of Allah

The ninety-nine Names of Allah, a.k.a. The ninety-nine Most aesthetic Names of God are the names of God which Muslims consider are disclosed in the Quran and Sunnah. There's, according to Hadith, an exceptional group of ninety-nine names but no numbering of them. Thus the precise list isn't uncontroversial, and the names of God transcend ninety-nine in the Quran and Sunnah. In one Islamic custom, the prophet Muhammad used to address God by all His Names:

"O God, I conjure You with all of Your aesthetic Names."

Muhammad is also rumoured to have said in a famed Hadith:

Verily, there are ninety-nine names of God, a hundred minus one. He who counts them would get into heaven.

Of note is that this hadith doesn't say that there are exclusive ninety-nine names, but ninety-nine names that are more honourable than the others. This induced citizenry to search them out in the Quran and Sunnah, and a list was collected. Over time it became common to recite the list in its totality. While some Muslims think that this list is marked by Muhammad himself, the specialist Muslim scholars contend powerfully that the list was just amassed by a Islamic scholar as an supplement to the actual hadith. If it was entirely an endeavor of a scholar, they're not necessarily the names suitable, and other assays might still be established. A modern scholar, Dr. Mahmoud Abdel-Razek, arrived at an attempt of this form and explicated in particular how come he disagrees in belief with al-Waleed about enlisting some of the names.

Nonetheless, enumerating the conventional names has evolved into a rite by some Muslims as an endeavour to enumerate them, while most other Muslims believe that the "numbering" isn't just the act of reading, but applying the dimensions that the names suggest.

The Quran relates to the dimensions of God as God's most aesthetical names. They are traditionally enumerated as ninety-nine in number to which is added up as the most eminent name, the supreme name of God, Allah.

MESSENGERS OF GOD

Muslims look on Prophets of Islam those non-divine men selected by God as prophets (nabi). All prophet imparted the same primary thoughts of Islam, including notion in one and only God and shunning of idol worship and sin. All came to advocate Islamism and assured of the approach of the last prophet and messenger of God: Muhammad. Each prophet had different group to whom their message was addressed, and successively, each prophet instructed minor variations in Sharia (or the exercise of religious belief) to their nations. These editions are applications of Islam and are not considered discrete versions of Islam.

Islamic custom admits that God sent out messengers to every state. In Islam, only Muhammad was sent out to bring God's message to the whole world, whereas other couriers (rasuls) were sent out to communicate their messages to a particular group of people or state.

Contrary to Jewish religion and Christianity, Islam differentiates between a direct courier of Supreme Being (rasul) and a prophet (nabi). Both function as divinely inspired receivers of God's disclosure. Nevertheless, additionally, rasuls are given a godly content or revelation for a community in book form. Although every rasul is a nabi, not every nabi is a rasul.

Muslims consider Adam as the first prophet and Muhammad as the final prophet; therefore Muhammad's title of respect Seal of the Prophets. In Islam, Christ is looked upon a nabi and a rasul because he experienced wahi (revelation) from God, through which God disclosed the Injil (religious doctrine) to him. Muslims consider that God has sent over 124,000 messengers everywhere the world as brought up in the Sahih Hadith. Five are agreed the highest awe for their tenacity and outstandingly firm dedication to God in the aspect of great suffering. These five are Nuh (Noah), Ibrahim (Abraham), Musa (Moses), Isa (Jesus), and Muhammad.

Muslims consider that God has sent out 124,000 (or 224,000) messengers all over the world, as mentioned by the prophet Muhammad (Sallallahu alaihi wa Sallam) in the Sahih Hadith. Historical narrations propose there lived a prophet named Khaled bin Sinan in pre-Islamic Arabia. The Quran mentions Al-Imran as the father of Maryam. Al-Khidr is not mentioned by name, but is traditionally assumed to be referred to in Quran 18:66. Biblical prophets Danyal (Daniel), Ishaia (Isaiah), Armya (Jeremiah), and Samuel are named by Ibn Kathir in his book as prophets. Luqman is named in the sura named after him but it is indecipherable whether he is a prophet or a wali. According to the most general shiite belief, Luqman was a mentor, not a prophet nor a wali. The accounted word hold that Luqman had a dream, and in that dreaming he was called for to opt between being a King and a scholar, and he decided the second.

More numerous historic figures may have been prophets, but this is a source of argumentation and arguing. Such figures include: Zarathustra, Buddha, Socrates, Merlin, Confucius, Krishna and Rama. However, Muslims will state that there's no way of acknowledging for certain because they are not observed by name in the Quran. An argumentation often used in support of the prophethood of such men is that they went with the word of God, but it was afterward corrupted, this accounting for the conflicts between Islam, and the various faiths with which each human is affiliated. The Hadith and Quran confirm such claims that allege that a messenger was sent to every people.

NIRVANA

Islam, contrary to several other faiths, believes in this world likewise as in the afterlife. It bids welfare of its followers not exclusive in this world but also in the next world. Therefore, Islam directs them to happy and useful life in this cosmos and educates them for success in a longer and lasting life which would begin after death. We haven't been furnished much cognition about the lifetime after death but we can make a few idea from the hints given in the Quran and customs of Prophet Muhammad as to what would take place. All living beings would expire. Edens and world and everything would be destructed on the Day of Judgement. Then every living being would be resurrected. God would judge the deeds of the human beings on the Day of Judgement. He would reward the good with Paradise and punish the wicked with Hell.

Death

"All humans will sample death", thus says the Quran. Consequently end is inevitable. There is no break away from it. You may be anywhere the demise will catch up with you when its time comes. Death doesn't spare anybody. It draws no distinction between high and low, between affluent and broke, between aged and young, between devout and sinner. Death placed its hands even on the Prophets who were the most privileged and the most blessed humans. No physician, no man of science, no wise man has been capable to contrive a method or medicine which could help one miss death. Death grabs a son from lap of his caring mother, a husband from the heart of his adoring wife, a rich man from his immense wealth, and a almighty king from his big empire. Death, in fact, is God's law that every animate thing and every human being must sample. Death asserts one's belief in God as He is Supreme Being who gives life-or-death.

Day of Judgment

The Day of Judgment or the Doomsday or the Day of Resurrection has been brought up hundreds of times in the Quran and with a lot names. In addition to these three names, it's been called the day of retribution, the crack of doom, the day of test, the hour, the day of devastation, the day of sorrow, the day of repentance, the day of breakup, the day of faithful, the day of expression of shortcomings, the day of agitating, the great event, the affecting cataclysm, the day of assembling, the predicted day, etc. In a way the names refer to the diverse aspects or properties of the same day which would be close to thousand worldly years. Nobody knows about this day except Supreme Being. When it would descend? What would precisely take place on this day? No human being not even a Prophet can tell. Nonetheless, we have been assured a few signs of the Hour by Prophet Muhammad which the Prophet identified before his associates during a discourse.

The Doom

The Day of Judgement would come suddenly, just as in a blink of an eye, even sooner than it. The day would be grueling in the paradises and the world. The sky will turn as liquid copper, the hills would turn as chips of fleece, mountains would be busted into dispelled debris and world would be left as an abandon plain without any arc nor toughness. Every breast feeding mother will forget her suckling and every pregnant one will be delivered of her charge. Every live animal will pass away all at once. Every thing will decease very fast. All this would come about on the first blowing of the horn.

Resurrection of the dead

The sacred Quran assures us that after our death, God would evoke us and give us liveliness again. This would be our resurrection (of heart and soul) which would befall on the Day of Resurrection, also called Day of Judgement. Every living human would savour death and on the Day of Resurrection it would be recreated to be paid compensation for its exploits done in this world. The disbelievers, in all years, have been laughing at the idea of resurrection arousing featherbrained questions before the prophets. Such doubts were also raised before Prophet Muhammad. The thought of resurrection, when they would be dead and cut down to bones and junk, looks to such people very unusual. The Quran assures them that Almighty God who gave them aliveness when they were nonentity would renovate them after their death as their resurrection isn't more difficult for the Lord of the Heavens and the Earth than their foremost creation. When Supreme Being means to do a thing He only says unto it: Be! and they are.

To get the disbelievers realize the process of revival of the dead, the Quran gives illustration of rain over and over which revives the dead and bare land and makes it raise all sort of flora, and forage to supply nutrient to the human beings and the animals. Also, the Quran gives us a few working cases, how the Prophets and god-fearing humans were in reality shown up the action of resurgence of the dead. To Prophet Christ, God gave miracle that he could raise the dead with divinities leave, while Prophet Abraham was shown the resurgence of the birds when he had killed them, and other man (Uzair) was himself given death and was revived thereafter.

The Judgement

After the resurrection, the masses would be brought in front God, the Almighty Creator of the cosmos and the Master of the day of reckoning, who'd judge between them. All human on that day will find itself faced with all that it has done of goodness and altogether that it has practiced of evil. No intervention will be acceptable for sinners nor any recompense or redeem will be admitted from such multitude although it's earthful of gold.

On the Day of Judgement, account book of Records would be set up, the Prophets and the spectators would be called in, human race would appear as intoxicated (though in reality not), the voices would be hushed up and God would pronounce between the men to honour the virtuous and penalize the sinful.

The innocent will be handed their statements of doings in their right hand, while the evildoers would be handed their list of evils in their left hands. The erstwhile will be euphoric while the last mentioned would be dejected as the former would be booming and aspirer of honour while the latter would be fearsome of the penalty. The evildoers would hope to be remitted to the Earth so that they may do good feats to earn their redemption but they'd not be admitted.

The Prophets would be called upon as attestors on their communities of following. The registers readied by Kiram-al-Katibeen (the two angels assigned by God with each human to set record of his life feats) would be brought out. Earth would also show her evidence. Even the body parts of a man would testify against him. God would pass sound judgement and His judgment would be concluding. The good would be honoured and the sinful would be penalized.

Paradise

On the day of reckoning the virtuous masses would be rewarded with heaven wherein they'll get in and abide everlastingly. They can live then in the society of their parents, wives and babies provided they're likewise devout and are rewarded with heaven. They would be received by Angels and would be greeted and served up by good-looking females and fine-looking young manly retainers. They'll bear green vests of best silver and gold fancywork and armlets of gold. They'd sit on thrones and lie in beautiful couches. They'd accept pure wine stimulating no drunkenness.

Promised land, according to the Quran, is a garden as broad as are the empyrean and the world. It has every imaginable approving underneath which rivers flow. Foods of all types, fruits of every varieties, vestal wine, water natural spring, channels with streaming honey and Milk River, pretty virgins with humble regard and adorable eyes as vestal as if they were hidden eggs, handsome boys, finest robes, thrones and couches of gold, etc. would be there in the Paradise in plenty. Its rightful owners are only those who believe and do good works. Those who do not believe and do evil deeds would never enter in it.

Hell

Those who discredit Allah, Allah's messengers and reject Allah's revealings, those who do wicked deeds and commit wickednesses, those who breach boundaries appointed by Allah and desecrate godly Laws, those who don't worship Allah exclusively and adjudge cooperators unto Him, those who follow the Devil and rise up against Supreme Being, will be held into Hell after their works are pronounced on the day of reckoning as they are the true owners of fire. They'll live there eternally; theirs will be a disgraceful fate.

Hell is full of fire and all horrifying and atrocious things -which human psyche can envisage - to penalize the offenders. When their skins are devoured by fire, they'll be allowed fresh skins to sample the agony. Theirs will be bed of inferno, and over them covers of Hell; sighing and howling will be their destiny and they'll be putting up therein so long as the paradises and the world abide or God wishes. They'll be induced to drink a purulence water which one can sip but can barely drink. Demise would bear on them by all sides, yet they cannot die. Clothes of flame will be cut down for them; seething liquid like liquefied lead will be hurled on their head. Offenders from the humanity and the Jinn will enter Hell. It's so large that it wouldn't be filled up to its full and would cry out for more.

REFERENCES

al- Utbi: *Al-Ta'rikh al-Yamini,* Cairo, 1869.

al-Biruuni, Abu-Rayhòan: *Tahòqiq md li-i-Hind,* Eng. tr. E. Sachau, *Alberuni's India,* London, 1910.

Baloch, Nabi Bakhsh Khan: "The Diwan of Abu 'Atòa of Sind", *IC*, xxiii (1949), 136-50.

Barani, Diya'-ad-din: *Ta'rikh-i Firuz Shahi,* Calcutta, 1862.

Ghulam Ahòmad Khan: *Majmu'a-i marfut-i khwajagan-i Chishti,* Delhi, 1906.

Ghulam Ahòmad, Mirza, of Qadiyan: *The Philosophy of the Teachings of Islam*, Rabwah, 1959.

Ghulam Muhammad: *Festivals and Folklore of Gilgat, Memoirs, Asiatic Society of Bengal*, Calcutta, 1905.

Ghulam Muh-d-din: *Sihòr al-Hind,* Delhi, 1876.

Misra, S. C.: *Muslim Communities in Gujarat*, Bombay, 1964.

Mohanlal, Munshi: "A Brief Account of Masud, Known by the Name of Shakarganj or Shakarbar", *JASB*, 1836.

Mrs Hassan Meer Ali: *Observations on the Mussulmauns of India*, London, 1917.

Mu'tamid Khan: *Iqbal Nama-i Jahangiri*, Calcutta, 1865.

Muhammad Malik Din: *Gagetteer of Bhawalpur*, Lahore, 1909.

Muhammadan Anglo-Oriental Educational Conference, *Majmu'a-i resolution ha-i dihsala*, Aligarh, 1896.

Muhòammad 'Ali: *English Translation of the Holy Qur'an with Commentary*, Lahore, various eds.

Muhòammad 'Ali: *The Ahòmadiyya Doctrines*, Lahore, 1932.

Muhòammad Hòasan Naqshbandi: *Hòalat-i masha'ikh-i Naqshbandiyya Mujaddidiyya,* Muradabad, 1904.

Muhòammad, Mirza: *Tuhòfat al-Hind,* BM Add. MS 16, 868.

Muhòsin Fani: *Dabistan-i madhahib,* Eng. tr. D. Shea and A. Troyer, Paris, 1843.

Muhòyi-d-din, Shaykh: *al-Balagh al-mubin,* Lahore, 1876.

Mujeeb, M.: *The Indian Muslims*, London, 1967.

Mushtaqi, Rizq-Allah: *Waqi'at-i Mushtaqi,* BM Add. 11633.

Mustawfa, Hòamid-Allah: *Ta'rikh-i Guzida*, Leiden, 1910.

Nadwi, Abu-l-Hòasan 'Ali: *Hindustani Musalman,* Lucknow, 1961.

Nadwi, Abu-l-Hòasanat: *Hindustan ki Qadim Islami Dargahen,* A'zamgarh, 1936.

Nadwi, Sulayman: "Muslim Colonies in India", *IC*, 1927.

Najm-al-Ghani Khan: *Madhahib-i Islam,* Lucknow, 1924.

Nizam-ad-din Burhanpuri, etc.: *Fatawa'i Hindiyya*, Urdu tr. by Sayyid Amir 'Ali, Lucknow, 1889.

Nizami, K. A.: ' *Abd-al-Hòaqq Muhòaddith Dihlawi,* Delhi, 1953.

Suhrawardi, Diya'-ad-din Abu-Najib ' Abd-al-Qahir: *Adab al-muridin,* Urdu tr. Delhi, 1901.

Tara Chand: *The Influence of Islam on Hindu Culture*, Allahabad, 1936.

5

Main Figures

MAIN FIGURES IN EARLY PERIOD

Prophet Muhammad

Muhammad was born in 570 AD. in Mecca and died on June 8, 632 AD. in Medina. His full name was Abu al-Qasim Muhammad Ibn Abd Allah Ibn Abd al-Muttalib Ibn Hashim. He's believed to be the last prophet of God by the Muslim faith and he was besides a unifier of a lot Arabian tribes. Muhammad was born after the death of his father Abd Allah. April 20, 570 is some of the times is established his birthdate. Muhammad was born tin a upper-middle-class family. He was firstly put under the attention of his paternal grandfather Abd al-Muttalib who was a previous leader of the esteemed Hashim clan (which was division of the tribe of Quraysh). As the climate of Mecca had a repute for health problems, Muhammad tended as an infant by a wet nurse from a wandering tribe and spent a lot time in the desert. (This was a primary practice amongst the middle and upper social class.) When he was six Muhammad's mother Amina passed away and when he was eight his grandfather Abd al-Muttalib also passed away. Muhammad at once came under attention of his uncle Abu Talib, the current leader of the Hashim clan, of the Quraysh tribe - the most cogent in Mecca.

Mecca was a desert city-state whose chief eminence was the Kaaba, reputedly established by Abraham, the conventional patriarch of the Jews. Most of Meccas inhabitants comprised idol worshippers. The city ran as a commercialized centre with no natural resources of its own, visited by many established dealers. Of all reports Muhammad played a very active purpose in the civil life of his city. His uncle Zubair established the order of gallantry called the Hilf al-fudul, which attended to the persecuted of the city, local dwellers and foreign visitors. Muhammad took part as an ardent member. Muhammad attended in some dispute settlement, most notably when the Kaaba became besmirched in a flood, and the Meccan leaders all desired the accolade of fixing the sanctified Black Stone in place when it was reconstructed. Muhammad became known as Al-Ameen, "the dependable" because of his immaculate repute in all his transaction. Muhammad was the magistrate chosen to solve the problem; his resolution comprised of unfolding a white sheet on the earth, laying the Black Stone in the midst, and calling for the tribal leaders to carry it to its place by holding the corners of the sheet. Muhammad himself then deposited the stone in its place.

About in 595 AD., on a trading travel, Muhammad met Khadijah, an affluent widow woman then forty years old. The boyish Muhammad (then twenty-five) so affected Khadijah that she proposed him marriage. The wedding proved a significant landmark in Muhammad's life. By Arabian custom minors didn't inherit, so Muhammad had obtained no inheritance from either father or grandfather, but by his wedlock he received a great fortune. The sira records that Khadija bore Muhammad six children. In final third of his life Muhammad set out to consider himself as a prophet. In 610 AD., Muhammad (now aged forty) described that when he sat in a cave in the hills outside Mecca mediating, the angel Gabriel presented him a message from Supreme Being. He was required to memorize all of his sights. Muslim historiography holds that as he was uneducated he could not pen them down. He did so, and after reluctantly disclosing his experiences to his wife Khadijah, he started out to acquire followers by the strength and calibre of the words he narrated. He accumulated agreeable acquaintances who accepted his claim to be a prophet and joined him in essential worship and prayers. By 615 AD., he had acquired a big following in Mecca.

Founding of Islam: Muhammad had a meditative turn of brain and habitually spent nights in a cave near Mecca in meditation and thinking. About 610, when pondering. Muhammad reportedly had a sight of the angel Gabriel and detected a voice telling him "you're the courier of God". (From this time till his demise, Muhammad reportedly experienced regular revelations. Some of the times when experiencing these messages, it's noted, Muhammad would perspire and go into a trance state.) Muhammad was agitated by this vision of Gabriel, but his wife Khadijah assured him. Around 613 AD. Muhammad began prophesying publicly. By extolling his message in public Muhammad acquired followers that included the sons and comrades of the richest men in Mecca. The religious belief he advocated came to be called Islam. Both the Quran and

Muhammad's expressions signal that Muhammad from an early stage considered Islam as an worldwide faith and not merely bounded to the Arabian community.

As the ranks of his following welled up, he became a terror to the local clans, particularly the Quraysh, his own clan, which had the obligation of looking after the Kaaba, which at these times comprised several thousand 'idols' that people revered as gods. As Muhammad advocated against this pantheon, he became deeply unpopular with the rulers, and his following endured from repeated assaults to individual and belongings. Tradition holds that some Meccans founded robust and brutal efforts to oppress the new Muslims: pushing them to lie on burning sand, placing large boulders on their chests, and pouring out blistering iron all over them. Many perished, but none relinquished their new faith. Muhammad himself wasn't the aim of this oppression since his family was plainly excessively all-powerful. This environment became bitter, and Muhammad advised his following to go to Abyssinia.

The Meccans tried to allure Muhammad to abandon his missionary work by offering him governmental power. As Muhammad's following grew, attacks were made to get him to dissolve or change his faith. He was offered a big portion in trade and wedding with some of most affluent families but he declined all such bids. Meccans ultimately demanded that Abu Talib deliver his nephew to be wiped out. When he refused, mercantile pressure was brought against Muhammad's clan and his admirers. Finally an assassination attack occurred. After the death of his uncle and of Khadija, Muhammad's own tribe drew back their protective covering of him. He was ill-treated, stoned, thorns and trash were thrown on him. All the same, no attempt succeeded in taking his spirit. He was forced to flee Mecca in 622; this is called the Hijrah, and this date marks the commencement of the Muhammadan calendar.

In 622 Muhammad and his Meccan following left Mecca for Medina where he had acquired a lot of converts. The Medinans evidently desired that Muhammad would combine them and prevent incidents such as the 618 Medinan Civil warfare in which many had lost their lives. A written document called the Constitution of Medina established a confederacy between Muhammad's Meccan followers and the eight Arab tribes of Mecca. Muhammad was mentioned as "the Prophet" but was not gifted any policy-making authority. Shortly prior to his demise Muhammad presented a noted final admonishment to his followers known as the Prophet's Final discourse. His death in June 632 at Medina, at sixty-three, kicked up a major crisis amidst his followers. Indeed this quarrel finally led to the sectionalization of the Islam between the Shia and Sunni sects. The Shia consider that the prophet put in Ali ibn Abu Talib as his heir, in a common discourse in his final haj in a place called Ghadir Khom, whilst the the Sunnites consider he didn't.

Muhammad's primary message stressed notion in single God, regard for morals above and beyond tribal liaisons, and prayer. Muslim account records that Muhammad was uneducated, although some scholars debate that Muhammad in all likelihood underwent some form of teaching, and point to his flourishing career as a merchant. When he grew up, he journeyed with many caravans as an executive whose duty was to see that the caravan arrived safely and with whole goods undamaged. He did these throughout most of his functional life. The Quran was in all likelihood set down during his lifespan. The Quran states that Muhammad narrated the entire Quran during his parting pilgrimage to Mecca in 632, meaning that it had an instituted order if not in reality framed onto parchment/paper. In politics, Muhammad's biggest contribution was as the first unifier of the Arabian multitudes. Abiding by directly in his custom of searching knowledge with trained techniques, Muslims revived and as well challenged Hellenic doctrine.

As a direct consequence, they also established what we now address the scientific method and conventional commendation and a science of history. Each of this comprised a direct upshot of Muhammad's focus on the true, literacy, cognition and documentation - and morals as the groundwork of education. This led finally to the legal practice of fiqh. Muslims also brought in a range of inventions, most notable including general anatomy, algebra, the decimal fraction numeric system and papermaking, to Europe and the Middle East. Notwithstanding a few martial and matrimonial behaviour troubling to contemporary minds, any bad influences may be largely due to Muslims imitating behaviours that Muhammad himself disavowed, much due to hadiths that at the least some sources disbelieve. These affects are certainly harder to assess. To what extent the current state of the Islamic World can be attributed to Muhammad as an individual or leader is extremely arguable, and probably even more laughable then charging Napoleon Bonaparte for the present-day state of the European Union. Although his political and historical influence is and stays deep, the most eternal legacy of Muhammad remains naturally as his function as the prophet of Islam. He himself cautiously separated his part as prophet from that as politician - the Quran isn't in in any case to be confused with his personal expressions (Ahadith) or actions (sira). His weaknesses, as he himself stated, were his own, and his accomplishments he accredited to Supreme Being.

Abu Bakr

Abu Bakr (573 AD.-634 AD.) was the nearest associate of the Prophet Muhammad, the prophet of Muslims. His full name was: Atiq ibn Abi Quhafa Abd Allah ibn Uthman ibn Amir al-Qurashi al-Taymi. He was two years junior that the Prophet, and was a close acquaintance of his. even prior to the revelation started when the Prophet was forty years old. He was the first male to accept Islam (Khadija, the Prophet's dear wife, was the first individual to accept Islamism). He was affluent and backed up Islam every way he could, through the brutal times in Mecca, wherever the prophet was at the start based. When the holy order was given to transmigrate to Medina, Abu Bakr in person went with the Prophet while his own clan were close by trying to assassinate him.

His trust was believed to be the most superior after Muhammad himself, and he was often confided with big obligations while the Prophet was alive. After the Prophet's demise, a committee was constituted and he was assigned as the first leader (generally titled Caliph) of the Islamic community. He had to appease a bloody rising by certain clans that were renegging on pacts with the Muslims. He also began the action of the compilation of the Quran into a composed book (Quran had been memorised word for word by thousands of folks, and most pieces were put down anyhow; it's just it hadn't comprised into an exclusive book). He passed away two years after the Prophet, in 634 AD.

Umar ibn al-Khattab

He was the 2nd of the supposed Four virtuous Caliphs (al-khulafa al-rashidun). Umar was an early convert to Islam, and close to Muhammad till the Prophet's demise in 632. Accordant to Sunnite custom, Muhammad's death was followed by a hot conflict among his followers over the issue of taking over - a quarrel which Umar defused by hailing Abu Bakr as authorized successor and first Caliph. When Abu Bakr died, Umar was his clear heir. In Umar's own rule, the Caliphate subdued large dominions in the Middle East, and Umar is supposed to have established the ground rules for caliphal governance. Umar also dabbled in calendar reform, establishing the Hijra Calendar, still used, which takes as its terminus a quo the hijra or coerced deportation from Mecca to Medina of the Prophet and his following, in 622 AD. Umar was killed in Medina in 644, but had antecedently set in place a committee to nominate his successor. The committee named Uthman ibn Affan.

Uthman ibn Affan

The 3rd of the supposed Four virtuous Caliphs (al-khulafa al-rashidun), Uthman followed Umar (Caliph 634-644) upon Umar's assassination. Favourising his personal family, the Umayyad, Uthman was before long accused with nepotism by his political adversaries. Disputation also surrounded his salary cut for soldiers, and his determination to order an authorized version of the Quran to be produced, and all other adaptations to be destroyed. A rebellion resulted, and Uthman was killed in Medina by units of the Caliphate ground forces from Egypt and Iraq.

Ali ibn Abu Talib

The 4th of the 4 virtuous Caliphs (al-khulafa al-rashidun). As the full cousin of the Prophet Muhammad, Ali was among the first to accept him as an actual prophet of Supreme Being. Ali later wedded Fatimah, the daughter of Muhammad, with whom he bore the sons Hassan and Husayn. Ali was a lot of times referred as a nominee for Caliph, but it wasn't till the demise of Uthman ibn Affan in 656 that he attained the Caliphate, being elected by the cizens of Mecca) and Medina. His candidature was disputed by, amongst other people, Muawiyah ibn Abu Sufyan, who followed Ali as Caliph, from 661 to 680. Ali died in 661, assassinated in Kufa by one of his political adversaries. In Shiite custom, Ali and his sons in the marriage with Fatimah are considered imams - actual, unfailing leaders of the Muslim community.

Al-Farabi

Abu Nasr Muhammad Ibn al-Farakh al-Farabi (870-950 AD.), was among the most distinguished men of science and philosophers of his time. Farabi was born in the humble village of Wasij in Turkmenistan from parents of Persian ancestry. After finishing his early academic years in Farab and Bukhara, Farabi arrived in Baghdad to follow up on higher studies in 901 A.D. He studied in Baghdad for well over forty years and developed command over several speeches and fields of cognition. Farabi made worthy contributions to the areas of mathematics, ism, medicine and even music. As a philosopher and Neo-Platonist he composed copious commentary on Aristotle's work. He is also accredited for categorising logical system into two separate groups, the first one comprising idea and the 2nd representing proof. Farabi wrote books on sociology and a celebrated book on music captioned Kitab al-Musiqa (The Book of Music). He played and formulated a wide-ranging number of instruments. Farabi is also famed for his presentation of the beingness of vacuum in Physics.

Farabi exercised outstanding influence on scientific discipline and cognition for numerous centuries. Regrettably, the book Theology of Aristotle, as was obtainable to him at that time was considered by him as actual, though afterwards it came out to be the work of some Neoplatonic author. In spite of this, he was considered the Second Teacher in philosophical system for centuries and his work, aspired at deduction of philosophy and sufism, made-up the way for Ibn Sinas work

Muhammad ibn Ali

Imam Muhammad al Baqir (676 - 743 AD.) was the 5th Shia Imam. He was born as Muhammad ibn Ali ibn Husayn. Muhammad al Baqir was born in Medina in 676, his male parent was Ali Zayn al Abidin, the 4th Shia Imam, his female parent was the daughter of Hasan named Fatimah. He was not mired in politics and was acknowledged for being a meditative human who committed his life to religious studies. When his brother, Zaid ibn Ali led a revolt against the Umayyads, Muhammad advised him against taking on the substantial military force of the Ummayads. Muhammad al Baqir's cognition left him to become an instructor, and he's all right thought of for his cognition in both spiritual and legal matters. His son, Jafar as Sadiq was a pupil of his, and without doubt he profited greatly from his father's knowledge. In spite of his distaste to politics, he was troubled continually by the Umayyad rulers. They were alarmed at his fame and the influence his academic works had. Additionally, the activities of his brother and other kinsmen made them doubting of him. He died on January 31, 743, some consider by poison. He was buried in Medina, in the Jannat ul-Baqi cemetary.

Muhammad ibn Ali Al-Taghi

Imam Muhammad at Taqi (April 12, 811 - November 27, 835 AD.) was the 9th Shia Imam. His name was Muhammad ibn Ali ibn Musa. Muhammad at Taqi was born in Medina to Ali ar Rida and a Nubian servile named Khaizuran. He was only nine when his father passed away, and per se, many doubed his power to carry the Imamate. Nevertheless, he hung on to his status with the help of Al Mamun whose backing proved valuble to the young Imam, and who brought him to dwell in Baghdad. In time, Muhammad was married to Al Mamun's daughter, Umm al Fadl. During his time in Baghdad he was known for posessing an astonishing quantity of cognition, particularly considering his young age.

After existing in Baghdad for a couple of years, Muhammad came back to Medina. Here, he found his kinship with his wife stressed, and upon the death of Al Mamun, he discovered his fortunes degenerate. The sucessor to his father in law, was Al Mamun's stepbrother. With the new Abbasid ruler in power, Muhammad was no more secure, and was not aided by the disapproval that Al Mu'tasm had for the Imam. Al Mu'tasm would call Muhammad at Taqi back to Baghdad where he desired to change him to the generous life style of the palace. Muhammad left his son Ali al Hadi with his mother in Medina and begin for Baghdad. He lived there for one more year, not charmed as al-Mu'tasm had desired, rather becoming a familiar scholarly person and popular with in debates. Al Mu'tasm would grow sick of him, and Muhammad at Taqi would pass away all of a sudden, likely through poison on November 27, 835. He was buried beside his grandfather, Musa al Kazim at Kazmain.

MAIN FIGURES IN MEDIEVAL PERIOD

Al-Tabari

Abu Jafar Muhammad ibn Jarir at-Tabari (838-923 AD.), Irani historiographer and theologist, was born in Amol, Tabaristan (south of the Caspian Sea), and studied in Baghdad, Syria and Egypt. "Tabari" implies from Tabaristan. He died in Baghdad in 923. Cast on his personal resourcefulnesses after his father's demise, he was cut down to heavy impoverishment till he was nominated private instructor to the son of the vizier Tibaidallah ibn Yaliya. He subsequently travelled to Egypt, but soon came back to Bagdad, where he remained as an instructor of custom and jurisprudence until his death. His life was bare and composed, and characterized by extreme industriousness. He is said to have often declined expensive presents. A Shafi'ite in law, he laid claim the right to criticize each and every schools, and ended by launching a school of his own, in which, nevertheless, he received the bloody ire of the Hanbalites.

His pieces of work are not numerous, but two of them are absolute comprehensive. The one is the Tarikh ur-Rusul wal-Muluk (chronicle of the Prophets and Kings), commonly called the Annals. These are accounts from the existence to AD. 915, and is famous for its detail and truth. It has been published under the editorship of MJ de Goeje in 3 serial, containing thirteen books, with two additional books bearing exponents, introduction and glossary. A Persian digest of this work, made in 963 by the Samanid scholar al-Balami, has been transformed into French by H Zotenberg. A Turkish version of this was brought out at Istanbul.

His second avid work was the comment on the Koran, which was branded by the equal comprehensiveness of detail as the Annals. The sizing of the work and the independency of assessment in it seem to have kept it from having a big circulation, but scholars such as Baghawi and Suyuti used it mostly. It has been brought out in thirty volumes at Cairo, 1902-1903 AD.

Ibn Kathir

Ibn Kathir was a Muslim scholarly person born in Busra. He was instructed by the Islamic Scholar Ibn Taymiyya in Damascus, Syria. He was born in the year 1301 AD. Ibn Kathir composed a renowned commentary of the Quran named "Tafsir Ibn Kathir" which associated certain Hadith, or expressions of the Prophet Muhammad, and sayings of the Sahaba (associates of the Prophet Muhammad) to verses of the Quran, in account. Tafsir Ibn Kathir is celebrated all over the Arab world and American mosques, and is among the most widely used accounts of the Quran today.

Ibn Kathir was celebrated for his great retentiveness which aided him learn many of the expressions of the Prophet Muhammad and the full Quran. Ibn Kathir is acknowledged as a judge, a master of Hadith, and a mufassir or Quran observer. Some view Ibn Kathir as a forerunner to the present-day Salafi or Wahhabi school of law, but Ibn Kathir himself as a Shafi scholar. This is suggested by two of his books, among which was "Layers of Shafi" a volume on the virtuousnesses of the Imam Shafi.

Additional books composed by Ibn Kathir include "Signs prior to the day of reckoning" and "The Birthday of the Prophet" which backs argumentations of the legality of observing Prophet Muhammad's birthday (seen as a deplorable conception or bida by a lot Muslims), and "Biographies of the Prophets". The current Wahhabi social movement of Islam lays claim a groundwork in the pennings of Ibn Kathir, and particularly his teacher Ibn Taymiyya. All the same, a lot of Ibn Kathir's pieces of writing go against Wahhabi beliefs such as his opinion of the legality of celebrating the Prophet Muhammad's birthday. Ibn Kathir turned blind barely before his death. When Ibn Kathir passed away he was entombed alongside his teacher Ibn Taymiyya in the Sufi Cemetery of Damascus, Syria in 1372 AD.

Hazrat Inayat Khan

Hazrat Inayat Khan, founding father of the Sufi Order International, arrived in the west as a spokesperson of numerous musical customs of his native India. As a Sufi instructor his message constituted love, harmoniousness, and beauty acquired from a lot of sufi teachings and an original approach to the concording of western and oriental spiritualty customs. He committed his early life to the mastery of the elaborations of classic Indian music, acquiring the title of Tansen from the Nizam of Hyderabad, a sponsor of the musical arts. In the fulfilment of his pursuance for a spiritual instructor, Inayat Khan took his Sufi induction from Shaykh al-Mashaykh Sayed Muhammad Abu Hashim Madani. Although he was an instigator of the four chief Sufi origins in India, Madani's common association was with the Chishti Order. At the close of his apprenticeship, Inayat Khan was ordered by his instructor to visit the West and work on building up a culture that blended the wiseness of the Orient and the coherent scientific mind-set of the west.

On September 13, 1910, Inayat Khan started out a spiritual pursuance over three continents. He at length settled in Suresnes, a suburban area of Paris. During his sixteen years in the west, he made a school of religious training established upon the conventional instructions of the Chishti Order, and impregnated with his imagination of the unity of religious ideals and a hope for the arousing of humanity to the immortal within. His sone Pir Vilayat Inayat Khan has carried on his father's teaching role. While contemporary sufi scholars and instructors state that his teachings were watered-down versions of the cryptical instructions of other sufi masters it's unchallenged that he was among the first individuals who brought in the teachings of the east to a western audience embedding a germ for additional development in later generations; a character which had as well been acted by religious instructors such as G. I. Gurdjieff, the Greek-Armenian mystic.

MAIN FIGURES IN MODERN PERIOD

Idries Shah

Idries Shah (1924-1996 AD.) was a writer and lyricist in the sufist custom. Idries Shah greatly broadened the western cognition of the sufi precepts. He had deep influence upon many intellects, notably Doris Lessing. His definition of Sufism was broad therein he was of the belief that it preceded Islamism and didn't depend upon the Quran, but was comprehensive in beginning, background and relevancy. He maintained that spiritual teachings should be conferred in forms and terms that are acquainted in the community wherever they're to settle. He considered that students should be given work supported their individualist capabilities, and disapproved schemes that implement the same practises to all. In his personal work he applied instructions accounts, and witticism, to great outcome.

Hamza Yusuf

Hamza Yusuf Hanson adopted Islam in 1977 and is among the most well-vesed Muslim scholars in the west. He passed a lot of years learning in the Middle East and Africa under several scholars. Presently, he is the director of the Zaytuna Institute, in California, which is committed to the resurgence of Islamic scientific discipline and the conservation of traditional pedagogies. Shaykh Hamza Yusuf Hanson was born in Walla Walla, Washington and brought up in Northern California. He turned Muslim in 1977 in Santa Barbara, California and afterwards moved to the Mideast and studied Arabic language and Islam for four years in the United Arab Emirates and later in Medina, Algeria, Morocco, and West Africa for many years.

He received education permits in assorted Islamic disciplines from respective known scholars in different countries. After ten-year of studies abroad, he came back to the USA and took degrees in nursing from Imperial Valley College and spiritual studies at San Jose State University. He has journeyed everywhere in the world holding talks on Islam. He is the co-founder of Zaytuna Institute, which is committed to the resurgence of conventional study techniques and the sciences of Islam. Shaykh Hamza has interpreted a lot of authoritative texts from Arabic and currently teaches at Zaytuna Institute in Hayward, California.

Ali Shariati

Ali Shariati (1933-1977) is an Iranian sociologist, born in Mazinan, a suburban area of Mashhad in Iran. His father was an active nationalistic sermonizer, who'd afterwards take part in his social movements. As an youngster he went to high school and primary school in Mashhad. In his years at the Teacher's Training College, he came into contact with youth who were from the lowly economical levels of the society and sampled the poorness and grimness that subsisted in Iran at that time. Simultaneously he was exposed by many facets of Western thinking as apparent in his writing. He got his degree from Sorbonne University in France, and then carried on his studies and acquired a doctor's degree in sociology from the University of Mashhad. It has been contemplated that he was wiped out by the SAVAK. Shariati is counted as one of the most authoritative ideological leaders of the Muslim Revolution of Iran.

REFERENCES

al-Hamdani, Abbas H.: *The Isma'ili Da'wa in Northern India*, Cairo, 1956.

al-Hujwiri, 'Ali ibn-'Uthman: *Kashf al-mahòjub,* R. A. Nicholson, London, 1936.

Bashir al-din Mahòmud Ahòmad: *Introduction* to Shir 'Ali Eng. tr. *of The Holy Quran*, Rabwah, 1955.

Bausani, A.: "Note su Shah Waliullah di Dehli", *Annali*, n.s., 1961.

Ghulam Sarwar: *Khazinat al-asfiya',* Cawnpore, 1902.

Ghulam, Halim: *Tuhòfa-i ithna-'ashariyya,* Lucknow, 1879.

Ghuldm Shah 'Ali: *Maqamat-i Mazò'hari,* Delhi, 1891.

Gilani, A. C. S.: *Ghalib, His Life and Persian Poetry*, Karachi, 1956.

Khayr-ad-din, M.: *Tadhkirat al-'ulama'*, Calcutta, 1934.

Khushal Khan Khattak: *Poems from the Divan*, tr. D. N. Mackenzie, London, 1965.

Khusraw, Amir: *Matòla 'al-anwar,* Lucknow, 1884.

Kühnel, Ernst: *Moghul-Malerei*, Berlin, 1956.

Laoust, H.: *Les Schismes clans l'Islam*, Paris, 1965.

Law, N. N.: *Promotion of Learning in India During Muhammadan Rule by Muhammadans*, London, 1916.

Lawrence, W. R.: *The Valley of Kashmir*, London, 1895.

Lentz, W.: "Sammlungen zur afghanischen Literatur — und Zeitgeschichte", *ZDMG* (1937), 711-32.

Leyden, J.: "On the Roshenian Sect and its Founder Bayazid Ansari", *Asiatic Researches*.

Lokhandwalla, Sh. T.: "The Bohras, a Muslim Community of Gujarat", SI, 1955.

Madani, Hòusayn. Ahmad: *Naqsh-i hòayat,* Delhi, 1953.

Mancri, Sharaf-ad-din Ahòmad ibn-Yahòya: *Maktubat,* Lucknow, 1868; Cawnpore, 1911.

Massignon, L.: *Essai sur les origines du Lexique Technique de la Mystique musulmane,* Paris, 1922.

Mawdudi, A. A.: *Towards Understanding Islam*, Lahore, 1960.

Mawdudi, Abu-l-A'la: *Ta'limat,* Lahore, 1955.

Mazòhar, Mirza Jan-i Janan: *Kalimat-i Tòayyibat,* Delhi, 1891.

Menant, D.: "Les Bohras du Guzarate", *RMM*, 1910.

Mihr, Ghulam-Rasul: *Sayyid, Ahòmad Shahid*, Lahore, 1952.

Ministry of Education, Government of Pakistan: *Report of the Commission on National Education*, Karachi, 1959.

Muhammad Malik Din: *Gagetteer of Bhawalpur*, Lahore, 1909.

Muhammadan Anglo-Oriental Educational Conference, Majmu'a-i resolution ha-i dihsala, Aligarh, 1896.

Muhòammad Hòasan Naqshbandi: *Hòalat-i masha'ikh-i Naqshbandiyya Mujaddidiyya,* Muradabad, 1904.

Muhòammad, Mirza: *Tuhòfat al-Hind,* BM Add. MS 16, 858.

Temple, R. C.: *The Legends of the Punjab*, Bombay, 1884.

The Founder of the Ahòmadivya Movement, Lahore, n.d.

6

Scriptures

The main scriptures of Islam are the Quran and the Hadith. The Quran is the reference of Allah's disclosures to human beings, carried through his messenger, Muhammad. The Hadith isn't considered a direct source of disclosure; rather, it is supposed to contain the records of the traditions, practices and decisiveness of the earlier Muslim community. Muslims consider that the Quran was given to Muhammad by God through the angel Gabriel. The Hadith is an accumulation of the expressions and deeds of Muhammad, accustomed supplement the Quran. Regrettably, the Hadith's truth and reliableness is highly questionable. Even many Muslims differ on the comparative dependability of different Hadith collections.

DIVINE WORDS

The Prophet of God said that Adam and Moses (in the cosmos of spirits) kept up an argument before God, and Adam defeated Moses; who said, 'Thou art that Adam whom God produced by the ability of his hands, and breathed into thee from His personal spirit, and made the angels accede before thee, and gave thee an abode in His own Paradise: after that thou threwest man upon the earth, from the fault which thou committedst.' Adam said, 'Thou art that Moses whom God elected for His prophecy, and to converse with, and He gave to thee twelve tables, in which are explained everything, and God made thee His confidant, and the bearer of His secrets: then how long was the Bible written before I was created?' Moses said, 'Forty years.' Then Adam said, 'Didst thou see in the Bible that Adam disobeyed God?' He said, 'aye.' Adam said, 'Dost thyself then reproach me on a affair which God wrote in the Bible forty years prior to producing me?'

A few heavenly words of prophet Muhammad are: it's not righteousness that ye turn your face towards the east or the west, but righteousness is (in) him who believeth in God and the Day of Judgment, and the angels and the Book, and the Prophets, and who giveth riches for the love of God to his phratry and to orphans and the needy and the son of the road and them that ask and for the absolving of slaves, and who is clamant in prayer, and giveth the alms; and those who carry out their concordat when they covenant, and the enduring in adversity and affliction and in time of ferocity, these are they who are true, and these are they who fear God.

Say: We trust in God, and what hath been sent to thee, and what was sent to Abraham, and Ishmael, and Isaac, and Jacob, and the tribes, and what was given to Moses, and to Jesus, and the prophets from their Lord-we arrive at no differentiation between any of them-and to Him are we reconciled: and whoso desireth other than surrender (Islam) for a religion, it shall certainly not be accepted from him, and in the life to come he shall be among the losers. Observe the prayers, and the middle prayer, and stand instant before God. And if ye fear, then afoot or mounted; but when ye are safe remember God, how he taught you what ye did not know. When the call to supplication soundeth on the Day of faithful (Friday), then rush along to remember God, and desert business; that is finer for you if ye only knew: and when supplication is done, pass around in the land and seek of the amplitude of God.

Turn thy face towards the sanctified Mosque; where ye be, turn your faces thitherwards. Give alms on the course of God, and let not your hands cast off you into devastation; but do goodness, for God loveth those who do goodness; and achieve the pilgrimage and the visit to God: but if ye be besieged, then send what is easiest as an offering. They will ask thee what it is they must give in alms. Say: Let what good ye give be for parents, and kinsfolk, and the orphan, and the needy, and the son of the road; and what good ye do, verily God knoweth it. They'll ask thee what they shall spend in alms; say, The excess. If ye give alms openly, it's well; but if ye hide it, and give it to the poor, it is better for you, and will take away from you some of your sins: and God knoweth what ye do.

O ye who trust, make not your almsgiving of no effects by taunting and irritation, like him who spendeth what he hath to be seen of men, and believeth not in God and the Day of Judgment: for his semblance is as the semblance of a stone with earth upon it, and a gruelling rain falleth upon it and leaveth it bare; they accomplish nothing with what they earn, for God guideth not the people that disbelieve. And the likeness of those who expend their wealth for the sake of pleasing God and for the certainty of their souls is as the likeness of a garden on a hill: a hard rain falleth on it and it bringeth forward its fruit two times; and if no heavy rain falleth on it, then the dew falleth; and God seeth what ye do. Genial words and pardon is better than alms which annoyance followeth; and God is affluent and remorseful.

The centers of men are at the disposition of divine unto one heart, and He turneth them about in in any case that He pleaseth. O conductor of hearts, turn our hearts to obey Thee. The first matter which God created was a pen, and He said to it, 'Write.' It said, 'What shall I write?' And God said, 'Write down the measure of every individual thing to be created.' And it wrote all that was and all that will be to infinity. There is not one amidst you whose sitting-place isn't composed by God whether in the fire or in Paradise. The associates said, 'O Prophet! since God hath assigned our place, may we entrust in this and desert our spiritual and moral duty?' He said, 'No, because the blessed will do beneficial works, and those who are of the deplorable will do sorry works.'

RELIGIOUS SCRIPTURES

The Holy Quran

It's not hard for a fair and just human to understand that the purpose of a Quran of God is to conduce people to God, and to make them trust in Him as a sure thing, and to bar them from doing sin by impressing the loftiness and reverence of God upon their hearts. Of what use is a book which cannot cleanse a heart, nor can bestow such pure and perfect understanding as should make one hate sin. The attraction of sin is a dangerous leprosy which cannot be healed till the manifestations of the living understanding of God, and the signs of His awe and greatness and power, descend like rain and till a person perceives God with His terrible powers as a goat perceives a tiger which is only two steps away from it. Man needs to be freed from the fatal passion of sin. The grandness of God should so engage his heart that it should free him of the overcoming want of passion which falls upon him like lightning and at once depletes his store of righteousness.

Those unpurified rages which attack repeatedly like epilepsy and destruct all sense of piousness cannot be annihilated by a self-conceived belief of God, nor can they be conquered by one's own reasoning or be blocked by a satisfaction whose suffering has not been felt by one. This is not a matter of apathy but in the estimation of a wise person it is worthy of consideration above all else as to how he might safeguard himself against the ruin which confronts him on account of his daring and his lack of relationship with God, the root of which is sin and disobedience. It is obvious that a person cannot give up a certain pleasure for the sake of conjecture. It is only a certainty that can rescue one from another certainty. For instance, if we are certain that there are a number of deer in a forest whom we can easily catch, we are incited by that certainty to enter the forest for that purpose; but if we're also sure that there are hundred lions in the woodland and thousands of pythons, we would be deterred from making the attempt. Thus sin can't be warded off without this degree of foregone conclusion.

It's exclusive iron that can break iron. There ought be that sure thing of the grandness and reverence of God which should shred the draperies of rashness, and should make the body shake, and should make demise appear near. The heart should be so overcome by fear that all relationship with the sinful ego should be cut asunder and one should be drawn by hidden hands towards God and the heart should be filled with certainty that God Who is truly present doesn't leave a audacious offender without punishment. What shall a searcher after accurate honour do with a book which doesn't fulfill this need?

God, in whose assembling is man's redemption and eternal felicity, cannot be ascertained without abiding by the Holy Quran. The agency of getting complete cognition through which one can see God, and the purifying water which withdraws all doubts, and the mirror through which one can lay eyes on that eminent Being, is the converse with God which we have just mentioned. He whose soul seeks the truth should arise and search for it. We say truly that if souls were prompted by true search and hearts felt true thirst, people would look for this way and would seek for it. Be sure that this seal is not set by God, but as man has deprived himself of this privilege, he seeks excuses for its absence. As it is not possible that we should be able to see without eyes or should be able to find out without ears or should be able to address without a tongue, in the same way, it is not imaginable that we should be able to behold the endorsement of the Beloved without the Holy Quran.

The direct path and the chief means which is full of the lights of foregone conclusion, and is the complete guide for our sacred wellbeing and our cerebral advancement, is the Holy Quran which is charged with the closure of all the spiritual competitions of the world. It contains a large quantity of the water of life for us and comprises many rare and priceless jewels which are hidden in it and are being displayed every day.

It is an superior measure whereby we can differentiate between truth and falsehood. It is the one bright lamp which shows the way of truth. Beyond any doubt the hearts of those who have a kinship with the straight path are drawn to the Holy Quran. God has so fashioned their hearts that they lean towards their Beloved like a lover and find no rest elsewhere, and hearing a patent and clean leading from Him, they hear to nothing else. They admit joyously and thirstily every truth contained in it.

At last it becomes the way of elucidation of the heart and brightening the moral sense and of fantastic revelations. It leads everybody to the pinnacles of advancement agreeing to their capacities. The righteous have always been in need of walking in the light of the Holy Quran. Whenever Islam has been confronted with any other religion in consequence of some new condition of the age, the sharp and effective instrument that has at once come to hand is the Holy Quran. In the same way, whenever philosophical thought has been given promotion in opposition to it, the Holy Quran has destructed that vicious plant and has so humiliated it as to provide a mirror to its students which shows up that true philosophical system which is contained in the Holy Quran. The Holy Quran is an extraordinary pearl. Its outside is light and its inside is light and its above is light and its below is light and there is brightness level in every word of it. It is a sacred garden whose collective fruits are within easygoing reach and through which streams flow. Every fruit of good luck is found in it and every torch is alighted from it.

The reflexion Khataman Nabiyyin which has been employed to the Holy Prophet, demands that the Holy Writ that was unveiled to him, should be the most complete of all books and should consist all excellences; and indeed and so it is. The rule is that whatsoever degree of spiritual power and inner perfection is obsessed by the person upon whom the word of God descends, the same degree of power and majesty is possessed by that word. As the spiritual power and inner perfection of the Holy Prophet, peace be on him, were of the highest degree, which no one exceeded or will exceed, therefore the Holy Quran occupies that high base and rank which hasn't been reached by any of the previous book and Word of God. The capability and sacred ability of the Holy Prophet were the greatest of all, and all excellences had reached their culmination in him.

Hence, the Holy Quran that was disclosed to him is also complete and as the excellences of Prophethood achieved their climax in him, the excellences of the miracle of the word reached their culmination in the

Holy Quran. Thus he was the Khataman Nabiyyin and his Book was the Khatamal Kutub. From the viewpoint of every aspect of a marvellous word, the Holy Quran is at the broadest stage. The perfection of the Holy Quran is seen and its miraculous character is proved from every point of view, that is to say, from the points of view of excellence of composition, of the sequence of its subjects, of its teaching and its perfection and of the fruits of its teaching. That's why the Holy Quran has not called for its match from any special viewpoint, but has issued a all-purpose gainsay taking a match from any viewpoint. From whichever viewpoint it is looked at, it is a miracle.

The blessed Quran is a miracle the likes of of which never was and never will be. The door of its graces and approvings is always exposed, and it's shining and demonstrate in every age as it was in the time of the Holy Prophet. It ought also be minded that the language of everyone agrees to his high resolve. The broader the resolve and purpose and the purpose of the speaker, the same will be the case with his speech. Glorious revelation also follows the similar rule. The broader the resolve of the individual to whom Divine disclosure is vouchsafed, the higher will be the reference of the revelation. As the circle of the resoluteness and capability and purpose of the Holy Prophet, was very extensive, the disclosure that came to him had the same high rank. No one else will ever so accomplish the equal stage of resolve and courageousness inasmuch as his message was not for any limited time or for any particular people, as was the case with the Prophets before him.

The good truths concerning to religion, and all the learning concerning to the subject of theology, and convincing argumentations in support of the truth collectively with the secrets and perceptivities that are set out in the Holy Quran, are such human modules jointly are not able to detect them nor can the intelligence of an intelligent person alight on them on its own. A considerateness of past ages has shown that no philosopher or mentor was able to detect all that knowledge; but in this case there is a wonder upon wonders, namely, that knowledge and insight were conferred upon one who was entirely ignorant. He had never seen a schoolhouse nor read a book nor accompanied with any learned or judicious person. He lived his life amidst wild people, was born and brought up amongst them and companioned with them.

Whatever comes to life by the exercise of God's complete mightiness, whether it is a part of conception or it is a Holy Book, virtually disclosed by Him, it's essential that it should have the quality that no one out of universe should have the power to bring out its like. This is established in two ways; one is by way of deductive reasoning. God is One and without associate in His Being and dimensions and works, and this does not admit of any partnership with Him in any of his conceptions or words or actions, for if such partnership were admissible in respect of any of His creations or words or processes, then it would be permissible in all His attributes and actions, and as such it would be permissible that there should be another God. That which possesses all Divine attributes would be God and that which possesses some of the attributes of the Divine, would be a collaborator of God in respect of those dimensions, and this is unlike reason. It follows that it is necessary that God should One without associate in all His attributes and words and actions, and His Being should be free from all those mutual exclusiveness which would lead to someone being His collaborator. Secondly, it's established by observance of all those things which have been produced by God that none of them could be produced by humankind, not even the smallest of them like a fly or a mosquito or a crawler.

On discovering their anatomy and constitution, one sees such marvels that provide absolute proof of the beingness of the Maker of the cosmos. Besides all these argumentations, it's clear to every sensible individual that were it permitted that some one other than God could have the power to create that which God has produced by His power, then no part of creation could be cited as cogent evidence of the existence of the True Creator and the matter of His recognition as the Creator would become dubious; for if some of those things that have been created by God Almighty could be created by someone else, then there is no rationality why someone else cannot create everything that God has created. Now that it is demonstrated that it is essential that that which God has produced should be unrivalled and its matchlessness is absolute proof of its being from God, this is a complete falsification of the suggestion that it's not essential that the Divine word should be uncomparable, or that its being unrivalled is no cogent evidence of its being from God.

The Holy Quran is a Holy Scripture which has announced its own matchlessness and has claimed its own grandness, its wiseness, its truth, the great thing about its constitution and its sacred lights. It is not accurate that the Muslims have themselves bring up these excellences on behalf of the Quran. It sets out its own merits and excellences and puts forward its matchlessness and peerlessness as a challenge to the whole of creation and cries out loudly: Is there any protester? Its truths and fine points are not confined to two or three which would allow room for doubt on the part of an naive person, but are like the soaring sea and are visible in every direction like the stars of paradise. There is no truth outside of it. There is no wiseness that is not comprised in it. There is no light that is not obtainable through following it. These things are not without proof and are not mere words. It is an established and distinctly proved verity which has been gleaming through 1,300 years. We have set out this truth in great detail and have elaborated the fine points of the Quran at so much length as to nominate a soaring sea for the gratification of a searcher after verity.

One of the important reasons of masses going astray in this age is that in the hearts of most people the grandness of the Holy Quran no more rules. One group of Muslims has become the follower of deceptive doctrine. They attempt to determine every topic by intellect. They lay claim that the highest supreme authority available to man for the resolution of quarrels is rationality. When they find that the existence of Gabriel and other angels that are mentioned in religious books, and the existence of heaven and hell as is demonstrated in the Holy Quran, cannot be proved by reason, they immediately reject them and begin to have recourse to weak accounts. They interpret angels as meaning powers, and revelation only as a faculty, and heaven and hell as meaning merely spiritual comfort or pain. They do not seem to realize that reason alone is not the instrument for discovery of the unknown. Indeed high verities and extreme insights are far above the reach of reason and are established only through true visions. If the criterion for truths were to be reason alone, the great wonderments of Godhead would remain concealed and man's understanding would remain incomplete and imperfect and he would not be rid of doubts and suspicions. The end of this biased understanding would be that in the absence of counselling from above and with no cognition of the lines of opinion that are set in movement by the Power on High, all kinds of doubtfulnesses would arise with reference to the existence of the Almighty Himself. The thought that rationality alone is adequate for unravelling all the enigmas of the True God Almighty is completely inexcusable.

The 2nd group has cast aside rationality wholly and has also left aside the Holy Quran which is the head of all cognition of matters Divine and has taken crisp hold of accounts and insignificant sayings. They should leave aside the expressions of others, and even if they should find a hadith which opposes the Holy Quran, they should cast aside it at once, as Almighty has articulated in the Holy Quran: In what preaching, leaving aside the Holy Quran, will they trust (7:186)? It is apparent that the Holy

Quran is an agency of the greatest class which is conclusive and sure. Most ahadith are hypothesis, and guess does not help anything in direct contrast with truth.

The benevolent One has taught the Quran. He has disclosed the Book which is the verity and is a equalizer for considering the truth. It is direction for human beings and bears the expounding of counselling. It separates between truth and falsehood by its reasoning. It is a critical discourse and free from doubt. We have revealed it to thee so that it might decide matters pertaining which there is difference and so that believers may be provided with counselling and clemency. It comprises all the truths which were contained in the previous books in a scattered form. Falsehood cannot approach it from fore or aft. It contains clear proof for people and is a guidance and a mercy for those who have faith. Then leaving apart Allah and His auguries, in what discussion will you believe? (It conforms to that if a hadith is at odds with Holy Quran, it must be disapproved. If it can be rendered as being in unison with the Holy Quran, it could be acceptable).

This is the wealthiness regarding which it had been prophesied that the Messiah would circulate it much that masses will have their fill of it. The prognostication doesn't mean that the Messiah would accumulate together substantial riches pertaining which it's been said: Your material possession and your issue are a trial (8:29); and that he would deliberately put people on trial by handing out riches among them. In his first advent also the Messiah felt no attraction towards worldly wealth. He has stated in the Gospel that the property of a believer are not gold and silver, but are the jewels of truths and understanding. This is the material possession that is bestowed by God Almighty on the Prophets, which they hand out. It is concerning this property that the Holy Prophet said: I am a distributor and Allah is the Bestower. It is related in the ahadith that the Promised Messiah would come into the world when knowledge of the Quran will be lost and ignorance will prevail. That is the time which is mentioned in the hadith: If faith goes up to the Pleiades it will be cut down by a man of Persia. It's been disclosed to me in a vision that the culmination of that age will begin in the Hijri year which agrees to the value of the letters of the rhyme: And We have the might to take it away (23:19); which adds up to 1274.

Think this well and do not pass over it hastily and supplicate God that He should open your intellects to it. The ahadith state that in the last mentioned days the Quran will be borne away from the world and its cognition will be lost and ignorance will dominate and the eagerness and pleasantness of trust will deviate from the hearts. Among them is the hadith that if faith will go up to the Pleiades and will disappear from the earth, a man of the Persians will offer his hand and will bring it down. This hadith shows clearly that when ignorance and inconstancy and error, which are depicted as smoke in the other ahadith, will become far-flung and true faith will become so uncommon as if it had been drawn up to the skies, and the Holy Quran will be deserted as if it had been raised towards Almighty, at that time, a man of Persian Empire will take hold of the trust from the Pleiades and will come down with it to the world. Make sure, hence, that he's the son of Virgin Mary who was to descend.

NON-RELIGIOUS SCRIPTURES

The Hadith

Hadith are unwritten traditions referring to the words and feats of the Muslim prophet Muhammad. Hadith collectings are considered as significant tools for ascertaining the Sunnah, or Islamic way, by all conventional schools of legal philosophy. Lingually the word 'hadith' signifies: that which is fresh from amidst matters or a piece of truth brought either in a small quantity or large. The Arabic plural form is ahadith. In English scholarly usage, hadith is often both singular and plural form. And hadith is what is addressed by the speaker. Tahdith is the non-finite, or verbal noun, of the primary verb form.

In Islamic language, the term hadith pertains to accounts about the affirmations or activities of the Islamic prophet Muhammad, or about his implied commendation of something said or done in his bearing. Authoritative hadith specialist Ibn Hajar says that the designated meaning of "hadith" in sacred custom is something attributed to Muhammad, as opposed to the Quran. Other affiliated words possess similar meanings: "khabar" (word, truth) often denotes to accounts about Muhammad, but occasionally refers to traditions about his associates (sahaba) and their heirs from the following generation (tabi'in); conversely, "athar" (shadow, trace) usually concerns to traditions about the associates and heirs, though sometimes implies customs about Muhammad. The word sunnah (tradition) is also used in relation to a standard custom of Muhammad or the early Islamic community.

A hadith comprises of two facets: the textual matter of the account (matn) carrying the de facto narration; and the chains of tellers (isnad, or sanad), which documents the itinerary through which the report has been channelized. The "sanad" is so named due to the trust of the hadith specialists upon it in determining the legitimacy or weakness of a hadith. The sanad consists of a 'chain' of the narrators each bringing up the one from whom they heard the hadith until bringing up the originator of the matn along with the matn itself. The first people who experienced hadith were the associates; so they conserved and comprehended it, knowing both its generalization and particulars, and then carried it to those after them as they were required. Then the genesis coming after them, the following experienced it thus carrying it to those after them and so forth.

Hadiths were in the beginning spoken customs of Muhammad's actions and traditions. From the first Fitna of the 7th century masses queried the roots of hadiths. This resulted in a list of vectors, e.g. "A stated that B told him that Muhammad told." Hadith were finally written down, appraised and assembled into large collections mostly during the reign of Umar II during 8th century, and also in the 9th century. These workings are mentioned to in affairs of Muslim law and chronicle to this day.

Customs of the life of Muhammad and the former account of Islam were handed down by word of mouth for more than a hundred years after Muhammad's death in AD. 632. Muslim historiographers say that caliph Uthman (the third caliph, or heir of Muhammad, who had at one time been Muhammad's secretarial assistant), was the first to inspire Muslims to write the Quran in a given form, and to record the hadith. Uthman's labours were cut short by his assassination, at the hands of grieved soldiers, in 656 AD. The Islamist community (Muslim Ummah) then fell into a lengthy civil war, which Islamic historians call the Fitna. After the fourth caliph Ali ibn Abi Talib was assassinated in 661, the Umayyad dynasty assumed hold of the Muslim empire. Ummayad rule was disrupted by a second civil war (the Second Fitna), restored, and finished in 758 when the Abbasid dynasty impounded the caliphate, and held it, at any rate in name, until 1258.

Muslim historians say that hadith collection and valuation carried on during the first Fitna and the Umayyad period. Nonetheless, much of this activity was presumptively unwritten transmission from early on Muslims to later gatherers, or from instructors to pupils. If any of these early scholars committed any of these collections to writing, they have not endured. The histories and hadith collections we have nowadays were written down at the start of the Abbasid period, more than a hundred years after Muhammad's death. Scholars of the Abbasid period were faced with a vast principal of miscellaneous customs, some of them unconditionally opposing each other. Many of these traditions backed differing views on a variety of disputable affairs. Scholars had to settle which hadith were to be believed as reliable and which had been contrived for political or theological proposes. To do this, they employed a number of processes which Muslims now call the scientific discipline of hadith.

At the commencing of the 7th century, those encountering the hadith set about to doubt the roots of the saying. The hadith were at length registered in written form, had their Isnad appraised, and were accumulated into big collectings during the 8th century. The consuming absolute majority of Muslims believe hadith to be all important accessories to and elucidations of the Quran, Islam's holy book. In Muslim legal philosophy, the Quran contains many rules for the demeanour expected of Muslims but there are no specific Quranic rules on many religious and pragmatic matters. Muslims believe that they can look at the way of life, or sunnah, of Muhammad and his associates to discover what to imitate and what to avoid. Muslim scholars also find it useful to know how Muhammad or his associates explained the revealings, or on what occasion Muhammad experienced them. Some of the times this will clarify a passage that otherwise seems apart. Hadith are a root for Muslim chronicle and life history. For the big majority of pious Muslims, bona fide hadith are also a source of spiritual inspiration.

The science of hadith is a technique of textual critique formulated by early Islamic scholars in ascertaining the veracity of reports assigned to Muhammad. This is accomplished by examining the text of the account, the scale of the report's transmittance, the paths through which the account was transmitted, and the case-by-case tellers involved in its transmittance. On the foundation of these standards, various categorizations were contrived for hadith. The earliest all-embracing work on the science of hadith was Abu Muhammad al-Ramahurmuzi's "al-Muhaddith", while other important work was al-Hakim al-Naysaburi's "al-Ma`rifat `ulum al-hadith". Ibn al-Salah's "`Ulum al-hadith" is conceived the authoritative definitive reference on the science of hadith.

Hadith are broadly categorised as sahih (good, reliable), daif (feeble), or mawdu‘ (fictional). Other categorizations applied as well include: hasan (beneficial), which denotes to a differently sahih account suffering from small inadequacy, or an imperfect report fortified due to a lot of other confirming reports; and munkar (ignored) which is a report that is rejected due to the presence of a sole and generally uncertain transmitter. Both sahih and hasan reports are considered satisfactory for usage in Islamic legal discourse. Classifications of hadith may also be based upon the scale of transmission. Reports that pass through many reliable transmitters at each point in the isnad up till their collection and arrangement are known as mutawatir. These reports are believed the most important as they pass through so many unlike routes that connivance between all of the transmitters becomes an impossible action. Reports not meeting this touchstone are known as ahad, and are of several different types. Another area of focus in the study of hadith is biographical analysis (ilm al-rijal, lit. "science of people"), in which details about the transmitter are inspected. This includes examining their date and place of birth; genetic associations; instructors and pupils; religiousism; ethical behaviour; literate output; their travels; as well as their date of death. Established upon these measures, the dependability (thiqat) of the transmitter is evaluated. Also ascertained is whether the person was really capable to conduct the report, which is deducted from their contemporaneousness and geographical proximity with the other transmitters in the chain. Illustrations of biographic lexicons include Ibn Hajar al-Asqalani's "Tahdhib al-Tahdhib" or al-Dhahabi's "Tadhkirat al-huffaz."

REFERENCES

al-Juwayni, 'Ala'-ad-din: *Ta'rikh-i Jahankusha*, Leiden/ London, 1912-37; Eng. tr. J. A. Boyle (*The History of the World Conqueror*), Manchester, 1958.

Allah Diya: *Siyar al-aqtòab,* Lucknow, 1889.

Bernier, F.: *Travels in Mughal India*, Eng. tr. London, 1891.

Binder, L.: *Religion and Politics in Pakistan*, Berkeley, 1961.

Goetz, H.: *Indian and Persian Miniature Painting*, Amsterdam, 1958.

Grierson, G. A.: *Bihar Peasant Life*, Calcutta, 1885.

Habib, M.: "Shaikh Nasruddin Mahòmud Chiragh-i Delhi as a Great Historical Personality"', *IC*, xx (1946), 129-53.

Hadi, Mirza Muhòammad: *Nur-Allah Shustari, Shahid-i Thalith,* Lucknow, 1925.

In 'am al-Hòaqq: *Muslim Bengali Adab,* Karachi, 1957.

Iqbal Husain: "Chandra Bhan Brahman", *IC*, 1945.

Iqbal, Muhammad: *Islam and, Ahmadism*, Lahore, 1936.

Ishaq, Muhammad: "India's Contribution to the study of Hadiith Literature", *Dacca University Bulletin*, 1955.

Isma'il, Shah (Shahid): *Tadhkir al-akhwan,* Lahore, 1948.

Ismi: *Futu as-salatòin,* Madras, 1948.

Ivanow, W.: *Guide to Ismda'ili Literature*, London, 1933.

Ja'bfar Sharif: Islam in India or the Qanun-i Islam, Eng. tr. G. A. Herklots, 1832; revised by W. Crooke, Oxford, 1921.

Jahangir: *Tuzuk,* Aligarh, 1864; Eng. tr. A. Rogers, London, 1909.

Jamali, Hòamid ibn-FaU+1EODl-Allah: *Siyar al-'Arifin,* Delhi, 1893.

Jamil, M. Tahir: *Hali's Poetry*, Bombay, 1938.

Juzjani, Minhaj-as-siraj: *Tabaqat-i Nasri,* ed. A. H. Habibi, Kabul, 1964.

Kalam-Allah, Shah: *Kashkal-i Kalimi,* Delhi, 1890.

Kamal Khwaja al-din: *The Ideal Prophet*, London, 1925.

Kashani, 'Izz-ad-din: *Misbahò al-hiddya,* Lucknow, 1904.

Kaul, J. L.: *Interpretations of Ghalib*, Delhi, 1957.

Khafi Khan: *Muntakhab al-lubab,* Calcutta, 1869-1925.

Khaja Khan: *Studies in Tasawwuf*, Madras, 1923.

Muhosin Fani: *Dabistan-i madhahib,* Eng. tr. D. Shea and A. Troyer, Paris, 1843.

Muḥòyi-d-din, Shaykh: *al-Balagh al-mubin,* Lahore, 1876.

Mujeeb, M.: *The Indian Muslims*, London, 1967.

Mushtaqi, Rizq-Allah: *Waqi'at-i Mushtaqi,* BM Add. 11633.

The Imperial Gayetteer of India, London, 1907-1909.

Titus, Murray T.: *Islam in India and Pakistan*, Calcutta, 1959.

7

Teachings

Traditionally Islam is explicated in termini of the ethical value of actions starting from forbidden to compulsory. These verbal descriptions apply to both the ruler and the subordinate. Islam does not thence begin from the conception of a fundamental law, which is a way of obligating the rulers to obey predictable decrees. Instead Islam is the natural law for everybody - as is the rule for the king as for the subordinate. Many of these ethical rules can be articulated in terms of rights and obligations when we believe who is implied. For instance the obligation to confer with citizenry on who should be the following political leader can be put in conditions of the right to be conferred. An obligation of the husband to provide for the wife can be named as the right of the married woman for provisos.

Generally a ban could add up to a right of some class not to have that act materialize (e.g. Don't steal - the right to material possession) and an obligation may add up to a right that it does take place (e.g. the obligation to attend after the sick, hapless and aged adds up to a right of these people over the rest of the population). Some of these rights and duties are conveyed very expressly by original roots; others have been deducted more indirectly. The state has a role of implementing justice and this means that the rights and responsibilities are accepted between people and between groups of various forms. There is been a common accord among Muslim scholars on the rights that implement to all people irrespective of religious belief and on the subject that there are rights and obligations that are intrinsic to your specific faith.

SPIRITUAL TEACHINGS

"Lord is One and there is no god but Supreme Being," is the foremost and the first commandment of Islam. Oneness of God or integrity of

Almighty is the centre of Islamism and Islam's sacred Book, the Quran, emphasizes these composition in about every of its 2nd or 3rd verse. All followers of Islamism has not only to trust in single God in his affection but has also to convey this notion by his tongue and present it through with his exploits. No body can accede into Islamic faith unless he or she announces there is no god but God and trusts truly in this announcement in his or her heart. In the abstract language of the religious belief, the belief in One God is called Tauheed. This conception of integrity of God is beautifully conveyed in Chapter 112 of the sacred Quran which is titled al-Ikhlas or at-Tauheed. It says: "Say: He is Allah, the matchless! Allah, the forever Besought of all! He begetteth not nor was begotten. And there is no one comparable to Him." Tauheed is trust in Allah with all His mights and dimensions.

The suitable or subjective name of God, accordant to Islam, is "Allah" while He has a lot of additional prenominal names (of which only ninety-nine have been named in the Quran). The word "Allah" is an Arabic language word which contains "Al" and "Ilah". "Al" is the decisive article which means "the", whilst "Ilah" stands for "the being who's revered". When these two words were brought together, the letter "I" at the commencement of the second word was cast off for easier pronunciation and thus the word "Allah" ensued. So "Allah" means "The God", i.e. "the God who's revered by all creatures and to whom all turn and implore for fulfillment of their "want".

God, according to the Quran, which is the sacred Holy Scripture of Islam, is the all-powerful, omnipotent, almighty, ubiquitous, all-knowing, omniscient and All-Seeing God of the all of the cosmos. He is the benevolent, the kind, the tolerant. There's no God except Him. He is peerless and He exclusively is to be adored. He has no collaborator, no parents, no progeny. He is the active, the ageless, the benefactor, the guardian. He is the Sovereign-Lord of the paradises and the world and shares His reign with none. He is the Lord of everything in the cosmos. Whatever is in the paradises and the world belongs to Him. He makes everything, then multiplies it. He gives life and death and is the Master of the day of reckoning. He would raise every human after his demise and would honour the innocent for good deeds with promised land and would penalize the sinful for wicked deeds with Hell. He sent messengers and disclosed books for the counselling of humankind.

Islam doesn't give any philosophic or technological arguments for the beingness of God. Its revealed Good Book, the Quran, doesn't try to establish God by theological abstract thought. It provides creations of God and His Signs and omens spread in the universe, in the nature around us and in ourselves, as the cogent evidence of beingness of God. "Lo! in the conceptions of the heavens and the earth, and the difference of night and day, and the ships which run on the sea therewith which is of use to men, and the water which Allah sendeth down from the sky, thereby reviving the earth after its death, and dispersing all kinds of beasts therein, and (in) the ordinance of the winds, and the clouds obedient between heaven and earth: are signs (of Allah's beingness and reign) for people who have common sense."- says the Holy Quran (2:164). "And of His signals is this: He produced you of dust, and behold you as humans, ranging wide! and of His signals is this: He produced for you helpmates from yourselves (women) that ye could find rest in it, and He enacted between you love and clemency. Behold! here in so are omens for common people who reflect". (al-Quran 30:21)

REDEMPTION

The Buddhist, Christian and Hindu philosophical systems of redemption have a lot in common. In all, the accent is upon release from sinfulness, upon deliverance from evil. In each, the aim is a go back to the former state of sinlessness and blissfulness. As sin is supposed to be inseparable from life and the phenomenal world is believed to be the abode of evil, it follows that liberation can be achieved only by renouncing the world. This doctrine appears in its most vestal form in Buddhism. It has been to some extent diluted in Christianity and Hinduism. It must be admitted that during certain periods of time of human history, the school of thought attracted large numbers of men and cast its spell even on men of learning and intelligence.

It's a reality that during these periods, men had tolerated critical defeat and were disenchanted with life. Having nothing to hope for in this world, they centred their hopes on the other world where they might get all that they lead missed in this world. This doctrine is the product of the disenchantment and defeatism. It is clearly abhorrent to men who are sane and normal. It is in direct opposition to reason, to experience and to the advancement of human race. Hope cannot be killed-it springs anew in the human heart. When man had found his natural buoyancy, he flinches with horror from such a dismal doctrine. He tends to look on the world of matter as a field for varied fruitful activities. He declines to think that his soul will be destroyed by the flimsiest link with the world. The doctrine as well means that the cosmos has no aim or purpose.

If admitted whole-heatedly, it will bear witness to be best for life and of the hope for advancement. If ever it turns the predominant creed, humanity will be condemned to stagnancy and decline. All the health instincts in man rise up against such a bare conception. To believe in a God Who has created a world which should be shunned is derogative both to God and man. The Quranic concept of redemption is of a different kind, and, achieved to the creative and active forces in man. To begin with, the world of substance is considered as substantiating an aim which is consistent with the design built-in in the human being.

Furthermore, in the Quran, the stress is on the positivist content of redemption. It is not considered as a negation of pain and release from evil. It comprises in the sense of fulfillment, the belief of realization and the thrill of elaboration. Man is endowed with a number of capabilities. By developing these he reaches his full height and characterizes for still higher stages awaiting him. Man must discover in what direction his self can develop and then he must create the circumstances, active as well as cultural, which favour the development.

His main task in this life is to develop his self by conquering the forces of nature and applying them for the evolution of mankind. Life is a ceaseless struggle against forces hostile to it -forces hostile to it-forces which would destroy it if they were not successfully opposed. In the external environment, there are wide variations in temperature. Sometimes it is too cold for man, sometimes it is too hot. Homeostatic mechanisms in the body usually keep the blood heat at the normal level. Without them, the human body will burn or freeze to end. Again, the body is assaulted by a mixture of deadly microbes which tend to destruct it. As long as human lives, he preserves the battle against these annihilating forces. The battle discontinues only on demise. It is, nonetheless, not only on the bodily plane that the battle is continued.

On the ethical plane also, he has to battle against forces of devastation which would decompose and break up his self. Here the problem is harder and complex, as the ego has to get by with the annihilative forces of the extrinsic cosmos as well as the whims of debasing animal nature which arise in man if not arrested. Man naturally looks around for help as he very often finds it hard to keep the enemy at bay. The Divine Guidance in the Quran offers man efficient help in the moral battle. This help is given according to a definite program. The first part of the syllabus may be characterized and protective. It helps man to guard himself against both the open and subtle attacks of annihilating forces.

This form of help is termed Maghfirah in the Quran. Ghafrun stands for "to cover" and Mighfar, which is deduced from it means the helmet which protects the head of the warrior from the blows of the foe. The Quran protects the human self just as efficaciously from the blows of destructive forces. Man flinches when he finds himself facing the alarming array of the powers of devastation. He begins to weaken and to give way to desperation. The Divine programme prevents him from yielding to batil by replenishing his store of moral energy and by breathing in faith in his heart that the haqq, though weak at the moment, will finally, prevail over batil. Many may feel vulnerable against the forces of batil but when the Divine Revelation has instilled in his heart Iman and courageousness, he enters the sphere with regenerated assurance and hope. This is how the first part of the program helps him. The second part, Taubah, in the language of the Quran, is healing. Numerous may have yielded to batil and may have abided by the wrong course. Even then, the Quran enunciates, their case is not desperate. Taubah extends them a certain remedy.

Taubah is deduced from the root word Taba which means to come back. Taubah, hence doesn't imply fruitless ruefulness or ineffectual remorse. It signifies that when human realizes that he has been abiding by the dishonourable course, he should have the courageousness to block and reconstruct his steps. In this sense Taubah means heart-searching, reassessment of the situation and revaluation of the policy he has been abiding by. Suppose a man suddenly realizes that the path he has been adopting is taking him farther away from his actual destination. If he is wise, he will not merely sit down and give himself up to unrestrained grief. It will decisively hasten back to his beginning point and when he has reached it, he will, after deserved deliberateness, choose a new path Taubah, on the ethical plane, constitutes the same sensible way of acting. But Taubah has in it an ingredient of Divine help.

The man who has recognized his error and is eager to correct it, is not left to his own resources. Overgenerous Divine help is given to him in the shape of inspiration which never errs. Otherwise, the sense of having blew his time and the feelings of doubtfulness about the results of his further efforts will press to a great extent on him and will hamper his efforts to regain the right path. The Divine help, the attendant of Taubah, freshens up and invigorates him so that he acts with increased energy. In short, Maghfirah aids a man in avoiding the blows of shaar, but when he is hit, Taubah helps to fix the harm done. It should be need that Taubah is not a inactive act of ruefulness; it is confirming effort at refurbishment of the lost attitude, with re-formation of energy born out of hope and sureness. Taubah is not merely detachment from what was harmful; it is the invalidation of its effects.

We have since debated two dissimilar aspects of redemption. It will be assured that the concept of redemption set-forth in the Quran is a positive accomplishment as against the antagonistic and desolate conception of escape preferred in certain quarters. The latter springs from a mislaid belief of man's nature and from a misconception of his kinship to the world. It throws man into the agitation with the handicap of tainted soul in depraved world, giving the only recourse of renouncing the fight and taking flight from it. Why set such a fruitless stage in the least. Divine purpose runs through the world, a aim of which is akin to the purpose for which is empowered with the self.

No doubt, the odds are set against him. But the obstructions care there not to frustrate him, but to call forth the best in him. They are configured to put him on his mettle and allow the unconquerable spirit he owns to reveal itself in all its glory. Man develops his powers in the course of defeating obstructions. Defeat forces him to construct his personality. Rebuffs and reversals toughen and temper him and by confronting them he acquires a mature personality. So we see that even the world from time to time appears to be relentless and brutal, in the end it comes out to be man's friend and not his enemy.

Surely human beings often goes astray. As a free being, it's his prerogative. When he commits an error, he has to pay the toll for it and in the action he realizes that he is fully answerable for his action and that the exemption he enjoys is actual and not illusive. To err is human, and it is normal for man to commit an error occasionally. If he acts wrongly, his self is stained, but the stain can be got rid of. If he realizes his errors and sincerely tries to make amends for his wrong-doing, he can recover his poise. This is the truth that is distinctly set fourth in the Quran. The Quran is a gospel of hope. It prevents man to give way to despair. A man may have led a wrong life for years but if he decisively turns his face in the right direction and continues acting rightly, he won't find the path to self-fulfillment blocked for all time.

Right actions nullify wrong actions. The man who is saved is not one who has never committed an error, which is out of the question, but one whose right actions outweigh his wrong actions. What exactly is meant by saving one's self or losing it? These phrases become apprehensible only if looked at in reference to the goal-seeking action of the human self. The biggest urge in man is for self-development and self-fulfillment. When he is making advancement towards this destination, he feels euphoric and recognizes that he is on the way to qualify himself for advancement to a broader level of beingness.

For the self lives in and through action, and the action innate to it is always in an upwardly direction. Inactiveness is the demise of the self, so is motion in a downwardly direction. When the self of man is making constant advancement toward the end, it may be with infrequent deflections and lapse, but it slowly moves ahead, until it finds itself in a state which is represented by Jannah, or heaven. The beautiful imagery with which it is represented, has misled many into believing that it is a place which provides satisfaction for the, senses.

It is not a place but a state of mind, a state charged with the sense of fulfillment and the belief of high aspiration. It is related to the feeling that the mountain climber feels when, after wearily climbing the hillside and avoiding boulders, he at last reaches the eminent pinnacle. More majestic peaks float into his imagination and invite him to fresh conquerings. For him it is at once the end of a travel and the commencing of another. His joy at successful action accomplishment is combined with the thrill of exhilaration at the uncovering of fresh areas for venture. Such is the frame of mind of those who have fully recognized themselves on the human plane and are ready to go up to a broader one.

The cognitive state at once contrary to this has been assigned as Jahannam. It is the Arabic form of the Israelite word Gehenna. In the beginning Gehenna signified the valley of Hannom, where human sacrifices to Baal and Moloch were offered. Jahannam represents that condition of beingness in which the self's meaningful activity is brought to a dead end. Drained and debilitated by continuous and lasting wrong doing, the self loses its capability for progress and for moving towards a broader state of being. Its urge for progress is crushed and the enervated self gives up itself to repent and self-reproach. It has voluntarily relinquished its right to take part in the pursuit of the good. If it ever feels the hope to rejoin the match of free egos, the hope is too weak to pull it out of the slough of desperation and inactiveness.

Such is the picture of promised land and hell that the Quran introduces for the man. According to the aspect maintained by the Quran, redemption is not dismissal from "evilness"; evil in ourselves or in the cosmos. To accomplish redemption is to prove one's worthiness for acceding on a broader level of beingness. Honour and penalty are wrongly believed as coming from extrinsic source.

They're the natural outcomes of what we do and believe and demonstrate themselves in the enrichment or poorness of our self. Heaven and Hell don't subsist outside us, someplace in the external place. They are states of us. Hell is the state in which the self feels its advancement barricaded. Heaven is the state in which the way to growth lies open to the self. To discontinue to aim is to be condemned to Hell, to be able to aspire is to be in Heaven. There is, therefore, no room for intervention and salvation in Islam. What we become, we become through our own activities. We cannot carry the burden of any other person and no one can relieve us of the burden we bear.

The concept of sin also must be redeveloped so as to bring it into concordance with the above view. Sinfulness shouldn't be considered as the contamination of evil that clutches the individual from birth, being either the legacy of our fathers or the result of one's own former life. Sin is the ill effect on our self of our own wrong doing. It can be destroyed by our own correct action and not by the activity of any one else. If we have committed wrong unwillingly, carelessly or even with our eyes clear, we can draw consolation from the contemplation that we bear the amend in our hands.

In the end we can specify wrong- as a human action which deprives the self, restricts its freedom, endangers its independency and dampens its urge for development. To react to it by ineffective fury, powerless sorrow or penance serves no function. The proper reaction is to make a decided attempt to regain our poise and follow the justly course with increased energy. We would also do well to bear in mind that our final success depends not on our innocence but on the prevalence of our proper actions over improper ones. "Feel of sinfulness" is one of the main sources of sadness. The healthy position to a weakened self infused by the Quran is a sure precaution against unhappiness and debility of aim. It may be added that Jannah and Jahannam are not held over until after demise; they demonstrate themselves in this lifespan and carry on thenceforth.

DEVOTION TO GOD

God is absolute. We earthly human beings having only bounded and confined cognition cannot specify Him nor discover Him. All we know about Him is by His signs which are spread out in the nature round us and through Prophets and revealed books. The Quran, the which is the Holy Scripture, tells us: "Allah is the brightness of the paradises and the earth.

The likeness of His light is as a recess wherein is a lamp. The lamp is in a glass. The glassful is as it were a bright star. This lamp is ignited from a sanctified tree, an olive neither of the East nor of the West, whose oil would almost glow forth (of itself) although no fire touched it. Allah guideth unto His light whom He will. And Allah speaketh to humanity in parables, for Allah is apprehender of all things"- (24:35). "Allah! There's no God save Him, the live, the immortal. Neither sleep nor slumber overtaketh Him. Unto Him belongeth whatever is in the paradises and whatsoever is in the world......." (al-Quran 2:255).

Supreme Being is ubiquitous accordant to Islam. He is all over. There's no limited place wherever we can allege that He lives. According to the Quran, to God belong the East and the West, whitherso you turn, there is the bearing of Him. God is with you wherever so ever you go." And when My servants question thee concerning Me, then surely I am nigh. I answer the prayer of the suppliant when he crieth unto Me. So let them hear My call and let them trust in Me, in order that they may be led aright", tells God to Prophet Muhammad (al-Quran 2:186). "We verily created man and We know what his soul whispereth to him, and We are nearer to him than his jugular vein", says God in the Quran (50:16), "There is no mysterious league of three but He is their fourth, nor of five but He is their sixth, nor of to a lesser degree that or more but he's with them wheresoever they may be; and afterward, on the Day of Resurrection, He will inform them of what they did. Lo! Allah is apprehender of all things." (al-Quran 58:7).

Islam is purely a monotheistic faith. It considers God is One and there's no God except Him. Unity of Almighty is the cardinal teaching of Islamism. The belief in the unity of God is the first and the foremost amongst the five columns or articles of Muslim religion which every follower of Islam is under responsibility to concede and bind to. None can enter into Islamic fraternity nor one can remain a Muslim until and unless he announces by tongue and also truly considers in his bosom that there is no God but Allah. "Your God is One God; there is no God save Him, the benevolent, the gracious", says the Holy Quran (2:163). It is Allah alone whom the Muslims worship: "Praise be to Allah, Lord of the worlds, the Beneficent, the Merciful. Owner of the Day of Judgment, Thee (alone) we worship; Thee (alone) we ask for help"_ is the prayer of the Muslims in every worship.

Addressing the Christians, the Quran says: "O people of the Book! Do not overstate in your religion nor utter aught concerning Allah save the truth. The Messiah, Jesus son of Mary, was only a messenger of Allah, and His word which He conveyed unto Mary, and a spirit from Him. So believe in Allah and His messengers, and say not "Three"_ cease! (it is) better for you! Allah is only One God. Far is it removed from His transcendent majesty that He should have a son. His is all that is in the heavens and all that is in the earth…" (4:171).

God, the all-powerful Lord of the universe, has neither parents, nor any spouse, nor any son, nor any daughter. The Quran says:" Praise be to God, Who hath not taken unto Himself a son, and Who hath nc partner in the sovereignty, nor hath He any protecting friend through dependence" (17:111). God is alone and one. He neither begets nor was begotten. "Say: He is Allah, the One! Allah, the eternally besought of all! He begetteth not nor was begotten. And there is none comparable unto Him", commands the Holy Quran (112:1-4)God has no partners and associates in His sovereignty and dominion nor in His attributes. Polytheism is condemned, holding partners unto God is the biggest and unpardonable sin. "Lo! Allah pardoneth not that partners should be ascribed unto Him, He pardoneth all save that to whom He will. Whosoever ascribeth partners unto Allah hath wandered for astray" -Thus warns the Holy Quran (4:116)

No earthborn human being - neither an average one nor even the glorious one like a prophet - can see God. Human eye cannot see God as eye - sight is limited. Prophet Moses expressed his desire to see God but, as the Quran tells us, lightening seized him and he fell down unconscious. Prophet Muhammad ascended the heaven but when he was asked had he seen God, he replied: God is light, how can I see Him? The Quran says: "Vision comprehendeth Him not, but He comprehendeth (all) vision. He is the Subtile, the Aware"- (6:103). "and it was not (vouchsafed) to any mortal that Allah should speak to him unless (it be) by revelation or from behind a veil, or (that) He sendeth a courier to reveal what He will by His leave. Lo! He is Exalted, Wise." (42:51)

God has cognition of every thing whatever is in the heavens and in the earth. He knows your secrets and what you hide in your breasts. He is knower of the obvious and the invisible, seen and the invisible, indeed of every thing of past, present or future. "Lo! nothing in the earth or in the heavens is hidden from Allah" says the Quran (3:5)." "And with Him are the keys of the inconspicuous. None but He knoweth them. And He knoweth what is in the land and the sea. Not a leaf falleth but He knoweth it, not a grain amid the darkness of the earth, not of wet or dry but (it's noted) in a clear record"-(al-Quran 6:59). The Quran further tells us:

"Lo! Allah! with Him is the knowledge of the Hour (Day of Judgement). He sendeth down the rain, and knoweth that which is in the wombs. No soul knoweth what it will earn tomorrow, and no soul knoweth in what land it will die. Lo! Allah is Knower, Aware"- (31:34)

God is the best and the biggest Lord. He is the only one who's the mastermind and the Maker of the cosmos, the heavens and the earth, and of everything which is obvious or inconspicuous to human eye and which is known or anonymous to man. Heavens and earth, sun and stars, moon and planets, night and day, light and dark, air and wind, storms and clouds, rain and water, oceans and rivers, mountains and hills, flowing streams and burbling springs, glaciers and icebergs, life and death, plants and gardens, fruits and vegetables, corn and crops, forests and trees, animals and animals, birds and fish, milk and honey, fire and water are all His conceptions. He produced man of potter's earth, Angels of light and Jinn of fire. The Quran assures us that God produced all thing in couples and produced life of water. When God destines to do a thing, He simply says unto it: Be! and it is.

God is the supreme Lord of the whole world. Reign over paradises and the earth and over everything belongs to God. He has no partner in sovereignty. Control over altogether belongs to Him. He dominates over everything. He is the governor and the Perfector. He is the Supreme lawmaker and Supreme-Judge. He is All-Mighty and omnipotent. He's the root and spring of power. It is He who bestows honour and power on anyone He will. None can benefit or harm except God. If God destines to give you benefit, none can deduct it, if He intends you harm, none can protect you. He confers daughters upon whom He will and brings sons upon whom He will or makes infertile whom He will.

God produced man of the most effective stature and made him the best of many of His creatures. He produced Adam of potter's earth and asked the Angels to bow down before him. All did except the Satan who was proclaimed outcast. However, God took on Satan's challenge and gave him hiatus till the Day of Resurrection. So Satan misdirects the man from correct course. He, first of all, misadvised Adam and made him to eat from the forbidden tree and thus got him booted out from heaven. Since the Devil misleads Adam's children to the course of evil and of Hell, God sent messengers and revealed books for the guidance of man. It is against this backdrop that great Prophets like Noah, Abraham, Moses, Jesus and Muhammad (peace be upon them) were sent and books like Torah, Gospel and the Quran were revealed. Those who follow the Prophets, revere God, do good deeds and lead their lives in accord with counselling unveiled by God through His couriers would be honoured on the day of reckoning with heaven wherein they would lead peaceful life eternal. But those who disapproved the Prophets, don't believe in God, do wicked deeds and follow the Satan would be penalized on the day of reckoning and would be cast off in Hell wherein they'd burn and seethe and have the worst conceivable life.

God assigned Caliph (viceroy or lieutenant) to the earth. It is a great responsibleness, indeed a test, for man how he conducts. God has conferred many favours on man. The Quran assures us that many matters have been produced for service to and welfare of man. The Quran says: Allah is He Who created the heavens and the earth and causeth water to descend from the sky, thereby producing fruits as food for you, and maketh the ships to be of service unto you that they may run upon the sea at His command, and hath made of service unto you the rivers. And maketh the sun and the moon, constant in their courses, to be of service unto you, and hath made of service unto you the night and the day. See ye not how Allah hath made serviceable unto you whatsoever is in the skies and whatsoever is in the earth and hath loaded you with His favours both without and within? Yet of mankind is he who disputeth concerning Allah, without knowledge or guidance or a Scripture giving light.

God is avid helper of man. His privileges and amplitudes on human beings are numberless. Some of His privileges have been enumerated by the Quran in its above verses, whereas there are innumerable favours of God which are not even recognized by man. God's favours within the man are man's eyes with which he sees, ears with which he listens, hearts with which he contemplates, hands with which he does everything and feet with which he walks. So man is a great handwork of Supreme Being and his every limb is of vast purpose to him.

God is the greatest and the best Sustainer, Provider, Preserver, Protector and Nourisher of all created-beings. He provides subsistence, food and other means of living to all living beings. The Quran says: "He placed therein (in the earth) firm hills rising above it, and blessed it and measured there in its sustenance in four days, alike for all who ask". The Quran reminds the man of Allah's favour in providing food: "Who hath appointed the earth a resting place for you and the sky a canopy; and causeth water to pour down from the sky, thereby producing fruits as food for you". (2:22). Allah provides sustenance to everyone. "And there is not a beast in the earth but the sustenance thereof dependeth on Allah.... " (al-Quran 11:6). It is God who increases and decreases subsistence. "Allah enlargeth livelihood for whom He will, and straiteneth it for whom

He will. Allah preserves the heavens and the earth. ".... His throne includeth the heavens and the earth and He is never weary of preserving them......" (al-Quran 2:255). ".... Have they not seen the birds obedient in mid air? None holdeth them save Allah ...." (al-Quran 16:79).

All creatures and all things worship and glorify God in their own way. "Have they not observed all things that Allah hath created, how their shadows incline to the right and to the left, making prostration unto Allah, and they are lowly? And unto Allah maketh prostration whatsoever is in the heavens and whatsoever is in the earth of living creatures, and the Angels (also), and they are not proud. They fear their Lord above them, and do what they are bidden". says the revealed book of Islam (16:48-50). "The seven heavens and the earth and all that is therein praise Him, and there is not a thing but hymneth His praise; but ye understand not their praise....... (al-Quran 17:44). "Haste thou not seen that unto Allah payeth adoration whosoever is in the heavens and whosoever is in the earth, and the sun, and the moon, and the stars, and the hills, and the trees, and the beasts, and many of mankind ......" (al-Quran 22:18).

Man is God's finest conception and God has built man viceroy in the earth, has arranged many of His creatures to assist man and has conferred on man many privileges, which we have brought up above. So man owes more thankfulness to God than other animals. Hence, there are many responsibilities of man towards his Lord. He should believe in Him and should worship Him alone. He should glorify God and hymn His praise. He should love God and remember Him always, sitting, walking, lying. He should fear God and be kind and merciful to others. He should beg to God exclusively and look for assistance entirely from Him. He should trust in God and seek His refuge from Satan the castaway. He should follow the Prophets and lead his life in accordance with their teachings. It's only then that humanity would come through and would rationalize his creation. He can then trust for honour when God revives the dead on the day of reckoning.

ETHICAL ACTIONS

Islam instructs that the only God is Allah, and that it's a sin (shirk) to make other matters or masses equal to Allah by looking up to them, idolizing them, or placing inappropriate endeavour and trust into finding them. Other actions that are stringently prohibited include slaying, thievery, fornication, loaning money for profits, the practice of magic, cowardice in fulfilling Allah's wishings, saying unsound things about others, and using drugs or alcohol. The revered book, the Koran, advertizes faith in God, advancing justice for everybody, forgiving others, and being humane, kind, benevolent, modest, and broad-minded. Muslims are also required to take obligation for the welfare of all life, and to be fearless in following God's laws and in standing up to unjustness and despotism.

The family unit is the center place where Muslim exercises are communicated. Bringing up children in the faith is exceedingly all important, and big families are close. The conception of compassionateness and care for others is a cardinal Muslim notion, and all humans are considered to be equal.

Islam instructs that all humans have rights, accorded by Allah, and that Muslims would be going against Allah if they did not defend those rights, whether of Muslims or non-Muslims. Men and women in Islam have equal rights, although they may take assorted roles in family life. Women are expected to dress with modesty, so that they do not arouse men other than their husbands. Some Muslims believe that this gives women much greater freedom, sparing them from encroaching looks, and making them apprized for who they're as people. A lot of of the states that have tyrannical practices, such as imposed solitude (separation and privacy of women), are implementing ethnic instead of religious rules.

An Islamic wedding is believed to be a bringing together of equals. Nevertheless, the functions of men and women are dissimilar, and men are expected to provide for the family while women nurture babies and support their husband and family unit. Muhammad advised couples to choose their partner for their spiritual piousness. In theory, polygamy (wedding more than one wife) is allowed in Islam, but the husband must keep every wives equal, not just financially, but in the reception of his time and care, and the first wife must give her total consent. In reality, this is difficult, and, aggregated with attachment to the civil law of many countries that teach monogamy, it is correct to say that polygamy isn't common. Opinions on the use of contraception vary greatly among different Muslims.

Abortion is legitimate if the life of the mother would be at danger if she continued with the maternity (according to the Surah 6:151). Divorcement is strongly discouraged, but in itself is a simple procedure, and remarrying is allowed. Muslims don't support chastity for spiritual reasons. Carnal knowledge between man and wife are considered to have been given to multitude by God, and are consequently a natural, alimentary part of life not to be bottled up. According to the Koran (Surah 4:16-18), gayness is forbidden. Consuming alcohol or other recreational drugs is strictly forbidden in Islam. Smoking is not mentioned in the Koran, but it is considered in the same way - ultimately, the body belongs to Allah, and should not be degraded and harmed. According to the teachings of Islam (Surah 53:42-47), only Allah knows why people are suffering or when they will die, and it is a great sin both to take life and to try to alter God's will. As such, mercy killing is prohibited, and self-destruction is not acceptable to Muslims. Those who commit suicide are considered to suffer further after demise because they will be far more cognizant of the sorrow and distress of those they left behind, but impotent to help. In fact, people who attempt suicide may be suffering from mental disease and be agitated to such an extent that they are considered not responsible for their activities; in these cases Muslims believe that they'll experience Allah's pardon.

Spiritual obligation to gift (zakat) is the third of the Five mainstays of Islam. Muslims ought to give 2.5% of their excess revenue and goods. Zakat is seen as a admonisher not to hold tight what is neither important nor one's material possession (as everything belongs to God). It's far more significant to help to dispense riches among all people, especially the destitute. The motivation for giving zakat is different to that of benevolent giving (sadaqah). There are many Islamic charities, and Muslims have an obligation to care for anyone suffering need (Surah 3:91, 2:195). Muslims believe that God gave people free will, and that their wrong choices bring evil into the world. They may also be lured to do wrong by the Devil (Iblis) (Surah 15:29-31, 15:39). Muslims believe in abiding by the justness set out for them in the Koran. If a crime is committed against somebody, they can forgive the culprit, and ask for a lesser penalty to be given. This is considered to be the best course (Surah 42:40).

The capital punishment is given for murder or for open attacks on the Islamic faith (Surah 17:33). A thief may have his hand chop off, and drunkenness may carry a penalty of caning (beating). However, conditions surrounding the crime are taken into consideration. For instance, if a person steals as their family is famishing, it is the obligation of the community to feed them and find them work. Muslims trust that in communities where Islam is abided by thoroughly, law-breakings are very uncommon. In Islam, religious and secular law are the same thing - Sharia. Ideally, religion and day-to-day life are inseparable. An Islamic state would be one patterned on the community Muhammad laid down at Medina. The Koran sets out very distinctly the correct way of running an

Muslim state; this admits support for the rights of spiritual or racial minorities living inside it. Muslims consider that no human agency should expect them to act against the will of Allah.

As Muslims consider that the cosmos belongs to God, and that masses will be held responsible for their activities on Day of Judgment, they are expected to protect and care for the surroundings and to care for brutes with care and esteem. Cruelty to animals is forbidden, as are blood sports, but animals may be killed in the appropriate manner for food or for other uses. Experimenting on animals to produce cosmetics and other luxury goods is forbidden, but in some circumstances, some Muslims might accept experimentation on animals to save human life. Muslims believe that God created the whole cosmos.

He created all animals; angels from light, man from clay, and jinn (spirits) from fire. He caused rain to break up the soil, and caused the floras to develop and produce fruit. After producing Adam from seven kinds of clay, and placing him in promised land, God created Eve from Adam's side. God told the angels to prostrate to Adam, but Iblis (the Devil) declined. In this way, Iblis began his noncompliance, and his endeavours to lure people from following God's will. Iblis tempted Adam and Eve to eat fruit that had been prohibited by God; when they disobeyed God, they were sent out of heaven and into the world. Muslims believe that those who follow God's bids will be honoured by returning to heaven after Day of Judgment.

MESSAGE OF HARMONY AND LOVE

Islam aspires to build a law-abiding society at all cost. It is because broader human aims cannot be accomplished in the absence of law-abiding conditions. The sacred as well as ethical advancement of the individual is possible only in amicable atmosphere. Hence the atmosphere of peace is essential for the building of good society. Scholarly research too is possible only in peaceful conditions. The task of the propagation of truth too can be performed only in peaceful ambience. That is why one of the teachings of Islam in rapprochement is the best. In that regard Islam tells us to constitute peace even at the cost of direct sacrifice and patience. An event of the first phase of Islamic history provides us with an example of this unilateralism. This is known as Sulh Hudaibiya. This was in actual fact a no-war pact that was barred by accepting all the demands of the rival group. To bring about an atmosphere of peace within the society Islam has given a number of teachings. For example, the Prophet of Islam observed a believer is one from whom people feel protected as regards their lives and belongings. Another hadith has this to say: By God, he is not a believer from whose nuisance his neighbour is not safe. Islam aims at making all individuals peace-loving to the ultimate extent. That is why we are enjoined to greet one another by saying Assalam-o-Alaikum' that is, peace be upon you. According to another saying of the Prophet, the best Islam is to greet everyone you come across, whether or not you are acquainted with the person. The frequent reduplication of this phrase 'peace be upon you' is in de facto an external expression of the hope for peace within. Islam wishes to infuse this feeling within every human that he should become a true lover of peace, to the point that this feeling starts welling up in his heart, finding expression whenever he meets a person. Islam is a peaceful religion from commencement to end. And it's but normal that it should be so, as all the best consequences it aims to accomplish, can be accomplished only when an ambience of peace is maintained at both interior and external level.

This course of serenity is abided by by the entire universe. It is known in science as the law of nature, which is enforced upon it by God. Whereas man has to acquire this path of peace of their own free will. This has been conveyed in the Quran in these words: "Are they seeking a religion other than God's, when every soul in heaven and earth has submitted to Him, willingly or by compulsion? To Him they shall all return".When peace is the religion of the entire universe, it should, therefore, be the religion of man too, so that, in the words of Jesus Christ, the will of the Lord may be done on earth as it is in heaven. In a similar vein, the Quran tells us that: "The sun is not allowed to overtake the moon, nor does the night outpace the day.

Each in its own orbit runs." When God created heaven and the earth, He so ordered things that each part might perform its function peacefully without clashing with any other part. For billions of years, therefore, the entire universe has been fulfilling its function in total harmony with His divine plan. Peace is no external commodity to be artificially imposed upon man. Peace is inherent in nature itself. The system of nature set up by God already rests on the basis of peace. If this system is not disrupted, it will continue to stay the course set for it by the Almighty. It is true that the only condition to maintain the human system on the path of peace is to keep it free from the elements of corruption. That is why the Quran states: And do not corrupt the land after it has been set in order. In order to preserve the peace built by nature, from commotion, two important enjoinings have been established by Islam. One at the human level, accents the exercise of patience, and the other, at the cultural plane, prohibits taking the offense.

Antagonistic response on the part of the someone is the biggest factor responsible for breaking up peace in daily life. It repeatedly happens that in social life one goes through bitterness on account of other people. On such occasions, if one reacts negatively, the matter would escalate relevant of a head-on collision. That's why Islam repeatedly orders us to tread the course of patience. The Quran says: Surely the patient will be paid their wages in full without measure. The reason for the rewards for patience being so great is that patience is the key factor in maintaining the desired system of God. In the words of the Quran the patient man is the helper of God. The other enjoining, designed to conserve peace in human society is to forbid the engaging of an aggressive war. No one in Islamism relishes the right to wage war against another. There are no grounds on which this could be considered justifiable.

There is only one kind of war permitted in Islam and that is a protective war. If a nation by diverting from the principles of nature wages war against another nation, then, a defensive war, with certain conditions, may be engaged by the country under fire. To add together, Islam is a religion of peacefulness. The Arabic root of Islam is 'silm' which implies peace. The Quran states: '…and Gods calls to the home of peace'. It is thus God's will that men and women should jointly build a society of peace in His world. Peace is common to all religions. Let us all endeavour then to build peace in the world, for that is the bedrock on which all human advancement rests.

REFERENCES

al-Qaqashandi: *Subhò al-a'sha*, Cairo, 1913-20.

Altòaf ar-Rahòman: *Ahòwal-i 'ulama-i Farangi Mahòall,* Lucknow, N.D.

Binyon, L.: *The Court Painters of the Great Moghuls*, London, 1921.

Blumhardt, J. F.: *Catalogue of the Hindustani Manuscripts in the Library of the India Office*, Oxford, 1926.

Halim, A.: "Mystics and Mystical Movements of the Sayyid Lodi Period", *Journal of the Asiatic Society of Pakistan*, 1963.

Hamdani, H. F.: "The Letters of Mustansir Billah", *BSOAS*, 1933-1935.

Hamid Ali: "The Customary and Statutory Laws of the Muslims in India", *IC*, 1937.

Harikishan Kaul: *Census Report, Punjab*, Lahore, 1912.

Hashimi, Nasir-ad-din: *Dakan men Urdu,* Hyderabad, 1936.

Havell, E. B.: *A Handbook of Indian Art*, London, 1920.

Hòali, Altòtaf Hòusayn: *Muqaddima-i shi'r wa sha'iri,* Lahore, 1953.

Hòasan 'Ali 'Izzat: *Mufarrihò al-qulub,* 10 Pers. MS 2809.

Hòasani, 'Abd-al-Hòayy: *Ath-thaqafa al-Islamiyya fi-i-Hind,* Damascus, 1958.

Hòasani, 'Abd-at-Rahòman: *Mir'at-i Madariyya,* BM Add. MS 168.

Hòjji Khalafa: *Kashf az-Zòunun,* Leipzig, 1835-52.

Hollister, J. N.: *The Shi'a of India*, London, 1953.

Hunter, W. W.: *The Indian Musalmans*, London, 1871.

I'jaz Husayn: *Mukhtasar ta'rikh-i adab-i Urdu,* Karachi, 1956.

Ibn-Kathir: *Al-Bidaya wa-n-nihaya,* Cairo, 1932-9.

Ibn-Nadim: *Al-Fihrist* (ed. Flügel), Leipzig, 1871-2.

Ibrahim 'Adil Shah 11: *Nawras* (ed. Nazir Ahmad), Lucknow, 1955.

Ibrahim Mir Siyalkoti: *Ta'rikh-i ahl-i adith,* Lahore, 1953.

Ikram, S. M. and Spear, P.: *Cultural Heritage of Pakistan*, Karachi, 1955.

Ikram, S. M.: *Ab-i Kawthar,* Lahore, 1952.

Imdad-Allah, Hòjji: *Maktubat-i Imdadiyya,* ed. Ashraf 'Ali Thaawi, Lucknow, 1915.

Mu'tamid Khan: *Iqbal Nama-i Jahangiri*, Calcutta, 1865.

Mustawfa, Hòamid-Allah: *Ta'rikh-i Guzida*, Leiden, 1910.

Nadwi, Abu-l-Hòasan 'Ali: *Hindustani Musalman,* Lucknow, 1961.

Nadwi, Abu-l-Hòasanat: *Hindustan ki Qadim Islami Dargahen,* A'zamgarh, 1936.

Wa'izòshifi: *Rashhòat*, Cawnpore, 1912.

Wahid Mirza: *The Life and Works of Amir Khusrau*, Calcutta, 1935.

8

Moral Value System

Islam has established some comprehensive basic rights for humankind at large, which are to be abided by and honoured under all conditions. To accomplish these rights Islam provides not only lawful precautions but also a very competent moral arrangement. Thus whatsoever leads to the welfare of the someone or the society is virtuously good in Islam and whatever is harmful is virtuously bad. Islam attaches much importance to the love of God and love of man that it warns against too much of formalism. We're given a beautiful verbal description of the righteous and God-conscious man in these verses. He should obey healthful ordinances, but he should fix his gaze on the love of God and the love of his fellow men. This is the standard by which a particular mode of behaviour is judged and categorized as good or bad. This criterion of assessment provides the core around which the whole moral conduct should revolve. Before making any moral enjoinings Islam seeks to firmly embed in man's heart the strong belief that his dealings are with God who sees him at all times and altogether places; that he may hide himself from the entire world but not from Him; that he may delude everyone but cannot delude God; that he can take flight from the grasp of anybody else but not from God.

Thus, by arranging God's joy as the target of man's life, Islam has equipped the broadest imaginable criterion of ethics. This is bound to provide boundless boulevards for the moral evolution of human race. By making Divine revealings as the primary source of cognition it gives permanence and stability to the moral measures which afford reasonable scope for actual adjustments, adjustments and innovations, though not for perversions, wild edition, atomistic relativism or ethical fluidness. It provides a sanction to ethics in the love and awe of God, which will impel man to obey the moral law even without any external pressure. Through belief in God and the day of reckoning it provides a force which enables an individual to assume the ethical behaviour with earnestness and sincerity, with all the devotion of heart and soul. It does not, through a assumed sense of originality and innovation, provide any novel moral virtues nor does it seek to understate the grandness of the well-known moral norms, nor does it give exaggerated importance to some and disregard others without cause. It takes up all the commonly known moral merits and with an equilibrium and balance it assigns a suitable place and function to each one of them in the total scheme of life. It widens the scope of man's individual and collective life - his domestic affiliations, his civic conduct, and his actions in the political, economical, legal, instructive, and cultural domains. It addresses his life from home to society, from the dining-table to the battlefield and peace conferences, literally from the cradle to the grave.

In brief, no area of life is excused from the comprehensive and complete application of the ethical precepts of Islam. It makes ethics rule sovereign and ascertains that the affairs of life, instead of dominated by selfish desires and petty interests, should be regulated by norms of morality. It stipulates for man a system of life which is based on all good and is free from all evil. It invokes the people, not only to practice virtue, but also to build chastity and annihilate vice, to bid good and to forbid wrong. It wants that the verdict of scruples should prevail and virtue must not be curbed to play second banana to evil. Those who answer to this call are amassed collectively into a community and given the name "Muslim". And the individual aim underlying the establishment of this community ("Ummah") is that it should make an coordinated attempt to constitute and implement goodness and conquer and annihilate evil.

MORAL VALUES

Spiritual thinking focused its research on certainty in life, and on the causes on individual beingness, to know inscrutable mystery of life. When religion focus on ethical values such as permissible and impermissible, on good and evil, on honour and punishment, then it enters the details of society life. Religion regulates beliefs and behaviours related to sacred things, and that they resemble unity of believers. Religion then has more than one job. From the individual side, it assists them to feel protection, stableness and safe, to determine their identity, and group belongingness and their acceptation to values and notions that religion regulates. From the side of society it helps in regulating emotions and their sustainability, and this is one of the pillars of community continuity and sustainability.

Covering all dealing of sociologists in the field of ethical values, we discover that it remind us, in details or concise, moral values as they had been seen in the old Greek heathenism, or in Hebraism, or Christian religion, then it turn suddenly to its shapes, and forms in modern Europe, brushing aside discussing their aspects, shapes and forms in Islam. But some Europeans during the 19th century tried to distill ethical values and precepts from the Holy Quran, but such tests never arrived at the stage of shaping pragmatic bases, or to offer them in the shape of a perfect composition of ethical values, also that they are built upon erroneous translation for the Holy Quran significations.

There's some other worst position which is detected among seculars, who analyze values in Islam then equate them to the values of Arab life before Islam, or to what had been expressed in the Torah or the Bible, then they settle that if values are agreeing between Islam and what its precedents, then this is an indicant that Islam disclosed them from former faiths, and if there is difference, then this is an indicator that values are not absolute but relative. The aim of this is to distort the shape of Islam, and to decide that it didn't bring any thing new to human life.

They didn't know that matching could come from that Islam is the source of values as it is in the former religions, because it came from Allah who sent all messengers and prophets, and they didn't know also that stating that values are comparative is mistaken, and that it's more correct to say that some societies are bounding their potentials and capacity to reach to the absolute right. The need for studying values from an Islamic perspective could be felt if we came to know that doubts cast by some intellectuals that Muslims are to forsake their ethical and spiritual values if they are to seek technological and scientific progress and to seek merge to western life, and that it is inconceivable for Muslims to build upon values, because the absence of values is the root that brought in industry and science and that values shall limit space for accomplishing civilization.

This isn't truthful, because some states accomplished civilizations while they protect their individuality and esteems such the Japanese. There are Islamic scholars who cling to their Islamic values, theological system and conduct and they achieved vast advancement in technological and scientific fields. The Holy Quran is a methodological analysis of ethics and virtuousness, that is stated the rules of morals, and drew the path of right behaviour that achieves happy life to all society individuals. Allah states in the Holy Quran (Surely, this Quran guides to what is most right; and gives to the believers who do good deeds the glad tidings that they shall have a great reward) (Al-Isra: 09), and that (And if there comes to you guidance from ME, then whoso will follow MY guidance, will not go astray, nor will he come to grief;) (Taha: 123), and the Holy Quran is the constitution of morals in Islam. Such morals search for change through struggle and not on the concept of sociology, but on its Islamic concepts that aim to build on moral values not on physical benefits. It is change to the best in beliefs and in systems. It is changing polytheism to oneness, ignorance by knowledge, unemployment by work, poverty by richness, weakness by strength, and selfishness by solidarity, and vulgar by chastity, and all other values that Islam is calling for in the process of building human society.

The criteria of progress and backwardness in Islam concept is unique. It is linking development to faith and guidance, and backwardness to infidelity and ashtray, even if they are linked to physical civilization and scientific benefits. If we search in the formation of Muslim society, we shall see that it is built on a course that came from Lord of All Creations. This course is the base society is built on, and formed as it is ordered by Allah to his slaves, not on those sought by other people. In view of this Shariaa, Muslim community had been built, and work and production relations, and rules of life, individual and group moral bases, and principles of behaviour, work laws, and all other society important aspects, that determine its path toward progress and development had been formed. This Islamic society is the society that enjoys its formation capacities that are distinguished from other human societies according to the following features: First: that it is a heavenly society that is built on Islamic political orientation, and relation between its persons is built upon this ideology. It is clear the compactness of the Muhammadan Message on embedding ideology of Islam in Muslims life for thirteen years, then He addressed orders and forbiddances that are met with full obey from all Muslim society individuals at that time.

It's clear also the concentration of the Holy Quran on the significance of ideology and religion in what had been Stated by Allah (O ye who believe ! believe in Allah and his Messenger and in the Book which He had revealed to His Messenger, and the Book which He revealed before it. And whoso disbelieves in Allah and His angels, and His Books and His Messengers and the Last Day, has surely strayed far away).

Second: it's an international community. It is a society that is not built upon race, nationality, or social. These are features that go away when their roots are absent. It is a society that is open for every last people from all races, languages or colours. Society that is built upon the orderings of Allah (Say, 'O mankind, truly I am a Messenger to you all from Allah). Third: it is collaborative society. One of the chief and most authoritative features of it is cooperation and solidarity, all its individuals are one unity, cooperatives, loving, and support each other on the hardships of life and crises.

The Noble Prophet said that (Believer to believer are like one building, one ties the other). Fourth: it is an advisory society. The chief benefit of this is that every human believes that he support other people seeking their welfares, and that Muslim is like a mirror for his brothers Muslim, and that one of the main obligations of all Muslims is promotion of virtue and prevention of vice, as Allah States (And the worshipers, men and women, are acquaintances of some other. They enjoined good and prohibit wickedness and observe Prayer and pay the Zakaat and obey Allah and His Messenger. It is these on whom Allah will have mercy. Surely, Allah is Mighty and Wise) (Al-Tawba: 71).

Sure that all those who try to study Muslim social history shall find that moral values are a part of the religion principles, could not be split of it. And that main principles of Islam urge all Muslims to stick to moral values, for this is the main pillar for Muslim nation victory, towards its development and sustainable human and materialistic civilization. If we look in ethical value and sovereign cases, we shall find that they broke down before Muslims historical collapse, and we know that the Islamic religion call to adhere to moral values through stick of religious and moral values. Religion calls for control of human behaviour and direct it toward correct behaviour and morals follow this behaviour, so, in most cases, we shall find religious controls mix with moral controls, on the contrary of non-Muslim societies, which follow its moral controls from society culture or from mind.

Religion in the concept of Islam is the course which gives moral values their sacred and honest, which makes individual feels that he is a monitor on his own values and behaviour, and that creates a self-deterrent. This is what is called in Islam the "religious impediment". Islam determines ethical values which society is to abide by, and give it a clear balanced reference of arrangements that all humans are to follow, and it strictly applied a group of controls that find its durability and cogency from religion controls, that in majority cases is left for human moral sense and his awe to his Lord. So untruthful, enviousness, malevolency, defamation, haughtiness, scant, and all kinds of such behaviours are banned in Islam, and controvert to good moral values, so curbs are applied to forestall individual from acting in and of itself.

MORALITY IN LIFE

The root of values in Islam differ from source to source. If we think of Islamic values, then the root would be sacred Quran and aristocratic Prophetic Sunnah, and this entails that values should be conclusive and balanced, and if we mean Muslims values in their societies then their roots would be numbers and could differ from one society to anther, but there could be a lot more common points. Such roots of values in Muslims societies could be pertained back to customs and habits, resembling other states, or rational and civilization quoting, origination in religion and other kinds of sources. Characteristics of such values can be summed as follows:

a. They're logic: that they adjust with the nature of good individual opining. No one among philosophers tried to decline one of these values cast in the sacred Quran. Allah said his Holy Book, it is a powerful Book, falsification cannot approach it either from ahead it nor from behind it. It is a revealing from the Wise, the laudable.

b. They're truthful: that they match real world and human nature and adapt with alteration in all positions and during all eras. They are not arbitrary paragons or impossible imageries, or unusual from human nature.

c. They're of value: that they are of value for both individual and society in this lifespan, and could lead to more welfares in the other life.

d. They're well-balanced: that they are not for persons or to society separately. Rather they're medium built on equilibrium and consistency, between human and society welfares.

e. They're the cornerstone of society: that they adapt between bodily and worldly needs, between psyche and body, between rights and obligations, under the superintendence of fair agency of the Holy Quran.

f. They're immortal: they're referred from the sanctified Shariaa of the Holy Quran and from the faith of Islam which Allah admitted as the exclusive religious belief for all humans.

g. They're internally uniform: the root of values in Islam is the Holy Book and Sunnah, from this point it shall not be conceived that there could be any sort of quarrel or conformity, as Allah Says (Will they not, then, contemplate upon the Quran ? Had it been from anybody other than Allah, they would surely have found out therein much variance). The most crucial thing here is that sources of values in Islam should be esteemed as coming from one unit.

By this point values in Islam could not be the matter that is gratifying for one person during any time entirely. In this case Islam addressed them desires that all Muslims are to face up and restrict. And that they could not be distilled from the human being experience or from the cultural activity. They are divine not left for the society, or to its activities or experiments. Values in Islam are good meaning without any kind of guidance such as love, it is for known types, and such as conviction which should not turn to dullness or inactivity. Values in Islam are the courses that determine positive and negative attitudes, and not left for motivations only, they are moved by faith sometimes. Values in Islam are not as communist term their values. Work is among the values of Islam, and not all values of Islam is what is thought of as to adapt with mid, for mind in Islam is a means for agreement decided values.

Ethical values in Islam aspire to ascertain human action in an Islamic society, and to encourage and control their behaviour to the benefit of the whole society and its humans, and to bring for all individuals a good conclusion in the other life. It aims to integration human attributes, behaviour, activity that aims to prepare followers of the Lord, whom Islam described them and clarified the path of goodness for them (It is not righteousness that you turn your faces to the East or the West, but truly righteous is he who believes in Allah and the Last Day and the angels and the Book and the Prophets, and spends his money out of love for him, on the similar and the orphans and the needy and the wayfarer and those who ask for charity and for redeeming the prisoners; and observes prayer and pays the Zakat; and those who accomplish their promise when they have made one, and the patient in impoverishment and afflictions and the firm in the time of war; it is these who have proved truthful and it is these who are truly God-Fearing.), and formed their medium passage in dealing in their lives (And seek, in that which Allah has given thee, the Home of the afterlife; and neglect not thy lot in this world; and do good to others as Allah has done good to thee; And seek not to create mischief in the land.

Verily, Allah loves not those who create mischief). Ethical values in Islam then, whether they are case-by-case such as earnestness, patience, charity love, psyche battling, or common such as auto- feeling, responsibility, and call for Islam, are entailed to bestow individual and society welfare, and protect human welfare. From this point we ascertain the principal bases of the value theory in Islam as to the following aims:

a. 1st aim: unity and worshipping: (basal foundations of Muslim life is that human should seek to attain the Oneness of the Lord, which is a strict respond to all what humans are thinking about the continent, life, and living, life before and after him, and that is what all humans should use to seek true worshipping to the Lord. This is the system disclosed from the Holy Book and Prophetic Sunnah.

b. 2nd aim: to develop the trustworthy individual(for arrangement of value in Islam attempt to develop the individual with a strong building, who seek to achieve the Say of Allah, Praise the Lord, (Say, 'My Prayer and my forfeiture and my life and my demise are all for Allah, the Lord of the creations). This is a portray that differs from the portray of good citizen in other current systems. The good person in human systems could kill, be unjust, and could attempt to built his self society on the account on other societies, but the good human in Islam is like Abu Bakr and Omer, who urge to ward off anguish, burning or killing babies, and to avoid bolting down trees or destruction of churches.

c. 3rd aim: is poising as Muslim value orientation is built upon equilibrium as the rationale of everything. Allah Says (and He has produced everything, and has ascertained its proper amount.), and Allah Says (And there's not an affair but are limitless gems thereof with us and we sent it not down except in a known measure). For all this Islam seeks to integrate all life expressions worldly-minded or sacred, and attempt to shape individual aim along with the society aims and call for all to incorporate words with exploits, and to balance between human wants therein life and his wants in the other life.

d. Exact ethical motive: Islam makes the moral side a criterion for beneficial feats, and the main side in values is the main aims for the message of Islam. The Noble Prophet came to complete good morals, and Islam cares for evolution of moral feeling in human nature, and makes rightness the guide of human behaviour both publically and in private, as Islam assures the ethical side in all worships.

MORAL VALUES FOR LEADER

According to Muslim conception, mightiness or dominance is a great trust or obligation. It is a big trial for those who are confided with it. The Quran says: "He it is who hath placed you as viceroys of the earth and hath exalted some of you in rank above others, that He may try you by the (trial of) that which He hath given you. Now the doubt comes up as to who's entitled for exercising power and authority to rule. As power is a trust, it should be given to the trust-worthy. It is the devout and virtuous people, and not the wicked and proud, who can be confided with power. Thus mightiness and dominance in an Islamic dispensation belongs to the virtuous, devout and capable citizenry. According to the Quran, only pious, righteous and believing slaves of Allah have been entrusted to govern as deputies or viceroys of God. Wherever the wicked are ruling it is against this basic principle and hence their decree would be only factual and not lawfully, according to Islam. Such loathsome persons are actually the supplanters and not authorized rulers.

For the head of Muslim state or governance, who has been traditionally addressed caliph, Ameer-ul-Mumineen (commander of the trustworthy) or Sultan, the magistrates of Islam have decreed some reservations in the light of the Quran and the Sunnah of the Prophet Muhammad and in the light of the conventionalities set by the devout caliphs. These qualifications should be possessed by a nominee for this reputable post. The nominee shouldn't only be a Muslim but he should also be a active Muslim not pandering in any major sin like adultery, drinking, betting, usury, shirk (polytheism), and noncompliance to parents. He should be devout with superior ethical character and should be known for integrity, honesty, justice, kindness, forgiveness, humility, chivalry, diligence, trust-worthiness and sense of responsibility.

He should be an adult and sane citizen of the Islamic state and should not be greedy for the post. Al-Mawardi, a distinguished Islamic political philosopher of Middle Ages, lays down the following qualifications for the position of Imam: (1) justness, (2) Learning, (3) mental balance, (4) good condition, (5) wiseness, (6) courageousness, (7) Quraishite ancestry. Nevertheless, concerning the qualification of Quraishite descent, many other jurists differ with Al-Mawardi and spurn his views. The designation of the head of state (called Imam or ameer or Caliph in Islamic language) is a very crucial question. Islam prefers election instead of denomination through nomination or ancestral principle.

Prophet of Islam, alike some other messenger of Allah, was authorized by the Divine Allah Himself as Prophet. After his migration from Mecca to Medina, he founded a humble Islamic state at Medina and became its first head. Despite hard and ceaseless opposition from the non-believers and the Jews, this state grew into a mighty one before the demise of Prophet in 632 A.D. Prophet Muhammad did not appoint his successor nor left any definite directions on the question of selection or appointment of his successor. In the absence of any nomination by the Prophet, the associates of Muhammad rightly deduced that the selection of chief of state has been left at the discreetness of the Muslim Ummah, which was to be worked out in accordance with the flavour of the Quranic enjoinment: "They determine their affairs with mutual reference" (42:38).

As soon as the news of the death of the Prophet became known, the assistants (ansars), especially the chiefs of Banu Khazraj, went forward to hold a group discussion at a place called 'Saqifa Bani Saadah' to elect heir. Hearing this, Abu Bakr, Umar and Abu Obaidah hastened to the place of assembling. After some discourse in group discussion of Saqifa, Abu Bakr was selected as the first caliph of Islam. Umar proposed his name, Abu Obaidah seconded it and the people present in the conference endorsed and accepted. On the following morning, when Abu Bakr took his seat on the pulpit in the mosque where the Holy Prophet had been accustomed to address his followers, Umar called upon the Faithful to swear allegiance to Abu Bakr and those who had been present at the meeting the night before, renewed the oath of allegiance they had then made and the rest of assembly followed their example. The people were guided in their choice by factors like seniority, merit, nobility of birth and his Quraishite origin.

The first caliph Abu Bakr was thus elected publicly with the general consent of the Muslim community. Umar was subsequently made caliph. When he felt that death was approaching him, Abu Bakr consulted his companions for nomination of his successor. Though he was personally convinced that Umar was the fittest person to be the caliph yet he did not, forthwith, announce his nomination. He called certain companions and consulted them about nomination of Umar. People like Abdul Rahman-bin-Auf told Abu Bakr that Umar was of blistering temper and wasn't appropriate. To this, Abu Bakr replied that his hot temper will cool off when he is trusted with public obligations. Then the caliph consulted Usman and other associates who gave their opinion in favour of Umar. Abu Bakr then assembled the people in the Mosque of the Prophet and declared the nomination of Umar, calling the people thus:

"Are you consenting to accept him your Amir whom I appoint as my heir? God is my evaluator, I have left no stone unturned in coming to (the best) decision in this matter. I am not nominating anybody related to me. I nominate Umar son of Khattab as my successor. Therefore, listen you all to him and obey him." From the crowd the people called out: "We have listened and we consent." Here we find that Abu Bakr only suggested and recommended the name of Umar after audiences with those in whom the people had trust, and then it was put to the vote of the Muslim folks who acknowledged him.

Caliph Usman was selected yet in a different way. When Umar was badly maimed and he was approaching his demise, he set up a regency or council of seniors comprising of six most notabilities of the Muslim Ummah, namely, Abdul Rahman-bin-Auf, Saad-bin-Abi Waqqas, Usman-bin-Affan, Ali-bin-Abi Talib, Zubair-bin-Awwam and Talha. The caliph rigorously prohibited the nomination of his son Abdullah and apprised the members of the council to decide his heir inside three days of his destruction. He also declared that whosoever tried to become Amir without the approval of Muslim multitude was to be decapitated. The council appointed Abdul Rahman-bin-Auf, one of its members who had expressed his intention not to be interested in the post, to decide the issue. Abdul Rahman conducted a survey and went around Medina to ascertain the public opinion.

He even met the visitors and pilgrims to know their views. From his enquiries, he came to the conclusion that either Ali or Usman can be the caliph as they commanded the people's approval. He, thereafter, gathered the people in the Mosque of the Prophet after morning prayers, to nominate the caliph from among Ali and Usman. Addressing Ali and Usman he said. "You have to follow the Quran and Sunnah and practice of Abu Bakr and Umar". To this, Usman accorded but Ali answered that he would, without doubt, abide by the Quran and Sunnah, however he would follow the previous two caliphs only to the extent to which his cognition and ability allowed him. Thus Usman was appointed by Abdul Rahman and other members of the council and so forth afterwards he was elected by the Ummah.

Usman's tragical assassination produced a serious situation for the Muslim Ummah. So some associates assembled in the house of Ali and persuaded him to assume the obligation of caliphate, but Ali turned down. When the companions took a firm stand that there was no more appropriate individual than him and that the Muslim Ummah needed him in her vital moments, Ali agreed on the consideration that he should be accepted as Amir openly by the community in the masjid of the Prophet. Therefore, the people assembled in the Mosque of the Prophet at Medina and unanimously elected Ali as caliph of the Islamic state. From the foregoing discussion, it is crystal clear that different modes of election for the head of state were adopted by the companions of the Prophet during the pious caliphate. Since, the law does not specify any particular method of appointment of the head of state, therefore, the companions regarded this issue as something which can be rightly varied in accordance with the best interests of the Muslim Ummah.

However, the legal consequences which flow from the conduct of the companions of the Prophet and right-guided caliphs are: that the head of state should be elected with the popular will and not imposed forcibly from above; that no particular class has monopoly of this post and that elections should be fair and free. Distinguishable techniques can be assumed to assess the popular opinion about the candidates in different conditions at different places. In the present-day Muslim state, the modern system of elections can be assumed. The head or Chief Executive may be elected immediately through common elections in which every adult citizen is eligible to vote. He may be elected indirectly by an elected college constituting the spokespersons of the people.

As soon as an Ameer or Caliph of the Muslim state is elected, all the citizens offer Baiat or loyalty to him. The Baiat or oath of dedication is not only a kind of confirmation or ratification of his election but is also an accord, a compact or a contract whereby the people convey their firmness that they'd obey him and abide with him through thick and thin. The prophet also used to secure the oath of allegiance or Baiat from the believers, male and female, on their conversion to Islam and on very important issues faced by the Muslim community, e.g. on the occasion of Treaty of Hudaibyia he took Baiat from the companions Verse 12 of Chapter 60 of al-Quran mentions oath of allegiance of the women. According to Marmaduke Pickthall, "this is called the women's oath of allegiance. It was the oath exacted from men also until the second pact of al-Aqabah when the duty of defence was added to the men's oath."

The Quran gives paramount importance to the Ulul-amr (the rulers) of the Islamic state and the obedience to them has been made second only to the obedience which is due to God and His messenger. Thus the followers of Islam are obliged to obey their rulers and stand united with them through thick and thin. Nevertheless, there are boundaries to this respect: first of all that the rulers ought be from amidst the Muslims and secondly that they should not be transgressors and unruly to God and

God's messenger. If the rulers breach the limits of God and openly disobey instead make fun the enjoinings of Islam, they need not be obeyed.

Abu Bakr, when he was attained the first caliph of the Islamic state, explicated this point. He said; "If I am right, help me. If I am wrong, correct me. Obey me so long as I follow the commandments of Allah and the Prophet, but turn away from me when I deviate." The main obligations and purposes of the Ameer or the ruler of Muslim state, as concisely expressed, are: dispensation of justness; administration of law and order; administration of Islamic system especially system of Salat and Zakat and ordering good and banning wrong; security of state and its citizens against the hostility of foes, interior or extrinsic; enforcement of Islamic laws and Hudood; looking after the welfare of the people especially the poor, the ill, the orphans, the widows. Al-Mawardi has attractively summed up the functions and obligations of the Imam as follows:

1. To guard and maintain the Faith of Islam against unorthodoxies and conceptions.
2. The dispensation of justness concording to precepts of Muslim shariah law.
3. The upkeep of law and order in the country.
4. The enforcement of Hudood (the criminal code of the Quran).
5. The defence of frontiers against foreign encroachment.
6. The administration and executing of Jihad against disbelievers in order to build the domination of Islam over all other faiths.
7. The infliction and collecting of Zakat and Kharaj.
8. The authorization of stipends and allowances from Bait-al-Mal (state exchequer) to the destitute, hapless and handicapped.
9. The naming of effective and reliable persons to the significant public offices.
10. The Imam should in person look into the government functions and should have his fastness on the government protecting the concern of his subject, and cautiously check into the foreign policy issues.

MORAL DUTIES OF SUBJECTS

The Quran, the book of Islam, brings about the behavior of Prophet Muhammad and the demeanour of Prophet Abraham as example or an perfect behaviour for the Muslims. The Muslims have been ordered to follow the practice of conduct of these great Prophets of Allah and to emulate their illustration for establishing their own behaviour and persona. The conduct of a great saintly woman, Mary, the mother of Prophet Jesus, and that of another woman, wife of Pharaoh is also be followed by the believers especially by the believing women. Even the examples of good character set up by the companions of the Prophet of Islam and other great Muslims should inspire the ordinary believers who can derive immense benefit from them.

Particularly the conduct of the Prophet Muhammad is a model for a Muslim. Muhammad was the most perfect man endowed with each and every virtue which goes to make up good conduct. The Quran calls his conduct very sublime and great. Even before the call to prophethood, he had been given the titles of al-Sadiq (the truthful) and al-Ameen (the trustworthy) by his compatriots. The sacred Quran and Hadith literature furnish a lot of examples of superior conduct of the Prophet of Islam which was an eminent factor in fetching the hearts of the people to Islam.

Code of behavior decreed by Islam for its following consists certain dos and don'ts which establish one a good human. Long lists of such activities which are honorable and advocated can be composed from the Quran and the Sunnah as there are hundreds of rhymes and Ahadith in both of the sanctified sources of Islamic teachings. However, because of restraints of place, we'd bring out only few of the verses of the Holy Quran and traditions of Prophet Muhammad without comments, which lay down certain rules of good behaviour.

If these are acted upon, they would help to earn pleasure of Allah and goodwill of one's fellow beings. Manner, according to dictionary meaning, is the way or mode in which a thing is done or a thing occurs or happens. It's a manner of life, external bearing, flair of vocalization, conduct in social intercourse. It is also one's way of doing or behaving, own style of behaving or deporting, manner of writing or intellection, friendly behaviour or behaviour presently conceived as civilized or unmannerly, admirable or infuriating.

Manners can be respectable or unfit, modest or immodest. Good and modest manners delight others while unfit and immodest manners make one unpopular. Islam likes benevolent manners for its following. The Quran enjoins that none is better than a Muslim in oral communication, while the Prophet of Islam said that he was sent to dispatch courtesy. In this division we shall talk about manners associating to various actions of life such as manners of entering houses, sitting in assemblies, eating and drinking, dress, etc. in the light of Islamic teachings. The Quran prohibited excess or wastage in eating and drinking. It permits eating from your houses and the houses of your relatives and friends. You may eat together or apart. When you are asked over, you must not stay longer in the home of your server as it may bother him but he might be timid in telling you to go. Therefore, you may break up and hang around not for conversation after accepting your meal.

The Prophet has given thorough commands about the fashions of eating and drinking. Consume with right hand, observe Allah's name when you begin eating, praise Allah when you've completed, and eat up from what is adjacent to you. Eat simple food and exercise moderation. Do not eat from the vessels and dishes of silver and gold. Preferably eat together. According to Holy Quran, God has revealed the garment to protect you from the heat and coats of mail to protect you in your wars. Clothing also covers your nakedness and preserves your physical beauty. You must take your proper dress particularly when you go to your places of worship. Let not the Satan seduce you as he stimulated Adam and Eve, to get out of promised land, tore away from them their robe and caused them see their shame. In the brightness of the Quranic commandments, we can realize the aim and importance of apparel.

Islam hasn't limited or decreed any code of dress up and has allowed the subject to be determined by the humans and the society concording to their atmospheric condition, traditions and surroundings. However, some cardinal rules have been established which require that dress shouldn't be too short or too flimsy to cover up the privates decently from nudity. The dress should be elementary and not very costly. The men should not wear silk. The Prophet liked the clothes of white and green colour and he discouraged the use of red clothes by the men. Lengthening of trousers beyond ankles was strongly forbidden as it gives an air of vanity and makes the robes dirty. Women have been prescribed veil and they should cover their body fully. Fragrance was liked by the Prophet and its practice has been advocated. Use of shoes and socks is suitable.

The Quran inspires the worshipers to recognize others by a better salutation than the one with which they were greeted; while Prophet Muhammad ensured them of vast honours in the afterlife and many benedictions in this world which are brought by greeting. Greeting removes badly feeling, malevolence and hate between the people and promotes brotherhood and fraternity. It also demolishes sense of vanity and superiority complex in the upper class people and promotes equality. Prophet Muhammad directed his followers that irrespective of the social status, one riding shall salute one walking, one walking shall salute one sitting; the small party shall salute the big party, and the junior in age shall greet the senior one. These guidances of the Prophet cut at the origins of cultural differentiations and prejudice which separate the masses into classes.

Hence it is the obligation of a believer to greet the other believer whenever he rans into him. The better man is he who greets first. Greeting brings big honours and when it is companioned with appealing of benedictions and mercy of Allah on the other it increases the honours. The best form of Islam is your devoting of food to the destitute ones and your greeting all whom you know and whom you know not. When you enter a house you are obliged to greet the inmates of the house. The best form of greeting is saying "peace be on you" and then handshaking. When you go to the house of a person for an interview or to see or meet him, you should first ask him for permission. If you are permitted you will enter the house after greeting the inmates of the house. If you are refused permission you would go back gently.

Permission is to be sought thrice. If it is refused or no reply is given you are obliged to return. The proper way of seeking permission is to say: "Peace be on you. May I come in?" Permission should not be given to a person who does not begin with a greeting. Asking for permission is, however, not necessary in case of a person who has been called for or sent for and he comes with the messenger. Seeking permission is essential even in case of close relations. If you attend the household of your parents or mother with whom you live, you should take permission. Even your retainers and your children are called for to ask for your permission whilst they want to enter your rooms at the time of seclusion.

For sitting in gatherings, Islam has decreed certain ways. According to the Quran, the individuals already sitting should give elbow room for an entrant when he requests for place to sit down in. This broadly happens when the place is already replete and the entrant finds no room. In such a situation it is obligatory for the believers to oblige their brother. When a person enters he should greet others. The Prophet enjoined his followers not to sit keeping their hands behind back and leaning against the palms of their hands. Before sitting they should draw their clothes closer with their hands. One must not sit in the middle of a circle. The late arriver should sit at the ending of the assembly. One must not sit between two individuals without their permission. One must not ask that the others should arise in his respect. Nobody should make a man stand up from his seat and then sit in that.

MORAL VALUES IN SOCIETY

Here we give a few primary ethical teachings of Islam for various facets of a Muslim's life. They address the broad spectrum of personal ethical conduct of a Muslim in addition to his social obligations.

God-Consciousness

The Quran cites it as the most eminent quality of a Muslim: "The most ethical among you in the sight of God is the one who's most God-conscious." (49:13) humbleness, modesty, control of passions and hopes, truthfulness, wholeness, patience, staunchness, and carrying out one's promises are honourable values which are accentuated again and again in the Quran. We read in the Quran: "And God loves those who are firm and steadfast." (3:146) "And vie with one another to attain to your Sustainer's forgiveness and to a Paradise as vast as the heavens and the earth, which awaits the God-conscious, who spend for charity in time of plenty and in time of hardship, and restrain their anger, and pardon their fellow men, for God loves those who do good." (3:133-134) "Establish regular prayer, enjoin what is just, and forbid what is wrong; and bear patiently whatever may befall you; for this is true constancy.

And do not swell your cheek (with pride) at men, nor walk in insolence on the earth, for God does not love any man proud and boastful. And be moderate in your pace and lower your voice; for the harshest of sounds, indeed, is the braying of the ass." (31:18-19) In a way which sums up the moral behaviour of a Muslim, the Prophet said: "My Sustainer has given me nine commands: to remain conscious of God, whether in private or in public; to speak justly, whether angry or pleased; to show moderation both when poor and when rich, to reunite friendship with those who have broken off with me; to give to him who refuses me; that my silence ought be absorbed with thought; that my looking should be an admonishment; and that I should control what is right."

Social Responsibilities

The commandments of Islam pertaining to social obligations are established on benignity and thoughtfulness of others. Since a broad injunction to be genial is likely to be brushed aside in particular situations,

Islam lays stress on particular acts of kindness and specifies the responsibilities and rights of various kinships. In a widening circle of relationship, then, our first obligation is to our immediate family - parents, husband or wife and children, then to other relations, neighbours, acquaintances and friends, orphans and widows, the destitute of the community, our associate Muslims, all our fellow humans and creatures.

Parents

deference and attention for parents is very much emphasized in the Islamic education and is a very significant part of a Muslim's aspect of religion. "Your maintainer has ordained that you worship none but Him, and that you be kind to parents. Whether one or both of them attain old age in your lifetime, do not say to them a word of contempt nor repel them, but address them in terms of honour. And, out of forgivingness, lower to them the extension of humbleness and say: My maintainer! Bring upon them Your mercy, just as they cared for me in childhood." (17:23-24)

Neighbours

The Prophet has pronounced: "he's not a believer who eats his fill whilst his neighbour alongside him is empty-bellied"; and: "He doesn't think whose neighbours are not secure from his harmful conduct." In reality, according to the Quran and Sunnah, a Muslim has to exonerate his ethical obligation not only to his parents, relations and neighbours but to the total humanity, animals and trees and plants. For instance, hunting down of birds and animals for the interest of game is not allowed. Likewise, cutting trees and plants which bear fruit is prohibited unless there is a very pressing motive for it.

PRACTICAL ASPECTS

On the primary moral features, Islam builds a broader organization of morals by virtuousness of which humanity can recognize its biggest potential. Islam distills the soul from self-serving ego, authoritarianism, abandon and undiscipline. It produces God-conscious human beings, devoted to their paragons, obsessed by piousness, abstention and discipline and unyielding with untruth, It brings on feelings of moral obligation and nurtures the capability for self control. Islam brings forth benignity, generousness, clemency, understanding, serenity, disinterested good will, principled fair-mindedness and truthfulness towards whole cosmos in whole situations. It nurtures august qualities from which only goodness may be expected.

REFERENCES

Amanat Allah: *MuHòafiz al-iman mill maka'id la-madhhaban,* Allahabad, 1877.

Amir Ahòmad: *Sirat al-Ashraf,* 2 vols, Lucknow, 1949.

Brahman, Chandra Bhan: *Chahar Chaman*, BM Add. MS 16, 863.

Bray, D.: *Census Report: Baluchistan*, Calcutta, 1913.

Ghulam Ahòmad Khan: *Majmu'a-i marfut-i khwajagan-i Chishti,* Delhi, 1906.

Ghulam Ahòmad, Mirza, of Qadiyan: *The Philosophy of the Teachings of Islam*, Rabwah, 1959.

Ghulam Muhammad: *Festivals and Folklore of Gilgat, Memoirs, Asiatic Society of Bengal*, Calcutta, 1905.

Ghulam Muh-d-din: *Sihòr al-Hind,* Delhi, 1876.

Ghulam Sarwar: *Khazinat al-asfiya',* Cawnpore, 1902.

Ghulam, Halim: *Tuhòfa-i ithna-'ashariyya,* Lucknow, 1879.

Ghuldm Shah 'Ali: *Maqamat-i Mazò'hari,* Delhi, 1891.

Gilani, A. C. S.: *Ghalib, His Life and Persian Poetry*, Karachi, 1956.

Goetz, H.: *Indian and Persian Miniature Painting*, Amsterdam, 1958.

Grierson, G. A.: *Bihar Peasant Life*, Calcutta, 1885.

Habib, M.: "Shaikh Nasruddin Mahòmud Chiragh-i Delhi as a Great Historical Personality"', *IC*, xx (1946), 129-53.

Hadi, Mirza Muhòammad: *Nur-Allah Shustari, Shahid-i Thalith,* Lucknow, 1925.

Halim, A.: "Mystics and Mystical Movements of the Sayyid Lodi Period", *Journal of the Asiatic Society of Pakistan*, 1963.

Hamdani, H. F.: "The Letters of Mustansir Billah", *BSOAS*, 1933-1935.

Hamid Ali: "The Customary and Statutory Laws of the Muslims in India", *IC*, 1937.

Hardy, P.: *Historians of Medieval India*, London, 1960.

Harikishan Kaul: *Census Report, Punjab*, Lahore, 1912.

Hòali, Altòtaf Hòusayn: *Muqaddima-i shi'r wa sha'iri,* Lahore, 1953.

Hòamid Qalandar: *Khayr al-majalis*, Aligarh, 1960.

Hòasan 'Ali 'Izzat: *Mufarrihò al-qulub,* 10 Pers. MS 2809.

Nadwi, Sulayman: "Muslim Colonies in India", *IC*, 1927.

Najm-al-Ghani Khan: *Madhahib-i Islam,* Lucknow, 1924.

Nizam-ad-din Burhanpuri, etc.: *Fatawa'i Hindiyya*, Urdu tr. by Sayyid Amir 'Ali, Lucknow, 1889.

Nizami, K. A.: ' *Abd-al-Hòaqq Muhòaddith Dihlawi,* Delhi, 1953.

Wajia 'Ali Shah: *Sòawt-i mubarak*, Lucknow, 1853.

Wakil Ahòmad: *Nusrat al-mujtahdin,* Lucknow, 1896.

Wali-Allah, Shah *Hòusn al-'aqida* (Urdu tr. *Mera aqida*), in *Ar-Rahim* 1964.

Walter, H. A.: *The Ahmadiyya Movement*, Calcutta/ London, 1918.

9

Movements

Nineteenth century in Islam is distinguished for the growth of a number of very significant reform social movements. The decay and resultant loss of Islamic political power and integration of British authority in most parts of the world had produced a totally fresh situation that had no case in point in the eternal and patterned chronicle of the community in India. It was now face to face with a number of very grave problems on whose answer depended the future of the Islamic community. A lot social movements came up to meet the challenge and proffer answers for some of these narked problems accordant to their own insight. Here we will be introduce you to major initiatives to regenerate Islam

RELIGIOUS MOVEMENTS

Wahhabi Movement

The 1st religious movement was founded by Saiyid Ahmad of Rai Bareli (1786-1831), which is broadly specified as Wahhabi movement. If the whole position is kept in mind and a comparability is made with the political theory and practices of the Arab Wahhabis, it would seem incorrect to call the movement as Wahhabi movement. The designation, all the same, has acquired wide currency and therefore casting it off is likely to create disarray. Furthermore, there are grounds to believe that in spite of a number of differences in their beliefs as well as approach, they were most probably influenced by the Arabian Wahhabis. The argument that since Wahhabis were driven out before Saiyid Ahmad paid his visit to Mecca for pilgrimage is far from convincing. The fact that they had lost political power at that time in Mecca does not mean that their ideological influence was also totally eliminated from there. Traces of Wahhabi influence could be easily discerned from the ideology of the movement. Still it would be hardly justified to designate the movement as Wahhabi movement. The Wahhabi movement of India was in many ways a continuation of the reform movement of Shah Waliullah Dehlavi (1702-1760) and was directly inspired by it. Saiyid Ahmad was a disciple of Shah Abdul Qadir and Shah Abdul Aziz, the illustrious sons and successors of Shah Waliullah. Shah Waliullah and his direct heirs have, however, tried to meet the challenge at an intellect level. They considered that the Islamic society could be changed through intellectual counselling. But the latter was a man of deeds and tried to undertake the problem with fall back to arms and therefore he took another track from the one abided by by his instructors. But it would be of value to remember that he had started out his movement as a spiritual reform movement and acquired appreciable success in it.

It was only later that his movement acquired the character of armed struggle against the Sikhs and the British and assumed a markedly political character. But even then the reformist zeal of the followers of Saiyid Ahmad continued unabated. It would also appear that in the beginning he had contemplated to migrate from India to escape from the degrading position in which he found the Muslims here after the occupation of the country by the British. When it is rendered impossible to lead one's life according to the dictates of the religion, it becomes obligatory to migrate (hijrat) to some other land where religious prescriptions could be freely practiced. But he ultimately chose the other alternative of armed struggle (jihad) against the powers that he thought to be responsible for this situation with a view to change it. In 1821 Saiyid Ahmad went on Haj pilgrimage and came back in 1823. After his return from the pilgrimage, he soon commenced his struggle against the Sikhs and the British and was at last martyrized at Balakot fighting against the Sikh army at the outset of May 1831.

The spirit of epic resistivity of the British that he had aroused went on to prompt approaching generations of the Indians for long. It should also be useful to remember that after the death of Saiyid Ahmad many of his disciples continued to work for reform in various regions. For example, Maulana Inayat Ali made great impact on the Muslim society of Bengal through his reform activities. Moreover, the movement that came to be known as Ahl-i Hadith Movement, which, besides reviving the learning of Hadith, had made great contribution in the field of religious reform, also owes its origins to some of the followers of Saiyid Ahmad like Shah Ishmael, who seem to have come under the influence of the Wahhabis of Arabia. He and a number of other followers of Saiyid Ahmad rejected the idea of complete adherence to any particular school of Islamic jurisprudence and refused to tie themselves to any interpretation that they believed to be against the injunctions of the Quran and Hadith.

Rejecting the validity of the schools of law, they emphasised the need of direct use of textual sources of the faith. They came to be called ghair muqallid (nonconformists). Nawab Siddiq Hasan Khan (1832-1890) and Maulana Nazir Husain (died 1902) were leading lights of this movement. They made great donation in the field of spiritual reform and advancement of the learning and scholarship of Hadith literature. The movement was essentially inspired by the teachings of Shah Waliullah but its disciples neglected the moderateness and his purport of placation. Their inflexibility in matters that could not be conceived as the necessities of Islam, led to the emersion of what could be termed as yet another faction inside Islam.

Faraizi Movement

While the movement of Saiyid Ahmad had an all India quality, the other Current reform movement, the Faraizi movement, was restricted to the Area of Bengal. It was founded by Haji Shariatullah (1781-1840) in Bengal in 1818. He was born in Bandarkhola in the Faridpur territory of Bengal in an Unknown family. At the age of 18 he went on a pilgrimage to Mecca and in two Pieces stayed there for twenty years learning at the feet of celebrated scholars Especially Shaikh Tahir Sanbal Makki, the leading scholar of Mecca. He returned to India in 1802. By the time he visited Mecca for the second time, it had come under the supremacy of the Wahhabis and thus he came in contact with their political orientation. Wahhabi movement was founded in Arabian Peninsula by Muhammad bin Abdul Wahhab (1703-1792) who was born in the Najd region of Arabia.

During his studies he appears to have come under the charm of the great Islamic creative thinker, scholarly person and reformist, Ibn Taimiya (1263-1328) and it was most credibly due to his impact that he was fired with the ardour to reform the society of its many evilnesses. Tired of at the rearing degeneration and foundations, he established an energetic reform movement advocating the Muslims to come back to the Asceticism and pureness of former days of Islam.

The Wahhabi movement had profoundly molded not only the denizens of Arabian Peninsula but its affect was also experienced in far off countries through those who came to Mecca for broader training and also for pilgrimage. It would appear that Haji Shariatullah came under the charm of the Wahhabis during his long stay in the Holy City and returned to his native place fired with a zeal for reform. The circumstance of the Muslim community in Bengal would have only fortified his resolve for the urgent need of reform.

The origins of the Faraizi movement of Bengal could be traced in the spiritual, Social, economic and political circumstances dominating in the region in the first quarter of the nineteenth century. The outrageousness of the problem could be guessed from the observation of a contemporary British writer that the Muslims of Bengal were Muslims only in name only. Due to their long contact with the non- Muslim population, they had adopted many of their fashions, traditions and Rites some of which were in direct conflict with the fundamental principle of Islam. They adored sun, moon and fire, observed Holi, Diwali, Dasehra, Shivaratri and many other such religious festivals just like their neighbours.

They practiced dowry system and frowned at widow marriage. Dance and consumption of wine has become part and parcel of their festivals. The Sufism, which had played a very important role in the formation of the Bengali Muslim society, had degenerated and has become a source of many evils. Under the impact of Hindu caste system the Muslim society of Bengal was also divided into many social groups and the Islamic ideals of equality and universal brotherhood were given a go bye. The members of the so-called upper classes would not mix with the people of the supposedly lower classes. Even traces of untouchability could be discerned in the Muslim society of Bengal.

Similarly, their political and economic conditions had also steeply declined. Bengal was earlier considered as one of the most flourishing and prosperous provinces of India but after the British occupation it was totally ruined and its prosperity and wealth became a tale of the past. The lack of patronage led to a steep decline in the production and as a result of the British policy, it was ran aground to a halt and the former prospering craftsmen and producers were decreased to intense pauperism and poverty. Abrupt growth in the tax revenue demand and the use of exceedingly merciless techniques in its actualization totally Bankrupted the peasantry. All these elements must have mattered with Haji Shariatullah when he chose to set in motion his movement for the regenerate the Muslim society of Bengal.

The Faraizi movement has been diversely identified as a pious reform movement, farmer movement, a class war and a movement for the socio-Economical upheaval of the Bengali masses. But if the full situation is kept in bear in mind, there could be little doubt that the Faraizi Movement was fundamentally a religious reform movement, as the name of the movement would as well clearly Hint. They called themselves Faraizis because of their strict observance of religious duties (Faraiz) prescribed by Islam. As noticed earlier, the inspiration for reforming the Bengali Muslim society in all probability came from the Wahhabis of Arabia. During the lifetime of Haji Shariatullah, the Faraizis mostly confined themselves to the field of religious reform. But later during the stewardship of his son and successor, Dudu Miyan, the movement expanded the area of its activity to economic and political spheres as well. The reason for this shift in the policy and priorities of the movement is not far to seek. Majority of the people among whom they were working and whom they sought to reform and redeem, were leading an abysmally pathetic life of extreme poverty and unabashed exploitation.

They could not have possibly remained passive spectators of the wretched conditions in which the masses were living. The concern for the material well being of their followers and the anxiety to ensure a dignified life for them set them on the path of confrontation with the zamindars and indigo planters as well as the government. The struggle on behalf of the peasants and weavers with a view to ameliorate their conditions and restore their dignity was bitter and prolonged but its gains were nothing less than spectacular. It almost changed the face of Bengal. But in spite of its great achievements in the fields of economy, culture and politics, its main focus throughout the period continued to be religious reform of the Bengali Muslims.

The main philosophical basis of the movement was absolute compliance to the will of God as enshrined in the Quran and the Sunnah (customs) of the Prophet In addition to the traditions transmitted from the early period of Islam. For the intentions of superintending this big organization and ascertaining effective Execution of their policies, the Faraizis had constituted a detailed network that they delegated as khilafat system. It would seem that Haji Shariatullah was knowledgeable of the necessity of such an organization but he didn't have time to do it. It was left to his son and successor, Dudu Miyan, to do the needful in this regard. He did, however, organise a group of clubmen (lathial) to protect the interests of the peasants and the weavers. The Khilafat system that was later established by Dudu Miyan was very elaborate in which the entire area under the Faraizi dominance was divided into villages, units and circles. At every level a Khalifah was appointed and thus a hierarchy was established.

On the top of the hierarchy was Dudu Miyan himself who was known as Ustad and at the bottom was Gaon Khalifah i.e. the Khalifah at the village level. The responsibilities of the Khalifah included instruction of the followers regarding the fundamentals of Islam, construction of mosques and appointment of imams etc., conducting marriages and funerals, building maktabs (schools), settling Quarrels relating to matrimony, inheritance, common quarrels etc. For meeting out the expenses of these multifaceted activities they received one tenth of the Yield of the unit as earnings. The obligations of the Khalifahs of assorted levels were well defined. There seems to have been an effective courier system that ascertained effective communication between the centre and various stages of the Khalifahs. It was through the Khilafat system that the central Faraizi leadership asseverated its control over its huge following spread in several areas of Bengal, and kept themselves advised about the developings taking place there.

REFORM MOVEMENTS

Deoband Movement

Deoband is a settlement in Saharanpur district of U.P. about ninety miles from Delhi. It was here that the groundworks of a Darul Ulum (institution of higher learning) were placed. It was fated to play a crucial role in the Chronicle of the community and the country. In 1867 the humble maktab that has been functioning there for some time in the Jami Masjid of the town titled Chhatta Masjid, was raised to the position of an institute of higher learning.

Maulana Muhammad Qasim Nanautawi (1832-1880) and Maulana Rashid Ahmad Gangohi (1828-1905) who spearheaded this movement were products of the school of Shah Waliullah. Their intellect ancestry goes back to Shah Waliullah through more than one way. Both of them learned hadith at the feet of Maulana Ahmad Ali Saharanpuri and Abdul Ghani Naqshbandi who were disciples of Shah Muhammad Ishaq (1778-1875), successor and daughter's son of Shah Abdul Aziz (1746-1824). They also studied under the guidance of Maulana Mamlauk Ali, a disciple of Shah Abdul Aziz's disciple Maulana Rashiduddin Dehlavi. Moreover, they were murids of Haji Imdadullah (1817- 1899) who later migrated to Mecca and came to be known as Muhajir Makki.

Shah Muhammad Ishaq had played a key role in the organisation of the Jihad movement of Saiyid Ahmad Barelavi. Besides lending his moral support to the movement, he was charged with the important task of managing supplies for the mujahids which responsibility he performed with credit. But after its failure, he migrated to Mecca in 1840 and settled there. Haji Imdadullah came into his contact there and benefited form his company. Later, he became a murid of Maulana Nasiruddin, a grandson of Shah Rafiuddin, son of Shah Waliullah, and a pupil and son-in-law of Shah Muhammad Ishaq. Maulana Nasiruddin was also very intimately affiliated with the Jihad movement of Saiyid Ahmad and had Acted a very significant role in its resurgence after the disaster of Balakot in 1831.

It is clear from this little account that Maulana Muhammad Qasim Nanautavi and Maulana Rashid Ahmad Gangohi who were implemental in the creation of the Darul Ulum at Deoband were schooled and coached under the intellectual and reformist customs of Shah Waliullah and Jihad movement of Saiyid Ahmad Barelavi. They were fired with the ardour to reform the society from the many evils that had crept in the mainstream of the Islamic faith and were running down the Vital force of the Muslim society. At the same time they had also inherited the Illustrious custom of resisting and fighting the British with a view to push them out from the land of the country. And consequently when the first war of independence began in 1857, they whole-heartedly participated in it.

The centre of their activity was Shamli, a town in Muzaffarnagar district of U.P. They succeeded in ousting the British from the area for some time and organised its administration. Haji Imdadullah, Maulana Muhammad Qasim Nanautawi and Maulana Rashid Ahmad Gangohi looked after various facets of the administration. After the failure of the uprising it was with great difficulty that they could escape the British Retribution. In fact Haji Imdadullah who was the moving spirit behind it, had to Get out to Mecca to avoid falling in the hands of British people. However, flames of this rebel spirit against the British authority continued to burn in the deep recesses of their hearts. When the battle for freedom began, the Ulama of Deoband wholeheartedly took part in it and were in its forefront. Jamiatul Ulama, which was constituted mostly by the graduates of the Darul Ulum, persisted in the thick of the battle for freedom and made substantial donation towards this goal.

Dars-i Nizami was assumed as the programme of the Madrasah. It was formulated by Mulla Nizamuddin of Sihali (1748). After the execution of his father, Mulla Qutbuddin in 1691, Aurangzeb allotted to the family a big house in Lucknow, which came to be popularly known as Farangi Mahal. This became A significant focus of learning and the family also came to be known as Farangi Mahali family. This family brought out many great scholars for several generationsand is still held in great respect. No doubt this syllabus is somewhat unbalancedas it gives much stress to subjects that could not be considered as essential.

Logic, philosophy and grammar claim more time than some of the more essential subjects. In spite of influenced attempts of stalwarts like Maulana Rashid Ahmad Gangohi, philosophy could not be dislodged form the syllabus. However, regarding Hadith it went beyond the recommendations of the Dars-i Nizami.

In fact biggest stress was given to the commandment of Hadith and all the six classical collections of the Hadith were taught and Shaikh ul Hadith (teacher of Hadith) occupied the most authoritative position among the teaching brotherhood.

Similarly, Fiqh became a speciality of the Darul Ulum and strict adherence to Hanafi School of jurisprudence became a trademark of the Deoband school of thought. This might have been conceived essential in those disorderly conditions for keeping the society together but in the long run it led to the sectarian conflict and rigidity that Shah Waliullah has so assiduously tried to cure and correct.

The Quranic Studies, however, didn't receive the same prominence in the syllabus as Hadith. It is also to be repented that in spite of the fact that the founders of the Darul Ulum were not opposed as such to the modern sciences but in practice English language could not find a place in its syllabus. This was a great defect and its effects continued to be felt for long as majority of the madrasahs till very newly under the influence of the tradition set by Darul Ulum did not think it essential to include English in their course of study.

Deoband eminently succeeded in fulfilling the objectives for which it was Founded. Within a very short span of time, Deoband was able to establish an Individuality of its own. It came to represent an especial school of thought of religious Custom that was made up of reformed religious practices and opinions. As noticed earlier, it was in fact continuation of the traditions willed by the heirs of Shah Waliullah but its stress was more on the reformed practices and Notions than on intellectual synthesis. Moreover, its scope and outreach was immensely widened and the possibilities of the penetration of its ideology were vastly built. They extended to the community what some scholars have termed as complex leadership.

What they advocated was a wise mixture of Law (Shariat) and the Path (Tariqat) as represented by various Sufi orders. This meant that while the importance of Sufism in the shaping of Muslim society was accepted, it was insisted that it continued within the boundaries set by the Shariat.

They therefore asserted that their followers should desert all those practices and notions, which were disallowed by the law or were suspect in its eyes. As the time passed the area of their influence expanded and step by step led to the Integration of their interpretation of reformed faith. It needs to be particularly noted that this was not bounded to the neighbourhood of Deoband or for that matter to north India but to the faraway areas of the country such as Chittagong, Peshawar and Tamil Nadu. Muslims living in another parts of the country progressively began to look to Deoband for leadership and counselling and direction in religious matters. Gradually Deoband assumed this onerous responsibility for it was exactly for what Darul Ulum was founded. The following factors were primarily responsible for bringing about this situation.

From the very commencement, Deoband succeeded in drawing scholars from different parts of the country. Many of them came from areas whose social Surroundings was immensely different from that of north India especially western U.P. where Deoband was placed. They could not easily address and understand Urdu language that served as the medium of direction. But by the time they graduated, they were trained and coached to successfully shoulder various Obligations connected with faith as Imams, preachers and teachers who could instruct and channelize the community in the spiritual affairs. They acted as Spokespersons and ambassadors of Deoband in their own areas and served as conduits by which Deobandi ideology was distributed. There were places where earlier no alim (plural Ulama) could be available but the position had altered. Now there were able folks in many regions to whom the local denizens could turn for counselling and advice in affairs of faith. As in most of the cases they had arisen from the same neighborhood, communicating with them was easy.

There were additional boulevards and tools that were employed by the Ulama of Deoband to take home their message to bigger number of masses. As noticed earlier, they did not cast away Sufism as the Ahl-i Hadith and the Wahhabis did. Several of those at the helm of matters there were Sufi Shaikhs as well. They had vast clientele of murids spread in the nook and corner of the country. The authority of a Sufi Shaikh over his disciples (murids) is complete and total.

This great authority they used not only for purging Sufism from many of the unIslamic elements that had found their way into its notions and practices but they also asserted on progressive interpreting of the faith. Likewise, Ulama of Deoband employed their pen and tongue with great result both to hold the religion and to broadcast their progressive ideas.

Several of them acquired to penning books in a big way. In addition to purely scholarly books, they also wrote multitude of books in Urdu on socio-religious compositions to extend to the people to regenerate their lives and build the society in accord with the bona fide teachings of the religion and desert those traditions and practices, which are not approved by the religion. They produced a huge corpus of literature on these subjects.

This also included considerably vast literature, which was prepared to refute and resist the missionary activities of the Christians and others as well as those Muslim factions and groups whom they believed as religiously aberrant. Deoband also produced many skilled arguers who played a substantial role in fighting Philosophical attacks on Islam from different quarters. They too used this skill to Sway and convert people to lead virtuously and scrupulously upright and correct life. It is apparent that the share of Deoband in the area of regenerating Muslim society is tremendous.

Aligarh Movement

The other reaction took the shape of Aligarh Movement. It was dissimilar from the movement that was founded by the founders of Deoband though both gave forth from the same fears. Those who spearheaded these movements came from immensely different backgrounds but some striking similarities could also be recognized. Syed Ahmad, popularly known as Sir Syed, was born on 17 October 1817 in a blue-blooded family, which had close dealings with the Mughal royal court. His ancestors had been affiliated with government service for long and he had chance to see and follow the Mughal Court, which was nothing more than a shadowy apparition of its illustrious past. From the religious point of view he was brought in an ambiance that blended the best customs associated with religious mysticism and regeneration. He was greatly charmed by the scholarship of Shah Waliullah and he's the one writer whom he citations most profusely in his writings.

It was evidently from his contact with the family of Shah Waliullah that he received his impetus for reformation of the Muslim society. Clearly the source of his inspiration was the same as that of the founders of Deoband. He, however, charted for himself a path which was Altogether dissimilar from them but the ardour and loyalty to reformation remained with him throughout his life. The difference of opinion fundamentally emanated from the fact that he was not only aware of the glorious heritage of Muslims and the need to preserve it but he was also fully conscious of the great changes that were going to take place in the Indian situation as a result of the collapse of the struggle of 1857 and the urgent need to make some sort of adjustment with the emerging situation.

This naturally set him on a path, which was qualitatively different from the one that was adopted by the Ulama of Deoband. The destruction that followed the Revolt shook him to the very roots of his existence. He was so deeply agitated at the large-scale killings of innocent people and far-flung ruin and destruction of property that for some time he Flirted with the idea of migrating from the country but the congenital goodness of his nature didn't permit him to opt for his personal safety and leave his people in distress. Ultimately he decided to work for the amelioration of their conditions and their uplift. The rest of his life he devoted to this noble cause.

The task of pulling his countrymen and more particularly the Muslim community, which had borne most of the brunt of the revenge of the rulers, was a far more difficult task. After much thinking over the problem, he came to the conclusion that lack of education was the biggest cause of the backwardness of the country and without attainment of advanced cognition there could be no hope of any Betterment in the situation. This realization determined his destination for the rest of his life and all his vigours were now addressed to accomplish this goal. It, however, took a lot of time to eventually acquire his scheme in this respect and work out a Elaborate program. Before achieving that aim, a step-by-step evolution in his thinking could be easily recognized.

He took the 1st provisional step in this way in 1859 when he was based at Muradabad as Sadrus Sudur. Here he founded a Farsi Madrasah in which Farsi, contemporary history, English language and Urdu were to be taught. Later, he raised contributions to build a Madrasah at Ghazipur in 1864 in which arrangements were made for instructing English, Urdu, Arabic, Persian and Sanskrit. Raja Hardeo Narain Singh was named as its sponsor. This was first academic institution to have been founded by evoking contributions from public, both Hindus and Muslims, even before Ulama at Deoband assumed this method for running the Darul Ulum. Later, this Madrasah was raised as Victoria High School. It was also at Ghazipur that he took by far the most important step to make the western knowledge accessible to the people. In 1863 he founded

Translation Society, which was later named as Scientific Society, with a view to arrange translation of standard works on modern arts, sciences, history, agriculture, mathematics and political economy etc. Some important contributions of the western scholarship were thus made available to the people who could not have access to them in their original form. In 1864 he was shifted to Aligarh, which was Fated to emerge as the centre of his movement for the arousing of the Islamic community and where Anglo-Muhammadan Oriental College and later the Aligarh Muslim University were to be situated. The office of the Scientific Society was also transferred to Aligarh and it carried on to run from here even when he was shifted to Banaras. It was from here that he set in motion Aligarh Institute Gazette in 1866 to popularize his thoughts.

Creation of an establishment for bestowing contemporary education, which was very dear to Sir Syed's heart, was a much harder task. As acknowledged earlier, the basic drafts were already drawn by Sir Syed while he was still in England.

But there were many hurdles in the direction and lot of preparation was yet to be done. As it was imagined to be a individual enterprise independent of government check, the problem of raising essential finances posed a big challenge. But Sir Syed was not a man to be discouraged by such challenges. He took big pain and acquired Fresh ways and techniques for collecting funds. This included as varied methods as door-to-door fund collection, drawing of lottery and singing of Ghazals in the exhibition. Without losing any time, he set the process for the establishment of the institution in motion. Committees were formed to work out details, take care of different aspects of the proposal and take steps for raising the funds.

The place where the college was to be established was also to be determined. Sir Syed sought public opinion to suggest the location of the institution. Majority opinion was in favour of Aligarh where offices of Scientific Society and Tahzib Akhlaq were already located. Within a period of less than four years since his return from England, on May 24, 1875 the base of Muhammadan Anglo-Oriental College was laid and day-to-day teaching began from 1 June same year. The Viceroy, Lord Lytton, formally laid the foundation stone on 8 January 1877. Sir Syed was still serving at Banaras. But he realised that his personal presence was necessary for the proper supervising and Carrying out of the project.

He applied for early retirement and returned to Aligarh in July 1876 to work regular for the realization of the dream that he had dreamt for the uplift of his community. It may, however, be remembered that though the college was basically meant to cater for the educational needs of the

Muslims as they were much more behind than their Hindu brothers in the field of modern education, its doors were all of the time open to the students of all communities. From the very commencement, the Hindus have comprised a sizeable number of both the staff and the students. Siddons, an Englishman, was the first Headmaster and Baijnath Prashad was the Second Master. Amongst the donors also a big number consisted of Hindus.

There were many Non-Muslims who made bighearted contributions for the purpose. They included Maharaja of Patiala, Maharaja of Vijyanagar, Maharaja of Banaras, Chaudhry Sher Singh, Raja Deo Narain Singh, Lala Phool Chand, Thakur Guru Parsad Sinha, Kunwar Jagat Singh, Rai Shankar Das and Sita Ram etc. Raja Jai Kishan was all of the time at the side of Sir Syed. Name plaques of these and many other people could be seen in Strechy Hall and on the frontals of the rooms in Sir Syed Hall. When Sir Syed Expired out of 349 students, 64 were Non-Muslims and out of the 22 members of the Committee, 6 were Hindus. It was good luck of Sir Syed that he could draw a band of earnest and Dedicated friends and admirers around himself. They included loyalists like Muhsinul Mulk, Viqarul Mulk, Samiullah Khan and many others. They were men of conviction, courage and vision. They were charged with the ardour to Assist for the upthrust of the community and were educated like Sir Syed to experience any sacrifice. They stood with Sir Syed in the thick and thin and backed him to the hilt as long as he was alive and afterward his death carried forward his delegacy with great purpose and single-mindedness to successful culmination.

Sir Syed attracted much antagonistic attention for his spiritual views. In this regard it would be of value to remember that Aligarh Movement wasn't a religious movement. It was fundamentally an educational and social reform movement. There was no unanimity among the notables of the Movement in this regard. Sir Syed never tried to bring down his religious ideas on others or include them in the curriculum of the College. The religious aspect of the College was entirely left to the care of a graduate of Darul Ulum at Deoband, Maulana Abdullah Ansari.

In his religious writings he basically wanted to defend Islam against the malicious propaganda of the European scholars that Islam was not compatible with the developments of the modern sciences and no progress could be made under its aegis. Sir Syed firmly believed that the universe was the Work of God while the Quran was the Word of God and therefore there could not be any inconsistency between the two and every active phenomenon should meet the laws of nature. He did not believe in miracles. The seemingly occult happenings mentioned in the Quran were sought to be explained in terms of a chain of causation. These and many of his other postulates appalled the Ulama and the common Muslims alike. Many of his pieces of writing on the subject area of spiritual reform also impinged on the religious susceptiblenesses of the people. While a number of his religious ideas such as dining with the Christian, are at present broadly Acceptable, others still carry on to attract unfriendly remarks from the scholars.

The truth, all the same, remains that while there was authentic background for criticism on some of his spiritual ideas; his attempt to defend Islam and Muslims against the European barrage was nothing less than massive. Sir Syed had aspired at the constitution of a university but this dream didn't Materialize during his lifespan but he had set the movement securely on course to achieve this goal. His distinguished heirs, Muhsinul Mulk and Wiqarul Mulk untiringly worked for the recognition of this aim. Sir Syed breathed his last in 1898 and M.A.O. College achieved the position of university in 1920. A century after his death Aligarh Muslim University is a vivacious modern university.

Sir Syed was a visionary and had correctly diagnosed the basic unease that was Exhausting the energy of the Muslim community and untiringly worked to set it on course to honour, dignity and prosperity. The difficulties that he had to surmount were enormous and many. But no amount of personal uncomfortableness, unfriendly Resistance and adverse circumstances could discourage him from his goal. With the help of a attached band of friends and admirers he achieved what might have seemed in the conditions to many as unattainable. It is difficult to Visualize the condition of the Muslims of the Subcontinent had there not been Sir Syed and his Aligarh Movement.

REVIVALIST MOVEMENTS

Forward-looking Muslims have brought out a significant body of broad-minded thoughts within Islam but some believe progressive Islamism and liberal Islamism as two distinct movements. These movements share a philosophy that counts for the most part on ijtihad. Broad-minded Muslims do not needfully pledge to the more culturally-based interpretings of the Quran and Hadith. They generally claim that they are returning to the principles of the early Ummah and to the ethical and pluralistic intent of their scripture. The reform movement uses monotheism (tawhid) "as an organizing principle for human society and the basis of religious knowledge, chronicle, metaphysics, aesthetics, and ethics, as well as social, economical and world order."

These are movements within Islamism, rather than an attempt at schism. As such, they believe in the basic dogmas of Islam, such as the Six Elements of notion and the Five mainstays of Islam. They believe their views to be fully compatible with the teachings of Islam. Their main difference with more conservative Islamic belief is in differences of interpreting of how to apply the core Islamic values to contemporary life. The liberal Muslim's focus on individual interpretation and morals, rather than on the genuine word of scripture, may have an antecedent in the Sufi tradition of Islamic mysticism.

However, this reformist approach has led liberal Muslims to adjust or characterize their criticism of various acts by radical Muslims, including act of terrorism. Such vague or certified criticisms have frequently been assaulted by western critics, particularly those who put forward that there's a so called "clash of civilizations".Over the trend of the 19th and 20th centuries, in accord with their progressively modern societies and outlooks, liberal Muslims have tended to re-explain many facets of their religion. This is especially true of Muslims who now find themselves enduring in non-Muslim countries. Such multitude may distinguish themselves diversely as broad-minded, advanced or progressive; but instead of meaning a specific agendum, these terms tend to comprise a broad spectrum of aspects which contend conservativist, orthodox interpretings of Islam in many different ways.

Muslim Brotherhood

The Muslim Brothers (The Society of the Muslim Brothers) is a multinational Sunni movement and the biggest political opposition organization in many Arab nations, especially Egypt. The world's earliest and biggest Muslim group was established by the Sufi school teacher Hassan al-Banna in 1928. These groups are committed to the credo:

Allah is our aim. The Prophet is our leader. Quran is our law. Jihad is our way. Passing away in the way of Allah is our broadest desire.

The Brotherhood's declared goal is to infuse the Quran and Sunnah as the "sole point of reference for arranging the life of the Muslim family, individual, community and state".

Since its origination in 1928 the movement has formally opposed hostile means to accomplish its goals, with some exclusions such as in the Israeli-Palestinian struggle or to bring down secular Baathist rule in Syria. This functionary attitude has been called into question, particularly by the Egyptian government who charged it of a movement of killings in Egypt after World War II. The Brotherhood has been depicted as both unjustly persecuted and perilously violent. Members have been arbitrarily arrested; in Egypt the government has obstructed the party's attempts to field candidates in elections, with arrests or torment of activists and obstruction of voting in Islamic Brotherhood strongholds.

However, supporters of the Brotherhood have demonstrated violence on their part in many occasions and have often clashed with supporters of other parties, specifically the NDP in Egypt. Outside of Egypt, the group's political activity has been described as evolving away from modernism and reformism towards a more traditional, "rightist conservative" stance. For example, the Muslim Brotherhood party in Kuwait opposes suffrage for women. Among the Brotherhood's more influential members was Sayyid Qutb. Qutb was the author of one of Islamism's most important books, Milestones, which called for the restoration of Islam by re-establishing the Sharia and by using "strong-arm power and jehad for getting rid of the organizations and authorities of the Jahili system," which he believed to include the entire Muslim world. The Brotherhood is supported by donations from its members who are asked to allocate part of their income to the movement. Most of these donations come from members dwelling in oil-rich lands, such as Saudi Arabia.

The Ahle Quran

Ahle Quran, a group shaped by Abdullah Chakralawi, swear altogether on the chapters and rhymes of the Quran. Chakralawi's position was that the Quran itself was the most perfect source of custom and could be solely followed. According to him, Muhammad could take in only one form of revealing (wahy), and that was the Quran. He reasons that the Quran was the only record of godly wiseness, the only root of Muhammad's commandments, and that it superseded the entire corpus of hadith.

Bazm-e-Tolu-e-Islam

It's a Pakistani based organisation whose followers can be found out throughout the Earth. The movement was started by Ghulam Ahmed Pervez, a Quranic scholar. Centering on Quranic teachings, he was amenable to re-explain Quranic verses and place minuscule or no stress on hadiths. Unlike other groups, Tolu-e-Islam followers don't rule out all hadiths; however, they only admit hadiths which "are in conformity with the Holy Quran" and "don't disfigure the personality of Muhammad and his associates." The administration is loosely controlled. It brings out books, brochures, and transcriptions of Pervez's speeches.

United Submitters, International

The term is intimately linked with the late Rashad Khalifa, founding father of the United Submitters International. While the USI don't pertain to themselves as "Muslim" or lay claim to be "Islamic," they follow the Quran exclusively. The group popularized the phrase: the Quran, the whole Quran, and nothing but the Quran. After Khalifa announced himself a messenger of God, he was declined as a renegade of Islam. He was assassinated in 1990. Beside following the Quran-only philosophy they also think that there is a numerical structure in the Quran founded on the number 19.

REFERENCES

Amir Khurd: *Siyar al-awhya,* Delhi, 1885.

Amritsari, Thand-Allah: *Ahl-i hòadith ka madhhab,* Amritsar, 1920.

Brockelmann, C.: *Geschichte der arabischen Literatur*, second edition, two vols., Leiden, 1943, 1949; three supplementary vols., Leiden, 1937-42.

Brown, Percy: *Indian Architecture (Islamic Period)*, Bombay, 1958.

Fakhr-ad-din Ahmad: *Izalat ash-shukuk,* Allahabad, 1880.

Fakhr-i Mudabbir: *Aadab al-hòarb wa-sh-shuju'a,* BM Add. MS 1653.

Faqir-Allah: *Rag Durpan*, 10 Pers. MS 1937.

Farid Bhakkari: *Dhakhira al-khawanin,* Karachi, 1961.

Farquhar, J. N.: *Modern Religious Movements in India*, London, 1924.

Fat'hò-ad-din: *Shajra-i Naqshbandiyya,* Rawalpindi, 1904.

Fergusson, James: *History of Indian and Eastern Architecture*, London., 1910.

Firishta, Abu-l-Qasim: *Gulshan-i Ibrahimi (Ta'rikh-i Firishta)*, Bombay, 1832; Lucknow, 1905; Eng. tr. J. Briggs (*History of the Rise of Muhammadan Power in India*), London, 1829.

Firuz Tughluq: *Futhòhòat-i Firuz Shahi*, ed. S. Abdur-Rashid, Aligarh, 1954.

Fisher, Humphrey J.: *Ahòmadiyyah: A Study in Contemporary Islam on the West Afirican Coast*, London, 1963.

Fyzee, A. A. A. (ed.): *A Shïte Creed*, Bombay, 1942.

Gait, E. A.: *Census Report: Bengal*, Calcutta, 1902.

Ghani, A. R. and Nur K. Ilahi: *Bibliography of Iqbal*, Lahore, 1955.

Ghani, A.: *A History of Persian Language and Literature in the Mughal Court*, Allahabad, 1929-1930.

Ghosh, J. C.: *Bengali Literature*, London, 1948.

Hashimi, Nasir-ad-din: *Dakan men Urdu*, Hyderabad, 1936.

Havell, E. B.: *A Handbook of Indian Art*, London, 1920.

Hòasani, 'Abd-al-Hòayy: *Ath-thaqafa al-Islamiyya fi-i-Hind*, Damascus, 1958.

Hòasani, 'Abd-at-Rahòman: *Mir'at-i Madariyya*, BM Add. MS 168.

Nizami, K. A.: "Some Aspects of Khanqah Life in Medieval India", *SI*, 1957.

Nizami, K. A.: *The Life and Times of Shaykh Farid-u'd Din Ganj-i Shakar*, Aligarh, 1955.

Nurul M. Karim: "Part played by Haji Shari'atullah and his son in the socio-political history of East Bengal", *Proceedings of the Pakistan History Conference*, Karachi, 1955.

O'Malley, L. S. S.: *Census Report: Bengal, Bihar, Orissa, Sikkim*, Calcutta, 1913.

Wellesz, Emmy: *Akbar's Religious Thought reflected in Mughal Painting*, London, 1952.

Wilkinson, J. V. S. and Gray, B.: *Persian Miniature Painting*, London, 1933.

10

Reformers

Modern-day Muslim reform movements often draw their beginnings to the founding era of Islam. Many verses of the Koran promote reform (islah), and a command of the prophet Muhammad anticipates that a renewer (mujaddid) will arise in each century to regenerate the community of Muslims. Prominent reformers shared a scripturalist desire to return Islam to the tenets of the sacred texts, as well as a corresponding distaste for popular practices and contemporary religious hierarchies that they viewed as deviating from these tenets. These recurrent movements for reform had varying impacts on Islamic thought. During the nineteenth century, a new wave of reform movements emerged as part of the resistance to European imperial expansion, on the proposition that this domination was due to Muslims' religious laxity. The nineteenth century also witnessed the rise of a new strain of Islamic reform, one that appealed to European models. Like earlier reformers, these modernists called Muslims to return to the sacred writing of Islam; unlike other reformers, however, they discovered a blessed conjunction between the spirit of these texts and current European values and institutions. This conjunction answered for for Europeans' power, and the acceptance of these ways would restore the resplendency of Islam.

One facet of present-day Western civilization that modernist Islamic reformers particularly treasured was the Protestant Protestant Reformation, which they interpreted as a move toward the ideals of Islam. Muhammad Abduh (Egypt, 1849-1905), Afghani's student and another major figure in the movement, described Protestantism as "calling for reform and a return to the simplicities of the faith-a reformation which included elements by no means unlike Islam". Similarly, the most prominent South Asian Islamic modernist, Muhammad Iqbal, suggested that Protestantism emancipated Europe from religious and political absolutism and embraced human goodness as opposed to original sin-"the basic propositions of Islam, as of modern European civilization." In the middle of the twentieth century, the analogy was reversed: instead of measuring the Reformation by the yardstick of Islamic ideals, Muslim reformers measured Islam by the yardstick of the Reformation. Iqbal came to feel that Muslims "are today passing through a period similar to that of the Protestant revolution in Europe" Abduh's influential disciple, Muhammad Rashid Rida phrased the analogy in exhortatory terms, mentioning the call for for Muslims to blend spiritual renewal and earthly renewal, the same way Europe has done with spiritual reformation and modernization.

Also in the mid-twentieth century, Islamic reformism split into two strands: one that upheld the equation of certain Western and early Islamic ideals, and one that rejected Western precedents. The liberal Islamic movement defended Western values such as democracy, human rights, and gender equality, using Islamic justifications-either specific injunctions from sacred texts on behalf of these positions, or silences in the texts that leave these matters to human invention, or the necessity and desirability of reinterpreting the texts within changing social contexts. A leading representative of this final approach, Abd al-Karim Sorush (Iran, b. 1945), has argued that religious interpretation must take account of intellectual developments outside of the sacred sources: "No reform can take place without re-shuffling the traditional suppositions, and no re-shuffling can emerge unless one is masterfully acquainted with both traditions and the newly developed ideas outside the sphere of revelation".

The second strand adopted certain modern values and practices but denounced their European provenance. For example, Hasan al-Banna (Egypt, 1906-1949), founder of the Muslim Brotherhood, the first and largest revivalist organization of the twentieth century, called for modern-style "social reform" including mass education, a war on poverty, and public health measures, yet his definition of reform associated all ills in Muslim societies with the rise of Western influence. More recently, Usama bin Ladin's Advice and Reform Committee, the Saudi Arabian opposition group that he founded while in exile in the Sudan in the mid-1990s, railed against political oppression and espoused the doctrines of human equality, rule of law, freedom of the press, human rights, and economic development, using the latest technologies to spread its message-while rejecting the notion that anything positive could be learned from the West.

Both strands of contemporary Islamic reform emerged largely from modern state school systems-Soroush was trained in pharmacology and philosophy, al-Banna in modern education, bin Ladin in engineering. With the expansion of secular education, the traditional seminary (madrasa) scholarship has lost the near-monopoly over religious interpretation that it attempted to enforce in earlier eras. Among the beneficiaries of educational expansion have been women, who were almost entirely excluded in earlier eras from advanced training in religious matters. As more Muslim women have gained secular education, small Islamic feminist movements have emerged in numerous countries. These movements criticize patriarchal cultural practices that they consider to be foreign to the original message of Islam, as well as patriarchal interpretations of the message that they consider to be a product of ongoing efforts by men to monopolize religious scholarship.

One of the common themes of Islamic reform movements, in the early twenty-first century as in past centuries, remains the denunciation of the seminaries' obscurantism and subservience to state authorities. This subservience has only been enhanced by the seminary reform projects of numerous colonial and postcolonial states. At the same time, the proliferation of Islamic authorities beyond the seminary has generated such a large variety of liberal and radical Islamic movements, all of them espousing "reform," that the word has been rendered almost meaningless. The term is so elastic, and so positively charged, that it is difficult in the early 2000s to find Muslim statements that reject reform in principle- even as criticisms of any particular reform are legion.

REFORMERS IN EARLY PERIOD

Al-Ghazali

Abu ?amid Muhammad ibn Muhammad al-Ghazali (1058-1111), known as Algazel to the western medieval world, was born and died in Tus, in the Khorasan province of Persia (modern day Iran). He was a Muslim theologian, jurist, philosopher, cosmologist, physician, psychologist and mystic of Persian origin, and remains one of the most celebrated scholars in the history of Sufi Islamic thought. He is considered a pioneer of the methods of doubt and skepticism, and in one of his major works, The Incoherence of the Philosophers, he changed the course of early Islamic philosophy, shifting it away from the influence of ancient Greek and Hellenistic metaphysics, and towards an Islamic philosophy based on cause-and-effect that were determined by God or intermediate angels.

Ghazali contributed significantly to the development of a systematic view of Sufism and its integration and acceptance in mainstream Islam.

He was a scholar of orthodox Islam, belonging to the Shafi'i school of Islamic jurisprudence and to the Asharite school of theology. Ghazali received many titles such as Sharaful Aemma, Zainuddin, Hujjatul Islam, meaning "Proof of Islam". He is viewed as the key member of the influential Asharite school of early Muslim philosophy and the most important refuter of Mutazilites.

However, he chose a slightly different position in comparison with the Asharites; his beliefs and thoughts differ, in some aspects, from the orthodox Asharite school.Al-Ghazali was responsible for formulating the Ashari school of atomism. He argued that atoms are the only perpetual, material things in existence, and all else in the world is "accidental" meaning something that lasts for only an instant. Nothing accidental can be the cause of anything else, except perception, as it exists for a moment. Contingent events are not subject to natural physical causes, but are the direct result of God's constant intervention, without which nothing could happen. Thus nature is completely dependent on God, which is consistent with other Ashari Islamic ideas on causation, or the lack thereof.

In the fourteenth century, Nicholas of Autrecourt considered that matter, space, and time were all made up of indivisible atoms, points, and instants and that all generation and corruption took place by the rearrangement of material atoms. The similarities of his ideas with those of al-Ghazali suggest that Nicholas was familiar with the work of al-Ghazali, who was known as "Algazel" in Europe, either directly or indirectly through Averroes.

Ibn Taymiyyah

Taqi ad-Din Ahmad ibn Taymiyyah (1263 - 1328), was a Sunni Islamic scholar born in Harran, located in what is now Turkey, close to the Syrian border. He lived during the troubled times of the Mongol invasions. As a member of the school founded by Ibn Hanbal, he sought the return of Islam to its sources, the Quran and the Sunnah. Ibn Taymiyyah is known for his devotion to jihad, or what he called the best of the forms of voluntary service man can devote to God. The ulema agree in proclaiming it superior to pilgrimage and to the 'umra, as well as to prayer and supererogatory fasts, as is shown in the Book and in the Sunna.

In the Mamluk's war against the Mongols (or Tartars), he issued a fatwa declaring jihad upon the Mongols not only permissible, but obligatory as the Mongols were not true Muslims. He based this ruling on the grounds that although the Mongols had converted to Sunni Islam they ruled using 'man-made laws' (their traditional Yassa code) rather than Islamic law or Shariah, and thus were living in a state of jahiliyya, or pre-Islamic pagan ignorance. `Every group of Muslims that transgresses Islamic law. must be combated, even when they continue to profess the credo.`

Ibn Taymiyyah held that much of the Islamic scholarship of his time had declined into modes that were inherently against the proper understanding of the Quran and the Sunnah. Ibn Taymiyyah believed that the first three generations of Islam- Muhammad, his companions, and the followers of the companions from the earliest generations of Muslims - were the best role models for Islamic life. Their practice, together with the Quran, constituted a seemingly infallible guide to life. Any deviation from their practice was viewed as bidah, or innovation, and to be forbidden.

Ibn Taymiyyah favoured an apparent (dhahir) interpretation of the Quran. He affirmed Allah's attributes - that he had "a hand and a face, that he loves and hates, and that he ascends and descends while remaining risen above in a throne over the heavens." His opponents charged that he taught anthropomorphism, that is, that he took references to Allah's hand, foot, shin, and face as being literally true - even though he insisted that Allah's "hand" was nothing comparable to hands found in creation. Some of his Islamic critics contend that this violates the Islamic concept of tawhid.

REFORMERS IN MEDIEVAL PERIOD

Jamal-al-Din Afghani

Sayyid Muhammad Ibn Safdar al-Husayn (1838-1897) was a political activist and Islamic nationalist in Iran, Afghanistan, Egypt, and the Ottoman Empire during the 19th century. One of the founders of Islamic modernism, and an advocate of pan-Islamic unity, he has been described as "less interested in theology than he was in organizing a Muslim response to Western pressure." In 1857, Jamaluddin Afghani spent a year in Delhi and after performing the pilgrimage of Haj in Mecca, he returned to Afghanistan in 1858. He became a counselor to the King Dost Muhammad Khan and later to Muhammad Azam. In 1869, the throne of Kabul was occupied by Sher Ali Khan, and Jamaluddin Afghani was forced to leave the country. In 1871, al-Afghani moved to Egypt and began preaching his ideas of political reform. His ideas were considered radical, and he was exiled in 1879. He then traveled to different European and non-European cities: Istanbul, London, Paris, Moscow, St. Petersburg and Munich.

In 1884, al-Afghani began publishing an Arabic newspaper in Paris entitled al-Urwah al-Wuthqa ("the trustworthy rope") along with Muhammad Abduh. The newspaper called for a return to the original principles and ideals of Islam, and for greater unity among Islamic peoples. This, al-Afghani argued, would allow the Islamic community to regain its former strength against European powers.

Al-Afghani was invited by Shah Nasser al-Din to come to Iran and advise on affairs of government, but fell from favour quite quickly and had to take sanctuary in a shrine near Tehran. After seven months of preaching to admirers from the shrine, he was arrested in 1891, transported to the border with Ottoman Mesopotamia, and evicted from Iran. Although al-Afghani quarrelled with most of his patrons, it is said he "reserved his strongest hatred for the shah," whom he accused of weakening Islam by granting concessions to Europeans and squandering the money earned thereby. His agitation against the Shah is thought to have been one of the "fountainheads" of the successful 1891 protest against the granting a tobacco monopoly to a British company, and the later 1905 Constitutional Revolution.

Although called a liberal by a contemporary English admirer, Wilfrid Scawen Blunt, Afghani did not advocate constitutional government. In the volumes of the newspaper he published in Paris, "there is no word in the paper's theoretical articles favouring political democracy or parliamentarianism," according to his biographer. Afghani simply envisioned "the overthrow of individual rulers who were lax or subservient to foreigners, and their replacement by strong and patriotic men." Afghani, above all else, called for unity amongst all Muslims. However, he did not believe that all Muslims ought to unify under one ruler, or Caliph. Rather, cooperation amongst Muslims was his answer to the weakness that had allowed Muslims to be colonized by the Europeans (namely Britain, Russia, and France).

He believed that, in fact, Islam (and its revealed law) was compatible with rationality and, thus, Muslims could become politically unified whilst still maintaining their faith based on a religious social morality. These beliefs had a profound effect on Muhammad Abduh, who went on to expand on the notion of using rationality in the human relations aspect of Islam (muamalat). Among the reasons why Al-Afghani is thought to have had a less than deep religious faith was his lack of interest in finding theologically common ground between Shia and Sunni, and his failure to marry. He is said to have "picked up female companionship when he wanted it without any show of religious scruples.".

Muhammad Iqbal

Sir Muhammad Iqbal (1877-1938) was a Muslim poet, philosopher and politician born in Sialkot, British India (now in Pakistan), whose poetry in Urdu and Persian is considered to be among the greatest of the modern era, and whose vision of an independent state for the Muslims of British India was to inspire the creation of Pakistan. He is commonly referred to as Allama Iqbal. After studying in England and Germany, Iqbal established a law practice, but concentrated primarily on writing scholarly works on politics, economics, history, philosophy and religion. He is best known for his poetic works, including Asrar-e-Khudi-which brought a knighthood- Rumuz-e-Bekhudi, and the Bang-e-Dara, with its enduring patriotic song Tarana-e-Hind. In India, he is regarding for the patriotic song, Saare Jahan Se Achcha. In Afghanistan and Iran, where he is known as Iqbal-e Lahori (Iqbal of Lahore), he is highly regarded for his Persian works.

Iqbal was a strong proponent of the political and spiritual revival of Islamic civilisation across the world, but specifically in India; a series of famous lectures he delivered to this effect were published as The Reconstruction of Religious Thought in Islam. One of the most prominent leaders of the All India Muslim League, Iqbal encouraged the creation of a "state in northwestern India for Indian Muslims" in his 1930 presidential address. Iqbal encouraged and worked closely with Muhammad Ali Jinnah, and he is known as Muffakir-e-Pakistan ("The Thinker of Pakistan"), Shair-e-Mashriq ("The Poet of the East"), and Hakeem-ul-Ummat ("The Sage of Ummah"). He is officially recognised as the "national poet" in Pakistan. The anniversary of his birth on November 9 is a holiday in Pakistan.

Hassan al-Banna

Hassan al-Banna (1906 -1949) was an Egyptian social and political reformer, best known for founding the Muslim Brotherhood, one of the largest and most influential 20th century Muslim revivalist organizations. Al-Bannas leadership was critical to the growth of the brotherhood during the 1930s and 1940s. In 1923, at the age of 16, Al-Banna moved to Cairo to enter the Dar al-Ulum college. Life in the capital offered him a greater range of activities than the village and the opportunity to meet prominent Islamic scholars (in large measure thanks to his father's acquaintances), but he was deeply disturbed by effects of Westernization he saw there, particularly the rise of secularism and the breakdown of traditional morals. The four years that Al-Banna spent in Cairo exposed him to the political ferment of the Egyptian capital in the early 1920s, and enhanced his awareness of the extent to which secular and Western ways had penetrated the very fabric of society. It was then that Al-Banna became particularly preoccupied with what he saw as the young generation's drift away from Islam.

He believed that the battle for the hearts and minds of the youth would prove critical to the survival of a religion besieged by a Western onslaught. While studying in Cairo, he immersed himself in the writings of the founders of Islamic reformism, including the Egyptian Muhammad Abduh, under whom his father had studied while at Al-Azhar. But it was Abduh's disciple, the Syrian Rashid Rida, who most influenced Al-Banna. Al-Banna was a dedicated reader of Al-Manar, the magazine that Rida published in Cairo from 1898 until his death in 1935.

He shared Ridas central concern with the decline of Islamic civilization relative to the West. He too believed that this trend could be reversed only by returning to an unadulterated form of Islam, free from all the accretions that had diluted the strength of its original message. Like Rida at the end of his life - but unlike Abduh and other Islamic modernists - Al-Banna felt that the main danger to Islam's survival in the modern age stemmed less from the conservatism of Al-Azhar and the Ulema (which he nevertheless criticized) than from the ascendancy of Western secular ideas. He was equally disappointed with what he saw as the failure of the Islamic scholars of al-Azhar University to voice their opposition to the rise of atheism and to the influence of Christian missionaries.

In his last year at Dar al-Ulum, he wrote that he had decided to dedicate himself to becoming "a counselor and a teacher" of adults and children, in order to teach them "the objectives of religion and the sources of their well-being and happiness in life". He graduated in 1927 and was given a position as an Arabic language teacher in a state primary school in Ishmaeliyya, a provincial town located in the Suez Canal Zone. It was to spread this message that Al-Banna launched the Society of the Muslim Brothers in March 1928. At first, the society was only one of the numerous small Islamic associations that existed at the time. Similar to those that Al-Banna himself had joined since he was 12, these associations aimed to promote personal piety and engaged in charitable activities.

By the late 1930s, it had established branches in every Egyptian province. A decade later, it had 500,000 active members and as many sympathizers in Egypt alone, while its appeal was now felt in several other countries as well. The society's growth was particularly pronounced after Al-Banna relocated its headquarters to Cairo in 1932. The single most important factor that made this dramatic expansion possible was the organizational and ideological leadership provided by Al-Banna.

In Ishmaeliyya, in addition to his day classes, he carried out his intention of giving night classes to his pupils' parents. He also preached in the mosque, and even in coffee-houses, which were then a novelty and were generally viewed as morally suspect. At first, some of his views on relatively minor points of Islamic practice led to strong disagreements with the local religious élite, and he adopted the policy of avoiding religious controversies. He was appalled by the many conspicuous signs of foreign military and economic domination in Ishmaeliyya: the British military camps, the public utilities owned by foreign interests, and the luxurious residences of the foreign employees of the Suez Canal Company, next to the squalid dwellings of the Egyptian workers.

He endeavored to bring about the changes he hoped for through institution-building, relentless activism at the grassroots level, and a reliance on mass communication. He proceeded to build a complex mass movement that featured sophisticated governance structures; sections in charge of furthering the society's values among peasants, workers, and professionals; units entrusted with key functions, including propagation of the message, liaison with the Islamic world, and press and translation; and specialized committees for finances and legal affairs.

In anchoring this organization into Egyptian society, Al-Banna relied on pre-existing social networks, in particular those built around mosques, Islamic welfare associations, and neighbourhood groups. This weaving of traditional ties into a distinctively modern structure was at the root of his success. Directly attached to the brotherhood, and feeding its expansion, were numerous businesses, clinics, and schools. In addition, members were affiliated to the movement through a series of cells, revealingly called usar (families. singular: usrah). The material, social and psychological support thus provided were instrumental to the movement's ability to generate enormous loyalty among its members and to attract new recruits. The services and organizational structure around which the society was built were intended to enable individuals to reintegrate into a distinctly Islamic setting, shaped by the society's own principles.

Rooted in Islam, Al-Bannas message tackled issues including colonialism, public health, educational policy, natural resources management, Marxism, social inequalities, Arab nationalism, the weakness of the Islamic world on the international scene, and the growing conflict in Palestine. By emphasizing concerns that appealed to a variety of constituencies, Al-Banna was able to recruit from among a cross-section of Egyptian society - though modern-educated civil servants, office employees, and professionals remained dominant among the organization's activists and decisionmakers.

Between 1948 and 1949, shortly after the society sent volunteers to fight in the war in Palestine, the conflict between the monarchy and the society reached its climax. Concerned with the increasing assertiveness and popularity of the brotherhood, as well as with rumors that it was plotting a coup, Prime Minister Mahmoud an-Nukrashi Pasha disbanded it in December 1948. The organization's assets were impounded and scores of its members sent to jail. Less than three weeks later, the prime minister was assassinated by a member of the brotherhood. This in turn prompted the assassination of Al-Banna, presumably by a government agent, in February 1949, when Al-Banna was still only 43 and at the height of his career.

REFORMERS IN MODERN PERIOD

Nasr Hamid Abu Zayd

Nasr Hamid Abu Zayd is an Egyptian Quranic thinker and one of the leading liberal theologists in Islam. He is famous for his project of a humanistic Quranic hermeneutics. From the beginning of his academic career, he developed a renewed hermeneutics view of the Quran and further Islamic holy texts, arguing that they should be interpreted in the historical and cultural context of their time. The mistake of many Muslim scholars was to see the Quran only as a text, which led conservatives as well as liberals to a battle of quotations, each groups seeing clear verses (when on their side) and ambiguous ones (when in contradiction with their vision). But this type of controversy led both conservatives and liberals to produce authoritative hermeneutics.

This vision of the Quran as a text was the vision of the elites of Muslim societies, whereas, at the same time, the Quran as a discourse played the most important part in the understanding of the masses. Nasr Abu Zayd calls for another lecture of the Holy book through a humanistic hermeneutics, an interpretation which sees the Quran as a living phenomenon, a discourse. Hence, the Quran can be "the outcome of dialogue, debate, despite, argument, acceptance and rejection". This liberal interpretation of Islam should open space for new perspectives on Islam and should account for social change in Muslim societies.

That is why Abu Zayd's analysis can find in the Quran several insistent calls for social justice. For instance, when Muhammad was busy preaching to the rich people of Quraysh, and did not pay attention to a poor blind fellow named Ibn Umm Maktûm who came asking the Prophet for advice, the Quran strongly blames Muhammad's attitude. As well, he finds a tendency to improve women's rights, arguing that the Quranic discourse was built in a patriarchal society, and therefore the addressee were naturally males, who received permission to marry, divorce, and marry off their female relatives, hence, it is possible to imagine that the Muslim females receive the same rights. The classical position of the modern ulama about that issue is understandable as "they still believe in superiority of the male in the family".

Abu Zayd promotes a view on modern Islamic thought by critically approaching classical and contemporary Islamic discourse in the field of theology, philosophy, law, politics and humanism. The aim of his research is to substantiate a theory of humanistic hermeneutics that might enable Muslims to build a bridge between their own tradition and the modern world of freedom of speech, equality (Minority rights, Women's rights, Social justice), human rights, democracy and globalisation.

Amina Wadud

Amina Wadud was born September 25, 1952 in Bethesda, Maryland. Her father was a Methodist minister and her mother descended from Muslim slaves of Arab, Berber and African ancestry dating back to the 8th Century. She is considered by many as a controversial Islamic feminist and scholar. She received her her B.S, from The University of Pennsylvania, between 1970 and 1975. In 1972 she pronounced shahadah and accepted Islam by choice, not knowing of her maternal ancestry. She received her M.A. in Near Eastern Studies and her Ph.D. in Arabic and Islamic Studies from the University of Michigan, in 1988. During graduate school, she studied advanced Arabic in Egypt at the American University in Cairo, she studied Quranic studies and tafsir at Cairo University, and took a course in Philosophy at Al-Azhar University.

She is currently visiting Scholar at the Starr King School of the Ministry, Berkeley CA. She achieved Full Professor of Islamic Studies at Virginia Commonwealth University (VCU) in Richmond, Virginia, in 2007. She is now retired from there as of 2008. She joined VCU after a three year contract as Assistant Professor at the International Islamic University Malaysia, between 1989 and 1993. Wadud's research specialities include gender and Quranic studies. She wrote a book on the subject, Quran and

Woman: Rereading the Sacred Text from a Woman's Perspective. The first edition of the book, published by Fajar Bakti, an Oxford University Press Subsidiary in Malaysia while one of the founding members of Sisters in Islam in Malaysia continues to be used all over the world as a basic text for activists and academics alike. After publishing her first book, she spoke at universities, grass roots level, government and non-government forum at various gatherings throughout the United States, Jordan, South Africa, Southern Africa, Nigeria, Kenya, Nepal, Pakistan, Indonesia, Canada, Denmark, Norway, Belgium,Netherlands, United Kingdom, Sarajevo, Spain, Malaysia, France, Italy, and Germany. Her latest book, Inside the Gender Jihad: Women's Reform in Islam, was published in 2006. It not only continues her Quranic analysis but also provides extensive details about her experiences as as Muslim, wife, mother, sister, scholar and activist.

Dr. Hassan Abd Allah al-Turabi

Dr. Hassan Abd Allah al-Turabi, commonly called Hassan al-Turabi (born 1932), is a religious and Islamist political leader in Sudan, who may have been instrumental in institutionalizing sharia in the northern part of the country. He has been called a "longtime hard-line ideological leader." Turabi was leader of the National Islamic Front, a politically powerful but not electorally popular political movement in Sudan. In 1979 he became Minister of Justice. In June 1989, a coup d'etat by allies, the "National Salvation Revolution", brought him and the National Islamic Front to power.

In March 1996 Turabi was elected to a seat in the National Assembly where he served as speaker of the National Assembly "during the 1990s." This period coincided with a decline in the influence of Turabi and his party's "internationalist and ideological wing" in favour of more pragmatic leaders, brought on by the imposition of UN sanctions on Sudan in punishment for Sudan's assistance to Egyptian terrorists in their attempt to assassinate Egyptian President Hosni Mubarak. Turabi was imprisoned in the Kobar (Cooper) prison in Khartoum on the orders of his one-time ally, current president Omar al-Bashir in March 2004. He was released on June 28, 2005.

Asma Jahangir

Asma Jilani Jahangir (born 1952) is a Pakistani lawyer and human rights activist. She has been the United Nations Special Rapporteur on Freedom of Religion or Belief since 2004 (first attached to the former Commission on Human Rights, now to the Human Rights Council).

Previously, she served as the UN Special Rapporteur on Extrajudicial, Arbitrary and Summary Executions. Born into a prosperous family with a history of activism (her father, Malik Jilani, was a former civil servant, entered politics upon retirement and spent time in jail and under house arrest for opposing military dictatorships), Jahangir herself became involved at a young age in protests against the military regime in Pakistan. She completed her law degree in 1978.

She cut her teeth during protests against the Hudood Ordinance put in place as part of Gen. Muhammad Zia-ul-Haq's Islamization program in Pakistan. She is a founding member of the Human Rights Commission of Pakistan, and has served as Secretary-General and later Chair of the organization. In 1980, Asma Jahangir and her sister, Hina Jilani, got together with few fellow activists and lawyers and formed the first law firm established by women in Pakistan. They also helped form the Women's Action Forum (WAF) in the same year. The first WAF demonstration was in 1983 when some 25-50 women took to the streets protesting the famous Safia Bibi case. Safia, a young blind girl, had been raped yet had ended up in jail on the charge of zina." In 1995, Jahangir received the Martin Ennals Award for Human Rights Defenders. In her capacity as a UN official, Jahangir was in Pakistan when a state of emergency was declared by President Pervez Musharraf.

REFERENCES

Anderson, J. N. D.: "Recent Reforms in the Islamic Law of Inheritance", *International and Comparative Law Quarterly*, 1965.

Arzu, Siraj-ad-din Ali Khan: *Tashòihò-i Ghara'ib al-lughat,* Cawnpore, 1868.

Brush, S. A.: "Ahmadiyyah in Pakistan", *MW*, 45 (1955), 145-71.

Burgess, J.: *The Muhammadan Architecture in Gujarat*, London, 1896.

Chishti, 'Abd-al-Hòalim: "Hasan ibn-Muhammad as-Saghani" in *Ma'arif,* Jan.-Sept. 1959.

Colebrook, H. T.: "On the Origin and Peculiar Tenets of Certain Muhammadan Sects", *Asiatic Researches*, vii (1801)

Cousens, H.: *Bijapur and its Architectural Remains*, Bombay, 1916.

Cragg, Kenneth: *Counsels in Contemporary Islam*, Edinburgh, 1965.

Crooke, W.: *Religion and Folklore of Northern India*, London, 1926.

Dames, M. Longworth: *Popular Poetry of the Baloches* London, 1907.

Dara Shukoh: *Safinat al-awhya'*, Urdu tr. Karachi, 1961.

Darmesteter, J.: *Chants populaires des Afghans*, Paris, 1888-90.

Daudpota, U. M.: *Sindhi Literature*, Karachi, 1951.

de Garcin Tassy: *Histoire de la Litterature Hindouie et Hindoustanie,* Paris, 1870.

Dörfer, Gerhard: *Türkische und mongolische Elemente in Neupersischen*, Wiesbaden, 1965.

Dughlat, Mirza Haydar: *Ta'rikh-i Rashidi,* Eng. tr. E. Denison Ross and N. Elias, London, 1898.

Dumasia, N. M.: *A Brief History of the Agha Khan*, Bombay, 1903.

Elliot, H. M. and Dowson, J.: *The History of India as Told by its Own Historians*, Allahabad, 1964.

Encyclopaedia of Islam, London, Leiden, 1960.

Encyclopaedia of Religion and Ethics, J. Hastings, Edinburgh, 1908-21.

Ethé, H.: *Catalogue of Persian Manuscripts in the India Office*, Oxford, 1903, 1937.

Faiz, Faiz Ahmad: *Poems*, tr. V. G. Kiernan, Delhi, 1958.

Hòjji Khalafa: *Kashf az-Zòunun,* Leipzig, 1835-52.

Hollister, J. N.: *The Shi'a of India*, London, 1953.

Hunter, W. W.: *The Indian Musalmans*, London, 1871.

Ibn-Kathir: *Al-Bidaya wa-n-nihaya,* Cairo, 1932-9.

Oman, J. C.: *The Mystics, Ascetics and Saints of India*, London, 1905.

Pakistan ki 'ilaqa'i zabanon par farsi ka athar, Karachi, n.d.

Philips, C. H.: *Historians of India, Pakistan and Ceylon*, London, 1961.

Punjab Notes and Queries, Allahabad, 1883-7.

11

Major Sects

Muslim factions are not simply sects or denominations, if it entails different approaches to the same faith. Members of one Muslim group don't generally accredit members of other groups as fellow Muslims, and open difference of opinion between sects is not unusual. Yet, in general, Islam is less divided than Christian religion and Jewish religion - the large majority of the world's Muslims are Sunnis. And Sufism is a mystical approach to Islam that is approved as orthodox by nearly all Muslims. Sunni Islam in most countries is dominant in the Middle East. Shiites on the other hand dominate Iran and are an absolute majority in Iraq. They are also authoritative in the Gulf states and a bulk in Baharain though the country is commanded by Shiites. Shiites are an crucial minority (fifteen percent) in Saudi Arabia. It is only in Western states and countries like India that Muslims enjoy true spiritual freedom and the right to exercise their faith freely and without worrying.

SUNNI ISLAM

Sunni Islam is the biggest denomination of Islam. The word Sunni comes from the word Sunnah, which entails the words and activities or example of the Islamic prophet Muhammad. Historically, Sunni Islam has often been specified only in counterpoint with other denominations or doctrines, such as Shia Islam, hanafiyah, Mu'tazila and others, believing itself to be the traditional form of Islam. As such, a case is sometimes made that Sunnism is as old as Islam itself, or at least dates back to the first civil war in Islam from 656 to 661. However, in terms of doctrine and theology, and in the sense of considering itself a separate denomination, Sunni Islam is younger than that, making it somewhat misleading to talk about Sunnites in a 7th century context. Sunni Islam was under the authority of the Caliph from Muhammad's death in 632 until the abolition of the caliphate by Mustafa Kemal Ataturk in 1924. Since then, no central international authority exists; many countries have a Grand Mufti or other official who holds the highest religious authority in the country.

However, during all of Islam's history, independent religious scholars, the ulama have held great influence in religious matters. During the first centuries of Islam, when the Umayyad and Abbasid caliphs were the worldly rulers of the Muslim world as well as the highest religious authorities of Sunni Islam, this led to some power struggles between the caliphate and the ulama. As the worldly power of the caliphate declined from the 9th and 10th century onwards, and as the religious law became more codified and exhaustive due to the efforts of the ulama, the caliphate's religious influence decreased as well. The precise portion of the world's Islamic population that binds to the various Shia sects, as contrary to the majority Sunni groups, is undetermined. Hence, employing several sources, one can arrive at an approximation of anywhere from a 7.5% to 10% Shiite counting on the sources.

Sunni Schools of Law

Sharia is known as the Islamic law. The Shariah is based on the Quran and the Sunnah, and those who attribute to different interpretings of the law can oftentimes be found attending to the same mosques. The four major Sunni schools of law:

- Hanafi School (established by Abu Hanifa)
- Maliki School (established by Malik ibn Anas)
- Shafi'i School (established by Muhammad ibn Idris ash-Shafii)
- Hanbali School (established by Ahmad bin Hanbal)

These four schools are slightly dissimilar from each other, but Sunni Muslims broadly believe them all equally legal. There are additional Sunni schools of law. Nevertheless, many are abided by by only low numbers of people and are comparatively anonymous due to the fame of the four major schools; also, many have failed out or were not sufficiently recorded by their followers to survive. Interpreting the Shariah to derive specific rulings (such as how to pray) is known as fiqh, which literally means understanding. A madhhab is a particular tradition of interpreting fiqh. These schools focus on specific evidence (Shafi'i and Hanbali) or general principles (Hanafi and Maliki) derived from specific evidences.

The schools were started by eminent Muslim scholars in the first four centuries of Islam. As these schools represent distinctly spelled out methodologies for interpreting the Shariaa, there has been little change in the methodology as such. Nevertheless, as the cultural and economical environment changes, new fiqh rulings are being made. The consensus is that the Shariah doesn't alter but fiqh rulings change all the time.

A madhhab isn't to be bemused with a religious order. There may be scholars comprising all four madhhabs living in bigger Muslim communities, and it is up to those who confer with them to decide which school they favour. Many Sunnis advocate that a Muslim should choose a single madhhab and follow it in all matters. However, rulings from another madhhab are considered acceptable as dispensations (rukhsa) in exceptional circumstances. Some Sunnis, however, do not follow any madhhab,. Indeed, some Salafis reject strict adherence to any particular school of thought, preferring to use the Quran and the Sunnah alone as the primary sources of Islamic law. Some Islamic scholars faced questions that they felt were not specifically answered in the Quran, particularly interrogatives with respect to philosophical conundra like the nature of God, the beingness of human free will, or the ageless beingness of the Quran. Various schools of theological system and philosophical system developed to answer these questions, each claiming to be true to the Quran and the Muslim tradition (sunnah). Amidst Sunnites, the following were the dominating traditions:

- Ashari, established by Abu al-Hasan al-Ashari (873-935). This theological system was adopted by Muslim scholars such as al-Ghazali. Ashariyyah theology accentuates divine revelation over human reason. Ethics, they say, cannot be derived from human reason: God's commands, as revealed in the Quran and the practice of Muhammad and his companions (the sunnah, as recorded in the traditions, or hadith), are the source of all morality. Regarding the nature of God and the divine attributes, the Ashari rejected the Mu'tazilite position that all Quranic references to God as having physical attributes (that is, a body) were metaphorical. Asharis asserted that these attributes were "true", since the Quran could not be in error, but that they were not to be implied as implying a coarse anthropomorphism. Asharis lean to stress divine omnipotence over human free will. They consider that the Quran is ageless and uncreated.
- Maturidiyyah, established by Abu Mansur al-Maturidi. Maturidiyyah was a minority custom until it was admitted by the Turkish clans of Central Asia (antecedently they had been Ashari and following of the Shafi school, it was entirely afterwards migration into Anatolia that they became Hanafi and

followers of the Maturidi credo). One of the tribes, the Seljuk Turks, migrated to Turkey, where later the Ottoman Empire was established. Their preferred school of law achieved a new prominence throughout their whole empire though it carried on to be followed almost entirely by followers of the Hanafi school while followers of the Shafi, Maliki, and Hanbali schools within the empire followed the Ashari school. Thus, where can be found Hanafi followers, there can be found the Maturidi creed.

The Quran as we have it now was composed by Muhammad's associates (Sahaba) in about 650, and is recognized by all Muslim denominations. However, there were many matters of belief and daily life that were not directly prescribed in the Quran, but were actions that were observed by the prophet and the community. Later generations sought out oral traditions regarding the early history of Islam, and the practice of Muhammad and his first followers, and wrote them down so that they might be preserved. These recorded oral traditions are called hadith. Muslim scholars sifted through the hadith and evaluated the chain of narration of each tradition, scrutinizing the trustworthiness of the narrators and judging the strength of each hadith accordingly. Most Sunni accept the hadith accumulations of Bukhari and Muslim as the most bona fide (sahih, or correct), and accord a small position to the collectings of other recorders. There are, nevertheless, four additional collections of hadith that are also held in special veneration by Sunni Muslims, making a total of six:

- Sahih al-Bukhari
- Sahih Muslim
- Sunan an-Nasaii
- Sunan Abu Dawud
- Sunan at-Tirmidhi
- Sunan ibn Majah

SHIA ISLAM

Shia Islam admits most Muslims who are not considered amongst the Sunni. The partition between Sunni and Shia, goes out to the death of the Prophet Muhammad when his followers were confronted with the decision of who'd be his heir as the leader of Islam. Shiites are those who followed Ali, the nearest relative of Muhammad, as Muhammad's heir. Today there are approximately 120 million Shi'ite Muslims in the world. The Shia consist of one major philosophical system known as the Jafaryia or the "Twelvers," and a couple of minor schools of thought, as the "Seveners" or the "Fivers." These names all advert to the number of imams they acknowledge after the death of Muhammad. The term Shia is generally meant to be similar with the Jafaryia/Twelvers.

Imamate

The distinguishing tenet and institution of Shia Islam is the Imamate, which includes the idea that the heir of Muhammad be more than merely a political leader. The Imam must also be a religious leader, which means that he must have the power to translate the interior secrets of the Quran and the Islamic law. The Twelver Shias further believe that the Twelve Imams who succeeded the Prophet were sinless and free from error and had been chosen by God through Muhammad. The Imamate began with Ali, who is also accepted by Sunni Muslims as the fourth of the "rightly guided caliphs" to succeed the Prophet. Shias venerate Ali as the First Imam, and his descendents, commencing with his sons Hasan and Husayn, carry on the line of the Imams until the Twelfth, who is considered to have ascended into a supernatural state to return to earth on Day of Judgment.

Shias point to the close lifespan connection of Muhammad with Ali. When Ali was six years old, he was asked over by the Prophet to live with him, and Shias consider Ali was the first individual to make the proclamation of trust in Islam. Ali also lived in Muhammad's bed on the night of the hijra, or migration from Mecca to Medina, when it was dreaded that the house would be assaulted by disbelievers and the Prophet stabbed to death. He fought in all the conflicts Muhammad did except one, and the Prophet chose him to be the husband of his favourite daughter, Fatima. In Sunni Islam an imam is the leader of congregational prayer. Among the Shias of Iran the term imam traditionally has been used only for Ali and his eleven descendants.

None of the Twelve Imams, with the exception of Ali, ever ruled an Islamic government. During their lifetimes, their followers hoped that they would assume the rulership of the Islamic community, a rule that was believed to have been wrongfully usurped. Because the Sunni caliphs were aware of this hope, the Imams generally were oppressed during the Umayyad and Abbasid dynasties. Therefore, the Imams tried to be as unnoticeable as possible and to live as far as was reasonable from the consecutive capitals of the Islamic empire.

During the 9th century Caliph Al Mamun, son of Caliph Harun ar Rashid, was favorably disposed toward the descendents of Ali and their followers. He welcomed the Eighth Imam, Reza (765-816), to come from Medina to his courtroom at Marv. While Reza was dwelling at Marv, Mamun delegated him as his heir in an evident effort to avoid conflict among Muslims. Rezas sister Fatima journeyed from Medina to be with her brother but took ill and died at Qom. A shrine developed around her tomb, and over the centuries Qom has become a major Shia pilgrimage and theology centre. Mamun took Reza on his military campaign to retake Baghdad from political rivals.

On this trip Reza died unexpectedly in Khorasan. Reza was the only Imam to reside or die in what is now Iran. A major shrine, and eventually the city of Mashhad, grew up around his tomb, which has become the most important pilgrimage centre in Iran. Several important theological schools are located in Mashhad, associated with the shrine of the Eighth Imam. Rezas abrupt demise was a blow to his followers, many of whom believed that Mamun, out of jealousy for Rezas expanding fame, had him poisoned. Mamun's suspected betrayal against Reza and his household tended to reinforce a feeling already prevailing amongst his followers that the Sunni rulers were untrusty.

The 12th Imam is thought to have been only five years old when the Imamate came upon him in 874 AD. at the demise of his father. The Twelfth Imam is commonly acknowledged by his titles of Imam-e Asr (the Imam of the Age) and Sahib az Zaman (the Lord of Time). Since his followers feared he might be assassinated, the Twelfth Imam was concealed from public view and was seen entirely by a few of his nearest deputies. Sunnis claim that he never existed or that he died while still a child. Shias believe that the Twelfth Imam remained on earth, but hidden from the public, for about 70 years, a period they refer to as the "lesser occultation" (gheybat-e sughra). Shias also believe that the Twelfth Imam has never died, but disappeared from earth in about 939 AD. Since that time the "greater occultation" (gheybat-e kubra) of the Twelfth Imam has been in force and will last until God bids the Twelfth Imam to apparent himself on earth once again as the Mahdi, or Messiah.

The Shia school of thought of the Imamate was not fully expounded until the 10th century. Other tenets were acquired still later. One characteristic of Shia Islam is the continual exposition and reinterpretation of doctrine. The most recent example is Khomeini's expounding of the doctrine of velayat-e faqih, or the political guardianship of the community of believers by scholars trained in religious law. The basic idea is that the clergy, by virtue of their superior knowledge of the laws of God, are the best qualified to rule the society of believers who are preparing themselves on earth to live eternally in heaven. The concept of velayat-e faqih thus provides the doctrinal basis for theocratic government, an experiment that Twelver Imam Shias had not attempted prior to the Iranian Revolution in 1979. In addition to the seven principal tenets of faith, there are also traditional religious practices that are intimately associated with Shia Islam. These include the observance of the month of martyrdom, Muharram, and pilgrimages to the shrines of the Twelve Imams and their various descendants. The Muharram observances, which culminate on the otherwise minor holiday of Ashura, commemorate the death of the Third Imam, Husayn, the son of Ali and Fatima and the grandson of Muhammad. He was killed near Karbala in contemporary Iraq in 680 AD. during a fight with troops supporting the Umayyad caliph. Husayn's death is immortalized by Shias with passion plays and is an intensely spiritual time.

Pilgrim's journey to the enshrines of Imams is a particular Shia custom. The most significant shrines in Iran are those for the Eighth Imam in Mashhad and for his sister Fatima in Qom. There are also important secondary shrines for other relatives of the Eighth Iman in Rey, adjacent to south Tehran, and in Shiraz. In virtually all towns and in many villages there are numerous lesser shrines, known as imamzadehs, which commemorate descendants of the imams who are reputed to have led saintly lives. Shia pilgrims visit these places because they think that the imams and their relatives have power to intercede with God on behalf of supplicants. The shrines in Iraq at Karbala and An Najaf are also venerated by Shias.

From the time that Twelver Shia Islam came forth as a clear-cut religious denomination in the early ninth century, its clergy, or ulama, have played a outstanding role in the evolution of its academic and legal tradition; however, the development of a distinct hierarchy among the Shia clergy dates back only to the early nineteenth century. Since that time the highest religious authority has been vested in the mujtahids, scholars who by virtue of their erudition in the science of religion (the Quran, the traditions of Muhammad and the imams, jurisprudence, and theology) and their attested ability to decide points of religious conduct, act as leaders of their community in matters concerning the particulars of religious duties. Lay Shias and small members of the clergy who lack such technique are asked to follow mujtahids in all matters referring to religion, but each believer is free to follow any mujtahid he selects.

Since the mid-nineteenth century it has been basal for a lot of mujtahids at the same time to attain prominence and to draw in large followings. During the twentieth century, such mujtahids have been allotted the title of ayatollah. Occasionally an ayatollah achieves almost universal authority among Shias and is given the title of ayatollah ol ozma, or grand ayatollah. Such authority was attained by as many as seven mujtahids simultaneously, including Ayatollah Khomeini, in the late 1970s. To become a mujtahid, it is necessary to complete a rigorous and lengthy course of religious studies in one of the prestigious madrasehs of Qom or Mashhad in Iran or An Najaf in Iraq and to receive an authorization from a qualified mujtahid. Of equal importance is either the explicit or the tacit recognition of a cleric as a mujtahid by laymen and scholars in the Shia community. There is no set time for studying a particular subject, but serious preparation to become a mujtahid normally requires fifteen years to master the religious subjects deemed essential. It is rare for any pupil to attain the status of mujtahid before the age of thirty; more ordinarily students are between forty and fifty years old when they attain this eminence.

Most seminary pupils do not finish the full programme of studies to become mujtahids. Those who leave the madrasehs after finishing the primary level can assist as prayer leaders, village mullahs, local shrine administrators, and other religious officials. Those who leave after completing the second level become preachers in town and city mosques. Students in the third level of study are those preparing to become mujtahids. The advanced students at this level are generally accorded the title of hojjatoleslam when they have completed all their studies. The Shia clergy in Iran wear a white turban and an aba, a loose, sleeveless brown cloak, open in front. A sayyid, who is a reverend descended from Muhammad, wears a black turban and a black aba.

Shah Ishmael, the founding father of the Safavid dynasty, who founded Twelver Shia Islam as the official religion of Iran at the beginning of the sixteenth century, was venerated by his followers as a Sufi master. Sufism, or Islamic mysticism, has a long custom in Iran. It developed there and in other areas of the Islamic empire during the ninth century among Muslims who believed that worldly pleasures distracted from true concern with the salvation of the soul. Sufis generally renounced materialism, which they believed supported and perpetuated political tyranny. Over time a great variety of Sufi brotherhoods was formed, including several that were militaristic, such as the Safavid order, of which Ishmael was the leader. Although Sufis were associated with the early spread of Shia ideas in the country, once the Shia clergy had consolidated their authority over religion by the early seventeenth century, they tended to regard Sufis as deviant. At various periods during the past three centuries some Shia clergy have encouraged persecution of Sufis, but Sufi orders have continued to exist in Iran. During the Pahlavi period, some Sufi brotherhoods were revitalized. Some members of the secularized middle class were especially attracted to them, but the orders appear to have had little following among the lower classes. The largest Sufi order was the Nimatollahi, which had khanehgahs, or teaching centres, in several cities and even established new centres in foreign countries. Early significant orders were the Dhahabi and Kharksar brotherhoods. Sufi fraternities such as the Naqshbandi and the Qadiri also subsisted amongst Sunni Muslims in Kordestan. There is no grounds of persecution of Sufis under the Republic, but the fraternities are considered suspicious and generally have kept a low visibility.

Iran also contains Shia sects that many of the Twelver Shia clergy look upon as unorthodox. Among these is the Ishmaeli, a sect that has several thousand disciples living chiefly in northeastern Iran. The Ishmaelis, of whom there were once several different sects, trace their origins to the son of Ishmael who predeceased his father, the Sixth Imam. The Ishmaelis were very numerous and active in Iran from the eleventh to the thirteenth century; they are known in history as the "Assassins" because of their practice of killing political opponents.

The Mongols destroyed their centre at Alamut in the Alborz Mountains in 1256. Subsequently, their living imams went into hiding from non-Ishmaelis. In the nineteenth century, their leader emerged in public as the Agha Khan and fled to British-controlled India, where he supervised the revitalization of the sect. The majority of the several million Ishmaelis in the live outside Iran. Another Shia sect is the Ahl-e Haqq. Its adherents are concentrated in Lorestan, but small communities also are found in Kordestan and Mazandaran. The origins of the Ahl-e Haqq are considered to lie in one of the mediaeval politicized Sufi orders. The group has been oppressed periodically by orthodox Shias. After the Revolution, some of the faction leaders were jailed on the ground of religious aberrance.

AHMADIYYA ISLAM

The Ahmadiyya Muslim Community is the larger community of the two arising from the Ahmadiyya movement founded in 1889 by Mirza Ghulam Ahmad of Qadian (1835-1908). The original movement split into two factions soon after the death of the founder. (The second branch is Lahore Ahmadiyya Movement, Ahmadiyya Anjuman Ishaat-i-Islam.) The Ahmadiyya Muslim Community is guided by the Khalifa (Caliph), currently Khalifatul Masih V, who is believed to be the spiritual leader of Ahmadis and the successor to Mirza Ghulam Ahmad. He is called the Khalifatul Masih (successor of the Messiah). Mirza Ghulam Ahmad was the founder of the Ahmadiyya movement. He declared that he was the "Promised One" of all religions, fulfilling the messianic prophecies found in world religions. He stated that his claims to being several messiahs converging into one person were the symbolic, rather than literal, fulfillment of the messianic and eschatological prophecies found in the literature of the major religions. The motto of the Ahmadiyya Muslim Community is "Love for All Hatred for None".

The Ahmadiyya Muslim Community is based upon one essential doctrine of unity which is split into three categories: Unity of God, Unity of Religion, Unity of Mankind. The Ahmadiyya writings describe a single, imperishable God, the creator of all things, including all the creatures and forces in the universe who is a Perfect Being. The existence of God is thought to be eternal, without a beginning or end, and is described as "a Living God" which means that he manifests himself everywhere, loves his creation, listens to their supplication, answers their prayers and speaks to them as he did in ages past. There is, according to Ahmadiyya belief, no intercession with God. In Ahmadiyya belief, God expresses His will in many ways, including through a series of Divine Messengers which are given to different peoples in different parts of the world. In expressing God's intent, these Divine Messengers are seen to establish religion in the world and to enable a relationship with God.

Ahmadiyya teachings state that God is too great for humans to fully comprehend, or to create a complete and accurate image, by themselves; human understanding of God is through his revelation via his Prophets. There is a strong emphasis on monotheism and Ahmadiyya does not adhere to any beliefs which distort this monotheism in any way (incarnations, polytheism, pantheism etc.). According to the Ahmadiyya teachings, the purpose of all things' creation is to worship God which is in accordance with the principle set out in the Quran. Though, according to Ahmadiyya belief, God has unlimited attributes, the Quran states 99 of these for God.

Thus, in accordance with Ahmadiyya belief, in order to fulfill the purpose of life, that is to worship God, one must mimic his attributes which are able to be copied, for example the attribute of Al-Wali or 'The Friend'. As according to Ahmadiyya belief, only the Prophets who were sent by God were fully able to mimic his attributes, and among them, only the Prophet of Islam, Muhammad, was able to fully mimic his attributes, then the Ahmadiyya deems it necessary to mimic the Prophets; by doing so, they are mimicking the attributes of God which are manifest in the Prophets. Ahmadiyya literature reveals a metaphor in which God is the sun atop of a lake and that the reflection of the sun on the lake is the Prophet.

The Ahmadiyya belief in God states that Allah is the proper name for God in Arabic, which literally means "the God" though the concept of God exists in other religions also and as a result of the Ahmadiyya belief of the Unity of Religions, the equivalent of the term Allah is also: El of the Canaanites, Elohim or Yahweh (Jehovah) of the Jews, Elah in the Aramaic language of Jesus Christ, Yazdan or Khuda of the Persian language, Ahura Mazda of the Zoroastrians, Brahman in Sankrit (of the Hindus), Deus in Latin, Theos in Greek, Dieu in French, Gott in German, God in English and others. Ahmadis believe in the five articles of faith believed in also by most Muslims but with some doctrinal differences. Ahmadis have a six article of faith called 'Taqdeer' or 'pre-destination' not believed in by most Orthodox Muslims as an article of faith.

1. Unity of God (Tauhid)
2. Angels (Malaikah)
3. Books
4. Prophets
5. The Day of Judgment
6. Divine Decree (Taqdir)

SUFISM

Sufism is less an Islamic sect than a mystical way of approaching the Islamic faith. It has been defined as "mystical Islamic belief and practice in which Muslims seek to find the truth of divine love and knowledge through direct personal experience of God." Islamic mystics are called Sufis and their way of life is Sufism. These terms evolved in Western languages in the early 19th century and derive from the Arabic term for a mystic, sufi, which in turn derives from suf, "wool." This likely refers to the woollen garment of early Islamic ascetics. Similarly, Islamic mysticism in general is called tasawwuf (to dress in wool) in

Arabic. Sufis are also referred to as fuqara, "the poor," the plural form of the Arabic faqir. The Persian equivalent is darvish. These are the roots of the English terms fakir and dervish, used interchangeably for an Islamic mystic.

Sufism has been a prominent movement within Islam throughout most of its history. It grew out of an early ascetic movement within Islam, which, like its Christian monastic counterpart, sought to counteract the worldiness that came with the rapid expansion of the Muslim community. The earliest form of Sufism arose under the Umayyad Dynasty (661-749) less than a century after the founding of Islam. Mystics of this period meditated on the Doomsday passages in the Quran, thereby earning such nicknames as "those who always weep." These early Sufis led a life of strict obedience to Islamic scripture and tradition and were known for their night prayers. Many of them concentrated their efforts upon tawakkul, absolute trust in God, which became a central concept of Sufism. Another century or so later, a new emphasis on love changed asceticism into mysticism. This development is attributed to Rabiah al-Adawiyah (d. 801), a woman from Basra who formulated the Sufi ideal of a pure love of God that was disinterested, without hope for Paradise or fear of Hell.

Other important developments soon followed, including strict self-control, psychological insight, "interior knowledge," annihilation of the self, mystical insights about the nature of man and the Prophet, hymns and poetry. This period, from about 800-1100 AD. is referred to as classical Sufism or classical mysticism. The next important stage in Sufi history was the development of fraternal orders, in which disciples followed the teachings of a leader-founder. The 13th century is considered the golden age of Sufism, in which some of the greatest mystical poetry was composed. Important figures from this period include Ibn alArabi of Spain, Ibn al-Farid of Egypt, Jalal ad-Din ar-Rumi of Persia, and Najmuddin Kubra of Central Asia.

By this time, Sufism had permeated the whole of the Islamic world and played a large role in the shaping of Islamic society. Sufi beliefs are based firmly in orthodox Islam and the text of the Quran, although a few Sufi teachers have strayed too close to monism or pantheism to remain within the orthodox fold. The core principles of Sufism are tawakkul (absolute trust in God) and tawhid (the truth that there is no deity but God). Tawhid is rich in meaning for mystics: it has been interpreted by some as meaning that nothing truly exists but God or that nature and God are but two aspects of the same reality. The love of God for man and the love of man for God are also very central to Sufism, and are the subjects of most Islamic mystical poetry and hymns.

Sufi practices have their foundation in purity of life, strict obedience to Islamic law and imitation of the Prophet. Through self-denial, careful introspection and mental struggle, Sufis hope to purify the self from all selfishness, thus attaining ikhlas, absolute purity of intention and act. "Little sleep, little talk, little food" are fundamental and fasting is considered one of the most important preparations for the spiritual life. Mystical experience of the divine is also central to Sufism. Sufis are distinguished from other Muslims by their fervent seeking of dhawq, a "tasting" that leads to an illumination beyond standard forms of learning. However, the insight gained by such experience is not valid if it contradicts the Quran.

The Sufi way of life is called a tariqah, "path." The path begins with repentance and submission to a guide (sheikh or pir). If accepted by the guide, the seeker becomes a disciple (murid) and is given instructions for asceticism and meditation. This usually includes sexual abstinence, fasting and poverty. The ulimate goal of the Sufi path is to fight the true Holy War against the lower self, which is often represented as a black dog. On his way to illumination the mystic will undergo such changing spiritual states (hal) as qabd and bast, constraint and happy spiritual expansion, fear and hope, and longing and intimacy, which are granted by God and change in intensity according to the spiritual "station" in which the mystic is abiding at the moment.

The culmination of the path is marifah (interior knowledge, gnosis) or mahabbah (love), which implies a union of lover and beloved (man and God). The final goal is annihilation (fana), primarily of one's own qualities but sometimes of one's entire personality. This is often accompanied by spiritual ecstasy or "intoxication."

After the annihilation of the self and accompanying ecstatic experience, the mystic enters a "second sobriety" in which he re-enters the world and continues the "journey of God." A central method on the Sufi path is a ritual prayer or dhikr ("remembrance", derived from the Quranic injunction to remember God often in Surah 62:10). It consists in a repetition of either one or all of the most beautiful names of God, of the name "Allah," or of a certain religious formula, such as the profession of faith: "There is no God but Allah and Muhammad is his prophet." A rosary of 99 or 33 beads has been in use since as early as the 8th century for counting the thousands of repetitions. In the mid-9th century some mystics introduced sessions with music and poetry recitals (sama) in

Baghdad in order to reach the ecstatic experience-and since then debates about the permissibility of sama, filling many books, have been written. Narcotics were used in periods of degeneration, coffee by the "sober" mystics (first by the Shadhiliyah after 1300).

Mystical sessions of music and poetry called sama (or sema) were introduced in Baghdad in the mid-9th century with the purpose of achieving an ecstatic experience. Narcotics have sometimes been introduced as part of the method, but this is considered a degeneration of the practice. The well-known "Whirling Dervishes" are members of the Mevlevi order of Turkish Sufis, based on the teachings of the famous mystic Rumi (d.1273). The practice of spinning around is the group's distinctive form of sama. The whirlers, called semazens, are practicing a form of meditation in which they seek to abandon the self and contemplate God, sometimes achieving an ectastic state.

The Mevlevi sect was banned in Turkey by Ataturk in 1925, but performances for tourists are still common throughout the country. The clothing worn for the ritual and the positions of the body during the spinning are highly symbolic: for instance, the tall camel-hair hat represents the tomb of the ego, the white cloak represents the ego's shroud, and the uplifted right hand indicates readiness to receive grace from God.

REFERENCES

Asad-Allah Tilhari: *Quwwat-i Hòanafiyya, Bada'un,* 1905.

Asbraf 'Ali Thanawi: *al-Intibahat al-mufida'an al-ishtibahat al-jadida,* Lahore, 1952.

Baloch, Nabi Bakhsh Khan: "The Diwan of Abu 'Atòa of Sind", *IC,* xxiii (1949), 136-50.

Barani, Diya'-ad-din: *Ta'rikh-i Firuz Shahi,* Calcutta, 1862.

Bashir al-din Mahòmud Ahòmad: *Introduction* to Shir 'Ali Eng. tr. *of The Holy Quran*, Rabwah, 1955.

Bausani, A.: "Note su Shah Waliullah di Dehli", *Annali*, n.s., 1961.

Bernier, F.: *Travels in Mughal India*, Eng. tr. London, 1891.

Binder, L.: *Religion and Politics in Pakistan*, Berkeley, 1961.

Binyon, L.: *The Court Painters of the Great Moghuls*, London, 1921.

Blumhardt, J. F.: *Catalogue of the Hindustani Manuscripts in the Library of the India Office*, Oxford, 1926.

Brahman, Chandra Bhan: *Chahar Chaman*, BM Add. MS 16. 863.

Bray, D.: *Census Report: Baluchistan*, Calcutta, 1913.

Brockelmann, C.: *Geschichte der arabischen Literatur*, second edition, two vols., Leiden, 1943, 1949; three supplementary vols., Leiden, 1937-42.

Brown, Percy: *Indian Architecture (Islamic Period)*, Bombay, 1958.

Brush, S. A.: "Ahmadiyyah in Pakistan", *MW*, 45 (1955), 145-71.

Burgess, J.: *The Muhammadan Architecture in Gujarat*, London, 1896.

Campbell, J. M.: *The Bombay Gazetteer*, Bombay, 1874-1904.

Chatterji, S. K.: *Indo-Aryan and Hindi*, Ahmadabad, 1942.

Chiragh 'Ali: *Rasd'il,* Hyderabad, 1918-19.

I'jaz Husayn: *Mukhtasar ta'rikh-i adab-i Urdu,* Karachi, 1956.

Ibn-Nadim: *Al-Fihrist* (ed. Flügel), Leipzig, 1871-2.

Ibrahim 'Adil Shah 11: *Nawras* (ed. Nazir Ahmad), Lucknow, 1955.

Ibrahim Mir Siyalkoti: *Ta'rikh-i ahl-i adith,* Lahore, 1953.

Qadiri, Shams-ad-din: *Urda-yi qadim,* Lucknow, 1930.

Qani', Ali Shir: *Tuhòfat al-karam,* Delhi, 1886.

Qidwa'i, J. A.: *Pashto Adab*, Karachi, 1951.

Qurayshi, 'Abd-ar-Razzaq: *Mirza Maz'har Jan-i Janan awr unka Urdu kalam*, Bombay, 1961.

12

Demographic Propagation

Approximation of the Muslim population (in year 2007) range from 1 billion to 1.8 billion in entire world. Around 85% are Sunni and 15% are Shia, with a small minority belonging to other factions. Some thirty-forty states are Muslim-majority, and Arabs account for around 20% of all Muslims worldwide. South Asia and Southeast Asia contain the most inhabited Muslim countries, with Indonesia, India, Pakistan, and Bangladesh bearing more than 100 million disciples to each one. According to U.S. government figures, in 2006 there were 20 million Muslims in China. In the Mideast, the non-Arab countries of Republic of Turkey and Islamic Republic of Iran are the largest Muslim-majority states; in Africa, Egypt and Nigeria have the most populous Muslim communities. Islam is the second largest religion after Christian religion in many European states.

ORIGIN

Muhammad was born in about 570 AD. in the settlement of Mecca, on the seacoast of the Red Sea of Saudi Arabia. He was the son of an Arabian merchant. And when he maturated up he had to accept the family business. At that time merchants in Mecca were prosperous. In Mecca there was a lot of money to be made out of the pilgrims who came from all over the east to visit the Kaabah. Built of three layers of stone, the Kabbah isbelieved to have been built by Abraham and his son Ishmael. Muhammad was already acknowledged to be very earnest, dependable and kind. These traits also left a mark over his professional life. Muhammad was agitated by the way masses around him led their life - specially the religious life.

His tribesmen, though Semite, like the Hebrews, had been riddled by irrational beliefs, and numerosity of faiths. They had an mixture of gods, whose effigies they engraved and idolized with unusual kinds of practices.

There was no uniformness in the faith. Nor was any discipline in the spiritual life. And Muhammad wanted to change all these. It is believed that Muhammad was one day visited by the archangel Gabriel who brought message from God, or in his language, Allah. Inspired by Allah, Muhammad chose to give up the occupation and went for a life of religious empowerment. It then committed himself to supplication, meditation, discourse and aiding the hapless. He was then around forty.

Muhammad disapproved the Arabs for idolizing a horde of gods, and told his hearings that Allah was the one and only true God. At first Muhammad's commandments annoyed the Arabs. Yet, unshaken, Muhammad carried on with his preaching. The situation turned so worse that his life was at stake. Following this, Muhammad had to leave his native town of Mecca. He journeyed further north to Medina. This emigration from Mecca to Medina in 622 AD. is an important milestone in the history of Islam. The year of the emigration is called Hegira. And it is the starting point from which the Muslim Era, called Hegira, is computed. Medina, however, welcomed his ideas. And Muhammad found a favourable climate for preaching and spreading his teachings. And he acquired a following of disciples. He preached rules of good and kind behaviour.

Ten years passed and Muhammad had attracted a sizeable number of diehard followers. This even included a humble but committed corps ready to fight to the end to defend his ideas. And Muhammad's religion became known as the Islamic religion and his followers were called Muslims. Islam spread when Muhammad's commandments were set down in a book called the Quran. This is the most sanctified book to the Muslims. Quran holds all the revelations that Muhammad received from Allah over a period of 23 years. According to Islamic history, after Prophet Muhammad's death, they were compiled under the direction of the first Sunni Caliph Abu Bakr about 1,400 years ago. And this is what we see in the present day's Quran. Muhammad taught his followers to destruct all his personal material possession when he died. Because, he considered that none but Allah should be revered. This is why Islam prohibits any form of idolism and god worship. In flow of time Islam took on believers all over the world.

EARLY RISE

Islam's historic evolution resulted in major political, economical, and military effects inside and outside the Muslim world. Within a century of Muhammad's first recitals of the Quran, an Islamic empire extended from the Atlantic Ocean in the west to Central Asia in the east. This new polity soon broke into civil war, and successor states fought each other and outside forces. However, Islam continued to spread into regions like Africa, the Indian subcontinent, and Southeast Asia. The Islamic civilization was one of the most advanced in the world during the Middle Ages, but was surpassed by Europe with the economic and military growth of the West. During the 18th and 19th centuries, Islamic dynasties such as the Ottomans and Mughals fell into the swing of European imperial powers. In the twentieth century fresh spiritual and governmental movements and new riches in the Muslim world led to both reincarnation and struggle.

Muhammad set about advocating Islam at Mecca before transmigrating to Medina, from where he combined the clans of Arabia into a single Arab Muslim sacred civil order. With Muhammad's demise in 632, discrepancy broke out over who would succeed him as leader of the Muslim community. Umar ibn al-Khattab, a prominent companion of Muhammad, nominated Abu Bakr, who was Muhammad's intimate friend and collaborator. Others added their support and Abu Bakr was made the first caliph. This choice was disputed by some of Muhammad's companions, who held that Ali ibn Abi Talib, his cousin and son-in-law, had been designated his successor. Abu Bakr's straightaway task was to retaliate a late defeat by Byzantine forces, although he first had to bring down an insurrection by Arab tribes in an episode known as the Ridda wars, or "Wars of Apostasy".

His demise in 634 ensued in the taking over of Umar as the caliph, followed by Uthman ibn al-Affan and Ali ibn Abi Talib. These four are known as al-khulafa ar-rashidun ("justifiedly Guided Caliphs"). Under them, the territorial dominion under Muslim rule expanded deeply into Persian and Byzantine territories. When Umar was assassinated in 644, the election of Uthman as successor was met with increasing opposition. In 656, Uthman was also killed, and Ali assumed the position of caliph. After driving back opposition in the first civil war (the "First Fitna"), Ali was assassinated by Kharijites in 661. Following this, Muawiyah, who was governor of Levant, captured power and began the Umayyad dynasty.

These conflicts over spiritual and political leadership would bring about to split in the Muslim community. The absolute majority accepted the authenticity of the three rulers before Ali, and became known as Sunnis. A minority differed, and considered that Ali was the only lawful successor; they became known as the Shia. After Muawiyah's death in 680, conflict over succession broke out again in a civil war known as the "Second Fitna". Afterward, the Umayyad dynasty prevailed for seventy years, and was able to conquer the Maghrib and Al-Andalus in the west as well as expand Muslim territory into Sindh and the fringes of Central Asia. While the Muslim-Arab elite engaged in conquest, some devout Muslims began to question the piety of indulgence in a worldly life, emphasizing rather poverty, humility and avoidance of sin based on renunciation of bodily desires. Pious Islamic ascetical exemplars such as Hasan al-Basri would inspire a social movement that would develop into Sufism.

For the Umayyad nobility, Islam was deemed a faith for Arabs only; the economic system of the Umayyad empire was established on the assumption that a absolute majority of non-Muslims (Dhimmis) would pay taxes to the minority of Muslim Arabs. A non-Arab who wanted to convert to Islam was supposed to first become a client of an Arab tribe. Even after conversion, these new Muslims (mawali) did not achieve social and economic equality with the Arabs. The descendants of Muhammad's uncle Abbas ibn Abd al-Muttalib rallied discontented mawali, poor Arabs, and some Shia against the Umayyads and overthrew them with the help of their propagandist and general Abu Muslim, inaugurating the Abbasid dynasty in 750. Under the Abbasids, Islamic civilization boomed in the "Islamic gold Age", with its capital at the cosmopolite city of Baghdad.

Through the late 9th century, the Abbasid caliphate started to break as several areas gained increasing stages of autonomy. Across North Africa, Persian Empire, and Central Asia emirates constituted as states broke away. The massive Arab empire broke down to a more religiously homogenised Muslim world where the Shia Fatimids contested even the religious authority of the caliphate. By 1055 the Seljuq Turks had eliminated the Abbasids as a military power, nevertheless they continued to respect the caliph's titular authority. During this time expansion of the Muslim world continued, by both conquest and peaceful proselytism even as both Islam and Muslim trade networks were extending into sub-Saharan West Africa, Central Asia, Volga Bulgaria and the Malay archipelago.

The Golden Age saw new legal, philosophical, and religious developments. The major hadith collections were compiled and the four modern Sunni Madh'habs were established. Islamic law was advanced greatly by the efforts of the early 9th century jurist al-Shafi'i; he codified a method to establish the reliability of hadith, a topic which had been a locus of dispute among Islamic scholars. Philosophers Ibn Sina (Avicenna) and Al-Farabi sought to incorporate Greek principles into Islamic theology, while others like the 11th century theologian Abu Hamid al-Ghazzali argued against them and ultimately prevailed. Finally, Sufism and Shi'ism both experienced major alterations in the 9th century. Sufism turned a fully fledged movement that had moved towards religious mysticism and away from its austere roots, while Shi'ism break up due to disagreements over the succession of Imams.

The spread of the Muslim territorial dominion brought on antagonism among medieval ecclesiastic Christian writers who saw Islam as an antagonist in the light of the battalions of new Muslim converts. This opposition resulted in polemic treatises which depicted Islam as the religion of the antichrist and of Muslims as libidinous and subhuman. In the medieval period, a few Arab philosophers like the poet Al-Maarri adopted a critical approach to Islam, and the Jewish philosopher Maimonides contrasted Islamic views of morality to Jewish views that he himself elaborated. Starting in the 9th century, Muslim conquests in the West began to be reversed. The Reconquista was launched against Muslim principalities in Iberia, and Muslim Italian possessions were lost to the Normans. From the 11th century onwards alliances of European Christian kingdoms mobilized to launch a series of wars known as the Crusades, bringing the Muslim world into conflict with Christendom.

Initially successful in their goal of taking the Holy land, and establishing the Crusader states, Crusader gains in the Holy Land were later reversed by subsequent Muslim generals such as Saladin; who recaptured Jerusalem during the Second Crusade. In the east the Mongol Empire put an end to the Abbassid dynasty at the Battle of Baghdad in 1258, as they overran in Muslim lands in a series of invasions. Meanwhile in Egypt, the slave-soldier Mamluks took control in an uprising in 1250 and in alliance with the Golden Horde were able to halt the Mongol armies at the Battle of Ain Jalut. Mongol rule extended across the breadth of almost all Muslim lands in Asia and Islam was temporarily replaced by Buddhism as the official religion of the land. Over the following century the Mongolian Khanates converted to Islam and this religious and ethnical absorption ushered in a new age of Mongol-Islamic deduction that shaped the further spread of Islam in central Asia and the Indian subcontinent.

The Seljuk Turks captured Abbassid lands and acquired Islam and become the actual rulers of the caliphate. They conquered Anatolia by defeating the Byzantines at the Battle of Manzikert, thereby precipitating the call for Crusades. They nevertheless broke rapidly in the second half of the 12th century producing various semi-autonomous Turkic dynasties. In the 13th and 14th centuries the Ottoman empire (named after Osman I) emerged from among these "Ghazi emirates" and established itself after a string of conquests that included the Balkans, parts of Greece, and western Anatolia. In 1453 under Mehmed II the Ottomans laid siege to Constantinople, the capital of Byzantium, which buckled shortly thereafter, having been deluged by a far greater number of Ottoman troops and to a little extent, cannonry.

Commencing in the 13th century, Sufism experienced a transformation, largely as a result of the efforts of al-Ghazzali to legitimize and reorganize the movement. He developed the model of the Sufi order- a community of spiritual teachers and students. Also of importance to Sufism was the creation of the Masnavi, a collection of mystical poetry by the 13th century Persian poet Rumi. The Masnavi had a deep influence on the development of Sufi religious thought; to many Sufis it is second in grandness only to the Quran. In the early 16th century, the Shi'i Safavid dynasty acquired control in Persia and built Shia Islam as an official faith there, and in spite of periodical setbacks, the Safavids remained all-powerful for two centuries. Meanwhile, Mamluk Egypt fell to the Ottomans in 1517, who then launched a European campaign which reached as far as the gates of Vienna in 1529.

After the invasion of Persia, and sack of Baghdad by the Mongols in 1258, Delhi became the most important cultural centre of the Muslim east. Many Islamic dynasties ruled parts of the Indian subcontinent starting from the 12th century. The prominent ones include the Delhi Sultanate (1206-1526) and the Mughal empire (1526-1857). These empires helped in the spread of Islam in South Asia, but by the early-18th century the Maratha empire became the pre-eminent power in the north of India. By the mid-18th century the British empire had formally ended the Mughal dynasty,, and at the end of the 18th century overthrew the Muslim-ruled Kingdom of Mysore. In the 18th century the Wahhabi movement took hold in Saudi Arabia. Established by the preacher Ibn Abd al-Wahhab, Wahhabism is a fundamentalistic political theory that decries practices like Sufism and the reverence of saints as un-Islamic.

By the seventeenth and eighteenth centuries, in spite of attempts at modernisation, the Turkish Empire had begun to feel threatened by European economical and military advantages. In the 19th century, the rise of nationalism resulted in Greece declaring and winning independence in 1829, with several Balkan states following suit after the Ottomans suffered defeat in the Russo-Turkish War of 1877-1878. The Ottoman era came to a close at the end of World War I and the Caliphate was abolished in 1924. In the 19th century, the Salafi, Deobandi and Barelwi movements were initiated. By the early years of the 20th century, most of the Muslim world outside the Ottoman empire had been absorbed into the empires of non-Islamic European powers.

After World War I losses, nearly all of the Ottoman empire was also parceled out as European protectorates or spheres of influence. In the course of the 20th century, most of these European-ruled territories became independent, and new issues such as oil wealth and relations with the State of Israel have assumed prominence. During this time, many Muslims migrated, as indentured servants, from mostly India and Indonesia to the Caribbean, forming the largest Muslim populations by percentage in the Americas. Additionally, the resulting urbanization and increase in trade in Africa brought Muslims to settle in new areas and spread their faith. As a consequence, Islam in sub-Saharan Africa likely doubled between 1869 and 1914. The Organization of the Islamic Conference (OIC), comprising of Muslim countries, was officially constituted in September 1969 after the burning of the Al-Aqsa Mosque in Jerusalem.

FACTORS RESPONSIBLE FOR RISE

The warfares of Islam in the Prophet's lifespan and in the lifetime of his direct heirs were all begun in self-protection, and were engaged with a humanity and thoughtfulness for the enemy. It wasn't the martial artistry of the early Muslims which enabled them to capture half the then known world and convert half that world so firmly that changeover stands unshaken to this day. It was their righteousness and their humanity, their manifest superiority in these respects of other men. At that time, Egyptians, Syrians, Mesopotamians and the Persians were slaves. And they had always been in that condition. The coming of Christianity to some countries had not improved their status. There was luxury among the nobles, and plenty of that kind of culture which is symptomatic, not of progress, but of corruption and decay.

The condition of the multitude was pitiable. The tidings of our Prophet's embassies to all neighbouring rulers, inviting them to give up superstition, abolish priesthood and agree to serve Allah only, and the evil treatment given to his envoys, made an impact in all those countries. The multitude was no doubt warned that Islam was something devilish and that the Muslims would destroy them. And then the Muslims swept into the land as conquerors, and by their conduct won the hearts of all those people. In the entire history of the world until then, the conquered had been absolutely at the mercy of the conqueror. No matter how complete his submission might be no matter if he was of the same religion as the conqueror. That is still the theory of war outside Islam. But it is not the Islamic theory. According to the Muslim Laws of War, those of the conquered people, who embraced Islam, became the equals of the conquerors in all respects.

The Muslims intermarried freely with the conquered people of Egypt, Syria, Mesopotamia, Persia and all North Africa - something none of their conquerors had ever done before. The advent of Islam brought them not only political freedom but also intellectual freedom, since he dispelled the blighting shadow of the priest from human thought. The citizenry of all those states, except Persian Empire, now claim Arabic as their indigenous language and, if called into question as to their nationality, would say, 'we are sons of the Arabs.' They all still consider the empire of Islamism as the realm of God on earth.

The consequence was what could be anticipated from so great a release of people who had never really had a chance before: a wonderful flowering of civilization that in the subsequent generations bore its fruit in works of science, art and literature. In spite of the incessant wars, this is the most joyous period in history. In judging it, you must not take every word literally that you may read from European writers. You must make allowances for enemy propaganda then and now.

The people, in a long period of uninterrupted prosperity, became unwarlike. There were little wars within the empire now and then. The defence of the frontier was confined to the fighting tribes, chiefly the Turks, who also formed the bodyguard of the Khalifa. These people soon became the masters, from guardians of the nominal rulers. They were men of simple, downright brutal character, of energy and common sense, who did not hide their contempt of the luxurious and feeble princes who succeeded one another on the throne of the great Mamun and Harun-ar-Rashid. One after another, they murdered or put them away with every circumstance of ignominy, but they did impregnate some humanness into the declining empire, which would have expired but for them, and keep at any rate its central states collectively in good order. Over the far provinces the Khalifas rule was now strictly formal.

Nominally, the Abbasid Khilafat of Baghdad lived on for a full five hundred years, but for the last three hundred and fifty years of its nominative length, the real autonomous power had passed to the Turks already, and its political prestigiousness was that of Turkish chiefs, and then of the Ayubis, Malik Adil, Malik Kamil and the rest. There was change of rulers, but the civilisation remained that of the Abbasids. Indeed it hardly, if that all, deteriorated and the condition of the common people throughout the Muslim empire remained superior to that of any other people in the world in education, sanitation, public security and general liberty. It's material prosperity was the envy of the Western world, whose merchant corporations vied with one another for the privilege of trading with it. In other countries, even in Europe, in the same period, the peasantry were serfs bound to the land they cultivated. The artisans still had a servile status, and the mercantile communities were only just beginning, by dint of cringing and of bribery, to gain certain privileges.

In the Muslim realm the merchants and the peasant and the artisan were all free men. It is true that there were slaves, but the slaves were the most fortunate of people. It was not unusual for a man who had no male descendant to marry his daughter to his slave who then take his name and carry on the honour of his house. The devotion of the slaves to their owners and the favour of which the master showed the slaves became proverbial. No colour or race prejudice existed in Islam. All people mingled in its markets and mosques and places upon a footing of complete equality and friendliness.

Some of the greatest rulers, saints and stages in Islam have been men as black as coal, like Jayyash, the saintly king of Yemen in the period of the Abbasid decline, and Ahmad Al-Jabarti, the great historian of Egypt in the time of Arnaut Muhammad Ali, founder of the Khadivial dynasty. And if anybody believes that there were no white people in that powerful fraternity, be it known that there are no men whiter than the blonde Circassians and the mountain kinfolk of Anatolia who very early found a base in the Muslim brotherhood. It was a civilization in which there were deviations of rank and riches, but these didn't equate to class differentiations as understood in the West, much less to Indian caste differentiations.

A famous characteristic of this civilization was its cleanliness at a time when Europe conjugated filth with holiness. In every town there was a hammam, public hot baths, and public springs for drinking and washing off purposes. A supply of pure water was the first considerateness wherever there were Muslims. And frequent washing became so much associated with their religion that in Andalusia in 1566, the use of baths was forbidden under severe penalties because it tended to remind the people of Islam. And an unfortunate gardener of Seville was actually tortured for the crime of having washed while at his work. Public food and water supplies were under strict inspection in all Muslim cities; and meat and other perishable food exposed for sale had to be covered with muslin as a protection from dust and flies. Communication was free between all classes of society and so was intermarriage, and everybody talked to everybody.

The teachers of the Arab universities were the foremost man of learning of their age. They were the teachers of modern Europe. These Ulama were not blind guides nor mere fanatics. The professors of those universities were the most enlightened thinkers of their time. In strict accordance with the Prophet's teaching, it was they who watched over the welfare of the people and pointed out to the Khalifa anything that was being done against the rights of man as guaranteed by the Quran. Indeed it was they who kept down the fanatic element, discouraged persecution for religious opinion, and saved Islamic culture from deterioration in a thousand ways.

They even forced ambitious Muslim rulers, in their un-Islamic strife, to refrain from calling on the people to assist them, to fight only with the help of their own purchased slaves and to respect all crops and cattle and non-combatants. They were capable, by the tremendous burden of their opinion with the masses, to penalize even rulers who breached the Sacred Law, in a way he which imparted them quickly to penance; and they demanded compensation for evildoing.

ISLAM IN INDIA

The Muslims are about twelve percent of India's population. But their influence on the Indian society was much firmer. The chief reason was that there were many Muslims rulers in different parts of India. Most of the Muslim rulers of India were encroachers from the west. Islam was established in Saudi Arabia. But most of Islam's broadcasters in India arrived from non-Arab countries (It must be noted that Arab traders and travellers had arrived into India even before Islam was established in Arabia. These Arabs probably had their own places of worship, later on transformed into mosques.).

The first spreaders of Islam in India were individuals who saw in spreading Islam a holy precept. They began coming to India from the 11 century. They arrived in India from Bukhara, Turkey, Iran, Yemen and Afghanistan. The most famous preacher of Islam in India was Khwaja Chishti, who arrived from Iran and his sect is called Sufism. But the accepted assumption in India is that most of Indias Muslims were converted to Islam through the sword. Meaning the Indians were given an option between death or adopting Islam.

The third option was getting examined in Islam religion along with heavy taxes- Jeziya (poll tax) and Kharaj (property tax). The process of converting Indians to Islam began in the 8 century, when the Arabs began invading north India and present day Pakistan. After the Arabs other Muslims invaded India. These invasions by Muslims in India were not continuous and not all Muslim invaders were Islamic fanatics. One of the Moghul emperors, Akbar, was very liberal and he even established a new religion, Din E Elahi, which included in it, beliefs from different religions. In some of the memorials constructed by Akbar symbolizations of different faiths are visible. In contrast with Akbar his great grand son, Aurangazeb, was a fanatical Muslim and during his full term the non-Muslims endured a lot. Many worshipping places of different faiths were demolished and changed into mosques.

Most of the Indian Muslims converted to Islam belonged to the lowlier classes of the Indian society. In addition to these Muslims there are also Muslims who belonged to the dominating families of the different Indian kingdoms. Some of these rulers were Hindus who in reality belonged to the warrior castes of the Hindu society and acquired Islam. Others are descendants of Muslim rulers who invaded India. The different Muslim rulers of India also brought to their kingdoms Muslim mercenaries, businessmen and slaves from different parts of the world like Russia; Afghanistan; Turkey; Arab countries and Africa. These people remained in India, married local Indians and converted them to Islam. Because of the different origins as stated and because of other reasons the Muslims of India refer to themselves not only as Muslims but also with other titles. In general the Muslims of India like the Muslim world is divided into two main sects, Sunni and Shia.

And just like in the whole Muslim world there is tension between these two sects. Each sect has many different schools. There are also Muslims who claim to be the descendants from the daughter of Prophet Muhammad and the men in this community add the title Syed before their names. Other claim to be the descendants from the first Muslims and add the title Sheik. Along with these Muslim world divisions, the Indian Muslims also have other divisions. Different communities who adopted Islam in different ways have different community names. In west India the Bohra and Khoja are Muslim communities who adopted Islam influenced by different Muslim preachers. The Khojas also split into different communities. The leader of the Khoja (Nizari) community is Aga Khan. The Nawait are descendants of Arab and Persian immigrants. In south India in the state of Kerala, the Mophilla community is descendants from Arab merchants. A well known Indian Muslim community is Pathan. The Pathan are Muslims who arrived from Afghanistan.

They normally have their surname as Khan. The Pashtun have an mental image of being courageous, guileless and upright. Many Indians who adopted Islam acquired the last name Khan and they claim that they are Pathans, which isn't all of the time true. The original Pathans claim that they originate from the Twelve Tribes of Israel. In the commencement of the 20 century, some progressive Muslims organizations developed in India who wanted to adapt Islamic philosophy to the modern world. These formations wanted to strike down polygamy and were in favour of women teaching.

ISLAM IN OTHER PARTS OF WORLD

By the early years of the twentieth century, most of the Islamic world outside the Ottoman empire had been engulfed into the empires of non-Islamic European powers. After First World War losses, nearly all of the Ottoman empire was also administered as European protectorates or arenas of influence. In the course of the 20th century, most of these European-ruled territories became independent, and new issues such as oil wealth and relations with the State of Israel have assumed prominence. During this time, many Muslims migrated, as indentured servants, from mostly India and Indonesia to the Caribbean, forming the largest Muslim populations by percentage in the Americas. Additionally, the resulting urbanization and increase in trade in Africa brought Muslims to settle in new areas and spread their faith. As a result, Islam in sub-Saharan Africa likely doubled between 1869 and 1914.

The 20th century saw the introduction of many new Islamic evangelist movements. Groups such as the Muslim Brotherhood in Egypt and Jamaat-e-Islami in Pakistan preach a totalitarian and theocratic choice to secular political ideologies. Sometimes called Islamist, they see Western cultural values as a menace, and promote Islam as a comprehensive solution to every public and private question of importance. In countries like Iran and Afghanistan (under the Taliban), revolutionary movements replaced secular regimes with Islamist states, while transnational groups like Osama bin Laden's al-Qaeda engage in terrorism to further their goals. In contrast, Liberal Islam is a movement that attempts to reconcile religious tradition with modern norms of secular governance and human rights.

Its supporters say that there are multiple ways to read Islam's sacred texts, and stress the need to leave room for "independent thought on religious matters".Modern critique of Islam includes accusations that Islam is intolerant of criticism and that Islamic law is too hard on apostates. Critics like Ibn Warraq question the morality of the Qu'ran, saying that its contents justify the mistreatment of women and encourage antisemitic remarks by Muslim theologians. Such claims are disputed by Muslim writers like Fazlur Rahman Malik, Syed Ameer Ali, Ahmed Deedat, and Yusuf Estes. Others like Daniel Pipes and Martin Kramer center more on picking apart the spread of Islamic fundamentalism, a danger they feel has been unheeded. Montgomery Watt and Norman Daniel brush aside many of the critiques as the product of old myths and polemicists. The rise of Islamophobia, according to Carl Ernst, had added to the antagonistic views about Islam and Muslims in the West.

DEMOGRAPHICS

Islam in Africa

Region	Muslims
Central Africa	15,347,332
East Africa	81,890,564
North Africa	179,623,477
Southern Africa	885,474
West Africa	134,577,785
Total	412,324,632

Islam in Asia

Region	Muslims
Central Asia	76,105,962
East Asia	39,609,350

Middle East	252,219,832
South Asia	456,062,641
Southeast Asia	239,566,220
Total	1,023,564,005

Islam in Europe

Region	**Muslims**
Balkans	8,165,137
Central Europe	521,284
Eastern Europe	21,826,829
Western Europe	13,577,116
Total	44,090,366

Islam in Americas

Region	**Muslims**
Caribbean	15,860
Central America	84,035
North America	5,115,892
South America	4,514,716
Total	9,730,503

Islam in Oceania

Region	**Muslims**
Oceania	372,968

Courtsey: *US State Department's International Religious Freedom Report, CIA World Factbook.*

REFERENCES

Arzu, Siraj-ad-din Ali Khan: *Tashòihò-i Ghara'ib al-lughat,* Cawnpore, 1868.

Asad-Allah Tilhari: *Quwwat-i Hòanafiyya, Bada'un,* 1905.

Asbraf 'Ali Thanawi: *al-Intibahat al-mufida'an al-ishtibahat al-jadida,* Lahore, 1952.

Ashraf, K. M.: "Life and Conditions of the People of Hindustan, 1200-1550", *JASB* 1935.

Azad Bilgrami, Mir Ghulam "Ali (ed.): *Khizana-i Amira*, Cawnpore, 1871.

Azad, Abu-l-Kalam: *Tadhkira,* Lahore, n.d.

Azad, Muhòammad Hòusayn: *Ab-i Hayat,* Lahore, n.d.

Aziz Ahmad: *Islamic Culture in the Indian Environment*, Oxford, 1964.

Azòfari, zòahir al-din: *Waqi'at-i Azfari*, Madras, 1957.

Babur: *Tuzuk,* Leyden and Erskine, London, 1921.

Bahra'ichi, Na'im-Allah: *Ma'lumat-i Mazhariyya,* Cawnpore, 1858.

Bailey, T. Grahame: *A History of Urdu Literature*, Calcutta, 1932.

Bains, A.: *Ethnography of the Castes and Tribes of India*, Strassburg, 1912.

Bakhtawar Khan: *Mir'at al-'alam,* BM Add. MS 7657.

Chiragh 'Ali: *Rasd'il,* Hyderabad, 1918-19.

Chishti, 'Abd-al-Hòalim: "Hasan ibn-Muhammad as-Saghani" in *Ma'arif,* Jan.-Sept. 1959.

Ikram, S. M. and Spear, P.: *Cultural Heritage of Pakistan*, Karachi, 1955.

Imdad-Allah, Hòjji: *Maktubat-i Imdadiyya*, ed. Ashraf 'Ali Thaawi, Lucknow, 1915.

In 'am al-Hòaqq: *Muslim Bengali Adab,* Karachi, 1957.

Qureshi, I. H.: *The Muslim Community of the Indo-Pakistan Sub-Continent*, 'S-Gravenhage, 1962.

Rahòman 'Ali: *Tadhkira-i 'ulama-i Hind,* Lucknow, 1914; Urdu tr. by M. Ayyub Qadiri, Karachi, 1961.

Ram Lajwanti Krishna: *Panjabi Sufi Poets*, Calcutta, 1938.

Rashidi, Hòusam-ad-Din: *Sindhi Adab,* Karachi, n.d.

Yusuf Husain: *L'Inde Mystique au Moyen Age*, Paris, 1929.

Zaehner, R. C.: *Hindu and Muslim Mysticism*, London, 1960.

13

Socio-Political Influence

Conventional political conceptions in Islam include leadership by heirs to the Prophet titled Caliphs, (Imamate in Shiah Islam); the grandness of following Islamic law or Sharia; the obligation of rulers to seek Shura or audience from their issues; and the grandness of rebuking unfair rulers but not encouraging insurrection against them. A sea change in the Islamic world was the abolition of the Ottoman caliphate in 1924, which some believed meant an end to the Islamic state both in "symbolic and practice terms". In the 19th and 20th century a common theme has been resistance to Western imperialism, particularly the British Empire, and sometimes the racist policies that discriminated against some Muslims.

The defeat of Arab armies in the Six Day War, the collapse of the Soviet Union and the end of communism as a feasible choice with the end of the Soviet Union and the Cold War has expanded the appealingness of Islam and Islamic fundamentalistic movements, especially in the circumstance of autocratic and corrupted regimens all across the Muslim world.

Islam is a faith which has survived for over fourteen centuries in many different states. In and of itself, various political movements in many different circumstances have used the banner of Islam to lend authenticity to their causes. Not surprisingly, practically every aspect of Islamic politics is subject to much disagreement and contention between conservative Islamists and liberal movements within Islam. I

slamist or Islamic parties exist in almost every democracy with a Muslim majority. In addition to the legitimacy given by medieval scholarly opinion, nostalgia for the days of successful Islamic empire simmered under later Western colonialism. This nostalgia played a major role in the Islamist political ideal of Islamic state, which primarily means a state which enforces traditional Islamic laws. The Islamist political program is generally to be accomplished by re-shaping the governments of existing Muslim nation-states; but the means of doing this varies greatly across movements and conditions. Many Islamist movements, such as the Jamaat-e-Islami in Bangladesh, have found that they could use the popular procedure to their vantage, and so focus on votes and coalition-building with other parties. Other more extremist movements such as Jamaatul Mujahideen Bangladesh adopt aggressive Islamic orientation.

In the aspect of the fantastic impoverishment, corruptness and disenchantment with established politics, the political ideal of the Islamic state has been criticised by many conjoining liberal movements within Islam and for instance by Ziauddin Sardar, as being impractical and not extending real solutions. Along with many other cultural phenomena, Islamic political thought has undergone its own globalization as adherents of many different strains have come together.

Even in such strictly controlled, secretive groups as Al-Qaida, there were believing Muslims of drastically varying backgrounds coming together, some of whom accepted the tactics and priorities of the group, and some not. While violent fanatics deployed by cynical leaders make highly visible attacks on Western concerns and even on 'homelands', this is believed by many to be no more than repercussion for an entire twentieth century full of distrustful assays by German, British, and American Empires to deploy Muslim idealists as a mere manoeuvre.

When Russian Federation joined the Council of the Islamic Conference in 2003, it accentuated that it had a long history of flourishing co-existence with Muslims, and a large amalgamated population of Muslims. President Vladimir Putin, notwithstanding a long and bloodied encounter with rebels in Chechnya, offered to act as a bridge or impersonal agent in dealings between Muslims and NATO, the EU and USA. This was a quite different rhetoric, a more pragmatic one likely reflecting the reality that the ex-Soviet republics of Uzbekistan, Kazakhstan, Turkmenistan, Azerbaijan had substantial Islamic political movements - similar to those in Turkey and Pakistan, relatively modern in tone and willing to participate in the US War on Terrorism to some degree, although not as direct combatants.

Some analysts believe that the old Cold War battlelines have been redrawn, with Russia choosing new friends - those with a record of success in coercing U.S.A. withdrawals from strategical districts with Islamic populations. In this view, the old Bolshevik alignment against colonialism is the dominant empty words.

Others admit the Russian assurance as earnest, and believe that Islamist movements of all stripes will at length come to adjustment with domestic secular forces, and Islam as a global anti-corruption, anti-colonialism, and anti-racism movement, less focused on Zionism and Palestine. George W. Bush for instance has noted the real need as economic development in Muslim countries, to break the cycle of poverty that tends to feed into extremist movements. In Afghanistan, Pakistan, Turkey and Iraq, the Bush administration has worked closely with nominally Islamic forces and ruling political parties in government. It denies intensely that it is involved in a warfare on Islam. However, polls of Islamic states indicate these self-denials are not believed.

SOCIO-POLITICAL IDENTITY

Both individuality and modernity are important parts of socio-political scene today and more so in case of Muslims. Muslims are considered much more concerned about religion and religious identity and supposed to be rejecting modernity. In fact social questions are quite complex and cannot be reduced to black and white ignoring grey areas in between. Another important thing is that we cannot subject the Muslim community to uniformity and homogeneity.

Muslims are immensely diverse not only in terms of sects, languages and cultures but also in terms of classes and socio-political attitudes. It is really dangerous to apply stereotypes on such immensely diverse community. It would also be equally wrong to think, as we often do, that all non-Muslims have accepted modernity and all that goes with it and that only Muslims resist it. Modernity, in such discourses, is never defined properly and is used in rather highly generalised sense. Some scholars have sub-divided modernity into 'hard modernity' and 'soft modernity'.

It is science and technology and in this sense all people, including Muslims have accepted modernity. No one rejects benefits of modern science and technology any more. If there was any resistance to it, it was in nineteenth century. In nineteenth century there were debates whether sun goes round the earth or vice versa. Hardly anyone debates this, not even semi-literate mullahs and imams. And no one ever rejected benefits of modern technology.

Soft modernity implies philosophical issues and critical examination of traditional beliefs. Here one can say there are significantly differing attitudes among Muslims. Soft modernity also includes secular education and acceptance of secularism. It is true there is comparatively more resistance to soft modernity among Muslims in general. Secularism is integral part of soft modernity and it is also important to note that secularism implies discourse of rights whereas religious discourse is discourse of duties. All authoritarian societies adopt discourse of duties rather than that of rights. Secular discourse, on the other hand, is entirely discourse of rights. A modern thinker asserts, not only political rights but also right to examine traditional beliefs critically. But this right can be availed of only when there is widespread high standard of education. Muslims, for various reasons, chief among them being poverty, lack widespread high degree of secular education and hence there is general resistance to discourse of rights, including right to critical examination of traditional beliefs.

But it should also be admitted that education is one factor among many. Socio-political interests also play an important role. Thus both among Muslims and non Muslims we find some highly educated ones aggressively promoting traditional beliefs and vehemently opposing any attempt to critically examine them. Whatever the reasons, women have to pay heavy price for rejection of soft modernity by men of the community. Women are entirely subject to the discourse of duty. The discourse of duty is, it can be said, doubly applicable to women in all the communities in India.

Women are subject to this discourse both in the name of religion as well as in the name of age-old customs and traditions. Women are much more unequal as they are denied benefits of soft modernity. Even among Hindus very few women are truly 'liberated' in this sense. Among Muslims women are even more unequal. They suffer from many disabilities more due to customs and traditions than religion. Islam is far more just to them than the traditions. But in traditional societies religion itself is subject to customs and tradition. Often it becomes important to liberate religion from traditions. In modern society question of religious identity has become far more important. A religiously plural country throws up complex problems in a democratic set up. A secular democratic society throws up the question of rights for different religious communities and also promotes competition for political power and economic resources. The elite of the communities mobilise masses by using religious identities and hence religious identities become quite important.

Communal problems came into existence in modern society, as concept of rights became more important than that of duty. Every community asserts its religious identity to put pressure on the system to wrest greater share in power. Our experiences in post-independence period show that minority community finds it difficult to match aggressive mobilisation by majority community. Thus for minority community religious identity becomes even more important. It becomes a mental refuge. Communal solidarity is seen as effective compensation for external pressure. And this communal solidarity puts its own demands on individual liberties.

Individuals have to fall in line under the weight of communal pressure and individual rights are compromised. It is an irony of the situation that on one hand the majority communal discourse puts Muslims under pressure for uniform civil code and makes it part of political agenda and on the other hand, creates conditions making it increasingly difficult for the community to accept change and 'soft modernity'. Here it should also be noted that it is wrong to depict one's religious community as more liberal and progressive and another community as more regressive and backward. It all depends on socio-political conditions particularly in multi-religious societies. If Muslims are less under majority communal pressure and find political atmosphere more congenial for their economic progress they will be more prone in a democratic society to accept change and soft modernity.

Also, more educated Muslims more easily opt for soft modernism than less educated and less secure Muslims. Some sects like the Bohras accept change more easily than other sects. These sects are economically and educationally better off though not all Bohras. There is poverty and illiteracy among them too. Thus there are regional, sectarian and economic factors influencing Muslim behaviour. Religion is invoked by these sections to accept or reject change as legitimising factor. Thus it will be seen that a sense of physical security and economic status can be far more influential than is generally recognised. However, communal discourse tries to blame it only on religion and that itself is communal approach to the complex problem of change and progress. The rationalists too err in this matter and tend to blame religion rather than these material factors for lack of acceptability of change.

ISLAM AND POLITICS

The Prophet Muhammad was a political leader besides the messenger carrying the risalah, instructor, Chief Justice, Head of the nation and Imam of the ummah. The Khulafaal Rasyidun, the justifiedly channelised leaders who came after him were also politicos following the Sunnah, way of the Prophet, establishing just administration, practising ihsan, the betterment of good and providing the leadership of 'ilm, knowledge and Iman, belief. However in the present time, due to 'politics' man faced suffering as a result of deceit and political ploys and scheming and devious politicians, whether in the form of past colonialists, treacherous rulers, tyrannical leaders and regimes preaching Machiavellian philosophy. It became common to label and describe committed Muslims as 'political' so that they are regarded warily and evilly for the aim of dissociating and advancing apart the people from them, meaning that society will banish and detest what is called 'political Islam'. It's been such symbols of Islam like the headscarf, the right attire and Congregationalist supplications are essayed to be judged 'political'.

Islam is always rejuvenated, its message spread across, its resurgence, its reverberating call heard by all even if it is given some limited freedom. Therefore the first battle is to obtain freedom to deliver the message of dawah, the risalah of tawhid (Unity of God), spread consciousness and enabling the existence of Islamic movements. True democracy is not the whims and desires of the tyrannical rulers or their cronies, it is not the place to jail and incarcerate its fighters and not the place to torture its proponents. Democracy is the simplest and proper way to achieve the aims of a noble life, to be able to invite all to Allah and Islam, to be able to call others to Iman without having our souls being imprisoned and our bodies sentenced to be executed by hanging. It is the space for a free and honourable nation to have the right to choose, evaluate the ruler, change governments without coups and without bloodshed.

The hypothesis, way and arrangement which appears extrinsic maybe acquired if it profits us and as long as it doesn't oppose clear Muslim decrees and the rules of Syariah. We assess, amend agreeing to our spirit, we don't acquire its philosophy, and we do not allow what is forbidden and vice versa. We do not relinquish or compromise what is ordained or compulsory - the wajib in Islam. The gist of democracy is that the public, the people can choose the rulers who are going to administer them; the people having the right to select, criticise and terminate; and the people are not forced to accept systems, trends, and policies which they do not agree to and they are not abused. They are free to hold elections, referendums, ascertaining absolute majority rights, protecting minority rights, having opponent, have multi parties, have press exemption and safeguarding the independency of the judicial system.

The beingness of assorted parties or motions is not forbidden as long as fusion is not achievable due to differences over objectives, approaches, understanding and the level of confidence and trust. Variety and specialisation are allowed as long as they do not become contradictory and confrontational. However everyone has to be in one united front when facing the challenges to aqidah, belief, syariah, ummah and the survival of Islam. Relations between parties and groupings should be in the atmosphere of non-prejudice, pardon, nobleness, advising truth and staunchness, wiseness and absorbing in healthy cordial debate.

Even when the Islamic State is established there is no reason to feel distraught at the existence of pluralism and differences. Without the shedding of blood, the most effective way as the outcome of long and painful struggles is the existence of political forces which the government in power is unable to contain or eliminate: that is presence of political parties. The ruling regime can get rid of individuals and small groups of opponents but it is difficult for them to defeat or wipe out larger organisations which are well structured, organised and rooted in the masses of society.

Political parties have the platform, machinery, newspapers and publications as well as mass influence. Political parties or political movements are necessary to fight oppression, to enable criticism, bringing back the government to to uphold truth and justice, bringing down or changing the government. These parties are capable of monitoring and appraising the government, offer advice and criticism. Voting in the elections is a form of testimony. A just testimony is considered as long as one is not convicted of crime. Whoever so votes or abstains from voting in the general elections causing the defeat of a trustworthy and deserving candidate but on the other hand allows the candidate who is less trustworthy and undeserving to win, one has gone against the command of Allah concerning giving testimony.

FUNDAMENTALISM

The word Muslim fundamentalism is chiefly used to distinguishes the notions of conventional Muslims that they should confine themselves to actual and conventional renditions of their sacred texts, the Quran and Hadith. It distinguishes an assortment of religious movements and groups in Muslim communities which may be entirely nonpolitical. An example is the Tablighi Jamaat, a missionary-like organization whose main goal is to increase the personal piety of its members. In this sense, Islamic fundamentalism is just a term for religious conservatism which forms part of the spectrum of Muslim society. It describes Muslim groups which advocate Islam as a political movement, especially Islamism, which advocate the replacement of state secular laws with Islamic law. All the above perspectives are opposed by liberal movements within Islam to varying degrees; in fact, fundamentalism and liberalism often define the two poles of public opinion in Muslim society.

This indicates that fundamentalism may be simply a kind of conservatism which finds expression in a religious context. Muslims believe that the Quran was dictated by Allah. Allah is traditionally used by Muslims as the Arabic name of God. The word Allah is not specific to Islam; Arab Christians and Jews, and the Catholic Maltese, also use it to refer to the monotheist deity; for exam, through the Arch-Angel Jabril, to Muhammad. Muhammad was the founding father of Islam, and is venerated by Muslims as the final prophet of God. Accordant to his conventional Muslim biographies the actual text of the Quran is indistinguishable to what was said by Muhammad to be the Quran.

As with disciples of other fundamentalistic movements, Islamic fundamentalists hold that the troubles of the cosmos stem from secular influences. Further, the course to serenity and justness in this world lies in a return to the first message of the religion, blended with a careful rejection of all Bidah ("innovation') and perceived anti-Islamic traditions. Sometimes this results in Islamism. Groups advocating Islam as a political movement are invariably responding to complex political and historical situations, usually with deep roots in the local environment.

For example, the rise of the conservative Jamaat-e-Islami party in Bangladesh would not have been possible without widespread public reaction against the corruption of the secular Awami League government in that country. Regrettably, this composite local political history is altogether lost in the oversimplified reductionism of terms like 'Muslim fundamentalism', which at the same time explains everything and nothing by faulting Islam for being the faith of the absolute majority.

Given the beingness of autocratic and corrupted regimens all over the Muslim world, it's not unexpected that for much of the twentieth century the dominating form of political dissent in these states has been radical Marxism instead of Islam as a political movement. However, the end of the Soviet Union and the Cold War largely discredited leftist ideologies and Arab Nationalism there by strengthening Islamic parties. Continuing Western support for the Israeli settlement of the West Bank has also increased the anti-American sentiments which Islamism represents. Many scholars of religion believe that, contrary to their own message, Islamic fundamentalists are not actually traditionalists. Typically, their message is that returning to the original version of the faith requires abandonment of a variety of traditional practices which they contend are medieval innovations, such as the practice of asking favours from "saints" (awliya). Nevertheless, scholars of Islam hold that the consequence is that the fundamentalists are producing innovations; they are making a form of Islam that never survived in the past.

Some Islamic fundamentalists seek to alter the polices of their nation so as to make their laws established on the Quran and Hadith. While there have historically been many non-violent Islamic fundamentalists, one Western intension of the term fundamentalism is the affirmation of views through violence or oppressiveness, rather than persuasion. As with disciples of other fundamentalist movements, Islamic fundamentalists hold that the problems of the world stem from secular influences. Further, the path to peace and justness lies in a return to the original message of Islam, combined with a conscientious rejection of all Bidah ("religious innovation") and perceived anti-Islamic traditions. Some scholars of Islam, such as Bassam Tibi, believe that, unlike their own substance, Islamic fundamentalists are not actually diehards. He refers to fatwahs issued by fundamentalists such as "every Muslim who pleads for the abatement of the sharia is an deserter and can be killed. The killing of those renegades cannot be pursued under Islamic law because this killing is rationalized" as going beyond, and unbraced by, the Quran.

CONTEMPORARY POLITICS

The point of reference for Islamic politics are the Quran and Sunnah. The chronicle of the battle of the Prophet and The Caliphs is the practical acknowledgment of such form of government. Although it has passed a span of 1500 years but the knowledge remains definite and precise. The Prophet had guaranteed the precision and purity of the Islamic teaching to be followed. If we refer to the Quran and the sunnah in doing politics, we will be safe. But it is really odd when electoral politicians give all kinds of excuses to allow them to deviate from the way of the Prophet in doing politics. They are prejudiced to the politics of the Prophet. So they make efforts to achieve the Islamic way of life by imitating and emulating the West. It never cross their minds that when they follow western politics, the result will surely be Western. It would never be Islamic.

What is most unfortunate, they go against and confront Islamic fighters who refuse to follow Western Politics and blame them for being indifferent to politics. They accept that Western politics is Muslim politics. Not getting tangled in such politics is believed wrong to them. They're so disoriented, they can no more think. They cannot distinguish between what is justly and what is untrue. Islamic politics is totally different from Western politics. This difference touches all aspects and angles which relate to politics. It is different in its meanings, methods, criteria, characteristics of leaders and followers, political actions and reactions and in the method of selecting leaders. Islamic politics is one of the many aspects of the Islamic way of life. It's esteemed a compulsory act upon the community. Islamic political science as a whole is applicative and can happen in the family, jamaah, state, nation and at cosmopolitan level.

Islamic politics is free from evil, transgressions, vice and sinful activities. It does not stress on selecting a leader and fighting for power once in every few years. But it gives priority on the personality and charisma of the leader to be appointed. And whether the leader can be fair and can impose justice everywhere. Would he be able to build a jamaah, state or country that is full of justice? Is he able to educate and nurture his people to be faithful to Allah, to be loyal, obedient, willing to work and responsible?

After which would he be able to build material development and the development of a physical civilisation for the needs of his people according to the Islamic syariah. And in following and emulating him, people would be safe from war, usury, oppressions and the satanic culture and would be protected from the society of sin and transgression. Islamic politics emphasises on the result or its objective. That is the formation of a Quranic society that is peaceful, harmonious and blessed by the Oft-Forgiving Allah.

Muslim politics was exercised by the Prophet. It did not commence with getting the ability to rule but it began by adding changes in persons and then the society to Islam through motivating, teaching, love and compassionateness. Because in an Islamic nation, good people is priority over good government. The government stands upon the people. Without the people, there is no government. Good people will choose good leaders and good governments. Those who oppose the execution of the Islamic rules and regulations are the same people who voted for them. What does this mean? It means that the people who are not Islamic educated or who do not truly understand Islam, not only do not support but they go against their own authorities whether they recognize it or not, though they themselves voted for the government and the authorities is only trying to apply the Muslim rules which is supposed to be their own inspirations.

That is the system of logic why Muslim politics must start with motive and teaching, through love and brotherhood. When the people are inducted and developed, there will be a shift towards the Islamic system, the Islamic country, even the Islamic world. This is the process in history. It happened to the pioneer of Islamic politics, i.e. the Prophet, the Caliphs, Sayidina Umar Abdul Aziz and Muhammad Al-Fateh. Their victories in the realms of history are very good lessons for us. Learn their history for our guidance. Never think that their history is not for us.

Everything that happened in Islamic history is relevant to Muslims of every era. Other than those already mentioned, where could we find just and fair leaders in history although there were some figures who tried? Yes, there was none! Other than the factor that they were not promised by God, the political methods that they used were not Islamic. It was borrowed or imitated from the infidels and the enemies. As a result, justice was denied, not only in the state or nation, but it also did not happen in the jamaah or the household. Virtuous and reasonable leadership can only materialize in the toifah (jamaah) of the Mujaddid (reformist) which comes about at one time in every hundred years.

REFERENCES

al-Hujwiri, 'Ali ibn-'Uthman: *Kashf al-mahòjub*. R. A. Nicholson, London, 1936.

al-Juwayni, 'Ala'-ad-din: *Ta'rikh-i Jahankusha*, Leiden/ London, 1912-37; Eng. tr. J. A. Boyle (*The History of the World Conqueror*), Manchester, 1958.

Allah Diya: *Siyar al-aqtòab,* Lucknow, 1889.

al-Qaqashandi: *Subhò al-a'sha*, Cairo, 1913-20.

Altòaf ar-Rahòman: *Ahòwal-i 'ulama-i Farangi Mahòall,* Lucknow, n.d.

Amanat Allah: *MuHòafiz al-iman mill maka'id la-madhhaban,* Allahabad, 1877.

Amir Ahòmad: *Sirat al-Ashraf,* 2 vols, Lucknow, 1949.

Amir Khurd: *Siyar al-awhya,* Delhi, 1885.

Amritsari, Thand-Allah: *Ahl-i hòadith ka madhhab,* Amritsar, 1920.

Anderson, J. N. D.: "Recent Reforms in the Islamic Law of Inheritance", *International and Comparative Law Quarterly*, 1965.

Azad, Abu-l-Kalam: *Tadhkira,* Lahore, n.d.

Azad, Muhòammad Hòusayn: *Ab-i Hayat,* Lahore, n.d.

Colebrook, H. T.: "On the Origin and Peculiar Tenets of Certain Muhammadan Sects", *Asiatic Researches*, vii (1801)

Cousens, H.: *Bijapur and its Architectural Remains*, Bombay, 1916.

Iqbal Husain: "Chandra Bhan Brahman", *IC*, 1945.

Iqbal, Muhammad: *Islam and, Ahmadism*, Lahore, 1936.

Ishaq, Muhammad: "India's Contribution to the study of Hadiith Literature", *Dacca University Bulletin*, 1955.

Isma'il, Shah (Shahid): *Tadhkir al-akhwan,* Lahore, 1948.

Raverty, H. G.: *Selections From the Poetry of the Afghans*, London, 1864.

Razvi, S. N. Haidar: "Music in Muslim India", *IC*, 1941.

Rieu, C.: *Catalogue of the Persian Manuscripts in the British Museum*, London, 1879-95.

Rizvi, S. A. A.: *Muslim Revivalist Movements in Northern India in the Sixteenth and Seventeenth Centuries*, Agra, 1965.

Zahid 'Ali: *Hamara Isma'ili madhhab awr uski hòaqiqat,* Hyderabad, 1954.

Zubayd M. G. Ahmad: *The Contribution of India to Arabic Literature*, PH.D. dissertation, University of London.

14

Religious Rituals and Traditions

During the ten years between his reaching in Medina and his death in AD. 632, Muhammad positioned the base for the perfect Islamic state. A core group of dedicated Muslims was constituted, and a community life was arranged according to the demands of the fresh religion. In addition to all-purpose ethical enjoinings, the requirements of the religion came to include a number of institutions that continue to characterize Islamic religious practice today. Foremost among these were the five pillars of Islam, the essential religious duties required of every adult Muslim who is mentally able.

The five pillars are each described in some part of the Quran and were already practiced during Muhammad's lifetime. They are the profession of faith (shahada), prayer (salat), almsgiving (zakat), fasting (sawm), and pilgrimage (Haj). Though some of these exercises had precedents in Judaic, Christian, and other Middle Eastern spiritual customs, taken collectively they differentiate Muslim religious practices from those of other faiths. The five mainstays are thus the most central rites of Islam and comprise the core practices of the Islamic faith.

RELIGIOUS RITUALS

Haj

The Haj is a pilgrimage to Mecca. It is the biggest yearly pilgrimage in the mankind. It is the fifth mainstay of Islam, a duty that must be accomplished at the least once in their lifespan by every able Muslim who can afford to do so. It is a presentation of the solidarity of the Islamic people, and their compliance to Allah. The pilgrimage happens from the 10th to the 15th day of Dhu al-Hijjah, the twelfth calendar month of the Islamic calendar. Because the Islamic calendar is a lunar calendar, eleven days shorter than the Gregorian calendar used in the Western world, the Gregorian date of the Haj is eleven days earlier from year to year.

The Haj is associated with the life of Muhammad, but the ritual of pilgrimage to Mecca is considered by Muslims to stretch back to the time of Abraham and Ishmael, prominent figures in both Islam and in Judaism. Pilgrims join processions of hundreds of thousands of people, who simultaneously converge on Mecca for the week of the Haj, and perform a series of rituals. As part of the Haj, each person walks counter-clockwise seven times about the Kaaba, the cube-shaped building which acts as the Muslim way of supplication (qibla); runs backward and forward between the hills of Al-Safa and Al-Marwah; drinks from the Zamzam Well; attends the plains of Mount Arafat to stand in vigil; and throws stones in a rite Stoning of Devil. The pilgrims then shave their heads, execute an animal sacrifice, and observe the four day worldwide festival of Eid-ul-Adha.

As of 2007, an approximated two million pilgrims took part in this annual pilgrimage. Crowd-control techniques have become deprecative, and because of the large numbers of people, many of the rituals have become more artificial. It is not essential to kiss the Black Stone, but merely to aim at it on each circle around the Kaaba. Throwing pebbles was done at large pillars, which for safety reasons were in 2004 changed to long walls with catch basins below to catch the stones.

The slaughter of an animal can be done either personally, or by appointing someone else to do it, and so forth. But even with the crowd control techniques, there are still many incidents during the Haj, as pilgrims are trampled in a crush, or ramps collapse under the weight of the many visitors, causing hundreds of deaths. Pilgrims can also attend Mecca to execute the rites at other times of the year. This is occasionally called the "lesser pilgrimage", or Umrah. However, even if they execute the Umrah, they are still compelled to perform the Haj at another point in their lifespans.

The Haj is founded on a pilgrimage that was old even in the time of Muhammad in the seventh Century. According to Hadith, components of the Haj trace back to the time of Abraham, around 2000 BC. The impression is that the Prophet Abraham was dictated by God (Allah) to leave his wife Hagar and his infant son Ismael alone in the desert. When he was gone, the baby became thirsty, Hagar ran backward and forward seven times looking for for water for her boy. The baby cried and hit the ground with his foot (some adaptations of the story say that an angel scratched up his foot or the tip of his wing along the earth), and water miraculously sprang onward.

This reservoir of water is today called the Well of Zamzam. Each year clans from all around the Arabia would converge on Mecca, as part of the pilgrimage. The exact faith of the tribes was not important at that time, and Christian Arabs were as likely to make the pilgrimage as the pagans. Muslim historians refer to the time before Muhammad as al-Jahiliyah, the "Days of Ignorance", during which the Kaaba contained hundreds of idols constituting totems of each of the tribes of the Arabian peninsula. The idols comprised multiple religions, from pagan gods like Hubal, al-Lat, Uzza and Manat, to symbols of Jesus and Mary and Allah (God).

Muhammad was known to regularly perform the Umrah, even before he began receiving revelations. Historically, Muslims would gather at various meeting points in other great cities, and then proceed en masse towards Mecca, in groups that could comprise tens of thousands of pilgrims. Two of the most famous meeting points were in Cairo and Damascus. In Cairo, the Sultan would stand atop a platform of the famous gate Bab Zuwayla, to officially watch the beginning of the annual pilgrimage. In 632 AD., when Muhammad led his followers from Medina to Mecca, it was the first Haj to be performed by Muslims alone, and the only Haj ever performed by Muhammad. He cleansed the idols from the Kaaba, and re-ordained it as the house of God. It was from this point that the Haj became one of the Five Pillars of Islam. Pilgrims generally travel to Haj in groups, as an expression of unity. Some airlines have special package holidays for Muslims going to Mecca. Ships also take pilgrims to Mecca so they can perform Haj.

During the Haj, male pilgrims are called for to dress only in a dress consisting of two sheets of white unhemmed cloth, with the top cloaked over the trunk and the bottommost bonded by a white waistcloth; plus a pair of sandals. Women are merely required to sustain their hijab - normal humble dress, which does not cover the hands or face.The Ihram clothing is intended to show the equality of all pilgrims in the eyes of Allah: there is no difference between a prince and a pauper when everyone is dressed the same. The Ihram also symbolizes purity and absolution of sins. A place designated for changing into Ihram is called a miqat. While the pilgrim is wearing the Ihram, they cannot shave, clip their nails, or use deodorant or perfume.

They may not swear or quarrel, kill any living thing, or engage in sexual intercourse. Upon arrival in Mecca the pilgrim, now known as a Haji, performs a series of ritual acts symbolic of the lives of Ibrahim (Abraham) and his wife Hajar (Hagar). The acts also symbolize solidarity of Muslims worldwide. The greater Haj (al-Haj al-akbar) begins on the eighth day of the lunar month of Dhu al-Hijjah. If they're not already wearing it on their arrival, pilgrims put on ihram clothing and then leave Mecca for the close town of Mina where they spend the rest of the day. The Saudi authorities has put up thousands of large white camps at Mina to provide fittings for all the pilgrims.

Umrah: During the first day of the Haj, the eighth day of the twelfth month, Dhu al-Hijjah, the pilgrims execute their first Tawaf, which calls for all of the pilgrims acceding The Sacred Mosque (Masjid Al Haram) and walk seven times anticlockwise around the Kaaba, kissing the Black Stone (Hajr Al Aswad) on each circuit. If kissing is not achievable due to the crowds, they may simply adjust themselves with the stone and point to it. Each complete circuit constitutes a "Shout" with 7 circuits constituting a complete tawaf. The place where pilgrims walk is known as "Mutaaf". Only the first three Shouts are compulsory, but invariably almost all perform it seven times. Eating is not allowed and the tawaf is normally performed all at once, the only exception being the drinking of water. Men are encouraged to execute the first three laps at a hastened pace, accompanied by four times, more intimately, at a easygoing pace.

After the completion of Tawaf, all the pilgrims have to offer two Rakaat prayers at the Place of Abraham (Muqaam E Ibrahim), a site near the Kaaba. However, again due to large crowds during the days of Haj, they may instead pray anywhere in the mosque. Although the circuits around the Kaaba are traditionally done on the groundlevel, Tawaf is now also performed on the first floor and roof of the mosque. After Tawaf on the same day, the pilgrims perform sai, running or walking seven times between the hills of Safa and Marwah.

This is a re-enactment of the frantic search for water for her son Ismael by Abraham's wife Hagar, before the Zamzam Well was revealed to her by Ismael, who started to cry for water and hit the ground with his feet, upon which the water of the Zamzam started coming up from under his feet. The circuit used to be in the open air, but is now entirely enclosed by the Masjid al-Haram mosque, and can be accessed via air-conditioned tunnels. Pilgrims are advised to walk the circuit, though two green pillars mark a short section of the path where they are allowed to run, along with an 'express lane' for the disabled. The safety procedures are in place because previous incidents in this ritual have resulted in stampedes which caused the deaths of hundreds of people.

As part of this ritual the pilgrims drink water from the Zamzam Well, which is made available in coolers throughout the Mosque. The pilgrims then return to their tents.

Arafat: The following morning, on the ninth of Dhu al-Hijjah, the pilgrims leave Mina for Mount Arafat where they stand in meditative watch, near a hill from which Muhammad gave his last preaching. This is looked at as the highlight of the Haj. Pilgrims must spend the afternoon inside a defined region on the plain of Arafat until after sundown. No specific rituals or prayers are required during the stay at Arafat, although many pilgrims spend time praying, and thinking about the course of their lives. If a pilgrim doesn't spend the afternoon on Arafat then their pilgrimage is conceived invalid.

Muzdalifah: As soon as the sun sets, the pilgrims leave Arafat for Muzdalifah, a region between Arafat and Mina, where 49 pebbles are gathered for the next day's rite of the stoning of the Devil (shaytan). Many pilgrims spend the night sleeping on the ground at Muzdalifah before returning to Mina. It is now the tenth of the month, the day of Eid ul-Adha.

Ramy al-Jamarat: At Mina the pilgrims execute Ramy al-Jamarat, hurling stones to signify their defiance of the Devil. This represents the trials felt by Abraham while he determined whether to sacrifice his son as called for by God. The Devil challenged him six times, and three times Abraham declined. Each pillar marks the position of one of these refusals. On the first occasion of when Ramy al-Jamarat performed, pilgrims will stone the largest pillar know as JamratalAqabah. On the second occasion, all three will be stoned. The stoning consists of throwing seven pebbles. Because of the crowds, in 2004 the columns were replaced by long walls. Pilgrims ascent ramps to the multi-levelled Jamarat Bridge, from which they can hurl their stones at the one jamarat.

Eid ul-Adha: After the Stoning of the Devil an animal is sacrificed. This represents God having mercy on Abraham and replacing his son with a ram, which Abraham then sacrificed. Traditionally the pilgrims butchered the animal themselves, or oversaw the butchering. Today many pilgrims buy a sacrifice coupon in Mecca before the greater Haj begins which allows an animal to be butchered in their name on the tenth, without the pilgrim being physically present. Centralized butcher houses will sacrifice a single sheep for each pilgrim, or a cow can represent the sacrifice of seven people. The meat is then packaged and given to charity and shipped to poor people around the world. Simultaneously as the sacrifices occur at Mecca, Muslims worldwide perform like sacrifices, in a four-day global festival called Eid ul-Adha.

Tawaf az-Ziyarah: On this or the next day the pilgrims re-visit the Masjid al-Haram in Mecca for a tawaf called the Tawaf az-Ziyarah or Tawaf al-Ifadah which represents being in a haste to respond to God and show love for Him, a compulsory part of the Haj. The night of the tenth is spent back at Mina. On the afternoon of the eleventh and again the following day the pilgrims must again throw seven pebbles at each of the three jamarat in Mina. Pilgrims must leave Mina for Mecca before sunset on the twelfth. If they are not able to leave Mina before sunset, they must execute the stoning ritual again on the thirteenth before returning to Mecca.

Tawaf al-Wada: Eventually, prior to leaving Mecca, pilgrims execute a farewell tawaf called the Tawaf al-Wada.

Journey to Medina: Although it's not mandatory as part of the Haj, many pilgrims also visit the city of Medina and the Mosque of the Prophet, which contains Muhammad's grave.

Purpose of Haj: The basic aim of the Haj pilgrimage is the same as that of any other fashion of adoration - atonement of the Lord - and yet, there is also something incomparable about it. There exists a special relationship, a peculiar affinity, between the Prophet - and, through him between his Ummat - and Hazrat Abraham. The Haj, in truth, constitutes both in its form and essence, the symbolization of the Will of God, and the idea underlying its ordainment is that every Muslim who can afford to undertake the pilgrimage should, at least, once in his life, betake himself to the place where he most glorious episode of Hazrat Abraham's life of utter dedication to his Creator had taken place, and cast himself, for the time being, in the role of that superbly self-effacing, all sacrificing Friend of the Lord. He should give a practical proof of his attachment to the path of that true friend, slave and devotee of the Divine and of his respectful devotion to the distinctive practices the Lord has ordained for the occasion and create within himself the sincere urge to dye his entire existence, inside in addition to as externally, in the hue of that venerable patriarch and give his soul a chance to take in its deal of the glorious spiritual resplendencies of the place.

There are many things occupying a place of importance in religion for which no definite procedure has been prescribed by the Shariat - only the principles governing them have been laid down - nor do they make an end in themselves. They are a means to an end. For instance, it is a religious obligation to learn the faith and to teach it to others, and to serve and to defend it to the best of one's ability, but, as you know, no precise method has been formulated for these as in the case of Namaz, Zakat etc.

These duties are also not an end in themselves - the study of faith is necessary because without it, people will not be able to discharge their religious obligations properly and, so on. They possess, as we have pointed out a few lines earlier, a definite, unalterable form and are also their own end.

Finally, the word 'Islam,' denotes submission. It is another name for surrendering oneself entirely to God. No other act of religion expresses this condition more eloquently than the four fundamental duties. This may be another reason why these have been made the basic ingredients of Islam. One more reason that suggests itself to (oneself) is that these duties, if performed in the right spirit, exert their influence on all the spheres of existence and are capable of transforming the whole life into one of faith and submission. The stipulation, of course, is that they retain some inner resemblance with the Namaz, Zakat, Roza and Haj of the Prophet and do not slip into a dead formality. It is without a doubt that these foundational duties are endowed to tremendous potentialities. If our prayers and our fasts and Zakat and Haj are not making themselves felt in our lives to any noteworthy degree, it is because they no longer pulsate with life.

One of the changes that come over the followers of the Prophets with the passage of time is that their acts of worship degenerate into rituals. The Muslims have not proved themselves to be above this rule. Such of them as have shut their eyes completely to the need of abiding by the compulsory items of worship and are, for practical purposes, leading a life of infidelity are outside the purview of our discussion at the moment. What they are going to end up in will come before them on the Day of Reckoning.

The mournful truth is that even with Muslims like us who observe the basic obligation of worship regularly, the case is that we are simply hugging their skeletons from which the spirit has departed. Very few of us can truthfully claim that the generalization we have just indulged in, does not apply to them. Or, at least those sections off the Ummat which still adhere to the fundamental obligations would be finding themselves in an entirely different state today. They would be their own example in the world for moral integrity, for social uprightness and for the excellence of their conduct in the practical and material walks of life. The lives of these men would be the most striking models of piety and goodness. Whoever came to know them would notice in them a peculiar charm and a unique fragrance.

This is not a flight of fancy but truth. The few deep-hearted men of genuine faith and endeavour that provide an exception to the general gloom - men whose merit and substance, with those offered up by the Prophet - even today make the finest specimens of humanity and people are struck by an inexplicable magnetism of spirit, and undeniable pervasive quality, as they come into contact with them. The tragedy of our times is that extremely rare as such men have become, the desire to seek them out and to profit by their company has become rarer. Should Allah grant one the good fortune to dedicate oneself to the task of Islamic regeneration, one's chief work would then lie in injecting fresh life and vitality into the foundational duties by bringing the Namaz, Zakat, Roza and Haj of the Ummat in line with the Namaz, Zakat, Roza and Haj of the sacred Prophet.

SOCIAL RITUALS

Birth Ceremonies

The new child is received into the Ummah, the community of Muslims. The headway of the family takes the baby and whispers the the Call to Prayer (the Adhan) into the left ear and the bidding to rise and revere in the right ear (the Iqamah)

God is Great

I bear witness that there is no God but God

I bear witness that Muhammad is the Prophet of God

Come to prayer

Come to success

God is great

There is no God but God

The meaning of this activity may be to ascertain that the life of the child begins with a proclamation of faith, it sets the scene for the future guidance of the child.

Tahnik: A small piece of mashed date or sugar is rubbed into the baby gums or placed on the tongue, usually by a honoured relative. This is to symbolize making the child sweet and compliant. A prayer usually follows this event.

Aqiqah: Seven days after birth comes Aqiqah, this consists of a feast and the naming ceremony. The baby's head is shaved and the weight of hair is made up in gold or silver, this money is donated to the poor, often extra money is given as a symbol of thanking Allah for the gift of the child. An animal is sacrificed as a symbol of thanksgiving for the gift of a child from Allah. Two animals are offered for a boy and one for a girl. In Britain this will take place at an abattoir by someone registered to slaughter animals, a fee has to be paid, the animal is killed in the Halal way to ensure it is kept holy. The meat is cooked and eaten, some will be given to the poor, once again as a symbol of thanksgiving for what Allah has given to the family. The name given to the baby is either the family name or one of the names of the prophets family, the name must not suggest any moral qualities, however, as Muslims believe that only Allah possesses moral qualities.

Khitan: For a boy circumcision must take place shortly after birth. Part of the foreskin is removed, this is both for reasons of hygiene and is continuing the tradition of the prophets before.

The Bismillah: The child will be taught to read the Koran at an early age so that it becomes second nature to read it in it's original language (Arabic). On the fourth birthday comes the Bismillah when the child learns the first lesson of the Quran by heart.

Marriage Ceremonies

Marriage (nikah) is a solemn and sacred social contract between bride and groom. This contract is a strong covenant as expressed in Quran. The marriage contract in Islam is not a sacrament. It is revocable. Both parties mutually agree and enter into this contract. Both bride and groom have the liberty to define various terms and conditions of their liking and make them a part of this contract.

Mahr: The marriage-gift is a divine injunction. The giving of mahr to the bride by the groom is an essential part of the contract. Mahr is a token commitment of the husband's responsibility and may be paid in cash, property or movable objects to the bride herself. The amount of mahr is not legally specified, however, moderation according to the existing social norm is recommended. The mahr may be paid immediately to the bride at the time of marriage, or deferred to a later date, or a combination of both. The deferred mahr however, falls due in case of death or divorce. One matrimonial party expresses 'ijab" willing consent to enter into marriage and the other party expresses 'qubul" acceptance of the responsibility in the assembly of marriage ceremony. The contract is written and signed by the bride and the groom and their two respective witnesses. This written marriage contract (Aqd-Nikah) is then announced publicly.

Sermon: The assembly of nikah is addressed with a marriage sermon (khutba-tun-nikah) by the Muslim officiating the marriage. In marriage societies, customarily, a state appointed Muslim judge (Qadi) officiates the nikah ceremony and keeps the record of the marriage contract. However any trust worthy practicing Muslim can conduct the nikah ceremony, as Islam does not advocate priesthood. The documents of marriage contract/certificate are filed with the mosque (masjid) and local government for record. Prophet Muhammad made it his tradition (sunnah) to have marriage sermon delivered in the assembly to solemnize the marriage. The sermon invites the bride and the groom, as well as the participating guests in the assembly to a life of piety, mutual love, kindness, and social responsibility. The Khutbah-tun-Nikah begins with the praise of Allah. His help and guidance is sought.

The Muslim confession of faith that 'There is none worthy of worship except Allah and Muhammad is His servant and messenger" is declared. The three Quranic verses and one Prophetic saying (hadith) form the main text of the marriage. This hadith is: 'By Allah! Among all of you I am the most God-fearing, and among you all, I am the supermost to save myself from the wrath of Allah, yet my state is that I observe prayer and sleep too. I observe fast and suspend observing them; I marry woman also. And he who turns away from my Sunnah has no relation with me".

The Muslim officiating the marriage ceremony concludes the ceremony with prayer for bride, groom, their respective families, the local Muslim community, and the Muslim community at large. Marriage (nikah) is considered as an act of worship (ibadah). It is virtuous to conduct it in a Mosque keeping the ceremony simple. The marriage ceremony is a social as well as a religious activity. Islam advocates simplicity in ceremonies and celebrations. Prophet Muhammad considered simple weddings the best weddings: 'The best wedding is that upon which the least trouble and expense is bestowed".

Primary Requirements

1. Mutual agreement (Ijab-O-Qubul) by the bride and the groom
2. Two adult and sane witnesses
3. Mahr (marriage-gift) to be paid by the groom to the bride either immediately (muajjal) or deferred (muakhkhar), or a combination of both

Secondary Requirements

1. Legal guardian (wakeel) representing the bride

2. Written marriage contract ("Aqd-Nikah) signed by the bride and the groom and witnesses by two adult and sane witnesses
3. Qadi (State appointed Muslim judge) or Mazoon (a responsible person officiating the marriage ceremony)
4. Khutba-tun-Nikah to solemnize the marriage

Walima: After the consummation of the marriage, the groom holds a banquet called a walima. The relatives, neighbours, and friends are invited in order to make them aware of the marriage. Both rich and poor of the family and community are invited to the marriage feasts.

Death Rites

When a Muslim is near death, those around him or her are called upon to give comfort, and reminders of God's mercy and forgiveness. They may recite verses from the Quran, give physical comfort, and encourage the dying one to recite words of remembrance and prayer. It is recommended, if at all possible, for a Muslim's last words to be the declaration of faith: I bear witness that there is no god but Allah.

Upon death, those with the deceased are encouraged to remain calm, pray for the departed, and begin preparations for burial. The eyes of the deceased should be closed, and the body covered temporarily with a clean sheet. It is forbidden for those in mourning to excessively wail, scream, or thrash about. Grief is normal when one has lost a loved one, and it is natural and permitted to cry.

When the Prophet Muhammad's own son died, he said: "The eyes shed tears and the heart is grieved, but we will not say anything except which pleases our Lord." One should strive to be patient, and remember that Allah is the One who gives life and takes it away, at a time appointed by Him. It is not for us to question His wisdom. Muslims strive to bury the deceased as soon as possible after death, avoiding the need for embalming or otherwise disturbing the body of the deceased. An autopsy may be performed, if necessary, but should be done with the utmost respect for the dead.

Washing and Shrouding: In preparation for burial, the family or other members of the community will wash and shroud the body. (If the deceased was killed as a martyr, this step is not performed; martyrs are buried in the clothes they died in.) The deceased will be washed respectfully, with clean and scented water, in a manner similar to how Muslims make ablutions for prayer. The body will then be wrapped in sheets of clean, white cloth (kafan).

Funeral Prayers: The deceased is then transported to the site of the funeral prayers (salat-l-janazah). These prayers are commonly held outdoors, in a courtyard or public square, not inside the mosque. The community gathers, and the imam (prayer leader) stands in front of the deceased, facing away from the worshippers. The funeral prayer is similar in structure to the five daily prayers, with a few variations. (For example, there is no bowing or prostration, and the entire prayer is said silently but for a few words.)

Burial: The deceased is then taken to the cemetery for burial (al-dafin). While all members of the community attend the funeral prayers, only the men of the community accompany the body to the gravesite. It is preferred for a Muslim to be buried where he or she died, and not be transported to another location or country (which may cause delays or require embalming the body). If available, a cemetery (or section of one) set aside for Muslims is preferred. The deceased is laid in the grave (without a coffin if permitted by local law) on his or her right side, facing Mecca. At the gravesite, it is discouraged for people to erect tombstones, elaborate markers, or put flowers or other momentos. Rather, one should humbly remember Allah and His mercy, and pray for the deceased.

Mourning: Loved ones and relatives are to observe a 3-day mourning period. Mourning is observed in Islam by increased devotion, receiving visitors and condolences, and avoiding decorative clothing and jewelry. Widows observe an extended mourning period (iddah), 4 months and 10 days long, in accordance with the Quran. During this time, she is not to remarry, move from her home, or wear decorative clothing or jewelry.

When one dies, everything in this earthly life is left behind, and there are no more opportunities to perform acts of righteousness and faith. The Prophet Muhammad once said that there are three things, however, which may continue to benefit a person after death: charity given during life which continues to help others, knowledge from which people continue to benefit, and a righteous child who prays for him or her.

OTHER RITUALS

Shahada

The absolute focus of Islamic piety is Allah, the supreme, all knowing, all-powerful, and above all, all-merciful God. The Arabic word Allah means "the God," and this God is understood to be the God who brought the world into being and sustains it to its end. By obeying God's commands, human beings express their recognition of and gratitude for the wisdom of creation, and live in harmony with the universe.

The profession of faith, or witness to faith (shahada), is therefore the prerequisite for membership in the Muslim community. On several occasions during a typical day, and in the saying of daily prayers, a Muslim repeats the profession, "I bear witness that there is no god but Allah and that Muhammad is his prophet." There are no formal restrictions on the times and places these words can be repeated. To become a member of the Muslim community, a person has to profess and act upon this belief in the oneness of God and the prophethood of Muhammad.

To be a true profession of faith that represents a relationship between the speaker and God, the verbal utterance must express genuine knowledge of its meaning as well as sincere belief. A person's deeds can be subjected to scrutiny by other Muslims, but a person's utterance of the profession of faith is sufficient evidence of membership in the Muslim community and cannot be challenged by other members of this community.

Five Daily Prayers

The second mainstay of Islam is the spiritual obligation to execute five prescribed daily prayers or salat. All adult Muslims are supposed to perform five prayers, preceded by rite cleaning or purgation of the body at different intervals of the daytime. The Quranic references also mention the acts of standing, bowing, and prostrating during prayers and facing a set direction, known as qibla. The Muslims were first asked to face Jerusalem during prayer, but already during Muhammad's lifetime they were required to face the Kaaba, an ancient shrine in the city of Mecca. The Quran also refers to the recitation of parts of the Quran as a form of prayer. However, even with its numerous references, the Quran alone does not give exact instructions for this central ritual of prayer.

The most detailed descriptions of the rituals for prayer derive from the example set by the prophet Muhammad and are preserved in later Islamic traditions. Some details of these rituals vary, however all Muslims agree that there are five required daily prayers to be performed at certain times of day: dawn (fajr or subh), noon (zuhr), midafternoon (asr), sunset (maghrib), and evening (isha). The dawn, noon, and sunset prayers do not start exactly at dawn, noon, and sunset; instead, they begin just after, to distinguish the Islamic ritual from earlier pagan practices of worshiping the sun when it rises or sets.

A prayer is made up of a sequence of units called bowings (rakas). During each of these units, the worshiper stands, bows, kneels, and prostrates while reciting verses from the Quran as well as other prayer formulas. With some variations among different Muslim sects, at noon, afternoon, and evening prayers, these units are repeated four times, while during the sunset prayer they are repeated three times, and at dawn only twice. The opening chapter of the Quran, al-Fatiha, is repeated in each unit in a prayer sequence. Each prayer concludes with the recitation of the profession of faith followed by the greeting "may the peace, mercy, and blessings of God be upon you."

Wherever Muslims live in substantial numbers throughout the world, the call to prayer, or adhan, is repeated five times a day by a muezzin (crier) from a mosque, the Muslim place of worship. Muslims are encouraged to pray together in mosques, but group prayer is only a religious obligation for the noon prayer on Friday. Women, travelers, sick Muslims, and those attending to the sick are granted license not to attend the Friday congregational prayer, although they may attend if they wish. The Friday noon prayer is led by an imam, who is simply a prayer leader; this prayer differs from the usual noon prayers of the other days of the week. As a required part of the ritual at this congregational meeting, two sermons precede the prayer. On other days, Muslims can pray anywhere they wish, either individually or in groups. They must observe the rituals of praying at certain times of day, facing in the direction of Mecca, observing the proper order of prayers, and preparing through symbolic purification.

Depending on the situation, this last ritual of ablution requires either total washing of the body or a less elaborate ritual washing of the hands, mouth, face, and feet. In addition to the five required daily prayers, Muslims can perform non-obligatory prayers, some of which have fixed ritual formats and are performed before or after each of the five daily prayers. Others are performed at night, either individually or with other Muslims. These additional formal and informal prayers give expression to the primary function of prayer in Islam, which is personal communication with God for the purpose of maintaining the abiding presence of the divine in the personal lives of Muslims.

The more formal aspects of prayer also serve to provide a disciplined rhythm that structures the day and fosters a sense of community and shared identity among Muslims. Salat is performed in "units" of prayer called rakaah. One rakaah consists of a series of positions (and movements from one position to the next), along with specific supplications and verses from the Quran which are read in each position. A rakaah begins in a standing position called qiyaam and ends with the musallee in a prostrate position (sujud). Different salat have different numbers of prescribed rakaat.

The salat must be performed with sincere devotion (khushoo), otherwise it is considered invalid. Salat is performed facing the direction of qibla (i.e. towards the Kaaba in Mecca), to the best estimation of the musallee if there is no certain way to determine the correct direction. The musallee begins the prayer by standing in qiyaam, facing qibla and silently reciting the niyyah (intention to pray) for the specific salat he is about to make. He then raises his hands and speaks aloud the takbir.

For fard as-salat, the first rakaah commences with the optional recitation of one of the opening supplications followed by the first chapter of the Quran, al-Fatihah. For subsequent rakaat and other types of salat, each rakaah commences with al-Fatihah. During the first two rakaah, following the recitation of al-Fatihah any other chapter or several verses of the Quran are additionally recited (qiraat) while in the standing position before the musallee moves into the bowing position (ruku). After one rakaah is complete (and on every subsequent odd rakaah), the musallee returns from the prostrate position (sujud) back to the standing position to begin another rakaah.

On every second rakaah, he first moves from sujud to an upright sitting position (jalsa) and recites the first portion of a supplication known as the tashahhud, before returning to the standing position to begin the next rakaah. On the final rakaah the musallee moves to the jalsa from the sujud position and recites the complete tashahhud. Sunni Muslims then conclude the prayer by turning their face toward the right shoulder and then toward the left shoulder, each time saying a salutation (taslim) to the angels that take note of your good (right shoulder) and evil (left shoulder) deeds. After the salat is completed it is common (but not compulsory) for Muslims to offer a supplication (dua) to God. This supplication, which essentially gives Muslims an opportunity to ask God for forgiveness and blessings, can be offered in any language.

Almsgiving

The third pillar of Islam is zakat, or almsgiving. A religious obligation, zakat is considered an expression of devotion to God. It represents the attempt to provide for the poorer sectors of society, and it offers a means for a Muslim to purify his or her wealth and attain salvation. The Quran, together with other Islamic traditions, strongly encourages charity and constantly reminds Muslims of their moral obligation to the poor, orphans, and widows; however, it distinguishes between general, voluntary charity (sadaqa) and zakat, the latter being an obligatory charge on the money or produce of Muslims.

While the meaning of terms has been open to different interpretations, the Quran regularly refers to zakat, identifying specific ways in which this tax can be spent. These specific uses include spending zakat on the poor and the needy, on those who collect and distribute zakat, on those whom Muslims hope to win over and convert to Islam, on travelers, on the ransom of captives, to relieve those who are burdened with debts, and on the cause of God.

The Quran provides less-detailed information about the kinds of things that are subject to the zakat tax or the precise share of income or property that should be paid as zakat. These determinations are provided in the traditions of the prophet Muhammad and have been the subject of elaborate discussions among Muslim legal experts, or jurists. For example, one-fortieth of the assets accumulated during the year (including gold, silver, and money) is payable at the end of the year, while one-tenth of the harvest of the land or date trees is payable at harvest time. Cattle, camels, and other domestic animals are subject to a more complex taxation system that depends on the animals in question, their age, the numbers involved, and whether they are freely grazing. Traditional zakat laws do not cover trade, but commercial taxes have been imposed by various Muslim governments throughout history.

Fasting

The fourth pillar of Islam is sawm, or fasting. Clear Quranic references to fasting account for the early introduction of this ritual practice. The Quran prescribes fasting during the month of Ramazan, the 9th month of the twelve -month Islamic lunar year. The month of Ramazan is sacred because the first revelation of the Quran is said to have occurred during this month. By tradition the month starts with the sighting of the new moon by at least two Muslims. For the entire month, Muslims must fast from daybreak to sunset by refraining from eating, drinking, and sexual intercourse. Menstruating women, travelers, and sick people are exempted from fasting but have to make up the days they miss at a later date.

According to various traditional interpretations, the fast introduces physical and spiritual discipline, serves to remind the rich of the misfortunes of the poor, and fosters, through this rigorous act of worship, a sense of solidarity and mutual care among Muslims of all social backgrounds. Thus Muslims usually engage in further acts of worship beyond the ordinary during Ramazan, such as voluntary night prayer, reading sections from the Quran, and paying voluntary charity to the poor. Muslims may even choose to wake before daybreak to eat a meal that will sustain them until sunset. After the fasting ends, the holiday of breaking the fast, 'id al-fitr, begins, lasting for three days.

At any time of year fasting is also required as a compensation for various offences and violations of the law. Many Muslims also perform voluntary fasts at various times of the year as acts of devotion and spiritual discipline. However, such additional fasting is not required by Islamic law.

REFERENCES

Abdullah, S.: *Adabiyyat-i Farsi men Hinduwon ka hòissa,* Delhi, 1942.

Abid Husain: *The Destiny of Indian Muslims,* London, 1965.

Abu-l-Layth Siddiqi: *Lakhna'u ka dabistan-i sha'iri,* Lahore, 1955.

Ahmad Ali Batalawi: *Nusrat al-mujtahidin,* Lucknow, 1895.

Ahòmad Shaykh Sirhindi: *Mabda wa ma'ad, Cawnpore,* 1891.

Akhund Darwiza: *Tadhkirat al-abrar wa-l-ashrar,* BM Or. MS 222.

al- Utbi: *Al-Ta'rikh al-Yamini,* Cairo, 1869.

al-Biruuni, Abu-Rayhòan: *Tahòqiq md li-i-Hind,* Eng. tr. E. Sachau, *Alberuni's India,* London, 1910.

al-Hamdani, Abbas H.: The Isma'ili Da'wa in Northern India, Cairo, 1956.

Aziz Ahmad: Islamic Culture in the Indian Environment, Oxford, 1964.

Azòfari, zòahir al-din: *Waqi'at-i Azfari*, Madras, 1957.

Cragg, Kenneth: *Counsels in Contemporary Islam*, Edinburgh, 1965.

Crooke, W.: *Religion and Folklore of Northern India*, London, 1926.

Ismi: *Futu as-salatòin,* Madras, 1948.

Ivanow, W.: *Guide to Ismda'ili Literature*, London, 1933.

Ja'bfar Sharif: Islam in India or the Qanun-i Islam, Eng. tr. G. A. Herklots, 1832; revised by W. Crooke, Oxford, 1921.

Jahangir: *Tuzuk,* Aligarh, 1864; Eng. tr. A. Rogers, London, 1909.

Rose, H. A.: *A Glossary of Tribes and Castes of the Punjab and North-West Frontier Province*, Lahore, 1911-19.

Rosenthal, E. I. J.: *Islam in the Modern National State*, Cambridge, 1965.

Roychoudhuri, M.: *The Din-i Ilahi,* Calcutta, 1941.

Sòabah-ad-din 'Abd-at-Rahòman: *Bazm-i Sòhòfiyya,* A'zamgarh, 1949.

15

Society

The foundations of the social organization of Islam rest on the notion that all humans are equal and comprise one single brotherhood. Islam says that if there's whatsoever actual difference between man and man it cannot be one of race, colour, state or speech, but of themes, notions and rationales. Two children of the same mother, though they may be equal from the point of view of a common ancestry, will have to go their different ways in life if their beliefs and moral conduct differ. On the contrary, two people, one in the East and the other in the West, even though geographically and outwardly separated by vast distances, will tread the same path in life if they share the same code of moral behaviour. On the basis of this fundamental tenet, Islam seeks to build a principled and ideological society very different from the racial, nationalistic and parochial societies existing in the world today.

The basis of co-operative effort among men in such a society is not the place of one's birth but a creed and a moral principle. Anyone, if he believes in Allah as his Master and Lord and accepts the guidance of the Prophets as the law of his life, can join this community, whether he is a resident of America or Africa, whether he belongs to the Semitic race or the Aryan, whether he is black or fair-skinned, whether he speaks a European language or Arabic. All those who join this community will have the same rights and social status. They will not be subjected to any racial, national or class distinctions. No one will be regarded as high or low. There will be no untouchability. There will be no special limitations upon them in arriving at weddings, eating and drinking and sociable contracts. No one will be looked down upon because of his parentage or work. No one will claim any typical rights by merit of his caste, community or ancestry. Man's virtue will not depend upon his family associations or riches, but only on whether he is better than other people in ethical demeanour or surpasses others in piousness and righteousness.

Such social order, surpassing as it does geographical limits and the roadblocks of race, colour and linguistic communication, is advantageous for all parts of the mankind; on its cornerstones can be raised the cosmopolitan fraternity of man. In societies based on race or nationality only those people can join who belong to a particular race or nation, but in Islam anyone who accepts its creed and moral standards can become a member, possessing equal rights with everyone else.

Those who do not accept this creed, while obviously not being received into the community, are treated with tolerance and humanity and guaranteed all the basic human rights. It is clear that if two children of the same mother differ in their ideas, their ways of life will be different; but this does not mean that they cease to be brothers. In the same way, if two nations or two groups of people living in the same country differ in their fundamental beliefs, principles and ideology, their societies will as well for certain disagree; all the same they'll continue to share the basic ties of humanity. Hence, the Muslim society offers to non-Muslims societies and groups the level best social and ethnical rights that can potentially be fitted in.

SOCIAL ORDER

Islam wards off extremes so as to conserve equilibrium and methodicalness in society. Justice to all is Islam's gist as it enables man to lead a good and blessed life and simultaneously fortifies bonds of human brotherhood and fortifies the social fabric. Justice in Islam is termed adl which means to divide two things equally or to keep the balance. This term is used in the Holy Quran for justice in all matters. Islam teaches the believers to be fair in their dealings.

Islam not only ordains the believers to do justice among themselves but also exhorts them to do full justice even in the case of their enemies. Justice and righteousness are the cornerstone of the Islamic way of life. The Holy Prophet was known for this justice even before he declared his prophethood. Throughout his life he urged his followers to be honest and upright and he himself set a perfect model of justice even to the followers of other religions and his foes.

In Islam, the state is not a divinity to be revered but an extraordinary establishment that is subject to the orders of law. Muslims are not affiliated in Islamic society because of their need for each other but rather, they are obliged to look after one another and to be responsible for the welfare of all. In accordance with the Divine law, the concept of social justice lays down certain conditions to treat man as an individual with liberty and equality as his birth right. It provides him with equal chances for building up his personality so that he is best fitted to fill the situation to which he is eligible, to give each human his due and to shape his relations with high society in terms of import and benefit.

Social Duties

This conception of social justice is accomplished by giving the individual a better understanding of his obligations in society and the honour thence as allowed under the Muslim dispensation. Teaching, being the measure and criterion in that context of use, was made obligatory by the Prophet on every Muslim. More specifically he said and knew that knowledge enabled one to distinguish right from wrong. By virtue of it, God exalts nations, makes them guides in good pursuits, and gives them leadership. The progress of society depends upon the interaction between the individual and society with the result that a balance is maintained in human affairs. Man as such should always keep in mind that God created the whole universe with a particular purpose and man has been asked to strive for its fulfilment.

The terms 'measure' and 'balance' refer to justice, the heavenly virtue which should be established among all men who constitute a society. Man has to act rightly with his associate beings and with the cosmos around him. which in the context of use of human involvements extends itself in the shape of cultural justice which weighs with exactness all corporeal and ethical exits.

Freedom in Society

Generally, human rights concentrate on equality and exemption. Human beings are all Slaves of God. In Islam, no favorable position, no differentiation and no distinction can be legally claimed by one over the other except by merit of piousness. All people are equal in their social status and this is fully manifested in the congregational prayers where there is no room for rank and special privilege.

All are equal in the sight of God whether he be a caliph or a slave. The Prophet Muhammad said that individuals were all equal like the teeth of a comb. Rights are generally followed by obligations but in Islam there are more responsibilities and less rights and this is meant to confine unlimited freedom lest it should be harmful to the concerns of society.

Justice to all is Islam's substance and this enables man to lead a full and blissful life while simultaneously fortifying the bonds of human brotherhood as well as the social framework. The social frame prevailing today in most Muslim countries is not Islamic. There are many places where conditions are monstrous and oppressive for the poor. There is rampant corruption, poverty and want around us. There are few who have acquired substantial wealth and thus enjoy the numerous amenities and luxuries of life whereas the majority do not even receive two square meals a day. Social order in an Islamic state lays stress on simple and austere efforts that are free from ostentation. The Holy Prophet Muhammad was just, he endeavoured to span the breach between the affluent and hapless, the high and the low. He preached a society in which there wouldn't be any victimization of one sphere over another. What Islam bearings at is a harmonious life which constitutes the balance of sociable forces.

Islam is far more than a scheme of theological system. It stands for a distinguishing refinement and a socio-political economical order based on pragmatic considerations. It is through the operation of Islamic principles that the fullest development of man's potentialities can be achieved. The optimum level of civilization which embodies the maximum for well-being can never be possible without spiritual and moral development. Islamic principles descending from Divinity are indeed perfect and absolute.

The Islamic approach is therefore just, natural, humane and also perfectly balanced and rational. Allah created mankind and He gave us a social order that has been embodied in the religion of Islam. Islam guides all mankind towards success both in this world and the hereafter and this has been the goal from the very first Prophet to the last Prophet of mankind. The perspective of Islam, apart from seeking success in the next world, is also strongly concerned with success in this world. Islam deals not only with the ways and means of devotion and worship towards Allah, but also with exercises which lead man towards Holy Communion with Him. Moreover, Islam helps human to solve temporal problems in terms of his relations in sociable and political life.

SOCIAL CONDUCT

Every religious belief lays great stress on moral facets of human behaviour in its own specific way. Broadly speaking there's great commonness between dissimilar faiths as far as ethical and ethical questions are concerned. In fact to mould a moral character is the most fundamental function of religion. All other functions are subsidiary to it. But it is also true that each religion has unique way of doing it and every religion puts differing emphasis on different aspects of human morality. Islam is also unique in this respect. It has its own honourable values and ethical conceptions, which are general as well as particular to Islam.

Islam has unequalled ethical motive of its own. It puts great deal of stress, for instance, on equality and justness and emphasizes self-respect of all humans. However, there are also universal moral values, which Islam lays emphasis on. The Quran gives us the concept of what it calls 'amal salih which, translated into English, would mean 'good deeds'. But this translation does not adequately convey the meaning. The key word here is 'salih'.

The root of the word is slh from which are derived many words with the meaning to be good, to repair, to mend, to improve, to be righteous, to be efficient, to be suitable, peace and friendliness, reconciliation etc. Muslims, as individuals and groups, have to fulfil certain basic duties which summarize the universal values of Islam. Whilst these obligations are abided by they bring justness, peacefulness and felicity in this world and they will so bring success and redemption in the afterlife.

Surat al-Isra was disclosed to Prophet Muhammad in Mecca after his nighttime Journey from Mecca to Jerusalem. In this surah Allah refers some basal loyalties of Muslims. Without accomplishing these commitments no person or group can succeed. Muslims have to live by these values and should invite the humanity to these raticnales. These principles are not limited to one race, clan or group; they are comprehensive in their range and practical application. These are as well called the Hikmah or the precepts of wisdom. It's advisable for every one to follow them. If followed properly they're able to increase the goodness and wiseness of all people. These precepts are:

1. To revere Allah alone: This means to recognize Allah as the ultimate reality and to recognize Allah as the Lord, to worship Him with all sincerity and to submit to Him in every aspect of life. A Muslim's life is nothing but total commitment to Allah. We are not only monotheists (people of Tawhid) but we are also theocentric people. Allah is the focus of our life and He is our total and elemental concern.

2. To be deferential and genial to the parents: This is to acknowledge the compassion and kindness of the parents, to be grateful to them and to do one's utmost to reciprocate that love and compassion. Filial piety and devotion is the second

most important commitment of Muslims. Deference and benignity to parents is not just a sociable duty for us; it is our spiritual duty and responsibility.

3. To be respectable to your relatives, to the hapless and the travellers: This is to remember that we are interconnected in this world. Our responsibilities are not only towards ourselves and our immediate families, but also to other relatives and to the society at large. We are all in need of each other and we are all fellow travellers in this path of life. We must see what we can do for others. Muslims must live a socially responsible life. Social obligation begins with the family, other relations and it includes all those who are in want.

4. To be thrifty with your money and not to waste your resources: One should be neither too tight with one's money nor too lose with it. Extravagance is not right, but also one should not become stingy and miserly. A Muslim is committed to the balanced life style. Money should be earned in Halal (lawful) ways and it should be spent in the right manner. This principle can be applied to all resources that Allah has given us. Prudent and careful use of resources is a very significant commitment of Muslims.

5. To take effective care of your youngsters: As we recognize the rights of the parents, we should also recognize the rights of children. Our children are our future. We must see that we raise healthy, intelligent and morally responsible children. Our commitment should be to raise them in safe and healthy environment. We must protect their life as well as their spirit and mind, their ethics and ways.

6. To steer clear of fornication and illegitimate relations: Sexual perversions bring the biggest harm to humans and societies. Observing the proper rules in this matter lead to health, happiness and good moral society. Muslims are committed to pure, clean and socially responsible life style. Islam teaches that one should not come even close to adultery or fornication. This means suitable dress code for males and females, suitable conduct in mixed societies and suitable control on cultural relations and amusement.

7. To regard every life and not to kill anybody unless in the interest of justice: This means that one should recognize the sanctity

of all life and should not do anything that may jeopardize life. One should avoid aggression and violence, because these things lead to murder. Every Muslim must be committed to peaceful ways. Conflicts should be resolved by dialogue and negotiations, not by killings and slayings. Nonetheless, justice must be asserted, because fair penalization brings safety and protects life.

8. To take care of the orphans: Orphans and all those who are defenceless must be taken care of. Their rights must be recognized and they should be protected from all harms. A Muslim must be deeply committed to the care of young, poor, infirm and handicapped. Kindness and compassion is the basic commitment of a Muslim. It includes everybody, including the brutes.

9. To fulfill the promises and your loyalties: Promises and contracts are an important part of human life and human civilization. When promises are not kept, people lose trust in each other and the whole society becomes weak. Muslims must be true to their words. Our commitment must be to speak the truth, to be honest and when we make an assurance we do our best to fulfill our pledges.

10. To be honest in business dealings and not to cheat in weight or measurement: Honest business brings progress, success and blessings. All business whether it is commercial, social or political must be done with a sense of justice and fairness. A Muslim is committed to fair dealing in everything and with every one. Dealing with a Muslim means dealing with full confidence. A Muslim businessman is the most truthful businessman. A Muslim worker is the most honest worker. A Muslim in any profession should bring honour to that profession.

11. To do things with knowledge and not to follow the hearsay or act on half- knowledge: The information agencies, the media have a great responsibility. A lot of injustice is done when the misinformation is given or the information is misused. Muslims should be committed to truth in information. They should promote truthful and honest reporting about everyone including their enemies. A report coming from a Muslim source should be the most trustworthy report. In a similar way Muslim should be extremely careful with their actions and reactions. They

should not react without proper evidence against anyone. They should show the world how the information is ascertained.

12. To be modest and have no haughtiness: moderateness and balance is the best thing in one's behaviour as well as in one's attitudes toward others. A Muslim is a dignified person, but he/she is humble. A Muslim is not boastful, arrogant or vainglorious. A Muslim gives thanks to Allah for all His gifts. For everything the elemental praise is for Allah and the real glory belongs to Allah.

    These are the canonical commitments of Muslims, as humans and as citizenry. These are the precepts of wisdom and the comprehensive values of Islam. When they are followed they bring justness, serenity and happiness in this world and they will indeed bring success and redemption in the afterlife.

Family Unit Life

In Islam, family is the foundation of the social organization. Family is not an irregular or unprompted organization of people, but it is a divinely decreed establishment. Family and wedding are regarded as noble and sacred; a social contract that confers mutual rights and obligations on the couple. The progress and welfare of society or its breakdown can be traced to the strength and unity or to the weakness of the family. The weakness is a crucial indicator of the weakness of society, reflected by problems like juvenile delinquency, drug abuse, alcoholism, teenage pregnancies, and divorce. The concept of an "extended family" is common in non-Western cultures, unlike the concept of a "nuclear family", which means a family consisting of just the parents and their children that is common in the West. "Extended family" means children, parents, grandparents, and sometimes in-laws share one household. Islam doesn't designate that a Muslim family should be either nuclear or expanded. With regards to relations inside the same family, the first and most significant is that of husband and wife, their children, and the grandparents.

Other relatives come in a second or third degree; although this is not to say that the individual has no obligation or responsibility at all towards these other relatives, whereas the first degree of relations has unequivocal and precise rights. Although the nature of duties and obligations among members of a family are instinctive in human nature, it is important to realize that Islamic law exists only to supplement and enforce these innate feelings and not to replace them. Islam acts as a guarantee that the rights and responsibilities that each member of the family has with regard to others will be fulfilled with justice and equality. In the absence of law, there could be problems arising from the fact that the innate nature of the father to treat all his children equally could be overridden by an attachment to one particular child, and so this child is especially favoured, for example in inheritance, leaving the other children with their rights denied.

Lineage or lineal duty has an essential role in the Muslim family because from it stems the duties, obligations, and responsibilities of family members. The most important Islamic teaching on this subject is that people must not claim a child as theirs if they adopted that child, and that children must not falsely claim to be the real son or daughter of a particular person if they are not, and that adopted children cannot be given the family name of their foster parents, because doing that would mask the adopted children's true identity.

And of course, natural children have more claim to any inheritance than adopted children. On the other hand, if an orphan or abandoned child is looked after by a family as an act of compassion; being given shelter, food, clothing, and other needs, then this is legal and indeed a great act of humanity for which Allah promises great rewards. Though the adopted children do not inherit on the same footing as the natural children, it is commendable for the adopter to bequeath something to them.

The importance of the family in Islam comes from its allocated function in preserving the human race by procreation. Also, it is responsible for protecting the morals of the society and individuals by providing the only legitimate avenue for the satisfaction of the sexual urge. Moreover, the family has an important role in providing the socialization and value orientation of children, and in providing social and economic security. Finally, making up a family motivates individuals to work hard, sacrifice their own welfare, and become beneficent for the sake of their family.

Charity

Charity, for which the saying used in the Holy Quran is "passing out of what God has given you", entails using your vitality, gift, imaginations, income, possessions, or whatsoever else, to help and do good to those in need. In Islam charity is very often brought up alongside prayer because just as the latter is man's relation with God, or man's duty towards God, the former (charity) represents his relation with his fellow-beings, and indeed with all the creation of God. Prayer expresses love for God, submission to Him, and a desire to bring out the Divine qualities that lie hidden in every person. Charity is an expression of sympathy and benevolence towards God's creation, putting into actual practice the lessons you learn in prayer. Innumerable examples can be given because doing any kind of good to anyone, even to yourself to make you more capable of benefiting others, by using what God has given you, is an act of charity.

Feeding the hungry, helping the poor, taking care of the destitute such as orphans, lending a hand to the disabled, helping an unemployed person to find a job, etc., are the more obvious examples of charity taught by Islam. But it also teaches that there are other, smaller acts of charity which one has the opportunity to do everyday. Aiding somebody in any way, showing the way to an unknown, speaking a kind word to cheer up someone, giving useful advice or bestowing knowledge to somebody, removing from the road something that could cause an accident, even plainly abstaining from wounding anyone, are all acts of charity in Islam.

Firstly, charity in Islam is much broader than giving money to the poor, and can be exercised just as well even where there is no poverty, as shown above. Secondly, giving charity, or the doing of any good to someone, must be done as a duty, not to degrade them or to ask for thanks. Thirdly, charity should be given solely out of love for God, out of the desire to do good to His creation. Being charitable is very strongly urged upon the Muslims, so much so that the Holy Prophet Muhammad has said that on every limb of the body, doing a charitable deed is due every day, whether it is with the hands, feet, or tongue. There is no person at all who cannot do a deed of charity to others.

According to the Holy Prophet, if someone has nothing to give, he should work and earn, and give out of that; if he still does not have anything to give, he should help someone in distress; and if he is unable, for some reason, to do even that, he should try to do any good he can and refrain from doing any harm to anyone. Just as acts of charity have the broadest possible significance in Islam, similarly the circle of those towards whom charity is to be exercised is the broadest that can be conceived. Starting with the people around us - our relations, friends, and neighbours - it extends to all Muslims, and to followers of other religions. In fact, a Muslim's charity covers even animals. The Holy Quran emphasizes that one should keep a special look-out for those who may be in need but who do not ask for help

TRADITIONAL VALUES IN SOCIETY

The substance of Islam brought by the Messenger of God, Muhammad was the final stage link up in the long chain of invitations toward God by the noble Prophets. Throughout history, this message has stayed the same: that human beings should recognise that their true Sustainer and Lord is One God, that they should submit to Him Alone, and that the lordship of man be eliminated. Except for a few people, mankind as a whole has never denied the existence of God and His sovereignty over the universe; it has rather erred in comprehending the real attributes of God, or in taking other gods besides God as His associates. This association with God has been either in belief and worship, or in accepting the sovereignty of others besides God.

Throughout every period of human history the call toward God has had one nature. Its purpose is 'Islam', which means to bring human beings into submission to God, to free them from servitude to other human beings so that they may devote themselves to the One True God, to deliver them from the clutches of human lordship and man-made laws, value systems and traditions so that they will acknowledge the sovereignty and authority of the One True God and follow His law in all spheres of life. The Islamism of Muhammad came for this aim, as well as the substances of the earlier Prophets.

The total world is under the sanction of God, and man, being a low part of it, inevitably obeys the natural laws regulating the universe. It is also essential that the same authority be accepted as the lawmaker for human life. Man shouldn't cut himself off from this authority to develop a separate system and a separate scheme of life. The growth of a human being, his conditions of health and disease, and his life and death are under the scheme of those natural laws which come from God; even in the consequences of his voluntary actions he is helpless before the universal laws. Man cannot change the practice of God in the laws prevailing in the universe. It is therefore desirable that he should also follow Islam in those aspects of his life in which he is given a choice and should make the Divine Law the arbiter in all matters of life so that there may be harmony between man and the rest of the universe.

It is therefore necessary that Islam's theoretical foundation-belief-materialize in the form of an coordinated and active group from the very commencement. It is essential that this group differentiate itself from the jahili society, becoming autonomous and clear-cut from the active and organized jahili society whose aim is to block Islam. The centre of this new group should be a new leadership, the leadership which first came in the person of the Prophet-peace be on him- himself, and after him was delegated to those who strove for bringing people back to God's sovereignty, His authority and His laws.

A person who bears witness that there is no deity except God and that Muhammad is God's Messenger should cut off his relationship of loyalty from the jahili society, which he has forsaken, and from jahili leadership, whether it be in the pretext of priests, conjurors or astrologists, or in the form of political, social or economical leadership, as was the case of the Quraish in the time of the Prophet. He will have to give his absolute allegiance to the new Islamic movement and to the Muslim leadership.

In this great Islamic society Arabs, Persians, Syrians, Egyptians, Moroccans, Turks, Chinese, Indians, Romans, Greeks, Indonesians, Africans were gathered together- in brief, peoples of all states and all races. Their various features were united, and with mutual cooperation, harmony and unity they took part in the construction of the Islamic community and Islamic culture. This marvellous civilization was not an Arabic civilization', even for a single day; it was purely an 'Islamic civilization'.

It was never a 'nationality' but always a community of belief'. Thus they all came together on an equal footing in the relationship of love, with their minds set upon a single goal; thus they used their best abilities, developed the qualities of their race to the fullest, and brought the essence of their personal, national and historical experiences for the development of this one community, to which they all belonged on an equal footing and in which their common bond was through their relationship to their Sustainer. In this community their 'humanity' developed without any encumbrance. These are features which were never accomplished by any other group of people in the entire account of mankind.

CASTE SYSTEM

There's no caste system in Islam, All men and women are born equal. In Islam, excellence depends upon the accomplishment of piousness or Allah-consciousness. There is no boundary to it. The more a person can acquire it, the higher position he will get in the society. Respectability in Islam depends on Allah-Consciousness and not on caste, race, wealth, power or position. Now only Islam can elevate their status to the point of honour and dignity by granting them equal status at par with the highest placed in the society. In fact, it is Allah who has given this guaranteed status to all who enter into His fold. No one can even think of taking it back or usurp in any from or shape even by the mightiest monarch, a Congress or a Parliament howsoever powerful it may be. The Quran ordains it and Allah's Prophet confirms it. Prophet Muhammad in his last discourse from the Mount of Arafat announced: "An Arab is no better than a non-Arab and a non-Arab is no better than an Arab; A red raced man is no better than a black, except in piety. Mankind are Adam's children and Adam was created from dust"

Islam forbids all kinds of differentiations on account of race, colour, birth or language. The society constituted by Prophet Muhammad was unequaled in this regard. It had Salman from Persia, Bilal from Ethiopia, Suhaib from Rome, all living together with respect and honour. Prophet Muhammad married his cousin, Zainab of the worthiest tribe of Quraish to Zaid bin Harith who was bought by his wife Khadija as slave. Caliph Omar used to call Bilal who was originally a slave as Sayyedna Bilal (Bilal My Lord) and used to accommodate him to sit by his side whenever he visited him during his Caliphate. Besides bringing the depressed at par in the society, Islam has its own wellbeing scheme that assures food, dress, protection, training, medical care, and justice to all the people within its fold who are hapless, destitute, impoverished, out of work or underemployed and disabled from its funds of Zakah and Sadaqah, a paramount source of transfer of resources from the haves to have-nots.

STATUS OF WOMEN

The intricate kinship between women and Islam is defined by both Muslim texts and the chronicle and civilization of the Muslim world. Sharia (Islamic law) allows for deviations between women's and men's roles, rights, and responsibilities. Muslim-majority countries give women varied degrees of rights with respect to marriage, split up, civil right, legal position, dress code, and education. Even where these differences are acknowledged, scholars and other commentators vary as to whether they are just and whether they are a correct interpretation of religious imperatives. Conservativists contend that differences of opinion between men and women are due to different position and obligations, while broad-minded Muslims, Muslim feminists, and others reason in favour of more forward-looking versions.

To assess the effect of Islam on the condition of women, many authors have discussed the status of women in pre-Islamic Arabian

Peninsula, and their determinations have been assorted. Some writers have argued that women before Islam were more liberated drawing most often on the first marriage of Muhammad and that of Muhammad's parents, but also on other points such as worship of female idols at Mecca. Other writers, on the contrary, have argued that women's status in pre-Islamic Arabia was poor, citing practices of female infanticide, unlimited polygyny, patrilineal marriage and others.

The position of women are mostly influenced by the extent of urbanization, industrialization, poletarization and political ploys of the state managers rather than culture or intrinsic properties of Islam; Islam, Moghadam argues, is neither more nor less patriarchal than other world religions especially Hinduism, Christianity and Judaism. Islam changed the structure of Arab society and to a large degree unified the people, reforming and standardizing gender roles throughout the region. Some have argued that in terms of women's rights, women generally had fewer legal restrictions under Islamic law than they did under certain Western legal systems until the 20th century. The calat on the ProphetFor example, restrictions on the legal capacity of married women under French law were not removed until 1965. However this argument is opposed by those who state that the consensus of Islamic Jurists has consistently held that in many cases a woman's evidence has half the value of that of a man, and that in some cases it is not admissible. To elucidate, in affairs of business concern, two men's testimonial is required, and where there is only one man, two women and one man are called for. In affairs of family, marriage, split up and such, however, one woman's evidence is enough to prove a case.

REFERENCES

Asad-Allah Tilhari: *Quwwat-i Hòanafiyya, Bada'un,* 1905.

Asbraf 'Ali Thanawi: *al-Intibahat al-mufida'an al-ishtibahat al-jadida,* Lahore, 1952.

Ashraf, K. M.: "Life and Conditions of the People of Hindustan, 1200-1550", *JASB* 1935.

Azad Bilgrami, Mir Ghulam "Ali (ed.): *Khizana-i Amira,* Cawnpore, 1871.

Azad, Abu-l-Kalam: *Tadhkira,* Lahore, n.d.

Azad, Muhòammad Hòusayn: *Ab-i Hayat,* Lahore, n.d.

Azòfari, zòahir al-din: *Waqi'at-i Azfari*, Madras, 1957.

Dames, M. Longworth: *Popular Poetry of the Baloches* London, 1907.

Dara Shukoh: *Safinat al-awhya'*, Urdu tr. Karachi, 1961.

Darmesteter, J.: *Chants populaires des Afghans*, Paris, 1888-90.

Daudpota, U. M.: *Sindhi Literature*, Karachi, 1951.

Jamali, Hòamid ibn-FaU+1EODl-Allah: *Siyar al-'Arifin,* Delhi, 1893.

Jamil, M. Tahir: *Hali's Poetry*, Bombay, 1938.

Juzjani, Minhaj-as-siraj: *Tabaqat-i Nasri,* ed. A. H. Habibi, Kabul, 1964.

Kalam-Allah, Shah: *Kashkal-i Kalimi,* Delhi, 1890.

Sabir, M.: "Cultural and Linguistic Affinities Between Turkey, Iran and Pakistan", in *Papers read at the R.C.D. Seminar on Common Cultural Heritage*, Tehran, 1965.

Sadiq, Muhammad: *A History of Urdu Literature*, London, 1964.

Saksena, R. B.: *A History of Urdu Literature*, Allahabad, 1940.

Saqi Musta'id Khan: *Ma'athir-i 'Aamgiri,* Calcutta, 1947.

16

Festivals

In the beginning, only two festivals were there in accordance with sharia law, the Eid-ul-fitr after the fastings of Ramazan and Eid-ul-Adha, concurring with pilgrim's journey to Mecca. All the same, many more festivals are celebrated to remember events (especially religious) which are beleived to be significant. For Muslims each and every religious festival have its own particular meaning. In fact, at the end of different manners of worship, Islam has established a kind of festival. The festival following the daily supplications of the week is Juma-tul-Mubarak (Friday), the one coming after the month of fast is called Eid-ul-Fitr, while the festival coming after the observance of Haj is know as Eid-ul-Adhia.

EID-UL-FITR

Eid-ul-fitr is a Muslim festival that symbolizes the end of Ramazan, the Muslim blessed month of fast. Eid is an Arabic language word implying "festivity", while Fitr stands for "to break the fast" (also mean "nature", from the word "fitrah") and so marks the ending of the fast period. Eid-ul-fitr starts the day after Ramazan ends, and is affirmed by the sighting of the new moon. Muslims give alms to the poor and wear their finest clothes. Eid-ul-fitr lasts three days and is called "The Smaller Eid" as compared to the Eid-ul-Adha that lasts four days and is called "The bigger Eid".

On the day of the festivity, a normal Muslim family arouses very early, does the first everyday supplication, and is expected to eat a bit, representing the end of Ramazan. They then go to special Congregationalist supplications held in masjids, large open areas, arenas and arenas. The prayer is generally brusque and is followed by a discourse (khu?ba). Worshippers greet and embrace each other with hugs in a spirit of peace and love after the congregational prayer. After the special prayers, festivities and merriment are commonly observed with visits to the homes of relatives and friends to thank God for all blessings. Eid-ul-fitr is a joyous occasion with important religious significance, celebrating the achievement of enhanced piety. It is a day of pardon, ethical victory, peace of faithful, companionship, fraternity and integrity. Muslims celebrate not only the end of fast but also thank God for the self-discipline and strength that Muslims believe almighty gave them. It's a time of charity and partaking, and many Muslims dress in festival attire.

As the day depends upon the sighting of the moon, the sighting can just be possible barely after sunset. Many Muslims ascertain with local mosques or other fellows of the community to see if the moon has been seen by official parties such as enlightened scholars. Though many Muslims believe that Quran says that the sighting of the moon ascertains the start of Eid, this is written in additional books. Basic greetings during this festival are the Arabic language greeting Eid mubarak (Blessed Eid) Happy Eid. Additionally, a lot of states have their unique greetings based on local dialect and customs. Muslims are encouraged to dress in their finest clothes and to attend a special Eid prayer that is executed in meetings at masjids or open areas like arenas, public square etc. When Muslims finish their fast on the last day (twenty-ninth or thirtieth), they recite Takbir.

"Allahu akbar, Allahu akbar, Allahu akbar

la ilaha illa Allah

Allahu akbar, Allahu akbar

wa li-illahi al-hamd"

Which when translated comes to:

God is the Greatest, God is the Greatest, God is the Greatest

There is no divinity but God

God is the Greatest, God is the Greatest

and to God goes all praise

The Takbir is said after verification that the moon of Shawwal has been seen on the eve of the last day of Ramazan. It keeps going until the start of the Eid prayer. Before the Eid prayer starts every Muslim, if feasible (man, woman or child), must give Zakat al-fitr, alms for the month of Ramazan. This corresponds to about two kilogram of a staple foodstuff (wheat, barley, etc.), or its cash equivalent, and is commonly collected at the masjid. This is distributed to needy local Muslims prior to the start of the Eid prayer. It can be given at any time during the month of Ramazan and is often given early, so the recipient can utilize it for Eid purchases. This is distinct from Zakat based on wealth, which must be paid to a worthy charity. The Eid supplication (salah) is accompanied by the khutba (sermon) then a prayer (dua) asking for pardon, clemency and help for the worries of Muslims across the world. The khutba also teaches Muslims as to the rites of Eid, such as the zakat (if they've not already given it). It's then usual to embrace the persons sitting on either side of oneself. People will also visit their relations, acquaintances and friends.

Afterward the prayers, a few people will go to the cemeteries (ziyarat al-qubur). Muslims spend the day giving thanks to the Almighty for all their benedictions, in addition to as merely having fun and delighting themselves. Children are generally given confectioneries or money. Women (especially relatives) are commonly given special presents by their loved ones. Eid is also the time for rapprochements. Feuds or quarrels, especially between family members, are often settled on Eid. Eid-ul-fitr marks the end of the fast of Ramazan. Ramazan is the sacred month par excellence. This has to do with the communal aspects of the fast, which expresses many of the basic values of the Muslim religion. Fast is considered by some researchers to glorify important differentiations, extolling the power of the sacred domain, while admitting the mastery of the physical domain.

The Muslim custom also connects events with the social occasion. For instance, on Eid-ul-fitr, the angel Gabriel came down with white apparels for from each one of prophet Muhammad's grandsons. At the end of the sacred calendar month of Ramazan, in which the Muslims are asked to observe fast from dawn to dusk and do additional prayers and observe spiritual values rigidly, the Muslims celebrate the sighting of the new moon (beginning of the new Islamic month). In Bangladesh, India and Pakistan, the night before Eid is called Chand Raat, or night of the moon. People visit markets and malls, with their families and children, for eleventh hour Eid shopping. Women, especially young girls, often paint each others' hands with traditional "henna" and wear bright bangles. The popular way of greeting in South Asia during festivity of this festival is to say Eid Mubarak to others. Children are encouraged to wish the elders. In substitution of this they also expect to get some cash money, called Eidi, from the seniors.

On the daybreak of Eid-ul-fitr, after taking a fresh bath, every Muslim is encouraged to wear fresh clothes, if they can afford it. As an alternative, they may don neat clean clothes. Men and boys go to masjid or open fields called Eidgah for special Eid prayers, thanking God for enabling a Muslim to observe the holy month meaningfully. The Muslims are ordained to pay Zakat al-Fitr (special charity money) or Fitra to the poor and needy before the Eid prayer, so that they can also join others to celebrate the Eid. After the prayers, the meetings are dispelled and the Muslims meet and greet each other including family members, children, seniors, acquaintances and neighbors. Some Muslims especially go to cemeteries to beg for the redemption of the deceased soul. Usually, children visit senior relations and neighbours to pay regards and greetings.

Among the special dishes in India, Pakistan and Fiji is sivayyan, a dish of delicate, cooked vermicelli noodles. In Bangladesh, sivayyan is called shemai, and is an intrinsic item of Eid dishes. After meeting the acquaintances and relations, many people go for parties, banquets, special fairs and celebrations in the parks (with picnics, pyrotechnics, etc.). In Bangladesh, India and Pakistan, many markets, malls, and eating places see huge crowd & high attending during this principal Muslim festival. A lot of people also use this chance to give out Zakat, the Islamic compulsory money tax on one's riches to the impoverished. In this way, the Muslims of South Asia observe their Eid-ul-fitr in a joyous mood by thanking the Almighty and bringing their families, acquaintances and the hapless and impoverished people closer in a democratic fashion.

EID-UL-ADHA

Eid-ul-Adha or the Festival of Sacrifice is a religious festival observed by Muslims worldwide as a remembrance of God's pardon of Abraham from his vow to forfeit his son, as ordered by Allah. (Islamic custom names Ishmael as the son who was to be sacrificed, whereas the Judeo-Christian custom names Isaac.) It's among the two Eid festivals observed by Muslims, whose foundation comes from the Quran. Like Eid el-Fitr, Eid-ul-Adha begins with a brusque supplication followed by a discourse (khutba). Eid-ul-Adha each year falls on the 10th day of the calendar month of Dhul Hijja of the lunar Muslim calendar. The celebrations last for two to three days or more depending on the state. Eid-ul-Adha occurs the day afterward, the pilgrims conducting Haj, the annual pilgrimage to Mecca in Saudi Arabia by Muslims from all over the world, descend from Mount Arafat.

It happens to be about 70 days after the end of the month of Ramazan. Eid-ul-Adha (Adha Eid) has other favourite names across the Muslim world, such as Eid el-Kibir (the 'Big' Eid) in Morocco, Algeria, Tunisia,

Egypt and Libya; Tfaska Tamoqqart in the Berber language of Jerba; Tabaski or Tobaski in West Africa; Babbar Sallah in Nigeria; Ciidwayneey in Somalia and Somali-speaking areas of Kenya and Ethiopia. In India and Pakistan it's also called Badi Eid (Big Eid). In Kashmir, where Kashmiri is expressed, it is called Baed Eid, and Keralites who speak Malayalam say Waliya Perunnal, both words also meaning "Big Eid." In Bangladesh it is called either Id-ul-Azha. In Republic of South Africa it is also addressed as Bakri Eid. In Indian state of Tamil Nadu, and in Sri Lanka, which has large concentration of Tamil-speaking Muslims, it is addressed as Peru Naal meaning 'The Big Day'. Occasionally, Tamil-speakers say Bakr Eid Peru Naal, meaning 'the Big Day of the Sacrifice'.

Men, women, and youngsters are required to dress in their best clothing to perform Eid prayer in any masjid. Muslims who can afford to do so sacrifice their best domesticated animals (commonly sheep, but also camels, cows, and goats) as a symbol of Abraham's sacrifice. The sacrificed animals, called "udhiya" as well known as "qurbani", have to fulfill certain age and quality standards or else the animal is beleived to be an unaccepted sacrifice. Generally, these must be at minimum a year old. At the time of sacrifice, Allah's name is recited along with the offering statement and a supplication as Muhammad said. According to the Quran, the meat is divided into three shares, one share for the poor, one share for the relatives and neighbours, and the last to keep to oneself.

A large portion of the meat must be given towards the poor and hungry people so they can all join in the feast which is held on Eid-ul-Adha. The remainder is cooked for the family celebration meal in which relatives and friends are invited to share. The normal generous practices of the Muslim religion are presented during Eid-ul-Adha by the combined effort to see that no deprived Muslim is left without sacrificial food during these days. Eid-ul-Adha is a solid assertion of what the Muslim community ethical code means in exercise. People in these days are expected to visit their relatives, beginning with their parents, and then their families and acquaintances.

Giving out meat among multitude is beleived to be an all important part of the festival during this time period, as well as intoning Takbir out loud before the Eid prayer on the first day and after prayers through out the four days of Eid. While Eid-ul-Adha is always on the same day of the Islamic calendar, the date on the Gregorian calendar varies from year to year since the Islamic calendar is a lunar calendar and the Gregorian calendar is a solar calendar. The Lunar calendar is approximately eleven days shorter than the Solar calendar. Every year, Eid-ul-Adha (like other

Muslim holidays) falls on one of two opposite Gregorian dates in a different part of the world, due to the fact that the boundary of crescent-shaped visibleness is dissimilar from the dateline.

RAMAZAN

Ramazan is a Muslim spiritual ceremony that happens during the 9th month of the Muslim calendar, considered to be the month in which the Quran started to be imparted. It is the Muslim calendar month of fast, in which Muslims do not eat or drink anything from break of day till end of day. Fast is meant to instruct the person patience and humility. Ramazan is a time to fast for the sake of God, to offer even more supplication than natural and call for pardon for the sinfulnesses of your yesteryear and ask for counselling in the futurity.

To abstain from every day evilnesses and try to purge oneself through temperateness and respectable deeds. The name "Ramazan" is the name of the 9th month; the word itself descended from an Arabic language word for acute heat, sunbaked earth, and dearth of food. It is beleived to be the most revered and sanctified month of the Muslim year. Supplications, sawm (fast), giving, and self-accountability are particularly accentuated at this time; religious observances associated with Ramazan are kept throughout the month. Laylat al-Qadr, which falls during an odd night in the last ten days of Ramazan(and so it can be either the twenty-one, twenty-three, twenty-five, twenty-seven, or the twenty-nine of Ramazan), marks the revealing of the 1st verses of the Quran and is believed to be the most blessed night of the year. Ramazan ends with the festival Eid-ul-fitr, on which banquets are held. During the month following Ramazan, called Shawwal, Muslims are encouraged to fast for an additional six days.

The most outstanding event of this month is the fast (sawm) followed by law-abiding Muslims. Each day during the month of Ramazan, Muslims round the world arise before break of day to eat the Suhoor meal (the pre dawning meal) and execute their fajr prayer. They interrupt their fast when the fourth prayer of the day, Maghrib (end of day), is due. During Ramazan, Muslims are expected to put more effort into abiding by the commandments of Islam and to avoid abhorrent and ungodly sights and voices. Sexual practices during fasting hours are also prohibited.

Pureness of both thought and action is important. The fast is destined to be an demanding act of deep private worship in which Muslims seek a advanced level of intimacy to God Almighty. The act of fast is said to redirect the heart away from worldly activities, its purpose being to cleanse the inner soul and free it from harm. Properly observing the fast is supposed to induce a comfortable feeling of peace and calm. It also allows for Muslims to practice self-control, sacrifice, and understanding for those who are less privileged, intended to make Muslims more benevolent and benevolent. Muslims can eat after the sun has set. Pregnant women, the senior, the sick, travellers and youngsters who have not achieved pubescence are all excused from fast as want of food and liquid in this position could be damaging to wellness.

Besides fast, Muslims are encouraged to read the entire Quran. Sunni Muslims tend to execute the reading of the entire Quran by means of particular prayers, called Tarawih, which are held in the masjids every night of the month, during which a whole section of the Quran (juz, which is 1/30 of the Quran) is recited, so that by the end of the month the entire Quran has been completed. Tarawih is an Arabic phrase referring to those extra prayers. This prayer is performed after salah of Ishaa, but before the witr rakat. Tarawih is not practiced by Shia Muslims, as they believe it was introduced into Islam by the second Caliph, Umar ibn al-Khattab. Muslims also pay Zakat during the month.

For those who qualify to pay Zakaat, as per the Islamic Nisab (that is those whose wealth exceeds their necessities), of the leftover of their wealth earned in that Islamic calendar year. Although Zakat can be paid any time of the year, it has to be calculated on a year to year basis, and many Muslims use Ramazan as the month for calculation and disbursement. Ramazan is also a time when Muslims are to slow down from worldly affairs and center on self regeneration, religious purifying and enlightenment, building a link between Almighty and themselves by supplication, prayer, giving, good efforts, forgivingness and assisting other people.

As it's a festival of charity and partaking, Muslims cook extraordinary foods and purchase gifts for their family and acquaintances and for charity to the hapless and impoverished who can't afford it; this can involve purchasing fresh clothes, shoes and additional items of want. There is also a social aspect involved - the preparing of special foods and inviting people for the Iftar meal. In many Muslim and non-Muslim countries with large Islamic populations, bazaars close down in the evening to enable masses to execute supplications and eat the Iftar meal (the meal to end the fast) - these bazaars then re-open and stay open for a good part of the night.

Muslims can be seen shopping, eating, spending time with their friends and family during the evening hours. Laylat al-Qadr (Shab-e Qadr), literally the "Night of Decrees" or "Night of Measures", is the day of remembrance of two very important dates in Islam that occurred in the month of Ramazan. Muslims believe that it was the night of the Laylat al-Qadr that the Quran's first verse was revealed. The exact night of the Laylat al-Qadr is only known to God. It has been assured to Prophet Muhammad one night, but on his way out to deliver the news he was disturbed by two Muslims' argument and that resulted in him forgetting the exact date of the night. The date was not disclosed only to promote Muslims to pray and work hard on the last 10 days and not only that night. That is why Muhammad suggested that it was on one of the last ten nights of Ramazan.

The Islamic festival of Eid-ul-fitr marks the end of the fasting period of Ramazan and the first day of the following month, after additional new moon has been sighted. The Eid falls after twenty-nine or thirty days of fast, as per the lunar sighting. Eid-ul-fitr means the Festival of breaking off the Fast; an exceptional festivity is made. Food is given to the hapless, everybody puts on their best, preferably new, clothes, and communal prayers are held in the early morning, followed by feasting and visiting relatives and friends. The prayer is two rakaahs only, and it is an optional prayer as opposed to the compulsory five daily prayers. According to one current school of thought, it is suggested that North American Muslims arrange their work schedule for Eid by requesting the two most likely days of Eid as vacations or merely as days away from work.

This allows for prize family time, and is related to the Christian tradition of taking Christmas Day and Christmas Eve off as holidays. This also allows for time off to celebrate the Eid prayer at a mosque and with family. The fast always ends after twenty-nine or thirty days of fast, and thus the request would be for the twenty-ninth and thirtieth day after the beginning of the fasting. Muslims are encouraged to fast six days in Shawwal, the month following Ramazan that begins after Eid-ul-fitr; these days need not be sequentially. Accordant to hadith, one who fasts the calendar month of Ramazan and six days during Shawwal will be honoured as if he fasted the whole year.

MUHARRAM

Muharram is the calendar month with which the Muslims commence their lunar Hijrah Calendar. It's among the four blessed months about which the Holy Quran enunciates, "The number of the months according to Allah is twelve (named) in the Book of Allah on the day He made heavens and the earth. Among these twelve months there are four blessed." These 4 months, accordant to the bona fide customs, are Dhul-Qadah, Dhul-Hijjah, Muharram and Rajab. All the observers of the Holy Quran are unvaried on this point, because the Holy Prophet, Sall-Allahu alayhi wa sallam, in his discourse on the occasion of his last Haj, announced: "One year comprises of twelve months, of which four are blessed months, three of them are in chronological sequence; Dhul-Qadah, Dhul-Hijjah, Muharram, and the fourth is Rajab."

The particular quotation of these four months doesn't signify that any other month has no holiness, because the month of Ramazan is confessedly the most sacred month in the year. But these four months were specifically termed as blessed months for the bare grounds that their holiness was accepted even by the gentiles of Mecca. In fact, every month, out of the twelve, is originally equal to the other, and there is no inherent sanctity that may be attributed to one of them in comparison to the other months.

When Allah Almighty chooses a particular time for His special blessings, the same acquires sanctity out of His grace. Thus, the holiness of these four months was accepted right from the days of Sayyidina Abraham, alayhi salam. Since the gentiles of Mecca assigned themselves to Sayyidina Abraham, alayhi salam, they abided by the holiness of these four months and in spite of their frequent tribal battles, they held it illegitimate to battle in these months.

In the Islamic law of Noble Prophet, Sall-Allahu alayhi wa sallam, the holiness of these months was upheld and the Holy Quran referred to them as the "blessed months". Although the fasts in the month of Muharram are not compulsory, yet one who fasts in these days out of his own will is eligible to a great honour by Allah Almighty. The Hadith quoted above means that the fasts of the month of Muharram are most rewarding ones among the Nafl or willing fasts. The Hadith doesn't mean that the award promised for fasts of Muharram can be achieved only by fast for the whole month. On the contrary, each fast during this month has merit. Therefore, one should avail of this opportunity as much as he can. Although Muharram is a sanctified month as a whole, yet, the 10th day of Muharram is the most sacred among all its days. The day is named Ashurah'.

According to the Holy Companion Ibn Abbas, Radi-Allahu anhu. The Holy Prophet, Sall-Allahu alayhi wa sallam, when migrated to Medina, found that the Jews of Medina used to fast on the 10th day of Muharram. They said that it was the day on which the Holy Prophet Musa (Moses), alayhis salam, and his followers passed over the Red Sea miraculously and the Pharaoh was submerged in its waters. On hearing this from the Jews, the Holy Prophet, Sall-Allahu alayhi wa sallam, said, “we’re more closely associated to Musa, alayhi salam, than you,” and told the Muslims to fast on the day of Ashura.

It’s also described in a number of trustworthy customs that in the first place, fast on the day of Ashura was compulsory for the Muslims. It was later that the fasts of Ramazan were made compulsory and the fast on the day of Ashura was made nonobligatory. Sayyidina Aisha, Radi-Allahu anha, has said: “When the Holy Prophet, Sall-Allahu alayhi wa sallam, came to Medina, he fasted on the day of Ashura and guided the people to fast. But when the fasts of Ramazan were made compulsory, the responsibility of fast was limited to Ramazan and the compulsory nature of the fast of Ashura was abandoned. Whoever so desires should fast on it and any other who so likes can avoid fast on it.”

However, the Holy Prophet, Sall-Allahu alayhi wa sallam, used to fast on the day of Ashura even after the fast in Ramazan was made obligatory. Abdullah ibn Musa, Radi-Allahu anhu, reports that the Holy Prophet, Sall-Allahu alayhi wa sallam, preferred the fast of Ashura on the fasts of other days and preferred the fasts of Ramadhaan on the fast of Ashura. In short, it is established through a number of authentic ahadith that fast on the day of Ashura is Sunnah of the Holy Prophet, Sall-Allahu alayhi wa sallam, and makes one entitled to a great reward. According to another Hadith, it is more recommended that the fast of Ashura should either be preceded or followed by another fast.

It means that one should fast two days: the 9th and 10th of Muharram or the 10th and 11th. The reason of this additional fast as mentioned by the Holy Prophet, Sall-Allahu alayhi wa sallam, is that the Jews used to fast on the day of Ashura alone, and the Holy Prophet, Sall-Allahu alayhi wa sallam, wanted to distinguish the Muslim way of fasting from that of Jews.

Consequently, he advised the Muslims to add a different fast to that of Ashura. Some customs intend another characteristic of the day of Ashura. Concording to these customs, one should be kinder to his family by providing more food to them on this day as compared to other days. These customs are not very reliable according to the science of Hadith. However, there are some fables and misconceptions with regard to Ashura that have managed to find their way into the minds of the ignorant, but have no support of authentic Islamic sources, some very common of them are these: This is the day on which Adam, alayhi salam, was created. This is the day when Abraham, alayhi salam, was born. This is the day when Allah accepted the repentance of Sayyidina Adam, alayhi salam. This is the day when Qiyaamah (doomsday) will take place.

Whoever takes bath on the day of Ashura will never get ill. Some other people attribute the sanctity of Ashura to the martyrdom of Sayyidna Husain, Radi-Allahu anhu, during his battle with the Syrian army. No doubt, the martyrdom of Sayyidina Husain, Radi-Allahu anhu, is among the most tragical episodes of our history. Yet, the holiness of Ashura can't be assigned to this event for the simple reason that the holiness of Ashura was laid down during the days of the Holy Prophet, much earlier than the birth of Sayyidna Husain, Radi-Allahu anhu.

EID-E-MILAD-UL-NABI

The festival of Eid-e-Milad-ul-nabi is also popularly known as Barah Wafat the 12th day. The day memorializes the birth and as well the death of Prophet Muhammad. Bara Wafat falls on the twelfth day of the third month Rabi-ul-Awwal in September-October. Here, Barah or twelve, stands for the twelve days of the Prophets illness. The festivities of birthday are low-keyed as the day also happens to be the death anniversary of Prophet Muhammad. The day is marked by holding spiritual sermons, reading the Holy book of Quran and giving alms to the poor. Prophet Muhammad was born in 571 AD. on April 12th, in Mecca in Arabia. Circa 610 AD., Prophet is said to have gained revelations from Allah through the angel Gabriel that he was His Messenger.

In 622 AD. Muhammad along with his followers went to Medina. This escape from Mecca to Medina is known as Hijrah and marks the commencement of the Muslim era. By 630 AD., Islam came to be admitted as a religion and Muhammad as ruler by a large number of masses. Nevertheless, in 632 AD. Muhammad conducted the pilgrimage to Mecca, preached his parting discourse and expired before long after.

Barah Wafat doesn't ask any kind of expansive festivities as the birth day and death anniversary of Prophet Muhammad coincidentally falls on the same day. Hence, Muslims spend this period in religious activities. Special prayers meets and sermons on Quran are also organized in mosques to mark the day of Milad. Learned men and scholars focus their sermons on the life and teachings of Prophet Muhammad and inspire people to follow the path of good life as shown in Quran. Hence, the festival gives a chance to people to introspect their deeds and think of ways of being a better person. Besides, in some places hymns are sung and elegies or marsiyas are recited in memory of the last days of the Prophet. Acts of charity are also done by devout Muslims and alms are distributed to the poor and the needy. Afterwards, citizenry invite acquaintances and relations for a banquet. In some mosques, however, a 'sandal rite' ceremony is performed over the symbolic footmarks of the Prophet etched in a stone. A stone impersonation of Buraq the horse on which Prophet Muhammad is said to have rose to his celestial home is placed near the footmarks and embrocated with sandal paste or fragrant powder. Likewise, the house and jewel casket bearing this are intricately adorned.

SHAB-E-BARAT

The festival of Shab-e-Barat is celebrated with éclat and exuberance by Muslims all over the world. Because, Muslims think that on the night of Shab-e-Barat almighty composes the fortunes of all humans for the approaching year by taking into accounting the feats committed by them in the yesteryear. The festival is celebrated either on the 13th or on the 14th day of Shaban, the 8th month of the Muslim year. This happens to be fifteen days before the beginning of Ramazan. Shab-e-Barat means the night of forgiveness or Day of Atonement. People pray to god both in preparation for Ramazan and for the forgiveness of the sins committed by them.

The festival is also known as Boraks Nigh. In Persian language, 'Shab' means night and 'Barat' means 'the night of commission or assignment'. In Arabic, nevertheless, the day is called Lailatul Baraat, meaning the night of emancipation. Some although see Shab-e-Barat as the night of good luck and a common legend says that on this night the Prophet travels to each house and allays the ails of agony of humanity.

The night of Shab-e-Barat too memorializes the entering of Muhammad into the city of Mecca. Nevertheless, Shia Muslims affiliate this night with the birth of their final Imam. Skies light up on the night of Shab-e-Barat as the festival is celebrated in the night. Houses and streets are are also illuminated by candles and strands of electric bulbs to provide a joyful ambiance to the festival. Colourful fire works keep dazzling the skies as the Muslims stay awake on the night of Shab-e-Barat. This is due to a belief that god writes the destinies of all living beings for the coming years in heavens during the night. Sweets, specially the delicious savaiyyan or the vermicelli is prepared and sent to friends and also to the relatives in their remembrance of those who died during the year. Some also execute acts of giving by dispersing treats to the hapless and impoverished in the name of their expired ancestors. Flowers are also offered to the tombs of the departed family members.

Fatihah or the benedictions are said over the meal in the name of the Prophet, his daughter Fatimah and her husband Ali. The sacred Book of Quran is also read to mark the day. Muslims hold a notion that if individual prays to Allah throughout the night and seek pardon for all the sinnings he could have committed, he could be forgiven. Therefore, the entire night of prayer is devoted to asking for forgiveness for the past year and for good fortune in the year to come. Some people also go to masjids for supplications and meditation. While some Muslims fast during the day and deliver nafal, the nonobligatory namaz at night. It might be noted that there is no reference of Shab-e-Barat in the holy book of Quran. However, Sura Dukhan does cites about Laila Mubaraka, which, accordant to the knowledgeable scholars of the Quran and the Hadith, is Shab-e-Barat.

REFERENCES

Chishti, 'Abd-al-Hòalim: "Hasan ibn-Muhammad as-Saghani" in *Ma'arif,* Jan.-Sept. 1959.

Colebrook, H. T.: "On the Origin and Peculiar Tenets of Certain Muhammadan Sects", *Asiatic Researches*, vii (1801)

Cousens, H.: *Bijapur and its Architectural Remains*, Bombay, 1916.

Cragg, Kenneth: *Counsels in Contemporary Islam*, Edinburgh, 1965.

Crooke, W.: *Religion and Folklore of Northern India*, London, 1926.

de Garcin Tassy: *Histoire de la Litterature Hindouie et Hindoustanie,* Paris, 1870.

Dörfer, Gerhard: *Türkische und mongolische Elemente in Neupersischen*, Wiesbaden, 1965.

Dughlat, Mirza Haydar: *Ta'rikh-i Rashidi,* Eng. tr. E. Denison Ross and N. Elias, London, 1898.

Dumasia, N. M.: *A Brief History of the Agha Khan*, Bombay, 1903.

Ibn-Kathir: *Al-Bidaya wa-n-nihaya,* Cairo, 1932-9.

Kamal Khwaja al-din: *The Ideal Prophet*, London, 1925.

Kashani, 'Izz-ad-din: *Misbahò al-hiddya,* Lucknow, 1904.

Kaul, J. L.: *Interpretations of Ghalib*, Delhi, 1957.

Khafi Khan: *Muntakhab al-lubab,* Calcutta, 1869-1925.

Oman, J. C.: *The Mystics, Ascetics and Saints of India*, London, 1905.

Pakistan ki 'ilaqa'i zabanon par farsi ka athar, Karachi, n.d.

Philips, C. H.: *Historians of India, Pakistan and Ceylon*, London, 1961.

Punjab Notes and Queries, Allahabad, 1883-7.

Sarwar Muhòammad: *Panjabidab,* Karachi, n.d.

Sayyid, Ahòmad Khan: *Tafsir al-Qur'an,* Lahore, 1880-1895.

Sell, E.: *The Religious Orders of Islam*, Madras, 1908.

Sen, D. C.: *History of Bengali Language and Literature*, Calcutta, 1911.

17

Religious Places

RELIGIOUS PLACES IN INDIA

Dargah Khwaja Sahib of Ajmer

It's a long-familiar historical fact that in propagating the moral and sacred values of Islam, great and competent contributions have been made by the walis (holy person) of Allah. It was their humanitarianism, temperament and piousness which converted the hearts of hundreds of thousands of masses. They touched the masses directly. They attended and admired them. They lived with them and inspired them in the realisation of Eternal Truth. The proof of this is more than evident from the history of the growth of Islam in India. Although India was penetrated in the first century of Hijra, the noble task of inspiring the people to its tenets and values was accomplished by Hazrat Khwaja Muinuddin Chishti, popularly known as Khwaja Sahib and Khwaja Gharib Nawaz.

He did it all through his own great moral power, glorious and appealing character, with love and dedication to mankind, without any worldly resources of wealth, power, force or support. Khwaja Sahib was a scholar of great repute. He interpreted the true Islamic message of love for mankind and through that, love for the Almighty Creator. He advocated the Quranic doctrine of integrity of religion and worked out its potentials for the whole of humanity. He was the most distinguished mystic of his time. He laid the groundwork of the broad-minded Chishti order of Sufis in India, and inspired millions of individuals to be his followers, and thus assisted the masses of the Indian sub-continent.

Khwaja Muinuddin Chishti, arrived in Ajmer at the age of 52 years (1190 AD.), on his divine mission, unique in the annals of Islam. His only armour for the success of his great mission was the greatest "invisible power" that pervades and sustains the whole universe. At that time, Ajmer was ruled by Prithvi Raj Chauhan, the famous Rajput king. In his court, he had a large number of powerful magicians with Ajai Pal as their leader. Khwaja Sahib stayed on a hill close to Ana Sagar lake now known as the Chillah Khwaja Sahib. When the news spread that a very pious Dervish had come to Ajmer, people began to flock to him in increasing numbers. Whoever came to him, received the kindest treatment and blessings. People were so much inspired by his divine teachings and simplicity that they began to embrace Islam. Many became his disciples. Even Ajai pal submitted himself to the divine powers of Khwaja Sahib, gave up all his magic and became his disciple.

Meanwhile, Shahabuddin Ghori again attacked India, in 1192 AD., and in the famous battle of Tarain, defeated Prithvi Raj. When Shahabuddin Ghori came to know of the presence of Khwaja Sahib at Ajmer, he personally came to see him at his place, and enjoyed the grace of his meeting.

Khwaja Sahib continued his noble magnificent mission, showing the Path of Truth to the people. He also sent his disciples and successors to the different part of the country who also served the people and preached the tenets of Islam. Dargah Shariff of Hazrat Khwaja Muinuddin Chishti is indeed an ornament to the city of Ajmer. It is one of the holiest places of worship in India not only for the Muslims but also for the people of other faiths who hold the saint the high esteem and reverence. As mentioned previously. The Khwaja Saheb, as a 'living spirit' of peace and harmony, enjoys universal respect and devotion ever since he set his holy feet on the soil of Hindustan.

He has unquestionably been one of the greatest spiritual redeemers of human sufferings. To the faithful and afflicted souls invoking his blessing, he has ever been a never-failing source of moral strength and spiritual enlightenment. Apart from the common people, even the mighty kings of India, both Hindu and Muslim, have paid submissive homage to the great saint and have sought his miraculous aid to solve their problems. The precious buildings and various rich endowments dedicated to the Dargah of Khwaja Saheb are living memorials to and reminders of his continued patronage enjoyed by the people of India throughout the past 750 years.

The Dargah lies at the foot of the northern extremity of Taragarh hill. Its main attraction is the mausoleum containing the tomb of the saint which is the sanctum of the Dargah. Among its other prominent attractions which catch the eye of a visitor immediately he enters the Dargah, are the two mighty Buland Darwaza, which were built with the donations of Sultan Ghyasuddin Khilji of Mandoo who ruled Malwa from 1469 to 1500 A.D. The other Buland Darwaza in the north, which is now the main entrance of the Dargah, was built by Nisam Usman Ali Khan of Hyderabad Deccan in 1915 AD. at a cost of Rs. 55,857/-. On the top of this gateway, there is the main Naqqar Khana (drum house) containing two pairs of huge naqqars (beating drums) which were presented by Emperor Akbar after his successful victory in a campaign of Bengal.

They are sounded to the accompaniment of music played on Nafeeries and Shahnias at certain fixed hours of every day and night of the year by musicians permanently employed on the staff of the Dargah. The Dargah includes many other attractive buildings, tombs, courtyards and Daalaans, some of which are exquisite specimens of the Moghul architecture and were erected during the Moghul period. Akbar was the 1st Moghul Emperor to visit the Dargah on foot when Ajmer came under his possession. He built the Akbari Masjid in the Dargah in 1571 AD. which is a big mosque (140x140) feet. It was furbished up by Nawab Ghafoor Ali of Danapur in 1901 AD. One of its wings now lodges the Moiniua Usmania Darul-Uloom, an Arabic language and Persain School, for religious teaching which is run under the direction of the Dargah.

Fatehpur Sikri

Fatehpur Sikri is in reality a historical capital city made out of twin village of Fatehpur and Sikri that are situated 45 kms from the city of Agra. The city is located amongst desolate ridge. Emperor Akbar built this city, to serve jointly with Agra, as the noble capital of Mogul empire. The story of this four centuries old city is no less exciting than the city itself. It has been described through the accounts of History that Emperor Akbar had no issues and that's why his lamentations new no border. Somebody counselled him to ask for an interview with the celebrated Sufi saint, Khwaza Salim Chisti who resided at Sikri village. He walked the distance with the royal entourage. Salim Chisti blessed him with a son who was called Salim in reverence to the saint. The same prince when sat on the throne, re-christened himself to Jahangir. Akbar commanded to build the city of Sikri to immortalize the arrival of the prince.

Hazratbal Mosque

Hazratbal Mosque is the most significant Muslim Religious place, located on the west shore of Dal Lake. Its pure white marble elegance is mirrored in the waters of the lake. Hazratbal's especial signification is derived from the fact that it puts up a hair of the prophet Muhammad.

This is exhibited to the public on religious occasions, usually accompanied by fairs. Apart from these occasions, Friday prayers are offered at Hazratbal and attended by throngs of people. Hazratbal is noteworthy for being the only domed masjid in Srinagar; the others having clear-cut pagoda like roofs. The shrine - masjid complex is situated on the west shore of the Dal Lake face-to-face to Nishat Bagh and commands a grand scene of the lake and the mountain beyond.

The chronicle of the shrine dates back to the early 17th century when the Mughal Emperor Shahjahan's Subedar, Sadiq Khan, arrayed a garden here & built a impressive building, Ishrat Mahal or Pleasure House in 1623. However, the Emperor, during his visit in 1634, ordered the building to be converted into a prayer House with some additions & alterations. During the time of Aurangzeb, when Moi-e-Muqqadus (The Holy Relic) arrived in Kashmir in 1699, it was first kept in the shrine of Naqashbad Sahib in the heart of the city. Since the place was found to be insufficient in view of the unprecedented rush of people who thronged the place to have a glimpse of the Moi-e-Muqqades, it was decided to shift the it to Hazratbal, then known as Sadiqabad. The building of the nowadays marble construction was started by the Muslim Auqaf Trust headed by Sheikh Muhammad Abdullah in 1968 and completed in 1979. The Moi-e-Muqqadas is exhibited on assorted affairs related with the life of Prophet & his foursome holy associates.

Khanqah of Shah Hamadan

Khanqah of Shah Hamadan or Khanqah-e-Moula is located in Srinagar, on the banks of the river Jhelum. One of the earliest Muslim shrines in Kashmir, the Khanqah was constructed by Sultan Sikander built in 1395. The Khanqah is a wooden construction whose chief beautiful feature is its attractively engraved eaves and dangling bells. The insides are richly engraved and painted, and the age-old chandeliers give it an air of luxuriousness. The Khanqah-i-Mualla is devoted to Muslim preacher Mir Syed Ali Hamdani. Also known as Shah Hamadan, the preacher came to Kashmir from the city of Hamadan in Persia in the 13th century. He is believed to be responsible for the spread of Islam in Kashmir. The Shah stayed in Kashmir for many years and then left for Central Asia via Ladakh. He also built a mosque at Shey (near Leh). The shrine gains an exceptional signification on 6th of Zilhaj (last month of Islamic calendar), the death anniversary of Mir Syed Ali Hamadni. On this day, devotees visit the shrine in multitudes to pay a tribute to Shah Hamadan.

The Khanqah of Shah Hamadan was the 1st masjid to be constructed in Srinagar. The Shah used to contemplate and offer his supplications daily on the banks of river Jhelum, at the same place where the shrine now bears. The Khanqah of Shah Hamadan in Kashmir has undergone ruination a couple of times. The year 1480 saw the shrine being ruined in a devastating fire. Later, the shrine was reconstructed and restored by the then ruler Sultan Hassan Shah. Again, in 1493 AD., Khanqah-e-Moula was demolished and reconstructed in two-stories. A fire again struck the shrine in 1731 AD. leading to first its destruction and then renovation by Abul Barkat Khan. This mosque, situated on the right bank of the Jhelum River, is an excellent example of indigenous wood architecture that draws inspiration from Buddhist, Hindu and Islamic architecture. Built by Sultan Sikandar and committed to the memory of Mir Sayyid Ali Hamdani, an Islamic saint from Hamadan, Persia, this masjid also serves as a khankah. In the Ain-i-Akbari of Abul Fazal, there's acknowledgment of a holy person living in Srinagar and establishing this monastery in his name.

The masjid has been raised to the earth and reconstructed 3 times. Destroyed by fire in 1480, it was rebuilt and expanded by Sultan Hassan Shah. In 1493 it was demolished and rebuilt as a two-story structure. Again in 1731 fire destroyed the mosque; Abul Barkat Khan reconstructed it. Most mosques and shrines (ziyarat) in Kashmir are based on an architectural pattern of a low, cubic space forming the prayer hall or burial chamber, which is then covered by a pyramidal roof and often supported by a series of pillars. Big masjids will have a 3rd factor known as the mazina which comprises of a public square, open marquee from which the muazzin would give the call to prayer (azan), and a sharp steeple which represents the minaret.

The Shah Hamadan mosque neatly fits this local typology of mosque architecture. It has a square plan measuring approximately 75'-6"(23m) on each side and sits on an irregular walled base composed of materials from ancient temples. It is a two storied, two-tiered structure with gently sloping, pyramidal roofs differentiating each tier. The roofs are further emphasized by heavy woodwork done on the cornices under the eaves. The first tier has double-arcaded verandahs running continuously around the building, the only break being for the canopied main entrance. The second tier is more of an arcaded balcony that protrudes on all four sides of the main structure.

The arcaded verandahs and balconies with their delicate wooden grilles (pinjras) and slender columns not only lend structural support to the roof but also effect an impression of this 52'-6" (16m) tall mosque soaring into the sky. The pyramidal roof of the second tier is capped off by an open pavilion for the muezzin, which in turn is crowned by a sharp pyramidal spire. The base of the spire has a protruding triangular, decorative window on each face and has a golden end ornament (alem) at the apex. Parts of the roof have over time been covered with seasonally flowering vegetation, creating a charming image of intricate woodwork and terraced flowerbeds.

Accessions over time were made; for instance a small accessory tabernacle and two rows of religious residence created in the interior. The rows consist of 14 cloisters, which flank the north and south side of the large 21x14 m prayer hall. The shrine of the saint is in a cloister in the northwest corner. A date, 1384 AD. (786 Hijra), marking the saint's death, is carved above the doorway. This tomb chamber is decorated with glass and glazed work.

An annual congregation forms at this shrine to celebrate the saint's death on the 6th of 'Zilhaj', the last month of Muslim calendar. The walls of the prayer hall are woodwork panels with stone skirting, some display the names of God carved in gold. At the centre of the prayer hall are four solid wooden pillars almost 7 m high, placed in a square configuration, to hold up the ceiling. They are decorated with painted wooden chips arranged in a fishbone pattern in the shafts, carved lotus motifs at the base and leaf patterns at the 16-sided capitals.

Nizamuddin Dargah

Located in the historical Nizamuddin village, about two kms from Humayun's grave, and not far from the easterly end of the Lodi Road, is the Dargah of Hazrat Nizamuddin. It's the shrine of a celebrated humanitarian Islamic Sufi and mystical saint, Sheikh Hazrat Nizamuddin Aulia Chishti. Sheikh Hazrat Nizamuddin was born at Badaun in the state of Uttar Pradesh in 1236. He was the adherent of the saint Sheikh Farid Shakarganj, who appointed him as his heir. Said to be a direct descendant of Sheikh Nizamuddin Chisti, he had a large following which included Alauddin Khilji, Muhammad bin Tughlaq and the great poet Amir Khusrau. The imperial progressions of the Mughal Emperors Babur, Humayun, Akbar, Jahangir, and Shah Jahan always stopped at Nizamuddin's shrine, while the Emperor paid his respects at the sacred dargah.

The honourable saint was favourite among people of all faiths because of his doctrine of repudiation and tolerance towards other religions. It is said that he prophesied Ghiyasuddin Tughlaq would never return to Delhi again and the ruler died soon after. Hazrat Nizamuddin died in 1325 and his shrine nowadays is a favourite pilgrimage site.

Hazrat Nizamuddin's original grave no more subsists. Faridun Khan, a nobleman, built the present construction in the mid-15th century, and it was furbished up and decorated by Firoz Shah Tughlaq, as well as by later rulers. A mosque and many other tombs of famous people surround the dargah, as they wished to be buried near the saint. It has a marble-paved courtyard where the sacred shrine of the saint can be seen. Shah Jahan later added the majestic pavilion with its marble arches and lattice screens known as jalis. Worshippers tie red threads to these jalis as signs of wishes they hope will be fulfilled.

The roof is surmounted by a dome, which is ornamented by vertical stripes of black marble with lotus cresting. It is said that Akbar constructed this imposing dome. The main grave is wrapped with a scented chadar or cloth, which is dark green in colour. Devotees offer their prayers at the shrine by showering rose petals and lighting incense sticks. Pilgrims congregate at the shrine twice a year for the festival or Urs held to mark the anniversaries of Hazrat Nizamuddin Aulia and the renowned poet Amir Khusrau. The best day to visit the shrine is on Thursday eve to feel the faith of the devotees, who visit the shrine, seeking fulfillment of their prayers.

Jama Masjid, Delhi

The Masjid-i-Jahan Numa, generally known as the Jama Masjid of Delhi, is the chief masjid of Old Delhi in India. Authorized by the Mughal Emperor Shah Jahan, builder of the Taj Mahal, and accomplished in the year 1656 AD., it is one of the greatest and best-known masjids in India. It is also at the beginning of a very busy and popular street/centre in Old Delhi, Chandni Chowk. Masjid-i-Jahan Numa means "the mosque commanding a view of the world", and the name Jama Masjid is a reference to the weekly congregation observed on Friday at the mosque. The courtyard of the mosque can hold up to twenty-five thousand worshippers. The masjid also houses many souvenirs in a cupboard in the north gate, including a transcript of the Quran written on deer skin.

The mosque was the final result of the attempts of over 5,000 workers, over a period of six years. The price incurred on the building in those times was ten lakh (1 million) Rupees. Shah Jahan built several significant masjids in Delhi, Agra, Ajmer and Lahore. The Jama Masjid's floorplan is very similar to the Jama Masjid at Agra, but the Jama Masjid is the bigger and more imposing of the two. Its majesty is further enhanced because of the high ground that he selected for building this mosque. The architecture and design of the Badshahi Masjid of Lahore built by Shah Jahan's son Aurangzeb in 1673 is closely related to the Jama Masjid in Delhi. The courtyard of the mosque can be reached from the east, north and south by three flights of steps, all built of red sandstone. The northern gate of the mosque has 39 steps.

The southern side of the mosque has 33 steps. The eastern gate of the mosque was the royal entrance and it has 35 steps. These steps used to house food stalls, shops and street entertainers. In the evening, the eastern side of the mosque used to be converted into a fair for poultry and birds as a whole. Before the 1857 War of Indian Independence, there was a madrasah near the south side of the mosque, which was dismantled after the mutiny.

The mosque faces west. Its three slopes are covered with open arched arcades, each having a eminent tower-like gateway in the middle. The mosque is about 261 feet long and 90 feet wide, and its roof is covered with three domes with alternate stripes of black and white marble, with its topmost parts covered with gold. Two lofty minarets, 130 feet high, and containing 130 steps, longitudinally striped with white marble and red sandstone, flank the domes on either side. The minarets are divided by three projecting galleries and are surmounted by open twelve-sided domed pavilions. On the back of the mosque, there are four small minarets crowned like those in the front.

Under the domes of the mosque, is a hall with seven arched entrances facing the west and the walls of the mosque, up to the height of the waist, are covered with marble. Beyond this is a prayer hall, which is about 61 meters X 27.5 meters, with eleven arched entrances, of which the centre arch is wide and lofty, and in the form of a massive gateway, with slim minarets in each corner, with the usual octagonal pavilion surmounting it. Over these arched entrances there are tablets of white marble, four feet long and 2.5 feet wide, inlaid with inscriptions in black marble. These letterings give the chronicle of the construction of the mosque, and glorify the sovereignty and merits of Shah Jahan. The slab over the middle arch contains simply the words "The Guide!" The mosque stand on a platform of about five feet from the pavement of the terrace, and three flight of stairs lead to the indoor of the mosque from the east, north, and the south.

The floor of the masjid is covered with white and black marble ornamented to copy the Muslim prayer mat; a thin black marble border is marked for the worshippers, which is three feet long and 1 ½ feet wide. In total there are 899 such spaces marked in the floor of the mosque. The back of the mosque is cased over to the height of the rock on which the mosque stands with large hewn stones.

Haji Ali Dargah

The Haji Ali Dargah is a mosque and dargah located on an islet off the coast of Worli in Mumbai. Lying as it does in the heart of the city, the dargah is one of the most recognizable landmarks of Mumbai. Although it is a mosque and dargah, it is very popular among Hindus from Mumbai itself, other parts of Maharashtra and southern Gujarat. It is believed that praying at the dargah helps fulfill one's wishes.The Sunni Barelvi Movement of India Controls the Dargah and Masjid as is the case of most of the Masjids of Mumbai.

The dargah was built in 1631 by a wealthy Muslim merchant and saint named Haji Ali who renounced all his worldly possessions before making a pilgrimage to Mecca. Legend has it that Haji Ali died on his way to Mecca and his body, in its casket, floated back to Mumbai. However, some believe that Haji Ali drowned at the place where the dargah stands today. As many as 40,000 pilgrims visit the shrine on Thursdays and Fridays.

The dargah is built on a tiny islet located 500 yards from the coast, in the middle of Worli Bay, in the vicinity of Worli. The islet is linked to the city precinct of Mahalakshmi by a narrow causeway. This causeway is not bound by railings, and is lashed by the sea during high-tide. Therefore, the dargah is accessible only during low tide. This 500-yard-walk on the causeway, with the sea on both sides, is one of the highlights of a trip to the shrine. The whitewashed structure occupies an area of 4,500 metres, and an 85 foot tower is the architectural highlight of the edifice. The tomb within the mosque is covered by a brocaded red and green chaddar (tomb cover sheet). It is supported by an exquisite silver frame. The main hall has marble pillars embellished with coloured mirror work: blue, green, yellow chips. The ninety-nine names of Allah are also written on the pillars.

RELIGIOUS PLACES OUTSIDE INDIA

Mecca

Mecca (Meccah Al-Mukarramah) is Islam's most blessed city and abode to the Kaaba shrine and the Grand mosque. The city is acknowledged for the annual Haj pilgrimage, which being one of the five pillars of Islam, attracts close to 2 million pilgrims. Islamic tradition attributes the beginning of Mecca to Ishmael's descendants. In the 7th century, the Islamic prophet Muhammad proclaimed Islam in the city, by now an important trading centre, and the city played an important role in the early history of Islam. After 966, Mecca was led by local sharifs, until 1924, when it came under the rule of the Saudis. In its modern period, Mecca has seen a great expansion in size and infrastructure. The modern day city is located in and the capital of Saudi Arabia's Mecca Province, in the historic Hejaz region. With a population of 1,700,000, the city is set seventy-three kms inland from Jeddah, in a constrict valley, and 277 meters above sea level.

According to Muslim custom, the account of Mecca goes back to Abraham when he constructed the Kaaba with the help of his son Ishmael, around 2000 BC. The denizens were expressed to have fallen away from monotheism through the charm of the Amelkites. Historians state that the Kaaba later became the repository of 360 idols and tribal gods of all of Arabias nomadic tribes. Until the 7th century, Meccas most important god would remain to be Hubal, having been placed there by the ruling Quraysh tribe. The city was also known to Ptolemy as "Macoraba". In the 5th century, the Quraysh tribe took control of Mecca, and became skilled merchants and traders. In the 6th century they joined the lucrative spice trade as well, since battles in other parts of the world were causing trade routes to divert from the dangerous sea routes to the relatively more secure overland routes.

The Byzantine Empire had previously controlled the Red Sea, but piracy had been on the increase. Another previous route, that from the Persian Gulf via the Tigris and Euphrates rivers, was also being jeopardized by victimization from the Sassanid Empire, as well as being interrupted by the Lakhmids, the Ghassanids, and the Roman-Persian Wars. Mecca's importance as a trading centre outperformed the cities of Petra and Palmyra.

By the middle of the sixth century, there were three outstanding colonies in northern Arabian Peninsula, right along the southwestern coast that borders the Red Sea, in a liveable area between the ocean and the great desert to the east. This area, known as the Hejaz, featured three settlements that had grown around oasis, where water was available. In the centre of the Hejaz was Yathrib, later renamed as Medina. 250 miles (400 km) south of Yathrib was Taif, a mountain town, and northwest of Taif was Mecca. Though the area around Mecca was completely barren, Mecca was the wealthiest and most important of the three settlements.

Islamic histories state that it had abundant water via the Zamzam Well, which was the site of the holiest shrine in Arabia, the Kaaba, and was also at the crossroads of major caravan routes. Actually the well of Zamzam was barely sufficient to support the small community there, the Kaaba was but one of many such Arabian Polytheistic temple found in the peninsula, and the city was the terminus for a single caravan route which ran from Mecca to Syria.

The harsh conditions of the Arabian peninsula usually meant a constant state of conflict between the tribes, but once a year they would declare a truce and converge upon Mecca in an annual pilgrimage. This journey was intended for religious reasons, to pay homage to the shrine, and to drink from the Well of Zamzam. However, it was also the time each year that disputes would be arbitrated, debts would be resolved, and trading would occur at Meccan fairs. These annual events gave the tribes a sense of common identity and made Mecca extremely important throughout the peninsula.

Muhammad's great-grandfather had been the first to equip a camel caravan, and they became a regular part of the town's economy. Alliances were struck between the merchants in Mecca, and the local nomadic tribes, who would bring leather, livestock, and metals which were mined in the local mountains. Caravans would then be loaded up in Mecca, and would take the goods to the cities in Syria and Iraq. Islamic tradition claims that goods from other continents also flowed through Mecca. From Africa and the Far East towards Syria supposedly flowed spices, leather, drugs, cloth, and slaves; and in return Mecca was to have received money, weapons, cereals, and wine, which were distributed throughout Arabia. The Meccans signed treaties with both the Byzantines and the Bedouins, and negotiated safe passage for caravans, which included such things as water and pasture rights.

These further increased Meccas political power as well as economic, and Mecca became the centre of a loose confederation of client tribes, which included those of the Banu Tamim. Other forces such as the Abyssinian, Ghassan, and Lakhm were in decline, and Meccan influence was the primary binding force in Arabia in the late 6th century. Muhammad was born in Mecca in 570, and thus Islam has been inextricably linked with Mecca ever since. Muhammad was born in a minor faction, the Hashemites, of the ruling Quraysh tribe. Islamic tradition states that he began receiving divine revelations here in 610 AD., and began to preach monotheism against Meccan paganism. After enduring persecution for 13 years, Muhammad emigrated in 622 with his followers to Medina.

The conflict between the Quraysh and the Muslims, however, continued: the two fought Battle of Badr, where Muslims defeated the Quraysh outside Medina; whilst the Meccans overcame the Muslims at the Battle of Uhud. Overall, however, Meccan efforts to annihilate Islam were unsuccessful, and during the Battle of the Trench in 627, the combined armies of Arabia were unable to defeat Muhammad.

In 628, Muhammad and his following peacefully marched to Mecca, seeking to enter the city for pilgrimage. Rather, however, both Muslims and Meccans entered into the Treaty of Hudaybiyyah, whereby Muslims and Quraysh would cease fighting and Muslims would be allowed into the city the following year. Two years later the Quraysh violated the truce, but instead of continuing their fight, the city of Mecca shortly surrendered to Muhammad. The prophet declared amnesty for the inhabitants, gave generous gifts to the leading Quraysh. Mecca was cleansed of all its idols and cult images in the Kaaba. Muhammad declared Mecca as the holiest site in Islam ordaining the it as the centre of Muslim pilgrimage, one of the faith's five pillars. Despite his conquest, however, Muhammad chose to return to Medina, leaving behind Attab bin Usaid to govern the city.

Muhammad's other activities in Arabia led to the unification of the peninsula, putting an end to the wars that had disrupted life in the city for so long. Muhammad died in 632, but with the sense of unity that he'd passed on to the Arabians, Islam began a rapid expansion, and within the next few hundred years stretched from North Africa well into Asia. As the Islamic Empire grew, Mecca continued to attract pilgrims not just from Arabia, but now from all across the Empire, as Muslims sought to perform the annual Haj. Mecca also attracted a year-round population of scholars, pious Muslims who wished to live close to the Kaaba, and local inhabitants who served the pilgrims. Due to the difficultness and expense of the Haj, pilgrims came by boat at Jeddah, and came overland, or conjoined the annual caravans from Syria or Iraq.

The absolute majority of Meccans are Sunni Muslims, with a minority of Shiite Pilgrims. The city has over 9000 Mosques. The Quran orders Muslims to face the sanctified precincts of Mecca during the Salat. At first though, the focus of the Qiblah was toward mosque al-Aqsa, Jerusalem. The determination of this sacred direction gave rise to an important study in medieval Islam, distinct and separate from mainstream Islamic tradition of mathematical geography and cartography. The cultural environment of today's Mecca has been influenced by a religious movement that began in central Arabia in the mid-eighteenth century. This movement is generally known as the Wahhabi movement. It has been also influenced by the Shafii school. Also, the conflict between progressives and religious researchers made a major affect on the Society of Mecca.

Since the seventh Century, Mecca has hosted millions of Islamic pilgrims worldwide in their way to Haj. This merge with pilgrims has also a major affect on the society and the religion of Meccans. The primary industry in Mecca in modern times is to support the annual pilgrimage of the Haj, as well as to support the pilgrims who visit the city at all other times of the year. Major stops in their visit include: The Kaaba is the ancient stone building towards which all Muslims pray. It was originally one of multiple such buildings in Arabia, but was the only one made of stone, and therefore is the only one still standing. Many Muslims believe that it dates back to the time of Abraham in 2000 BC. All pilgrims are called for to walk anticlockwise round the Kaaba seven times commencing at the Black Stone, in a rite called the Tawaf.

Muslims consider that the Zamzam Well was disclosed to Hagar, mother of Ishmael. She was urgently looking for water for her infant son, but could find none. Mecca is located in a hot dry valley with few other sources of water. According to tradition, the water of the Zamzam well is divinely blessed. It is believed to satisfy both hunger and thirst, and cure illness. The water is dished out to the public through coolers placed throughout the Masjid al-Haram and the Al-Masjid al-Nabawi in Medina. All pilgrims arrive at every effort to drink of this water on their pilgrimage.

Medina is a city in the Hejaz region of western Saudi Arabia, and serves as the capital of the Al Medina Province. It is the second holiest city in Islam, and the burial place of Muhammad. It is historically significant for being Muhammad's home after the Hijrah.

Medinas importance as a religious site derives from the presence of the 'Tomb of Prophet Muhammad' inside 'The Mosque of The Prophet'. The mosque was built on a site adjacent to Muhammad's home, and as Muslims believe that prophets must be buried at the very same place they leave this mortal world, Muhammad was thus buried in his house. The tomb later became part of the mosque when it was expanded by the Umayyad Caliph Al-Walid I. The first mosque of Islam is also located in Medina and is known as Masjid Quba (the Quba Mosque). It was destroyed by lightning, probably about 850 AD., and the graves were almost forgotten. In 892 the place was cleared up, the tombs located and a fine mosque built, which was destroyed by fire in 1257 AD. and almost immediately rebuilt. It was restored by Qaitbay, the Egyptian ruler, in 1487.

Like Mecca, the city of Medina only permits Muslims to enter, although the haram (area closed to non-Muslims) of Medina is much smaller than that of Mecca, with the result that many facilities on the outskirts of Medina are open to non-Muslims, whereas in Mecca the area closed to non-Muslims extends well beyond the limits of the built-up area. Both cities' numerous mosques are the destination for large numbers of Muslims on their Haj (annual pilgrimage). Hundreds of thousands of Muslims come to Medina annually to visit the 'Tomb of Prophet' and to worship at mosques in a unified celebration. Muslims believe that praying once in the Mosque of the Prophet is equal to praying at least 1000 times in any other mosque.

Jerusalem

Jerusalem is the capital of Israel and its largest city in both population and area, with 732,100 residents in an area of 125.1 square kilometers if disputed East Jerusalem is included. Located in the Judean Mountains, between the Mediterranean Sea and the northern tip of the Dead Sea, modern Jerusalem has grown up outside the Old City.

The city has a history that goes back to the 4th millennium BC., making it one of the oldest cities in the world. Jerusalem has been the holiest city in Judaism and the spiritual centre of the Jewish people since the 10th century BC., contains a number of significant ancient Christian sites, and is considered the third-holiest city in Islam. Despite having an area of only 0.9 square kilometer (0.35 square mile), the Old City is home to sites of key religious importance, among them the Temple Mount, the Western Wall, the Church of the Holy Sepulchre, the Dome of the Rock and al-Aqsa Mosque. The old walled city, a World Heritage site, has been traditionally divided into four quarters, although the names used today — the Armenian, Christian, Jewish, and Muslim Quarters — were introduced in the early 19th century. In the course of its history, Jerusalem has been destroyed twice, besieged 23 times, attacked 52 times, and captured and recaptured 44 times.

For Muslims, Jerusalem is the third most holy site in Islam. The name of Jerusalem derived from its original Jebusite name Ur-Salem or Urishalim. For Muslims the name suggests "peace" and corresponds closely to the Muslim concept of the sacred; a place where peace reigns and conflicts is excluded.

Going back to Jerusalem's history we find that it marked more by conflict than by peace. Hadrian destroyed the city, replacing it by a Roman creation from which Jews were banned. Then the Sassanids came and laid it waste. Under the Islamic era, Jerusalem enjoyed 13 years of peace until the Seljuk Turks came between 1070 and 1090 AD., in addition to the Crusader Kingdom between 1099 and 1187 AD. All that led to a sort of chaos and it brought a constant conflict between the conquerors in the city.

So the question that comes is how did Jerusalem become important in Islam, and to Muslims? Jerusalem was in the middle of Trade routes. Most of the merchants used to pass from there heading towards Asia Minor and the west. Not to forget Arabs from Mecca too. Islam holds a great estimation as the location of many vents associated with the life of Jesus. From that day, Jerusalem has had a very important spiritual meaning for Muslims, not only being the first Qibla but also the mystical experience of the prophet's ascendance to heaven. Jerusalem tried to be focused by Muslim Pilgrimage, but the significance of Jerusalem thereafter declined in favour of Mecca and Medina.

When Saladdin recaptured the city from the Crusaders, Jerusalem regained once again its glory, where Christians were guaranteed rights of worship, Muslim places of worship which had been desecrated were restored, even a small Jewish community returned to the city, and Jewish culture has seldom flourished as they did under Muslim rule, that's how the spiritual significance of Jerusalem has been absorbed by all three religions.

Muslims on the other hand have an obligation to honour other religions. There is recognition, a respect for both Judaism and Christianity as people of the book, mentioned in the holy Quran. I guess it would be a pity for Jerusalem, the supposed city of peace, were to be transformed into a city of war as a result of Israeli plans, which ignore its significance for Muslims.

Karbala

Karbala is a city in Iraq, located about 100 km. southwest of Baghdad. It is the capital of Karbala Province. Shia Muslims consider Karbala to be one of their holiest cities after Mecca, Medina, Jerusalem and Najaf. The city is best known as the location of the Battle of Karbala. Karbalas prominence in Shia is the result of the Battle of Karbala, fought on the site of the modern city on October 10, 680. Both Husayn and his brother Abbas ibn Ali were buried by the local Bani Asad tribe at what later became known as the Mashhad Al-Husayn. The city grew up around the tombs, though the date of construction of the first sanctuary is not known.

The city and tombs were greatly expanded by successive Muslim rulers, but suffered repeated destruction from attacking armies. The original shrine was destroyed by the Abbasid Caliph al-Mutawakkil in 850 but was rebuilt in its present form around 979, only to be partly destroyed by fire in 1086 and rebuilt yet again.

Like Najaf, the city suffered from severe water shortages that were only resolved in the early 18th century by building a dam at the head of the Hussayniyya Canal. In 1737, the city replaced Isfahan in Iran as the main centre of Shia scholarship. In the mid-eighteenth century it was dominated by the dean of scholarship, Yusuf Al Bahrani, a key proponent of the Akhbari tradition of Shia thought, until his death in 1772, after which the more state-centric Usuli school became more influential. It suffered severe damage in 1802 when an invading Wahhabi army sacked the city. Following the Wahhabi invasion, the city's sheikhs established a self-governing republic which was ended by a reimposition of Ottoman rule in 1843. This prompted many students and scholars to move to Najaf, which became the main Shia religious centre.

Karbalas development was strongly influenced by the Persians, who were the dominant community for many years. The Kammouna family (Arab) were custodians of the shrines for many years and effectively ran the city until it fell under the control of the British Empire in 1915. The Persian influence was deliberately reduced under British rule, with a series of nationality laws being introduced to squeeze out the Persian community. By 1957, they accounted for only 12% of the city's population. They were subsequently assimilated into the Iraqi population, accepting Iraqi nationality.

The association of the city with Shia religious traditions led to it being treated with suspicion by Iraq's Sunni rulers. Under Saddam Hussein's rule, Shia religious observances in the city were greatly restricted and many non-Iraqi Shia were not permitted to travel there at all.

REFERENCES

Elliot, H. M. and Dowson, J.: *The History of India as Told by its Own Historians*, Allahabad, 1964.

Encyclopaedia of Islam, London, Leiden, 1960.

Encyclopaedia of Religion and Ethics, J. Hastings, Edinburgh, 1908-21.

Ethé, H.: *Catalogue of Persian Manuscripts in the India Office*, Oxford, 1903, 1937.

Hadi, Mirza Muhòammad: *Nur-Allah Shustari, Shahid-i Thalith,* Lucknow, 1925.

In ‘am al-Hòaqq: *Muslim Bengali Adab,* Karachi, 1957.

Khaja Khan: *Studies in Tasawwuf,* Madras, 1923.

Khayr-ad-din, M.: *Tadhkirat al-'ulama'*, Calcutta, 1934.

Khushal Khan Khattak: *Poems from the Divan*, tr. D. N. Mackenzie, London, 1965.

Khusraw, Amir: *Matòla ‘al-anwar,* Lucknow, 1884.

Muhòsin Fani: *Dabistan-i madhahib,* Eng. tr. D. Shea and A. Troyer, Paris, 1843.

Muhòyi-d-din, Shaykh: *al-Balagh al-mubin,* Lahore, 1876.

Mujeeb, M.: *The Indian Muslims*, London, 1967.

Mushtaqi, Rizq-Allah: *Waqi'at-i Mushtaqi,* BM Add. 11633.

Shatòtòari, Baha'ad-din: *Risala-i Shatòtòariyya,* 10 Pers. MS 2257.

Shçr Khan Lodi: *Mir'at al-khayal,* Calcutta, 1831.

Shçrani, M.: *Panjab mçn Urdu*, Lahore, 1928.

Shibli Nu'mani: *Rasa'il,* Delhi, 1898.

The Imperial Gayetteer of India, London, 1907-1909.

Titus, Murray T.: *Islam in India and Pakistan*, Calcutta, 1959.

18

Art and Iconography

Icon-making and depiction of people however is severely forbidden in Islam. Muslims view icons as idols, and firmly prohibit the worship of an icon, or worship in front of it. Media studies and cultural studies, iconography refers the study of images or signs like for instance those image that have an important significance to a particular culture. Discussing imagery as iconography in this way implies a critical "reading" of imagery that often attempts to explore social and cultural values.

HISTORY

Islamic architecture encompasses a wide range of both secular and religious styles from the foundation of Islam to the present day, influencing the design and construction of buildings and structures in Islamic culture. The principal Islamic architectural types are: the Mosque, the Tomb, the Palace and the Fort. From these four types, the vocabulary of Islamic architecture is derived and used for buildings of lesser importance such as public baths, fountains and domestic architecture.

In 630C.E. the Islamic prophet Muhammad's army reconquered the city of Mecca from the Banu Quraish tribe. The Kaaba sanctuary was rebuilt and re-dedicated to Islam, the reconstruction being carried out before the prophet Muhammad's death in 632C.E. by a shipwrecked Abyssinian carpenter in his native style. This sanctuary was amongst the first major works of Islamic architecture. Later doctrines of Islam dating from the eighth century and originating from the Hadith, forbade the use of humans and animals in architectural design, in order to obey God's command (and thou shalt not make for thyself an image or idol of God.) and also (thou shalt have no god before me) From ten commandments and similar Islamic teachings. For Jews and muslims veneration violates these commandments.They read these commandments as prohibiting the use of idols and images during worship in any way.

In the seventh century, Muslim armies conquered a huge expanse of land. Once the Muslims had taken control of a region, their first need was for somewhere to worship - a mosque. The simple layout provided elements that were to be incorporated into all mosques and the early Muslims put up simple buildings based on the model of the Prophet's house or adapted existing buildings for their own use.

Recently discoveries have shown that quasicrystal patterns were first employed in the girih tiles found in medieval Islamic architecture dating back over five centuries ago. A specifically recognisable Islamic architectural style emerged soon after the time of Muhammad, developing from localized adaptations of Roman, Egyptian, Byzantine, and Persian/ Sassanid models. An early example may be identified as early as 691 AD with the completion of the Dome of the Rock (*Qubbat al-Sakhrah*) in Jerusalem. It featured interior vaulted spaces, a circular dome, and the use of stylized repeating decorative patterns (arabesque).

The Great Mosque of Samarra in Iraq, completed in 847 AD, combined the hypostyle architecture of rows of columns supporting a flat base above which a huge spiralling minaret was constructed. The Hagia Sophia in Istanbul also influenced Islamic architecture. When the Ottomans captured the city from the Byzantines, they converted the basilica to a mosque (now a museum) and incorporated Byzantine architectural elements into their own work (e.g. *domes*). The Hagia Sophia also served as a model for many Ottoman mosques such as the Shehzade Mosque, the Suleiman Mosque, and the Rüstem Pasha Mosque.

Distinguishing motifs of Islamic architecture have always been ordered repetition, radiating structures, and rhythmic, metric patterns. In this respect, fractal geometry has been a key utility, especially for mosques and palaces. Other significant features employed as motifs include columns, piers and arches, organized and interwoven with alternating sequences of niches and colonnettes. The role of domes in Islamic architecture has been considerable. Its usage spans centuries, first appearing in 691 with the construction of the Dome of the Rock mosque, and recurring even up until the seventeenth century with the Taj Mahal. As late as the 19th century, Islamic domes had been incorporated into Western architecture.

Another distinctive sub-style is the architecture of the Mughal Empire in India in the sixteenth century and a fusion of Arabic, Persian and Hindu elements. The Mughal emperor Akbar constructed the royal city of Fatehpur Sikri, located twenty-six miles west of Agra, in the late sixteenth century.

The most famous example of Mughal architecture is the Taj Mahal, the "teardrop on eternity," completed in 1648 by emperor Shah Jahan in memory of his wife Mumtaz Mahal who died while giving birth to their 14th child. The extensive use of precious and semiprecious stones as inlay and the vast quantity of white marble required nearly bankrupted the empire. The Taj Mahal is completely symmetric other than Shah Jahan's sarcophagus, which is placed off center in the crypt room below the main floor. This symmetry extended to the building of an entire mirror mosque in red sandstone to complement the Mecca-facing mosque place to the west of the main structure. Another structure that showed great depth of Mughal influence was the Shalimar Gardens.

ARCHITECTURE

Islamic Architecture was imported into India with the establishment of the Slave Dynasty. Earliest Islamic monuments in India were often built over existing Jain, Buddha or Hindu monuments and by recycling the material of the existing structures. Adhai-Din-Ka Jhonpara at Ajmer and monuments at Chanderi are typical examples of this type of construction. Mosques and tombs in India mostly represent Islamic Architecture. Mosques feature domed prayer halls at one end of an open a courtyard (sahn). The mihrab (arched niche) faces west, towards Mecca. The main form of adornment is surface decoration using geometry, arabesque and calligraphy. This is because hero worship is prohibited among the Muslim community. Jama Masjid at Delhi is a typical example of an Indian mosque.

Another type of Islamic building in India is the tomb or the mausoleum. These were evolved from the basic cube and hemisphere vocabulary of the early phase into a more elaborate form during the Mughal Period. The tomb chamber houses the commemorative plaque below, which is the grave. Well known examples for the Islamic Architecture are the Gol Gumbaz at Bijapur, Agra Fort, Buland Darwaza, Humayun's Tomb, Qutab Minar and Safdarjang Tomb.

Islamic architecture was later fostered by the rulers of the Sultanate of Delhi and it attained perfection in Taj Mahal, a contribution of the Mughals. Islamic architecture in India was at its zenith during the tenure of the Mughals. Vassal kingdoms of the Mughals encouraged the Mughal Architecture. Monuments at Pandua built by the Sultans of Bengal, structures at Jaunpur built by Sharqis, lace-like intricate carvings in mosques in Gujarat constructed during period of Gujarat Sultanate are typical examples of Islamic influence in India. Ancient Jain and Hindu motifs also found their way into the mosques in Gujarat.

Numerous kingdoms in the Deccan Region encouraged Islamic architecture. Awadh legacy in Faizabad and Lucknow; mosques, havelis and palaces in the erstwhile princely states of Dujana and Farrukhnagar in Haryana, Tonk in Rajasthan are other important centers in India exhibiting Islamic architecture.

Modern Islamic architecture has recently been taken on to a whole new level with such buildings being erected such as the Burj Dubai, which is soon to be the world's tallest building. The Burj Dubai's design is derived from the patterning systems embodied in Islamic architecture, with the triple-lobed footprint of the building based on an abstracted version of the desert flower hymenocallis which is native to the Dubai region. Nature and flowers have often been the focal point in most traditional Islamic designs. Many modern interpretations of Islamic architecture can be found in Dubai due to the architectural boom of the Arab World. Yet to be built is Madinat al-Hareer in Kuwait which also has modern versions of Islamic architecture in its super tall tower.

Common interpretations of Islamic architecture include the following: The concept of Allah's infinite power is evoked by designs with repeating themes which suggest infinity. Human and animal forms are rarely depicted in decorative art as Allah's work is considered to be matchless. Foliage is a frequent motif but typically stylized or simplified for the same reason. Arabic Calligraphy is used to enhance the interior of a building by providing quotations from the Qur'an. Islamic architecture has been called the "architecture of the veil" because the beauty lies in the inner spaces (courtyards and rooms) which are not visible from the outside (street view). Furthermore, the use of grandiose forms such as large domes, towering minarets, and large courtyards are intended to convey power.

Many forms of Islamic architecture have evolved in different regions of the Islamic world. Notable Islamic architectural types include the early Abbasid buildings, T-type mosques, and the central-dome mosques of Anatolia. The oil-wealth of the twentieth century drove a great deal of mosque construction using designs from leading modern architects. *Arab-plan* or *hypostyle* mosques are the earliest type of mosques, pioneered under the Umayyad Dynasty. These mosques are square or rectangular in plan with an enclosed courtyard and a covered prayer hall. Historically, because of the warm Mediterranean and Middle Eastern climates, the courtyard served to accommodate the large number of worshipers during

Friday prayers. Most early hypostyle mosques have flat roofs on top of prayer halls, necessitating the use of numerous columns and supports. One of the most notable hypostyle mosques is the Mezquita in Córdoba, Spain, as the building is supported by over 850 columns. Frequently, hypostyle mosques have outer arcades so that visitors can enjoy some shade. Arab-plan mosques were constructed mostly under the Umayyad and Abbasid dynasties; subsequently, however, the simplicity of the Arab plan limited the opportunities for further development, and as a result, these mosques gradually fell out of popularity.

The Ottomans introduced *central dome mosques* in the 15th century and have a large dome centered over the prayer hall. In addition to having one large dome at the center, there are often smaller domes that exist off-center over the prayer hall or throughout the rest of the mosque, where prayer is not performed. This style was heavily influenced by the Byzantine religious architecture with its use of large central domes.

SCULPTURE

The sculptural style that started as early as Turkish invasions took its shape due course of time and acquired a distinct national characteristic that marks it as Islamic architecture. Many fine early monuments of this period are found in delhi, the most famous one being the Jama Masjid, built by Qutub-Ud-Din Aibak near Qutab minar in the early thirteenth century. The most magnificent phase of Islamic Architecture was initiated by Mughals, under great emperor Akbar. The Agra Fort and the deserted capital city of Fatehpur Sikri and Sikandrabad near Agra are all fine examples of Muslim sculptural art and design. Taj Mahal being the most magnificent of all. From a historical perspective, the vast lands in which Turks existed, starting from pre-historical times have been places where great civilizations have grown and lived, consequently where sculpture production have been widespread. Turks living in Central and Asia Minor have made sculptures for different reasons in the pre-Islamic time. After the acceptance of Islam, sculpture with religious quality and worship purposes were prohibited. Since there was no prohibition against description of non-religious nature, it was especially possible to realize stylized plant, animal and human sculptures in Seljuk art.

Although Seljuks developed a sculpture dependent of architecture, the classical period of architectural conception of Ottomans was based on simplicity, monumentalism, geometric and abstract forms. For this reason Ottomans stayed distant to sculpture that could take place in this frame until the ends of the nineteenth century. They had only produced sculptural examples in tomb-stones, marking stones and bow figures of lions. The first messengers of sculpture that appeared with a western understanding towards the end of the nineteenth century were relief marbles made with a naturalist style describing flowers arranged in vases or fruits in plates on public fountains in squares at the Tulip Period, beginning of the eighteenth century.

Ottoman Sultans were pioneers of westernization movements in the culture of the Ottoman Empire in the nineteenth century. The example is Sultan Abdulaziz, in 1871, a sculptor brought from Europe, make his sculpture on horseback and animal sculptures to be put in the gardens of the palace. During the same period we come across to reliefs with human figures and sculptures in buildings built in Beyoglu, a westernized district of Istanbul, showing a parallel style with the contemporary European architecture. An exhibition of Italian wax sculpture was opened in Beyoglu in 1882. Human size examples of important people of the time and of historical characters were shown at the exhibition where the public was able to see them with a fee. The acceptance of sculpture as part of art in Turkey in modern sense is realized in 1883 with the founding of Sanayi-i Nefise Mektebi Alisi / School of Fine Arts. Osman Hamdi Bey was the founder and first principal of the school. Sculpture, that was less popular compared to painting,found the possibility of development after this date within the environment of the school.

CALLIGRAPHY

Islamic calligraphy, equally known as Arabic calligraphy, is the art of beautiful hand writing, and by extension, of bookmaking. This art has most often employed the Arabic script, throughout many languages. Calligraphy is especially revered among Islamic arts since it was the primary means for the preservation of the Qur'an. The work of calligraphers was collected and appreciated. Consideration of figurative art as idolatrous led to calligraphy and abstract figures becoming the main forms of artistic expression in Islamic cultures.

Arabic, Persian and Ottoman Turkish calligraphy is associated with geometric Islamic art (the Arabesque) on the walls and ceilings of mosques as well as on the page. Contemporary artists in the Islamic world draw on the heritage of calligraphy to use calligraphic inscriptions or abstractions in their work. While many religions have made use of figural images to convey their core convictions, Islam has instead used the shapes and sizes of words or letters. Because Islamic leaders saw in figural arts a possible implication of idolatry, Islam's early theocracy looked to the artistry of calligraphy for religious expression. In Islamic and Arabic cultures, calligraphy became highly respected as an art — the art of writing.

Arabic calligraphy is a primary form of art for Islamic visual expression and creativity. Throughout the vast geography of the Islamic world, Arabic calligraphy is a symbol representing unity, beauty, and power. The aesthetic principles of Arabic calligraphy are a reflection of the cultural values of the Muslim world. A thorough investigation into the aesthetic differences between Arabic and non-Arabic calligraphy might provide an approach for understanding the essential spirit of each culture.

Contemporary scholarship stipulates that Arabic belongs to the group of Semitic alphabetical scripts in which mainly the consonants are represented. Arabic script is derived from the Aramaic Nabataean alphabet. It is a script of twenty-eight letters and uses long but not short vowels. The letters are derived from only seventeen distinct forms, distinguished one from another by a dot or dots placed above or below the letter. Short vowels are indicated by small diagonal strokes above or below letters. When written without dots and diacritical points, Arabic script can look flat and barren. But when the dots and diacritical points are added, the script comes to life like a garden in spring.

Arabic lettering has achieved a high level of sophistication, and Arabic scripts can vary from flowing cursive styles like Naskh and Thuluth to the angular Kufi. On a traditional Islamic building, a number of different writing styles may appear on, for example, the walls, windows, or minarets. Most of the inscriptions are not only from the Qur'an but also the Hadith (the Prophet's words) and are in harmony with the religious purposes of the building. An inscription can give meaning to the building by clarifying its function.

Arabic calligraphy is a symbol representing power and beauty. Its history is the integration of artistry and scholarship. Through the abstract beauty of the lines, energy flows in between the letters and words. All the parts are integrated into a whole. These parts include positive spacing, negative spacing, and the flow of energy that weaves together the calligrapher's rendering. The abstract beauty of Arabic calligraphy is not always easily comprehended — but this beauty will slowly reveal itself to the discerning eye. Arabic calligraphy is not merely an art form but involves divine and moral representations — from which calligraphy acquires its sublime reputation.

Calligraphy has arguably become the most venerated form of Islamic art because it provides a link between the languages of the Muslims with the religion of Islam. The holy book of Islam, the Qur'an, has played an important role in the development and evolution of the Arabic language, and by extension, calligraphy in the Arabic alphabet. Proverbs and complete passages from the Qur'an are still active sources for Islamic calligraphy. The Arabic alphabet consists of twenty-eight letters and eighteen different forms of writing.

Calligraphy, the most Islamic of arts in the Muslim world, has also its figurative sides. By interweaving written words, made from an "Allah", a "Muhammad", a "Bismillah", etc., or using micrography, calligraphers produced anthropomorphic figures ('Ali, the Ideal Human of mystics, a praying man, a face), zoomorphisms (symbolical creatures, most from the Shi'a iconography, like the lion (Duldul, horse of 'Ali, horse ('Ali's Duldul), fish, stork or other bird (the qur'anic Hudhud)) and unanimated representations (a sword (Dhu al-Fiqar), a mosque, a ship (made from the letter and Arabic grammatical conjunction *waw*, symbol of mystical union). Calligrams are related to Muslim mysticism and popular with many leading calligraphers in Turkey, Persia and India from the seventeenth century onward.

In the teachings of calligraphy figurative imagery is used to help visualize the shape of letters to trace (such as "initial *ha'* looks in *nasta'liq* similar to two eyes like his Persian name implies: "ha' two eyes" *he' do tcheshm*). In literature and poetry seeing in letters a reflection of the natural world goes back to the Abbasid times.

PRESENT DAY EXAMPLES

- Chinli Kiosk, at Istanbul, Turkey.
- Dome of the Rock, at Jerusalem, Israel.
- Great Mosque, at Kairawan, Tunisia.
- Great Mosque of Damascus, at Damascus, Syria.
- Mosque of Al Mutawakkil, at Samarra, Iraq.
- Mosque of Sultan Ahmed, at Istanbul, Turkey.
- Sultan Hassan Mosque, at Cairo, Egypt.
- Suleyman Mosque, at Istanbul, Turkey.
- Taj Mahal, at Agra, India.
- The Alhambra, at Granada, Spain.

- The Selimiye, at Edirne, Turkey.
- Yaama Mosque, at Tahoua, Niger, Africa.
- Gol Gumbaz at Bijapur
- Agra Fort, at Agra
- Buland Darwaza, at Agra
- Humayun's Tomb, at Delhi
- Qutab Minar, at Delhi
- Safdarjang Tomb, at Delhi.

REFERENCES

Azòfari, zòahir al-din: *Waqi'at-i Azfari*, Madras, 1957.

Aziz Ahmad: *Islamic Culture in the Indian Environment*, Oxford, 1964.

Babur: *Tuzuk,* Leyden and Erskine, London, 1921.

Bada'uni, 'Abd-al-Qadir: *Muntakhab at-tawarikh,* Calcutta, 1868-1869.

Bahra'ichi, Na'im-Allah: *Ma'lumat-i Mazhariyya,* Cawnpore, 1858.

Bailey, T. Grahame: *A History of Urdu Literature*, Calcutta, 1932.

Cousens, H.: *Bijapur and its Architectural Remains*, Bombay, 1916.

Cragg, Kenneth: *Counsels in Contemporary Islam*, Edinburgh, 1965.

Crooke, W.: *Religion and Folklore of Northern India*, London, 1926.

Dames, M. Longworth: *Popular Poetry of the Baloches* London, 1907.

Dara Shukoh: *Safinat al-awhya*', Urdu tr. Karachi, 1961.

Darmesteter, J.: *Chants populaires des Afghans*, Paris, 1888-90.

Fyzee, A. A. A. (ed.): *A Shïte Creed*, Bombay, 1942.

Gait, E. A.: *Census Report: Bengal*, Calcutta, 1902.

Ghani, A. R. and Nur K. Ilahi: *Bibliography of Iqbal*, Lahore, 1955.

Ghani, A.: *A History of Persian Language and Literature in the Mughal Court*, Allahabad, 1929-1930.

Jamali, Hòamid ibn-FaU+1EODl-Allah: *Siyar al-'Arifin*, Delhi, 1893.

Jamil, M. Tahir: *Hali's Poetry*, Bombay, 1938.

Juzjani, Minhaj-as-siraj: *Tabaqat-i Nasri,* ed. A. H. Habibi, Kabul, 1964.

Kalam-Allah, Shah: *Kashkal-i Kalimi,* Delhi, 1890.

Kamal Khwaja al-din: *The Ideal Prophet*, London, 1925.

Khafi Khan: *Muntakhab al-lubab,* Calcutta, 1869-1925.

Khaja Khan: *Studies in Tasawwuf,* Madras, 1923.

Leyden, J.: "On the Roshenian Sect and its Founder Bayazid Ansari", *Asiatic Researches.*

Lokhandwalla, Sh. T.: "The Bohras, a Muslim Community of Gujarat", SI, 1955.

Madani, Hòusayn. Ahmad: *Naqsh-i hòayat,* Delhi, 1953.

Mançri, Sharaf-ad-din Ahòmad ibn-Yahòya: *Maktubat,* Lucknow, 1868; Cawnpore, 1911.

Massignon, L.: *Essai sur les origines du Lexique Technique de la Mystique musulmane,* Paris, 1922.

Storey, C. A.: *Persian Literature, A Bio-Bibliographical Survey*, London, 1927-58.

Suhrawardi, Diya'-ad-din Abu-Najib ' Abd-al-Qahir: *Adab al-muridin,* Urdu tr. Delhi, 1901.

Tara Chand: *The Influence of Islam on Hindu Culture*, Allahabad, 1936.

Temple, R. C.: *The Legends of the Punjab*, Bombay, 1884.

Wellesz, Emmy: *Akbar's Religious Thought reflected in Mughal Painting*, London, 1952.

Wilkinson, J. V. S. and Gray, B.: *Persian Miniature Painting*, London, 1933.

Yusuf Husain: *L'Inde Mystique au Moyen Age*, Paris, 1929.

Zaehner, R. C.: *Hindu and Muslim Mysticism*, London, 1960.

19

Islam in Modern World

When we use the term "modern", we mean neither present-day nor newest nor flourishing in the subjugation and supremacy of the natural world. Instead, for us "modern" means that which is cut off from the unknown, from the changeless precepts which in fact regulate all matters and which are made known to man through revealing in its most ecumenical sense. Modernity is thus contrasted with tradition, the last mentioned means all that which is of Divine Origin along with its manifestations and deployments on the human plane while the former by contrast implies all that is merely human and now ever more increasingly subhuman, and all that is divorced and cut off from the Divine Source. Obviously, tradition has always accompanied and in fact characterized human existence whereas modernism is a very recent phenomenon. As long as man has lived on earth, he has buried his dead and believed in the after life and the world of the Spirit. During the "hundreds of thousands" of years of individual life on earth, he's been conventional in mentality and has not "developed" as far as his relation with God and nature seen as the conception and reflection of God are concerned.

Compared to this long history during which man has continuously celebrated the Divine and performed his function as God's vicegerent (khalifah) on earth, the period of the domination of modernism stretching from the Renaissance in Western Europe in the 15th century to the present day appears as no more than the blinking of an eye. Yet, it is during this fleeting moment that we live; hence the apparent dominance of the power of modernism before which so many Muslims retreat in helplessness or which they join with a superficial sense of happiness that accompanies the seduction of the world.

The realism present in the Islamic perspective combined with the strong emphasis of the Holy Quran upon the gradual loss of perfection of the Islamic community as it moves away from the origin of revelation prevented the kind of utopianism present in modern European philosophy from growing upon the soil of Islamic thought. Moreover, the Muslim remained always aware that if there is to be a perfect state, it could only come into being through Divine help. Hence, although the idea of the cyclic renewal of Islam through a "renewer" (mujaddid) has been always alive as has the wave of Mahdism which sees in the Mahdi the force sent by God to return Islam to its perfection, Islam has never faced within itself that type of secular utopianism which underlies so much of the politico-social aspects of modern thought. It is therefore essential to be aware of the profound distinction between modern utopianism and Islamic teachings concerning the mujaddid or renewer of Islamic society or the Mahdi himself. It is also basic to distinguish between the traditional figure of the mujaddid and the modern reformers who usually, as a result of their feeble reaction to modern thought, have hardly brought about the renewal of Islam.

The Islamic tradition can never accept a thought pattern which is devoid of the perfume of the sacred and which replaces the Divine Order by one of a purely human origin and inspiration. The confrontation of Islam with modern thought cannot take place on a serious level if the primacy of the sacred in the perspective of Islam and its lack in modern thought is not taken into consideration. Islam cannot even carry out a dialogue with the secular by placing it in a position of legitimacy. It can only take the secular for what it is, namely the negation and denial of the sacred which ultimately alone is while the profane or secular only appears to be.

The successful encounter of Islam with modern thought can only come about when modern thought is fully understood in both its roots and ramifications and the whole of the Islamic tradition brought to bear upon the solution of the enormous problems which modernism poses for Islam. At the centre of this undertaking lies the revival of that wisdom, that hikmah or Haqiqah, which lies at the heart of the Islamic revelation and which will remain valid as long as men remain men and bear witness to Him according to their theomorphic nature and their state of servitude before the Lord (ubudiyyah), the state which is the purpose of human existence.

DIASPORA

These are some of the distinct features of Islam, which make it necessary for modern man to seek his salvation through this ideology.

First, it must be well understood that Islam is not a mere ideological vision. It is a practical system of life that fully appreciates all the genuine needs of humankind and tries to realize them.

Second, in trying to meet the genuine requirements of man, Islam effects perfect balance between all areas of life and activity. It starts with the individual maintaining a balance between the requirements of body and soul, reason and spirit and in no case allows one side to dominate the other. It does not suppress the human instincts in order to make the soul ascend the higher planes, nor does it allow man, in his efforts to fulfil his bodily desires, to stoop down to the low level of animalism and hedonism. On the contrary, it makes them both meet on a single higher plane, doing away with all the internal psychological conflicts that threaten the human soul or set a part of it against the other parts.

In the social sphere, it proceeds to achieve equilibrium between the needs of the individual and those of the community. It does not allow an individual to transgress against other individuals, or against the community. Nor does it allow the community to commit transgression against individuals. It also does not approve of one class or group of people to enslave another class or group of people. Islam exercises a beneficent constraint on all these mutually opposed forces, prevents them from coming into collision with one another, and harnesses them all to co-operate for the general good of humankind as a whole.

Thus, Islam strikes a balance between different sectors of society and between different aspects of existence, spiritual as well as material. Unlike Communism, it does not believe that economic factors, i.e. the material aspect alone, dominate human existence. Nor does it contribute to what the pure spiritualists or idealists say, claiming that spiritual factors or high ideals alone are sufficient to organize human life. Rather, Islam holds that all these diverse elements put together, form what is called human society; and that the best code of life is that which takes note of all these, making full allowance for body as well as reason and spirit, arranging them all in the framework of a harmonious whole.

Third, it must always be kept in mind that Islam has an altogether independent existence of its own as a social philosophy and an economic system. Some of its outward manifestations may on the surface appear to resemble those of Capitalism or Socialism, but in fact, it is far from being the one or the other. It retains all the good characteristics of these systems, yet is free from their shortcomings and perversions. It does not extol individualism to that loathful extent which is the characteristic of the modern West. It was from this germ that modern Capitalism sprang and institutionalized that concept of individual freedom, where man is allowed to exploit other individuals and the community only to serve his personal gain. Islam guarantees personal freedom and provides opportunities for individual enterprise, but not at the cost of society or ideals of social justice.

The reaction to Capitalism has appeared in the form of Socialism. It idolizes the social basis to an extent that the individual is reduced to an insignificant part of the social machine with no existence of his own. Therefore, the community alone enjoys freedom as well as power, the individual has no right to question its authority or demand his rights. The tragedy of Socialism and its variants is that they assign to the State absolute powers to shape the lives of the individuals.

Islam strikes a balance between the two extremes of Capitalism and Socialism. Being appreciative of their role, Islam harmonizes the individuals and the State in such a way that individuals have the freedom necessary to develop their potentialities and not to encroach upon the rights of their fellowmen. It also gives the community and the State adequate powers to regulate and control the socio-economic relationships to guard and maintain this harmony in human life. The basis of this whole structure as visualized by Islam is the reciprocity of love between individuals and groups; it is not erected on the basis of hatred and class conflict, as is the case with Socialism.

It may also be pointed out here that this unique system of life as visualized by Islam, did not originate as a result of any economic pressure, nor was it an outcome of some mutually conflicting interests of antagonistic groups of people. It was revealed to the world as the ordained system of life, at a time when men attached no particular importance to economic factors, nor did they know anything about social justice in the sense we know it in modern times. Both Socialism and Capitalism are much later developments. Islam presented its scheme of social reform much before any of the social movements of our times.

This historical announcement of fundamental human rights not only contains those rights voiced by many a revolutionary in our times, it adds to them some more as well, without necessitating any inter-class hatred, bloody revolutions, and without rejecting all those human elements in life that do not fall under the above three heads: food, housing and family.

These are some of the salient features of the Islamic code of life. They are sufficient to show that a religion with such laws and principles, that is comprehensive and includes the complete human existence, emotions, thoughts, actions, worship, economic dealings, social relationships, instructive urges and spiritual aspirations – all arranged in the framework of a single harmonious but unique system of life, can never lose its usefulness for mankind. Nor can such a religion ever become obsolete, as its objectives are the same as those of life itself and therefore, destined to live on so long as there is life on this planet.

Considering the existing state of affairs in the contemporary world, humankind cannot reasonably afford to turn its back upon Islam or reject its system of life. Humankind is still afflicted with the most savage and odious forms of racial prejudices. Surely, the world in the twentieth century has yet a great deal to learn from Islam. Long ago, Islam freed humanity from all racial prejudices. It did not content itself with the presentation of a beautiful vision of equality alone, but it achieved in practice an unprecedented state of equality between all people, black, white or yellow, declaring that none enjoyed any superiority over the others except in virtue and piety.

Finally, the world with the shadows of war still hanging over it cannot but turn towards Islam – the only way to establish and maintain real peace on this earth. The era of Islam has in a way just started, not ended; it is not a spent force, but a living dynamic force, its future is as bright as its great historical past is glorious, when it illumined the face of earth at a time when Europe was still groping its way in the dark recesses of Medievalism.

MODERN RELIGIOUS MOVEMENTS

Progressive Muslims have produced a considerable body of liberal thoughts within Islam. These movements share a philosophy that depends largely on ijtihad. Liberal Muslims do not necessarily subscribe to the more culturally-based interpretations of the Quran and Hadith. They generally claim that they are returning to the principles of the early Ummah and to the ethical and pluralistic intent of their scripture. The reform movement uses monotheism (tawhid) "as an organizing principle for human society and the basis of religious knowledge, history, metaphysics, aesthetics, and ethics, as well as social, economic and world order."

Over the course of the 19th and 20th centuries, in accordance with their increasingly modern societies and outlooks, liberal Muslims have tended to reinterpret many aspects of their religion. This is particularly true of Muslims who now find themselves living in non-Muslim countries.

Such people may describe themselves variously as liberal, progressive or reformist; but rather than implying a specific agenda, these terms tend to incorporate a broad spectrum of views which contest conservative, traditional interpretations of Islam in many different ways. Although there is no full consensus amongst liberal Muslims on their views, they tend to agree on some or all of the following beliefs.

SPIRITUAL REVOLUTION

Modern Muslim spiritual social movements often retrace their roots to the founding era of Islam. Several rhymes of the Quran encourage sacred (islah), and a command of the prophet Muhammad anticipates that a renewer (mujaddid) will come up in each century to to uplift the spirituality and the community of Muslims. Some crusaders, such as al-Ghazali, were merged into the orthodoxy of Islamic scholarship; others, such as Ibn Taymiyya, were largely neglected for centuries. During the nineteenth century, a new wave of spiritual movements came forth as part of the resistance to European imperial expansion, on the proposition that this mastery was due to Muslims' spiritual laxity. Outstanding movements and persons included Haji Shariat Allah and the Fara idi movement in Bengal, Ahmad Brelwi in India, Imam Shamil in the Caucasus, Abd al-Qadir in Algeria, and Muhammad Ahmad in the Sudan.

The nineteenth century also saw the acclivity of a new breed of Islamic spiritual movements, one that attracted European models. Like earlier reformers, these modernists called Muslims to return to the sacred writing of Islam; unlike other reformers, however, they described a happy conjunction between the spirit of these texts and current European values and institutions. In the mid-twentieth century, Islamic spiritualism split into two strands: one that upheld the equation of certain Western and early Islamic ideals, and one that rejected Western precedents. The liberal Islamic movement defended Western values such as democracy, human rights, and gender equality, using Islamic justifications-either specific injunctions from sacred texts on behalf of these positions, or silences in the texts that leave these matters to human innovation, or the requisite and desirableness of re-explaining the texts within dynamic cultural circumstances.

The second chain assumed careful contemporary values and exercises but stigmatized their European place of origin. For instance, Hasan al-Banna, founding father of the Muslim Brotherhood, the first and largest evangelist organization of the twentieth century, called for modern-style "social spiritual" including mass education, a war on poverty, and public health measures, yet his definition of spiritual associated all ills in Muslim societies with the rise of Western influence. Among the common themes of Muslim spiritual movements, in the early 21st century as in past centuries, remains the denouncement of the seminaries' obscurantism and obsequiousness to country authorities. This servility has only been heightened by the seminary religious projects of several colonial and postcolonial states.

FUTURE

Portion of the challenge Muslims face in the twenty-first century is to build up a theological system of reform and address the developing extremism that subsists in some Islamic societies. Most modern Muslim nation-states were formed only after Second World War. Muslims are fighting with a period of history in which they are attempting to define what it means to be a Muslim in contemporary society. If the purpose of education and civilization is to engender a sense of pridefulness, self-respect, and honour in individuals so that they improve their state and consequently that of society, Islamic education and civilization have done this. History records many instances when Islam realized this goal in far-flung lands. For instance, Isaac Taylor gave a speech at the Church Congress of England about Islam's results and effect on people, at which he said:

When Islam is adopted, paganism, fetishism, infanticide and witchery go away. Filthiness is substituted by cleanliness and the new convert develops personal self-esteem and dignity. Disrespectful dances and wanton relation of the sexes cease; female chastity is rewarded as a virtue; industry replaces idleness; license gives place to law; order and sobriety prevail; blood feuds, cruelty to animals and slaves are eradicated. Islam swept away corruption and superstitions. Islam was a revolt against empty polemics. It gave hope to the slave, brotherhood to mankind, and recognition to the fundamental facts of human nature. The virtues which Islam inculcates are temperance, cleanliness, chastity, justice, fortitude, courage, benevolence, hospitality, veracity and resignation. Islam preaches a practical brotherhood, the social equality of all Muslims. Slavery is not part of the creed of Islam.

Polygamy is a more difficult question. Moses did not prohibit it. It was practiced by David and it is not directly forbidden in the New Testament. Muhammad limited the unbounded license of polygamy. It is the exception rather than the rule. In resignation to God's Will, temperance, chastity, veracity and in brotherhood of believers they (the Muslims) set us a pattern which we should do well to follow. Islam has got rid of alcoholism, gambling and prostitution, the three banes of the Christian lands. Islam has done more for civilization than Christian religion. The conquering of third of the earth to his credo was a miracle.

Although Islam dominated two-thirds of the historical civilized world for at least eleven centuries, the Muslims' indolence and carelessness of what was going on around them made their civilization to decline. However, Islam itself did not-and cannot-decline. Military victories and a superiority complex induced Muslims to rest on their laurels and neglect further scientific research. They deserted themselves to living their own lives and recounting the Quran without analyzing its broader significances. In the meantime Europe was attaining large advancements in scientific discipline, which it had adopted from Muslim civilization.

ISLAM AS A GLOBAL RELIGION

Islam is a religious belief established upon the capitulation to Almighty who is One. The very name of the religious belief in Arabic language, means at once compliance and serenity, for it is in submitting to God's Will that human beings gain peace in their lives in this world and in the hereafter. The substance of Islam concerns God, who in Arabic is called Allah, and it calls itself to humanity's most unsounded nature. It concerns men and women as they were produced by God—not as fallen beings. Islam therefore considers itself to be not an innovation but a reassertion of the universal truth of all revelation which is God's Oneness. This truth was affirmed by the prophets of old and especially by Abraham, the father of monotheism.

Islam venerates all of these prophets including not only Abraham, who is the father of the Arabs as well as of the Jews, but also Moses and Christ. The Prophet and Messenger of God, Muhammad, was the last of this long lime of prophets and Islam is the last religion until the Day of Judgement. It is the final reflection of the Abrahamic custom. One should in fact properly speak of the Judeo-Christian-Islamic tradition, for Islam shares with the other Abrahamic religions their sacred history, the basal moral commandments incorporated in the Decalogue and first and last, belief in the One God. And it regenerates and reduplicates the true notions of Jews and Christians whose religious texts are named as divinely revealed books in Islam's own sacred book, the Quran.

The Muslim universe remains today a big land stretching along from the Atlantic to the Pacific, with a significant bearing in Europe and America, exalted by the commandments of Islam and seeking to affirm its own individuality. Notwithstanding the bearing of patriotism and various profane political orientation in their midst. Muslims want to live in the present time but without simply copying blindly the ways adopted by the West. The Muslim cosmos wishes to live at peace with the West besides the East but at the same time not to be mastered by them. It wants to commit its resourcefulnesses and energies to constructing a better lift for its people on the basis of the commandments of Islam and not to blow its resources in either inner or outer struggles. It seeks at last to produce better agreement with the West and to be better understanding each other better that they can serve up their own masses more with success and also contribute to a finer life for the whole humanity.

REFERENCES

Ahmad Ali Batalawi: *Nusrat al-mujtahidin,* Lucknow, 1895.

Bahra'ichi, Na'im-Allah: *Ma'lumat-i Mazhariyya,* Cawnpore, 1858.

Bailey, T. Grahame: *A History of Urdu Literature*, Calcutta, 1932.

Faiz, Faiz Ahmad: *Poems*, tr. V. G. Kiernan, Delhi, 1958.

Fakhr-ad-din Ahmad: *Izalat ash-shukuk,* Allahabad, 1880.

Fakhr-i Mudabbir: *Aadab al-hòarb wa-sh-shuju'a,* BM Add. MS 1653.

Faqir-Allah: *Rag Durpan*, 10 Pers. MS 1937.

Firishta, Abu-l-Qasim: *Gulshan-i Ibrahimi* (*Ta'rikh-i Firishta*), Bombay, 1832; Lucknow, 1905; Eng. tr. J. Briggs (*History of the Rise of Muhammadan Power in India*), London, 1829.

Firuz Tughluq: *Futhòhòat-i Firuz Shahi*, ed. S. Abdur-Rashid, Aligarh, 1954.

Fisher, Humphrey J.: *Ahòmadiyyah: A Study in Contemporary Islam on the West Afirican Coast*, London, 1963.

Kühnel, Ernst: *Moghul-Malerei*, Berlin, 1956.

Laoust, H.: *Les Schismes clans l'Islam*, Paris, 1965.

Law, N. N.: *Promotion of Learning in India During Muhammadan Rule by Muhammadans*, London, 1916.

Bibliography

Abdullah, S.: *Adabiyyat-i Farsi men Hinduwon ka hòissa,* Delhi, 1942.

Abid Husain: *The Destiny of Indian Muslims,* London, 1965.

Abu-l-Layth Siddiqi: *Lakhna'u ka dabistan-i sha'iri,* Lahore, 1955.

Ahmad Ali Batalawi: *Nusrat al-mujtahidin,* Lucknow, 1895.

Ahòmad Shaykh Sirhindi: *Mabda wa ma'ad, Cawnpore,* 1891.

Akhund Darwiza: *Tadhkirat al-abrar wa-l-ashrar,* BM Or. MS 222.

al- Utbi: *Al-Ta'rikh al-Yamini,* Cairo, 1869.

al-Biruuni, Abu-Rayhòan: *Tahòqiq md li-i-Hind,* Eng. tr. E. Sachau, *Alberuni's India,* London, 1910.

al-Hamdani, Abbas H.: *The Isma'ili Da'wa in Northern India*, Cairo, 1956.

al-Hujwiri, 'Ali ibn-'Uthman: *Kashf al-mahòjub,* R. A. Nicholson, London, 1936.

al-Juwayni, 'Ala'-ad-din: *Ta'rikh-i Jahankusha,* Leiden/ London, 1912-37; Eng. tr. J. A. Boyle (*The History of the World Conqueror*), Manchester, 1958.

Allah Diya: *Siyar al-aqtòab,* Lucknow, 1889.

al-Qaqashandi: *Subhò al-a'sha*, Cairo, 1913-20.

Altòaf ar-Rahòman: *Ahòwal-i 'ulama-i Farangi Mahòall,* Lucknow, n.d.

Amanat Allah: *MuHòafiz al-iman mill maka'id la-madhhaban,* Allahabad, 1877.

Amir Ahòmad: *Sirat al-Ashraf,* 2 vols, Lucknow, 1949.

Amir Khurd: *Siyar al-awhya,* Delhi, 1885.

Amritsari, Thand-Allah: *Ahl-i hòadith ka madhhab,* Amritsar, 1920.

Anderson, J. N. D.: "Recent Reforms in the Islamic Law of Inheritance", *International and Comparative Law Quarterly*, 1965.

Arzu, Siraj-ad-din Ali Khan: *Tashòihò-i Ghara'ib al-lughat,* Cawnpore, 1868.

Asad-Allah Tilhari: *Quwwat-i Hòanafiyya, Bada'un,* 1905.

Asbraf 'Ali Thanawi: *al-Intibahat al-mufida'an al-ishtibahat al-jadida,* Lahore, 1952.

Ashraf, K. M.: "Life and Conditions of the People of Hindustan, 1200-1550", *JASB* 1935.

Azad Bilgrami, Mir Ghulam "Ali (ed.): *Khizana-i Amira,* Cawnpore, 1871.

Azad, Abu-l-Kalam: *Tadhkira,* Lahore, n.d.

Azad, Muhòammad Hòusayn: *Ab-i Hayat,* Lahore, n.d.

Azòfari, zòahir al-din: *Waqi'at-i Azfari*, Madras, 1957.

Aziz Ahmad: *Islamic Culture in the Indian Environment*, Oxford, 1964.

Babur: *Tuzuk,* Leyden and Erskine, London, 1921.

Bada'uni, 'Abd-al-Qadir: *Muntakhab at-tawarikh,* Calcutta, 1868-1869.

Bahra'ichi, Na'im-Allah: *Ma'lumat-i Mazhariyya,* Cawnpore, 1858.

Bailey, T. Grahame: *A History of Urdu Literature*, Calcutta, 1932.

Bains, A.: *Ethnography of the Castes and Tribes of India*, Strassburg, 1912.

Bakhtawar Khan: *Mir'at al-'alam,* BM Add. MS 7657.

Baloch, Nabi Bakhsh Khan: "The Diwan of Abu 'Atòa of Sind", *IC*, xxiii (1949), 136-50.

Barani, Diya'-ad-din: *Ta'rikh-i Firuz Shahi,* Calcutta, 1862.

Bashir al-din Mahòmud Ahòmad: *Introduction* to Shir 'Ali Eng. tr. *of The Holy Quran*, Rabwah, 1955.

Bausani, A.: "Note su Shah Waliullah di Dehli", *Annali*, n.s., 1961.

Bernier, F.: *Travels in Mughal India*, Eng. tr. London, 1891.

Binder, L.: *Religion and Politics in Pakistan*, Berkeley, 1961.

Binyon, L.: *The Court Painters of the Great Moghuls*, London, 1921.

Blumhardt, J. F.: *Catalogue of the Hindustani Manuscripts in the Library of the India Office*, Oxford, 1926.

Brahman, Chandra Bhan: *Chahar Chaman*, BM Add. MS 16, 863.

Bray, D.: *Census Report: Baluchistan*, Calcutta, 1913.

Brockelmann, C.: *Geschichte der arabischen Literatur*, second edition, two vols., Leiden, 1943, 1949; three supplementary vols., Leiden, 1937-42.

Brown, Percy: *Indian Architecture (Islamic Period)*, Bombay, 1958.

Brush, S. A.: "Ahmadiyyah in Pakistan", *MW*, 45 (1955), 145-71.

Burgess, J.: *The Muhammedan Architecture in Gujarat*, London, 1896.

Campbell, J. M.: *The Bombay Gazetteer*, Bombay, 1874-1904.

Chatterji, S. K.: *Indo-Aryan and Hindi*, Ahmadabad, 1942.

Chiragh 'Ali: *Rasd'il,* Hyderabad, 1918-19.

Chishti, 'Abd-al-Hòalim: "Hasan ibn-Muhammad as-Saghani" in *Ma'arif,* Jan.-Sept. 1959.

Colebrook, H. T.: "On the Origin and Peculiar Tenets of Certain Muhammedan Sects", *Asiatic Researches*, vii (1801)

Cousens, H.: *Bijapur and its Architectural Remains*, Bombay, 1916.

Cragg, Kenneth: *Counsels in Contemporary Islam*, Edinburgh, 1965.

Crooke, W.: *Religion and Folklore of Northern India*, London, 1926.

Dames, M. Longworth: *Popular Poetry of the Baloches* London, 1907.

Dara Shukoh: *Safinat al-awhya'*, Urdu tr. Karachi, 1961.

Darmesteter, J.: *Chants populaires des Afghans*, Paris, 1888-90.

Daudpota, U. M.: *Sindhi Literature*, Karachi, 1951.

de Garcin Tassy: *Histoire de la Litterature Hindouie et Hindoustanie*, Paris, 1870.

Dörfer, Gerhard: *Türkische und mongolische Elemente in Neupersischen*, Wiesbaden, 1965.

Dughlat, Mirza Haydar: *Ta'rikh-i Rashidi,* Eng. tr. E. Denison Ross and N. Elias, London, 1898.

Dumasia, N. M.: *A Brief History of the Agha Khan*, Bombay, 1903.

Elliot, H. M. and Dowson, J.: *The History of India as Told by its Own Historians*, Allahabad, 1964.

Encyclopaedia of Islam, London, Leiden, 1960.

Encyclopaedia of Religion and Ethics, J. Hastings, Edinburgh, 1908-21.

Ethé, H.: *Catalogue of Persian Manuscripts in the India Office*, Oxford, 1903, 1937.

Faiz, Faiz Ahmad: *Poems*, tr. V. G. Kiernan, Delhi, 1958.

Fakhr-ad-din Ahmad: *Izalat ash-shukuk,* Allahabad, 1880.

Fakhr-i Mudabbir: *Aadab al-hòarb wa-sh-shuju'a,* BM Add. MS 1653.

Faqir-Allah: *Rag Durpan*, 10 Pers. MS 1937.

Farid Bhakkari: *Dhakhira al-khawanin,* Karachi, 1961.

Farquhar, J. N.: *Modern Religious Movements in India*, London, 1924.

Fat'hò-ad-din: *Shajra-i Naqshbandiyya,* Rawalpindi, 1904.

Fergusson, James: *History of Indian and Eastern Architecture*, London., 1910.

Firishta, Abu-l-Qasim: *Gulshan-i Ibrahimi (Ta'rikh-i Firishta),* Bombay, 1832; Lucknow, 1905; Eng. tr. J. Briggs (*History of the Rise of Muhammedan Power in India*), London, 1829.

Firuz Tughluq: *Futhòhòat-i Firuz Shahi*, ed. S. Abdur-Rashid, Aligarh, 1954.

Fisher, Humphrey J.: *Ahòmadiyyah: A Study in Contemporary Islam on the West Afirican Coast*, London, 1963.

Fyzee, A. A. A. (ed.): *A Shïte Creed*, Bombay, 1942.

Gait, E. A.: *Census Report: Bengal*, Calcutta, 1902.

Ghani, A. R. and Nur K. Ilahi: *Bibliography of Iqbal*, Lahore, 1955.

Ghani, A.: *A History of Persian Language and Literature in the Mughal Court*, Allahabad, 1929-1930.

Ghosh, J. C.: *Bengali Literature*, London, 1948.

Ghulam Ahòmad Khan: *Majmu'a-i marfut-i khwajagan-i Chishti,* Delhi, 1906.

Ghulam Ahòmad, Mirza, of Qadiyan: *The Philosophy of the Teachings of Islam*, Rabwah, 1959.

Ghulam Muhammad: *Festivals and Folklore of Gilgat, Memoirs, Asiatic Society of Bengal*, Calcutta, 1905.

Ghulam Muh-d-din: *Sihòr al-Hind,* Delhi, 1876.

Ghulam Sarwar: *Khazinat al-asfiya',* Cawnpore, 1902.

Ghulam, Halim: *Tuhòfa-i ithna-'ashariyya,* Lucknow, 1879.

Ghuldm Shah 'Ali: *Maqamat-i Mazò'hari,* Delhi, 1891.

Gilani, A. C. S.: *Ghalib, His Life and Persian Poetry*, Karachi, 1956.

Goetz, H.: *Indian and Persian Miniature Painting*, Amsterdam, 1958.

Grierson, G. A.: *Bihar Peasant Life*, Calcutta, 1885.

Habib, M.: "Shaikh Nasruddin Mahòmud Chiragh-i Delhi as a Great Historical Personality"', *IC*, xx (1946), 129-53.

Hadi, Mirza Muhòammad: *Nur-Allah Shustari, Shahid-i Thalith,* Lucknow, 1925.

Hòali, Altòtaf Hòusayn: *Muqaddima-i shi'r wa sha'iri,* Lahore, 1953.

Halim, A.: "Mystics and Mystical Movements of the Sayyid Lodi Period", *Journal of the Asiatic Society of Pakistan,* 1963.

Hamdani, H. F.: "The Letters of Mustansir Billah", *BSOAS*, 1933-1935.

Hamid Ali: "The Customary and Statutory Laws of the Muslims in India", *IC*, 1937.

Hòamid Qalandar: *Khayr al-majalis*, Aligarh, 1960.

Hardy, P.: *Historians of Medieval India*, London, 1960.

Harikishan Kaul: *Census Report, Punjab*, Lahore, 1912.

Hòasan 'Ali 'Izzat: *Mufarrihò al-qulub,* 10 Pers. MS 2809.

Hòasani, 'Abd-al-Hòayy: *Ath-thaqafa al-Islamiyya fi-i-Hind,* Damascus, 1958.

Hòasani, 'Abd-at-Rahòman: *Mir'at-i Madariyya,* BM Add. MS 168.

Hashimi, Nasir-ad-din: *Dakan men Urdu,* Hyderabad, 1936.

Havell, E. B.: *A Handbook of Indian Art*, London, 1920.

Hòjji Khalafa: *Kashf az-Zòunun,* Leipzig, 1835-52.

Hollister, J. N.: *The Shi'a of India*, London, 1953.

Hunter, W. W.: *The Indian Musalmans*, London, 1871.

Ibn-Kathir: *Al-Bidaya wa-n-nihaya,* Cairo, 1932-9.

Ibn-Nadim: *Al-Fihrist* (ed. Flügel), Leipzig, 1871-2.

Ibrahim 'Adil Shah 11: *Nawras* (ed. Nazir Ahmad), Lucknow, 1955.

Ibrahim Mir Siyalkoti: *Ta'rikh-i ahl-i adith,* Lahore, 1953.

I'jaz Husayn: *Mukhtasar ta'rikh-i adab-i Urdu,* Karachi, 1956.

Ikram, S. M. and Spear, P.: *Cultural Heritage of Pakistan*, Karachi, 1955.

Ikram, S. M.: *Ab-i Kawthar,* Lahore, 1952.

Imdad-Allah, Hòjji: *Maktubat-i Imdadiyya,* ed. Ashraf 'Ali Thaawi, Lucknow, 1915.

In 'am al-Hòaqq: *Muslim Bengali Adab,* Karachi, 1957.

Iqbal Husain: "Chandra Bhan Brahman", *IC*, 1945.

Iqbal, Muhammad: *Islam and, Ahmadism*, Lahore, 1936.

Ishaq, Muhammad: "India's Contribution to the study of Hadith Literature", *Dacca University Bulletin*, 1955.

Isma'il, Shah (Shahid): *Tadhkir al-akhwan,* Lahore, 1948.

Ismi: *Futu as-salatòin,* Madras, 1948.

Ivanow, W.: *Guide to Ismda'ili Literature*, London, 1933.

Ja'bfar Sharif: Islam in India or the Qanun-i Islam, Eng. tr. G. A. Herklots, 1832; revised by W. Crooke, Oxford, 1921.

Jahangir: *Tuzuk,* Aligarh, 1864; Eng. tr. A. Rogers, London, 1909.

Jamali, Hòamid ibn-FaU+1EODl-Allah: *Siyar al-'Arifin,* Delhi, 1893.

Jamil, M. Tahir: *Hali's Poetry*, Bombay, 1938.

Juzjani, Minhaj-as-siraj: *Tabaqat-i Nasri,* ed. A. H. Habibi, Kabul, 1964.

Kalam-Allah, Shah: *Kashkal-i Kalimi,* Delhi, 1890.

Kamal Khwaja al-din: *The Ideal Prophet*, London, 1925.

Kashani, 'Izz-ad-din: *Misbahò al-hiddya,* Lucknow, 1904.

Kaul, J. L.: *Interpretations of Ghalib*, Delhi, 1957.

Khafi Khan: *Muntakhab al-lubab,* Calcutta, 1869-1925.

Khaja Khan: *Studies in Tasawwuf,* Madras, 1923.

Khayr-ad-din, M.: *Tadhkirat al-'ulama'*, Calcutta, 1934.

Khushal Khan Khattak: *Poems from the Divan*, tr. D. N. Mackenzie, London, 1965.

Khusraw, Amir: *Matòla 'al-anwar,* Lucknow, 1884.

Kühnel, Ernst: *Moghul-Malerei*, Berlin, 1956.

Laoust, H.: *Les Schismes clans l'Islam*, Paris, 1965.

Law, N. N.: *Promotion of Learning in India During Muhammedan Rule by Muhammedans*, London, 1916.

Lawrence, W. R.: *The Valley of Kashmir*, London, 1895.

Lentz, W.: "Sammlungen zur afghanischen Literatur — und Zeitgeschichte", *ZDMG* (1937), 711-32.

Leyden, J.: "On the Roshenian Sect and its Founder Bayazid Ansari", *Asiatic Researches*.

Lokhandwalla, Sh. T.: "The Bohras, a Muslim Community of Gujarat", SI, 1955.

Madani, Hòusayn. Ahmad: *Naqsh-i hòayat,* Delhi, 1953.

Mançri, Sharaf-ad-din Ahòmad ibn-Yahòya: *Maktubat,* Lucknow, 1868; Cawnpore, 1911.

Massignon, L.: *Essai sur les origines du Lexique Technique de la Mystique musulmanc,* Paris, 1922.

Mawdudi, A. A.: *Towards Understanding Islam*, Lahore, 1960.

Mawdudi, Abu-l-A'la: *Ta'limat,* Lahore, 1955.

Mazòhar, Mirza Jan-i Janan: *Kalimat-i Tòayyibat,* Delhi, 1891.

Menant, D.: "Les Bohras du Guzarate", *RMM*, 1910.

Mihr, Ghulam-Rasul: *Sayyid, Ahòmad Shahid*, Lahore, 1952.

Ministry of Education, Government of Pakistan: *Report of the Commission on National Education*, Karachi, 1959.

Misra, S. C.: *Muslim Communities in Gujarat*, Bombay, 1964.

Mohanlal, Munshi: "A Brief Account of Masud, Known by the Name of Shakarganj or Shakarbar", *JASB*, 1836.

Mrs Hassan Meer Ali: *Observations on the Mussulmauns of India*, London, 1917.

Muhòammad 'Ali: *English Translation of the Holy Qur'an with Commentary*, Lahore, various eds.

Muhòammad 'Ali: *The Ahòmadiyya Doctrines*, Lahore, 1932.

Muhòammad Hòasan Naqshbandi: *Hòalat-i masha'ikh-i Naqshbandiyya Mujaddidiyya,* Muradabad, 1904.

Muhammad Malik Din: *Gagetteer of Bhawalpur*, Lahore, 1909.

Muhòammad, Mirza: *Tuhòfat al-Hind,* BM Add. MS 16, 868.

Muhammedan Anglo-Oriental Educational Conference, Majmu'a-i resolution ha-i dihsala, Aligarh, 1896.

Muhòsin Fani: *Dabistan-i madhahib,* Eng. tr. D. Shea and A. Troyer, Paris, 1843.

Muhòyi-d-din, Shaykh: *al-Balagh al-mubin,* Lahore, 1876.

Mujeeb, M.: *The Indian Muslims*, London, 1967.

Mushtaqi, Rizq-Allah: *Waqi'at-i Mushtaqi,* BM Add. 11633.

Mustawfa, Hòamid-Allah: *Ta'rikh-i Guzida*, Leiden, 1910.

Mu'tamid Khan: *Iqbal Nama-i Jahangiri*, Calcutta, 1865.

Nadwi, Abu-l-Hòasan 'Ali: *Hindustani Musalman,* Lucknow, 1961.

Nadwi, Abu-l-Hòasanat: *Hindustan ki Qadim Islami Dargahen,* A'zamgarh, 1936.

Nadwi, Sulayman: "Muslim Colonies in India", *IC*, 1927.

Najm-al-Ghani Khan: *Madhahib-i Islam,* Lucknow, 1924.

Nizam-ad-din Burhanpuri, etc.: *Fatawa'i Hindiyya*, Urdu tr. by Sayyid Amir 'Ali, Lucknow, 1889.

Nizami, K. A.: *' Abd-al-Hòaqq Muhòaddith Dihlawi,* Delhi, 1953.

Nizami, K. A.: "Some Aspects of Khanqah Life in Medieval India", *SI*, 1957.

Nizami, K. A.: *The Life and Times of Shaykh Farid-u'd Din Ganj-i Shakar,* Aligarh, 1955.

Nurul M. Karim: "Part played by Haji Shari'atullah and his son in the socio-political history of East Bengal", *Proceedings of the Pakistan History Conference*, Karachi, 1955.

O'Malley, L. S. S.: *Census Report: Bengal, Bihar, Orissa, Sikkim*, Calcutta, 1913.

Oman, J. C.: *The Mystics, Ascetics and Saints of India*, London, 1905.

Pakistan ki 'ilaqa'i zabanon par farsi ka athar, Karachi, n.d.

Philips, C. H.: *Historians of India, Pakistan and Ceylon*, London, 1961.

Punjab Notes and Queries, Allahabad, 1883-7.

Qadiri, Shams-ad-din: *Urda-yi qadim,* Lucknow, 1930.

Qani', Ali Shir: *Tuhòfat al-karam,* Delhi, 1886.

Qidwa'i, J. A.: *Pashto Adab*, Karachi, 1951.

Qurayshi, 'Abd-ar-Razzaq: *Mirza Maz'har Jan-i Janan awr unka Urdu kalam,* Bombay, 1961.

Qureshi, I. H.: *The Muslim Community of the Indo-Pakistan Sub-Continent,* 'S-Gravenhage, 1962.

Rahòman 'Ali: *Tadhkira-i 'ulama-i Hind,* Lucknow, 1914; Urdu tr. by M. Ayyub Qadiri, Karachi, 1961.

Ram Lajwanti Krishna: *Panjabi Sufi Poets*, Calcutta, 1938.

Rashidi, Hòusam-ad-Din: *Sindhi Adab,* Karachi, n.d.

Raverty, H. G.: *Selections From the Poetry of the Afghans*, London, 1864.

Razvi, S. N. Haidar: "Music in Muslim India", *IC*, 1941.

Rieu, C.: *Catalogue of the Persian Manuscripts in the British Museum,* London, 1879-95.

Rizvi, S. A. A.: *Muslim Revivalist Movements in Northern India in the Sixteenth and Seventeenth Centuries*, Agra, 1965.

Rose, H. A.: *A Glossary of Tribes and Castes of the Punjab and North-West Frontier Province*, Lahore, 1911-19.

Rosenthal, E. I. J.: *Islam in the Modern National State*, Cambridge, 1965.

Roychoudhuri, M.: *The Din-i Ilahi,* Calcutta, 1941.

Sòabah-ad-din 'Abd-at-Rahòman: *Bazm-i Sòhòfiyya,* A'zamgarh, 1949.

Sabir, M.: "Cultural and Linguistic Affinities Between Turkey, Iran and Pakistan", in *Papers read at the R.C.D. Seminar on Common Cultural Heritage*, Tehran, 1965.

Sadiq, Muhammad: *A History of Urdu Literature*, London, 1964.

Saksena, R. B.: *A History of Urdu Literature*, Allahabad, 1940.

Saqi Musta'id Khan: *Ma'athir-i 'Aamgiri,* Calcutta, 1947.

Sarwar Muhòammad: *Panjabidab,* Karachi, n.d.

Sayyid, Ahòmad Khan: *Tafsir al-Qur'an,* Lahore, 1880-1895.

Sell, E.: *The Religious Orders of Islam*, Madras, 1908.

Sen, D. C.: *History of Bengali Language and Literature*, Calcutta, 1911.

Shatòtòari, Baha'ad-din: *Risala-i Shatòtòariyya,* 10 Pers. MS 2257.

Shçr Khan Lodi: *Mir'at al-khayal,* Calcutta, 1831.

Shçrani, M.: *Panjab mçn Urdu*, Lahore, 1928.

Shibli Nu'mani: *Rasa'il,* Delhi, 1898.

Shustari, Nur-Allah: *Majalis al-mu'minin,* Tehran, 1852.

Sijzi, Amir Hòasan: *Fawa'id al-fu'ad,* Delhi, 1865.

Sikander ibn-Muhòammad 'Manjhu': *Mir'at-i Sikandari,* Baroda, 1961.

Simnani, 'Ali'-ad-dawla: *Chihil Majalis,* BM Or. MS 9725.

Simnani, Ashraf Jahangir: *Latòa'if-i Ashrqfi,* Delhi, 1882.

Smith, V. A.: *Akbar, the Great Mughal*, Oxford, 1919.

Smith, Wilfrid Cantwell: *Pakistan as an Islamic State*, Lahore, 1951.

Sorley, H. T.: *Shah Abdul Latif of Bhit*, London, 1940.

Stchoukine, Ivan: *La Peinture Indienne,* Paris, 1929.

Storey, C. A.: *Persian Literature, A Bio-Bibliographical Survey*, London, 1927-58.

Suhrawardi, Diya'-ad-din Abu-Najib ' Abd-al-Qahir: *Adab al-muridin,* Urdu tr. Delhi, 1901.

Tara Chand: *The Influence of Islam on Hindu Culture*, Allahabad, 1936.

Temple, R. C.: *The Legends of the Punjab*, Bombay, 1884.

The Founder of the Ahòmadivya Movement, Lahore, n.d.

The Imperial Gayetteer of India, London, 1907-1909.

Titus, Murray T.: *Islam in India and Pakistan*, Calcutta, 1959.

Wahid Mirza: *The Life and Works of Amir Khusrau*, Calcutta, 1935.

Wa'izòshifi: *Rashhòat*, Cawnpore, 1912.

Wajia 'Ali Shah: *Sòawt-i mubarak*, Lucknow, 1853.

Wakil Ahòmad: *Nusrat al-mujtahdin,* Lucknow, 1896.

Wali-Allah, Shah *Hòusn al-'aqida* (Urdu tr. *Mera aqida*), in *Ar-Rahim* 1964.

Walter, H. A.: *The Ahmadiyya Movement*, Calcutta/ London, 1918.

Wellesz, Emmy: *Akbar's Religious Thought reflected in Mughal Painting*, London, 1952.

Wilkinson, J. V. S. and Gray, B.: *Persian Miniature Painting*, London, 1933.

Yusuf Husain: *L'Inde Mystique au Moyen Age*, Paris, 1929.

Zaehner, R. C.: *Hindu and Muslim Mysticism*, London, 1960.

Zahid 'Ali: *Hamara Isma'ili madhhab awr uski hòaqiqat,* Hyderabad, 1954.

Zubayd M. G. Ahmad: *The Contribution of India to Arabic Literature*, PH.D. dissertation, University of London.

Index

F

G

H

I

J

K

L

M

N

O

P

Q

R

S

W

Z